Your
Graduate Training
in Psychology
Effective Strategies for Success

EDITORS

Peter J. Giordano • Stephen F. Davis • Carolyn A. Licht

Belmont University   Morningside College   Fordham University

Los Angeles | London | New Delhi
Singapore | Washington DC

Los Angeles | London | New Delhi
Singapore | Washington DC

FOR INFORMATION:

SAGE Publications, Inc.
2455 Teller Road
Thousand Oaks, California 91320
E-mail: order@sagepub.com

SAGE Publications Ltd.
1 Oliver's Yard
55 City Road
London EC1Y 1SP
United Kingdom

SAGE Publications India Pvt. Ltd.
B 1/I 1 Mohan Cooperative Industrial Area
Mathura Road, New Delhi 110 044
India

SAGE Publications Asia-Pacific Pte. Ltd.
33 Pekin Street #02-01
Far East Square
Singapore 048763

Acquisitions Editor: Christine Cardone
Editorial Assistant: Sarita Sarak
Production Editor: Libby Larson
Copy Editor: Kim Husband
Typesetter: C&M Digitals (P) Ltd
Proofreader: Sally Jaskold
Cover Designer: Janet Kiesel
Marketing Manager: Liz Thornton
Permissions Editor: Karen Ehrmann

Printed in the United States of America

Library of Congress Cataloging-in-Publication Data

Your graduate training in psychology: effective strategies for success/editors, Peter J. Giordano, Stephen F. Davis, Carolyn A. Licht.

p. cm.
Includes bibliographical references and index.

ISBN 978-1-4129-9493-4 (pbk. : alk. paper)

1. Psychology—Study and teaching (Graduate) 2. Graduate students. I. Giordano, Peter J. II. Davis, Stephen F. III. Licht, Carolyn A.

BF77.Y68 2012

150.71′1—dc23   2011029802

This book is printed on acid-free paper.

11 12 13 14 15 10 9 8 7 6 5 4 3 2 1

Contents

Preface ❖

E ach year, thousands of students are accepted into graduate training programs in psychology. After the excitement of this initial acceptance, however, these students are typically faced with a number of questions and concerns. These students are likely to confront questions like "How will graduate school differ from my undergraduate training?," "What is the best way to get off to a good start?," "How can I develop all the new skills I will need to be successful in graduate school?," or "What are comprehensive exams and how do I prepare for them?" The initial exuberance of gaining admission to graduate school can give way to feelings of anxiety, uncertainty, and possibly despair.

We've written this book to answer these questions and many more that students face *after* they enroll in graduate school. Many books target issues of admission to graduate school, but few are directed toward students who have been accepted to or are currently in graduate training programs. We have selected authors with experience and expertise in the topics of each chapter. Students will find that the chapters directly address the major issues confronting them, both master's- and doctoral-level students, during their graduate training in psychology.

This book is designed to illuminate the broad range of processes, practices, and procedural issues that face graduate students in psychology. Ordered chronologically, from the first year of graduate school ("Settling In") to what students need to know as they finish ("Winding Down and Gearing Up"), students will learn the key skills needed to succeed in all aspects of their academic and professional careers while in school and after beginning a professional career. The chapters are designed to offer practical advice from authors who have "been there and done that."

One of the challenges of graduate training is that many of the rules for success are not written down in a manual. Students have to learn by observation and deal with the hard knocks of real life in graduate school. Our aim is to help students understand some of the unwritten rules for being successful. Such knowledge will benefit both students and faculty. Students benefit because, by taking the advice in this book, they will be more likely to complete their graduate training in a timely fashion and then successfully launch into rewarding professional careers. Faculty benefit because their students will be better equipped to successfully navigate the challenges during the various developmental stages of graduate training. In addition, during the middle phase of graduate school, what we have called the "Developing and Maturing" phase, graduate students must master specific skills that are complex and challenging. For example, students may begin teaching for the first time or must now prepare for comprehensive exams. Also, students will be devoting more and more time to research and writing. This middle portion of the book directly confronts these issues, and the chapter authors offer sound advice for advancing in these important domains. To augment the practical advice and suggestions for skill development, each chapter ends with a section called "Suggestions for Further Exploration." These sections give students some follow-up resources for their continued professional development.

This book is intended for graduate students enrolled in graduate psychology programs (both master's and doctoral programs) as well as faculty who are teaching and mentoring students in pursuing their graduate degrees. Faculty may want to assign this book in courses such as professional development seminars or seminars designed to orient graduate students to their graduate training program. The students should keep the book and refer to it throughout their graduate school experience because certain chapters become more relevant at specific junctures in their training.

If knowledge is power, then we hope this book will empower psychology graduate students to be extremely successful through all phases of their graduate training experience and beyond!

Peter J. Giordano

Stephen F. Davis

Carolyn A. Licht

About the Editors

❖

Peter J. Giordano is professor and chair of Psychological Science at Belmont University in Nashville, Tennessee. He earned his Ph.D. in clinical psychology from the University of North Carolina at Chapel Hill. A past recipient of the CASE Tennessee Professor of the Year Award and past National President of Psi Chi, he is a frequent workshop presenter on pedagogy in psychology and on student professional development issues. Contact: pete.giordano@belmont.edu.

Stephen F. Davis is Roe R. Cross Distinguished Professor Emeritus at Emporia State University. He served as the 2002–2003 Knapp Distinguished Professor of Arts and Sciences at the University of San Diego. Currently, he is Distinguished Guest Professor at Morningside College. In 2007, he was awarded the honorary Doctor of Humane Letters degree by Morningside College. Since 1966, he has published more than 315 articles and 30 textbooks and presented more than 900 professional papers; the vast majority of these publications and presentations include student coauthors. Among his research specialties are academic dishonesty and learning styles. Contact: davis122@suddenlink.net.

Carolyn A. Licht is currently working as a Supervising Psychologist/Coordinator of Psychiatric Residencies for the Office of Counseling and Psychological Services at Fordham University in New York. Previously, she served as a staff psychologist in the Family Care Center at Harlem Hospital, working in the pediatric and adult infectious disease medical clinics specializing in the care of individuals infected and affected by HIV, substance use, and trauma. She received her Ph.D. in clinical psychology with a child and family specialization from Fordham University's Graduate School of Arts & Sciences, Bronx, New York, in 2007, and was licensed in New York State in 2009 after completing her predoctoral internship at Jacobi Medical Center and her postdoctoral fellowship with Columbia University Medical Center working at Harlem Hospital. Contact: calicht@msn.com.

About the Contributors ❖

Jonathan B. Banks is a doctoral student in the experimental psychology program at the University of North Texas. His research interests include the impact of stress on cognition and the relationship between working memory and mind wandering. Contact: jonathan.banks@unt.edu.

Jeffrey S. Bartel is a visiting assistant professor in the psychology department of Washington and Jefferson College in Washington, Pennsylvania. His primary research interests are in adolescent social development, especially prosocial and gender role development. Contact: jbartel@washjeff.edu.

Bernard C. (Barney) Beins is professor and chair of psychology at Ithaca College. He received his doctorate from City University of New York in experimental psychology. He is author of about 150 articles, chapters, books, and pedagogical material and has given about 200 presentations. He recently received the Charles L. Brewer Distinguished Teaching of Psychology Award from the American Psychological Foundation. Contact: beins@ithaca.edu.

Victor A. Benassi is professor of psychology, professor of college teaching, and faculty director of the Center for Excellence in Teaching and Learning at the University of New Hampshire. He has taught courses in college teaching and supervised graduate students' teaching of psychology since the early 1980s. His research has addressed a variety of topics related to teaching and learning, judgment, superstitious belief, and perceived control. He received his Ph.D. in psychology from the City University of New York. Contact: vab@unh.edu.

Christia Spears Brown is an associate professor of developmental and social psychology in the Children at Risk Research Cluster at the University of Kentucky. Contact: christia.brown@uky.edu.

Robert Bubb is a teaching fellow and doctoral candidate in industrial and organizational psychology at Auburn University. He received a master's degree in psychology from Brigham Young University in 2008. His current research focuses on the efficacy of digital learning products in the classroom. Contact robb.bubb@auburn.edu.

Susan R. Burns is the associate dean for academic affairs at Morningside College in Sioux City, Iowa. She is a graduate of Emporia State University (Emporia, KS) and

Kansas State University (Manhattan, KS). She has presented and served as faculty sponsor for more than 150 presentations at the local, regional, and national levels and has authored more than 20 different scholarly publications. She recently coauthored a textbook, *Human Relations for the Educator: Meeting the Challenges for Today and Tomorrow,* and currently serves as the managing editor for the *Journal of Psychological Inquiry.* Contact: burns@morningside.edu.

William Buskist is the Distinguished Professor in the Teaching of Psychology at Auburn University and a faculty fellow at Auburn's Biggio Center for the Enhancement of Teaching and Learning. His primary responsibilities at Auburn center around preparing graduate students for academic/teaching careers. Contact: buskiwf@auburn.edu.

Radha G. Carlson is a clinical assistant professor in the department of psychology at the University of North Carolina at Chapel Hill as well as a staff psychologist at Central Regional Hospital. Contact: radhacarlson@gmail.com.

Erica M. Chin is a clinical psychologist and assistant clinical professor of medical psychology (in psychiatry) at Columbia University Medical Center. Dr. Chin also serves as the director of assessment and senior psychologist at the pediatric psychiatry department for New York Presbyterian Hospital. Contact: chineri@childpsych.columbia.edu.

Kimberly Christopherson is an assistant professor in the psychology department at Morningside College in Sioux City, Iowa. Her research interests include how to best use technology in the classroom and teaching, learning, and curriculum in higher education. Contact: christopherson@morningside.edu.

Daniel Corts is an associate professor of psychology at Augustana College in Rock Island, Illinois. His research covers diverse topics from language comprehension to college student development. Dan is coauthor of the forthcoming textbook *An Introduction to Psychological Science.* Contact: DanielCorts@augustana.edu.

Stephen F. Davis is Roe R. Cross Distinguished Professor Emeritus at Emporia State University. He served as the 2002–2003 Knapp Distinguished Professor of Arts and Sciences at the University of San Diego. Currently he is Distinguished Guest Professor at Morningside College. In 2007, he was awarded the honorary Doctor of Humane Letters degree by Morningside College. Since 1966, he has published more than 315 articles and 30 textbooks and presented more than 900 professional papers; the vast majority of these publications and presentations include student coauthors. Among his research specialties are academic dishonesty and learning styles. Contact: davis122@suddenlink.net.

Leah Skovran Georges is a doctoral student in the psychology and law program at the University of Nebraska–Lincoln. Contact: lskovran@gmail.com.

Gary S. Goldstein is associate professor of psychology at the University of New Hampshire at Manchester. He has 30 years' experience teaching in the college classroom and is a past winner of the UNH Manchester Excellence in Teaching Award. His research, which focuses on various dimensions of college teaching, has appeared in *The Journal on Excellence in College Teaching*, *Research in Higher Education*, *College Teaching*, and *Teaching of Psychology*. Contact: gsg@cisunix.unh.edu.

Valerie M. Gonsalves is a postdoctoral resident at Fulton State Hospital in Fulton, Missouri. She is a graduate of the University of Nebraska Clinical Psychology program. Contact: vmgonsalves@yahoo.com.

Regan A. R. Gurung is the Ben J. and Joyce Rosenberg Professor of Human Development and Psychology at the University of Wisconsin, Green Bay. His primary research interests involve scholarship on teaching and learning. Contact: gurungr@uwgb.edu.

G. William (Bill) Hill IV is professor emeritus of psychology and former executive director of the Center for Excellence in Teaching & Learning at Kennesaw State University. His professional interests and research focus on faculty development and effective teaching. He can be reached at bhill@kennesaw.edu.

Matthew T. Huss is a professor at Creighton University in Omaha, Nebraska. He also is a graduate of the University of Nebraska law and psychology and clinical psychology training programs. He is the author of more than 50 different scholarly publications, including a textbook on forensic clinical psychology. Contact: mhuss@creighton.edu.

Jared Keeley is an assistant professor of psychology at Mississippi State University in the clinical psychology master's degree program. In addition to clinical interests, he is actively involved in the scholarship of teaching and learning and is an advocate for graduate student training. Contact: jkeeley@psychology.msstate.edu.

Jason P. Kring is an assistant professor in the human factors and systems department at Embry-Riddle Aeronautical University in Daytona Beach, Florida. He is president of the Society for Human Performance in Extreme Environments and codirector of the Team Simulation and Gaming Laboratory at Embry-Riddle. Contact: jason.kring@erau.edu.

Christina M. Leclerc is an assistant professor of psychology at the State University of New York at Oswego. She earned her doctorate from North Carolina State University studying lifespan developmental psychology. Her research interests lie in examining the age-related changes in the neural mechanisms associated with the processing of emotional information. Contact: christina.leclerc@oswego.edu.

Michael J. Lee is administrative director of the Center for Excellence in Teaching and Learning at the University of New Hampshire, where he directs the program in college teaching. He earned his Ph.D. in English from the University of New Hampshire, where he also taught American literature for many years prior to his current position. Contact: mjl@unh.edu.

Laurie Reider Lewis is a licensed clinical psychologist specializing in the treatment of children, adolescents, and families. She obtained her undergraduate degree from

Binghamton University and her doctorate in clinical psychology from the Graduate School of Applied and Professional Psychology at Rutgers University. She completed her child-clinical psychology internship at New York-Presbyterian Hospital—Columbia University Medical Center, where she remains a faculty member in the Department of Psychiatry. Beyond her doctoral training in clinical psychology and applied experience, Dr. Lewis is a former elementary and middle school teacher and school counselor with a master's degree in education from Harvard University. Contact: drlaurierlewis@gmail.com.

Carolyn A. Licht is currently working as a Supervising Psychologist/Coordinator of Psychiatric Residencies for the Office of Counseling and Psychological Services at Fordham University in New York. Previously, she served as a staff psychologist in the Family Care Center at Harlem Hospital, working in the pediatric and adult infectious disease medical clinics specializing in the care of individuals infected and affected by HIV, substance use, and trauma. She received her Ph.D. in clinical psychology with a child and family specialization from Fordham University's Graduate School of Arts & Sciences, Bronx, New York, in 2007, and was licensed in New York State in 2009 after completing her predoctoral internship at Jacobi Medical Center and her postdoctoral fellowship with Columbia University Medical Center working at Harlem Hospital. Contact: calicht@msn.com.

Janet R. Matthews is professor of psychology at Loyola University New Orleans. She is a past chair of the Louisiana State Board of Examiners of Psychologists, is licensed in Louisiana with specialties in both clinical psychology and clinical neuropsychology, and is board certified in clinical psychology through the American Board of Professional Psychology and in assessment psychology through the American Board of Assessment Psychology, for which she currently serves on the board of directors. She is the current president of APA's Division 31 (State Provincial, & Territorial Psychological Association Affairs). Contact: matthews@loyno.edu.

Lee H. Matthews has a private practice that often includes consulting in such diverse facilities as a rural public hospital, a state psychiatric hospital, an inpatient geropsychiatry unit, and a grief recovery center. He is licensed in Louisiana with specialties in both clinical psychology and clinical neuropsychology, has board certification in clinical psychology (American Board of Professional Psychology) and assessment psychology (American Board of Assessment Psychology), and is listed in the National Register of Health Services Providers in Psychology. He currently serves on the Louisiana State Board of Examiners of Psychologists. Contact: psycres@aol.com.

Loretta Neal McGregor is the department chairperson and associate professor of psychology and counseling at Arkansas State University at Jonesboro. Her professional involvements include membership in the American Psychological Association, in which she is a member of Division Two, The Teaching of Psychology and in which she recently served as the associate director of society programming for the APA Program. She is also a member of the Southwestern Psychological Association. In this organization, she served as program chairperson, convention manager, and state representative. Contact: Lmcgregor@astate.edu.

Catherine Overson earned her PhD in social psychology at the University of New Hampshire in Durham in May 2011. Currently, she is interested in individual differences related to judgment of performance in the academic setting, with research aimed at identifying theoretically based individual differences in self-efficacy and study behaviors related to academic performance. Contact: coverson@unh.edu.

David S. Shen-Miller is an assistant professor of counseling psychology at Tennessee State University. He received his doctorate in counseling psychology from the University of Oregon in 2008 and from 2003 to 2006 served as the director of the University of Oregon Men's Center. His research interests include the psychology of men and masculinity, issues related to psychology training and supervision, and qualitative research. Contact: dmiller20@tnstate.edu.

Seraphine Shen-Miller is an assistant professor of psychological science at Belmont University. She received her doctoral degree in social and personality psychology from the University of Oregon. Her main area of research interest is the development of beliefs and values and their relations with psychological and social well-being. Contact: seraphine.shen-miller@belmont.edu.

Randolph Smith taught at Ouachita Baptist University in Arkansas for 26 years, chaired Kennesaw State University's psychology department for 4 years, and became chair of Lamar University's psychology department in 2007. His professional work centers on the scholarship of teaching. Randy served for 12 years as editor of the Society for the Teaching of Psychology's journal *Teaching of Psychology* and is currently editor of the *Psi Chi Journal of Undergraduate Research*. He has worked with high school teachers grading AP exams since the test's inception and has served as Faculty Advisor for TOPSS (Teachers of Psychology in Secondary Schools). In 2006, Randy received the American Psychological Foundation's Charles L. Brewer Distinguished Teaching of Psychology Award.

Holly E. Tatum is an associate professor and chair of the psychology department at Randolph College in Lynchburg, Virginia. Contact: htatum@randolphcollege.edu.

Krisztina Varga Jakobsen is an assistant professor in the department of psychology at James Madison University. Her research interests include cognitive development and effective teaching practices. Contact: jakobskv@jmu.edu.

Alex J. Watters is a student at Creighton University's Werner Institute in Omaha, Nebraska, where he is studying negotiation and conflict resolution. He also graduated summa cum laude from Morningside College, where he studied political science and global history. He is a motivational speaker who has shared his story to hundreds, most recently as the keynote speaker to the Morningside College class of 2014. Contact: waters.alex@gmail.com.

Lonnie R. Yandell is professor of psychology at Belmont University in Nashville, Tennessee. His passions are teaching his classes and working with students on research projects. Contact: lonnie.yandell@belmont.edu.

Introduction

If you are opening this book for the first time, you are about to embark on one of the most exciting adventures in your academic career—graduate school! It was not an easy path to reach this point. Long study hours in the library, frustrating moments writing papers, and anxiety in preparing and giving oral presentations have now paid off with your admission to graduate school. If you are like most students, you vividly remember when you first opened that letter or e-mail offering admission to a graduate training program. What an exciting moment; we still remember that exhilarating experience ourselves!

But once the excitement begins to wear off, you are now faced with a number of other questions and challenges. What will graduate school be like? What are the expectations in graduate school? How can I maximize my chances for success? Will I be up to snuff with regard to my writing, speaking, and research abilities? Are there things I can do from the outset that will contribute to my ultimate success—completion of my degree and finding my dream job—once all is said and done?

These are all important questions, and you are wise to start thinking about them from the outset. Our vision for this book is that it will answer these questions and many others like them. To this end, we have organized the book into three developmental phases in your graduate career. Section I deals with issues related to "Settling In" to your life as a graduate student. The next phase, "Developing and Maturing," is the theme of Section II. Last but not least, Section III is organized around issues of "Winding Down and Gearing Up (All at the Same Time)," that time in your graduate training when you are finishing up important requirements such as the dissertation and beginning to move toward your career after graduate school.

The book is not meant to be read cover to cover all at once. Because of the developmental organization of the book, certain chapters will be more relevant to your situation at specific points in time. We do, however, strongly recommend that you read the first three chapters very early in your graduate training. There are lots of unwritten rules and expectations once you begin graduate training, and it is to your advantage to know some of these rules as you start graduate school. The authors of these first three chapters offer insightful suggestions on how to get off to a great start.

From there, look to the other chapters for help with your particular needs as they arise. You will find *lots* of suggestions for how to maximize your success in graduate school. You have worked hard to get where you are and are now entering a challenging, stimulating, and very rewarding part of your life.

We wish you all the success in the world!

Peter J. Giordano

Stephen F. Davis

Carolyn A. Licht

SECTION I

Introduction—Settling In

Congratulations on your admission to a graduate training program in psychology! Years of hard work and careful planning have helped you land where you are. Now the journey begins in earnest. The first section of this book offers 10 chapters to help you start out on the right track and begin to settle in to a rewarding graduate school experience. The chapters are written by experienced psychology faculty from a variety of training and personal backgrounds. Chapters 1, 2, and 3 offer guidance on how to start out strong to maximize your eventual success. The next several chapters offer guidance on issues such as relationships; what to do if your career plans begin to change; and important considerations for minority graduate students, older, nontraditional, or international students, or graduate students with special needs. Chapter 9 offers insight for students enrolled in online graduate training programs. The final chapter in this section deals with the important issue of how to take good care of yourself during the inevitable stressors that you will encounter. If you read and take to heart the advice in these chapters, you will be off to a great start and begin to settle in to a successful training experience.

1

Settling in the Right Way ❖

Playing by the Rules

Jason P. Kring
Embry-Riddle Aeronautical University

Stephen F. Davis
Morningside College

Your first day of graduate school will be a whirlwind of introductions, hand-shakes, sightseeing tours, and dozens of pick-ups and drop-offs of forms and parking decals and more forms. Oh, and there will be a lot of information, piles of information, mountains of information! For most of the first week, it will feel like drinking water from a fire hose. Much of the information those first days of graduate school will tell you what to do and what not to do. These are the written rules of the graduate program, the department, and the university as a whole. There are rules for where to park on campus, policies on intellectual property rights, lists of required courses, and many, many deadlines for things like financial aid, the dissertation process, and ordering your cap and gown for graduation.

With all of that information, you should be well prepared to settle in for your first semester as a graduate student. Presumably, you will know exactly what you need to do to earn your degree and when to do it. However, even with the mountain of information handed to you on that first day, there is an even taller mountain of information that you will need to succeed that is not written down. These are the informal, unwritten rules of the "game." One of your authors often refers to doing well in graduate school and one's subsequent academic or professional career as "playing the game." Students who know how to play the game well typically excel in graduate school. This characterization of graduate school as a game is not meant to belittle or degrade its importance but rather to illustrate that, like many activities

5

in life, there are rules, tradeoffs, and strategies that can help you succeed. Much like learning the "tricks" to win a video game or board game (e.g., buy up as much property as you can in the beginning rounds of a game of Monopoly!), you can learn how to play the game of graduate school more intelligently and more effectively. And much like games you learned as a child, there are written rules (three strikes and you're out) and rules you hear from other players (hit the ball toward Jason, he can't catch worth a darn!).

Learning these rules, both written and unwritten, and then playing the game using these rules will give you a tremendous advantage in graduate school. In fact, taking some of these rules to heart may make the difference between completing your program successfully and stalling midway and then dropping out. Unfortunately, the possibility of the latter is more common than you might think. The Council of Graduate Schools (2005) reports ". . . previous studies suggest that, while the majority of students who enter doctoral programs have the academic ability to complete the degree, on average only 50 to 60 percent of those who enter doctoral programs in the United States complete their degrees" (p. 22). Why is this? Although there are innumerable reasons why graduate students drop out of a program, from financial to family issues, academic ability does not appear to be one of them. For some who do not finish, they simply may never have learned how to play the game well.

Learning the rules will also help you achieve what Bloom and Bell (1979) call "superstar" status. Superstar graduate students stand out from the crowd and exhibit a number of specific behaviors, including being visible in the department, working hard (and making sure faculty see you working hard), reflecting the values of the program, working closely with faculty, and what they termed the "W" factor whereby students made faculty feel worthwhile and rewarded as teachers. The superstar students are the ones faculty contact when opportunities arise, such as research participation or coauthoring a conference paper, and you want to make sure, as you settle in, that you start earning this label.

In this chapter, we hope to convey two simple but valuable lessons to help you settle in. First, you need to find the rules of the game. Second, you need to start playing by these rules sooner rather than later. In other words, the key to settling into your first semester in graduate school is to quickly and accurately figure out how to play by the rules; the formal, written ones and the informal, unwritten ones. Let's begin with how you find the rules of the graduate school game.

Finding the Rules of the Game

The formal rules of graduate school are relatively easy to find. They are contained in that large packet of information you received at orientation and quickly shoved into a desk drawer. They are contained in the dozens, perhaps hundreds, of e-mails you will soon begin receiving from the administrative staff, faculty, department chair, and university. Even more formal rules are to be found in the graduate catalog, with pages and pages of policies and procedures you need follow to earn your degree.

But how does one find the informal rules of the graduate school game? In some cases, basic trial and error will provide you with a number of valuable, perhaps painfully acquired, lessons you will turn into rules. One of your coauthors learned, on his first day of graduate school, that a grey t-shirt, a long walk across campus, and a "meet-and-greet" session with the incoming class of students does not mix well with the heat and humidity of a Florida summer. He eventually cooled down, and his sweat-soaked shirt began to dry, but for weeks he was known as the "sweaty guy from Colorado." Another good source of informal rules is the experience of students and teachers captured in journal articles, online blogs, and books like the one you are holding right now. For example, Walfish and Hess (2004) describe nine strategies for successfully completing the Ph.D. drawn from the comments of a recent graduate student in a clinical psychology program. These include "Don't make the mistake of thinking that graduate school is just like undergraduate school in terms of how you can behave and present yourself," "Always be nice to office staff (secretaries, office managers, receptionists) at your graduate program," and "Accept feedback gracefully" (pp. 145–147).

Similarly, in Chapter 4 of this book, Susan Burns describes perhaps your best source for informal rules: the relationships you will develop that first semester, from finding the right advisor to the value of peer mentors. These relationships are so important to learning how to play the game that you should start the process right away. As you go through that first day, look around you; the current students, the faculty, the department chair, and the administrative staff will all have some insight into playing the game well. Some of these suggestions may seem obvious ("Get to class on time, read the book, and participate in class discussions"), some will seem peculiar ("Dr. Smith gets really upset when you use the word *methodology*"), and some will seem downright ridiculous ("If you can incorporate a *Star Wars* reference into your answer, you'll score points with Dr. Jones"), but try and remember all of them. No single suggestion will make or break your graduate career, but taken together, they provide a collection of tricks to help you get ahead.

Unfortunately, keeping all of the informal rules straight is no easy task. Some of the advice from others will seem contradictory. During his doctoral program, for example, one of your coauthors was told by a professor to spend all of his time studying because "graduate students don't get Bs," yet not a day later, another professor told him to focus on gaining research experience, even if it meant getting Bs or Cs in his classes. In addition, there are informal rules for different aspects of your graduate experience. When settling in that first semester, you will hear suggestions to help you in at least four main areas: (a) emotional adjustment and stability, (b) physical health, (c) the social dynamics of the program, and (d) professional and scholarly development. Let's explore each of these areas in more detail so that you can be on the lookout for good advice and begin collecting the informal rules of the game from day one.

Emotional Adjustment and Stability

Without a doubt, the first semester of graduate school will be a period of adjustment for you. You may have moved to a new location, leaving family, friends, or significant others. You might be living on your own for the first time or be recently married and now must learn how to balance school with family commitments. Whatever your particular situation, the transformation from undergraduate student to graduate student is a major one, and part of settling in successfully is learning how to adjust emotionally. Students who have already made this adjustment are your best source for informal rules on how to handle the stress of increased workloads, where to turn for help and support, even the best places to hang out on a Friday night to meet others and relax. Learning how to deal with stress is also important in that you want to keep your emotions in check when in classes or at practicum sites. As Walfish and Hess (2004) note, "Everyone has bad days and good days and upsetting events occur, but try as much as possible to keep that from coming out when you are in the role of graduate student" (p. 145).

Physical Health

Similar to emotional stability, you need to learn how to keep yourself physically healthy. We know many students will pull the "all nighters," replacing sleep with studying and water with coffee and Red Bull, but in general, you should strive to stay rested, get physical exercise, and eat well. One of your coauthors often asks his students how much they slept the night before and what they had for breakfast. Although the data are anecdotal, students getting 3 to 4 hours of sleep and whose breakfast consists of a candy bar and a soda are far more likely to crash and fall asleep in class than those getting 6 to 7 hours and eating a well-rounded meal. Will you be labeled a superstar student if professors routinely see you sleeping in the back of the class? Furthermore, Beck (2003) notes that the habits you develop in graduate school will influence the habits you keep during your career, including a good balance between professional activities and personal needs (for more on this point, see Chapter 10 of this book).

In terms of exercise, finding ways to stay physically fit can serve two purposes. One, exercise is an excellent way to relieve stress. And two, physical activities, such as intramural sports or simply meeting a few friends at the gym, are an ideal way to meet fellow students and build your network of social support. For example, some of our students formed a running club. They meet once a week for casual runs with lots of conversation and fun while training for local races.

Social Dynamics of the Program

Almost every organization, from a Fortune 500 company down to a local Girl Scouts troop, has a unique social dynamic, and a graduate program is no different. The "politics" of a department influence who makes decisions and who gets along with whom and often organizes students, faculty, and staff into seemingly disparate and conflicting "cliques." Learning the rules of your program's particular political climate is crucial to avoiding uncomfortable situations or overstepping your boundaries. For instance, be wary of students, even faculty, who badmouth others in the department. Avoid the temptation to get involved in these debates because you don't want your own negative comments to make their way to the wrong person. Keep in mind, you may work with any of the faculty during your time in the program, even later in your career. The same can be said for fellow students. A terse comment, said in haste, could come back to haunt you.

On this point, it is worth noting that social networking websites, like Facebook, are just as open to scrutiny, if not more so, as face-to-face conversations in the department. Because many students and increasingly faculty are on these sites, one negative comment about a professor or student can travel with lightning speed. One of your coauthors has actually seen all of the following comments posted on a Facebook wall by students in his department (luckily, he was not the subject of these rants):

> *"Dr. Blank is such an idiot! He has no clue what he's talking about most of the time."*
> *"I didn't learn a thing in Dr. Blank's class! What a waste!"*
> *"I didn't study at all for that exam. Didn't need to, got the answers from blank."* (blank being another student whose identity was clear, thus incriminating both for cheating)
> *"Sitting in Dr. Blank's class right now. . . . BORING!!!!"*

And, as the old saying goes, actions speak louder than words. By actions, we mean evidence of actions represented by the pictures students post on social networking sites. One of the quickest ways for you to harm your reputation in the department and alter your role in the social dynamics of the program is to post a picture of a drunken escapade or inappropriate behavior, especially one that gets a lot of attention and discussion. We are not advocating students avoid having fun, but if the fun crosses a line, then be smart enough to not advertise it to your peers and professors.

Professional and Scholarly Development

A majority of the rules you need to learn for the graduate school game will focus on your development as a scholar and professional. If you look at chapters in Section II of this book, developing and maturing as a graduate student encompasses a number of skills and abilities. To settle in the right way, start looking, right away, for opportunities to gain experience in writing, teaching, clinical and counseling activities, research, and giving presentations.

As we have already mentioned, one rule of the game is getting to know the faculty because they provide opportunities to gain these experiences. For example, an invaluable skill is being able to give an effective verbal presentation. Although many students dread public speaking, the more you do it, the easier it becomes. You can practice your presentation skills, for instance, by giving a paper at a conference. You may have already done this as an undergraduate student, but if not, you should definitely start searching for conferences during your first semester and, with the submission deadline dates in mind, start planning how to gain the research or applied experience that will become the subject of your conference submission. Likewise, you can partner with a faculty member on one of his or her presentations.

Another excellent opportunity to practice your presentation skills while gaining valuable teaching experience as well is to volunteer as a graduate teaching assistant (GTA) in the department. There is perhaps no better way to learn how to speak in front of people than preparing and giving a class lecture. Obtaining a GTA position, however, is easier said than done. Faculty select GTAs based on which students demonstrate reliability, competence, and motivation in their classes; so, from the first day of the semester, know that your potential as a GTA is already being assessed.

Faculty are also a great resource for gaining experience in research, and you should start looking for these opportunities as you settle in. We advise you to start small and start humble. In your first semester in graduate school, it is unlikely a faculty member will select you to head his or her research lab or to run a major research project. Granted, you may have all the necessary skills and expertise (well, this is probably not the case, but we want you to feel confident as you settle in!), but you have to prove that you have the "right stuff." Doing so requires you to build up a string of successes, working from smaller, seemingly mundane tasks, like scheduling research participants for a study, to more difficult and exciting tasks, such as helping design or conduct a research study (or, better yet, having a hand in the always exciting data analysis process where your training in statistics is on display). You want to prove to your advisor that you are reliable, capable, and motivated, and the best way to do so is through your actions. In our experience, students who can be trusted with small tasks are the ones we choose to take on big tasks.

Research skills also involve learning how to acquire research funding. As you will see in Chapter 19 in this book, finding funding sources and developing research proposals is a key part of the research process in academia. Although many of our students avoid this component of research like the plague ("I have to conduct a thorough literature review? Yuck!"), the smart ones, the ones who understand the importance of keeping research dollars coming into a laboratory or department, seek out ways to get experience in the process. And although we cannot speak for all faculty, we are sure a good number would agree that a student who can help put together an effective research proposal is a tremendous asset and would be highly sought after in the department.

Getting to know the faculty and learning their areas of research interest and expertise will also greatly enhance your scholarly development, for these are the people who will involve you in activities that add lines to your curriculum vitae. Tenenbaum, Crosby, and Gliner (2001) found that help from advisors contributed positively to academic productivity in the form of presentations and publications, as well as students' satisfaction with their graduate experience.

Finally, getting to know the faculty will help you graduate, as one of them will ultimately serve as your major advisor and/or chair your dissertation committee. Yes, as you settle in, it is already time to start thinking about your dissertation. You don't need to have the experimental hypothesis solidified by the end of orientation, but it is never too early to start making plans for what you need to do to earn the degree, and one of most important things is selecting your dissertation chair. As described in Chapter 20 of this book, finding the right person to serve as your chair and, later, the right committee, is an integral part of the dissertation process.

Applying the Rules of the Game

At the beginning of the chapter, we described our hope that you would learn two valuable lessons for how to settle into graduate school the right way. The first was how to find the rules of the game, and we offered a number of suggestions to help you achieve this goal. Our second lesson can be summarized in two words: Start now! We realize the first semester of graduate school is hectic. There are many changes in both your personal and academic lives. Nevertheless, the sooner you start applying the rules of the game, the more successful your graduate experience will be. Don't make the mistake, for example, of waiting a semester, or even a year, before meeting the faculty and staff in the department. Don't delay seeking out opportunities to volunteer on research projects or make your interest in a GTA position known.

And keep in mind that building your reputation among your peers, the faculty, and the staff starts on day one. Take advantage of social activities organized by the department or other students as a way to let others get to know you. In short, once you have learned the rules of the game, start using them right away to speed your development into a superstar student.

As an illustration, let's look at the experience (albeit manufactured to make a point), of two very different students with two very different approaches to settling in. The first, we'll call him Jason, began his graduate career by showing up a week after orientation. When he did attend classes, about 50% of the time, he was often late and would quickly fall asleep in his back-row seat. His Facebook wall was replete with stories and pictorial evidence of late nights partying and days at the beach (when he should have been in class). During his first several semesters, Jason avoided the department and would only stop in to get a form signed by the chair or copy entire textbooks on the department copy machine. Participation in research and teaching were nonexistent as he focused on perfecting his tan and his surfing career, and when asked to join student clubs in the department, his response was always no. Of course, when it was time to start his dissertation, 6 years later, Jason was surprised and frustrated that none of the professors wanted to help him go from proposal to defense in 4 months. Sadly, Jason left the program ABD—all but dissertation—and took a job selling surf boards.

In contrast, the second student, we'll call him Steve, began his graduate career by attending all of the orientation-week functions and introducing himself to fellow students, both incoming and current, every member of the faculty, and the office staff. During his first semester, Steve attended every class, sitting up front and not only staying awake but engaging in class discussions and group projects. After class, he would spend time in the department, volunteering to assist professors with classes or organize student social activities, and continued to build relationships with faculty. In his first year in the program, Steve was hired as a GTA, volunteered in a research lab running participants, and coauthored two conference presentations. He soon found the perfect academic advisor, who would later become his dissertation chair, and began developing an idea for his dissertation. At the end of 5 years in the program, Steve's dissertation was complete and his curriculum vitae was full of dozens of conference presentations, coauthored book chapters, and a few highly prized peer-reviewed journal articles. After graduation, he was quickly hired as an assistant professor at another university and paid a salary of nearly $300,000 (okay, that last part is pure embellishment).

Conclusion

Of course the experiences of Jason and Steve represent extreme examples of playing the game. One never even tried to learn or apply the rules; the other not only learned the rules well but also applied them immediately. It is our hope that you will fall somewhere in between these examples (hopefully more toward Steve) as you begin graduate school. We also hope you find your own unique way to become a superstar student. Some students make their mark in the area of research, impressing faculty with their dedication and proficiency for writing research proposals, designing research projects, collecting and analyzing data, and publishing results in journals. Others focus on developing their teaching skills or gaining applied experience as counselors.

Wherever you choose to make your mark, learn how to play the game from the beginning. Graduate school can be one of most exciting and enlightening periods of your career, and starting out the right way, by learning how to play by the formal and even more important informal rules, can set you on a course to success.

❖ References

Beck, J. G. (2003). The graduate school experience: One faculty member's perspective. *The Behavior Therapist, 26,* 245–247.

Bloom, L. J., & Bell, P. A. (1979). Making it in graduate school: Some reflections about the superstars. *Teaching of Psychology, 6,* 231–232.

Council of Graduate Schools (2005). *Graduate education: The backbone of American competitiveness and innovation: A report from the Council of Graduate Schools Advisory Committee on graduate education and American competitiveness.* Retrieved from http://www.cgsnet.org/Default.aspx?tabid=240&newsid440=47&mid=440.

Tenenbaum, H. R., Crosby, F. J., & Gliner, M. D. (2001). Mentoring relationships in graduate school. *Journal of Vocational Behavior, 59*(3), 326–341.

Walfish, S., & Hess, A. K. (2004). It's not just about grades: One student's strategies for successfully completing the Ph.D. *Constructivism in the Human Sciences, 9,* 143–149.

❖ Suggestions for Further Exploration

Delamont, S., Atkinson, P., & Parry, O. (2000). *The doctoral experience: Success and failure in graduate school.* New York: Falmer Press (an e-book version [2005] is published by Taylor and Francis e-Library and available at www.ebookstore.tandf.co.uk). With a broader focus on doctoral programs in the social and natural sciences, this book offers many insights into helping you develop as a scientist and earn your Ph.D. Chapters cover valuable lessons on supervision in the research process, the different cultures and challenges between university departments and academic disciplines, and science in the laboratory and in the field.

Kuther, T. L. (2008). *Surviving graduate school in psychology: A pocket mentor.* Washington, DC: American Psychological Association. Kuther's brief yet informative book provides a wealth of practical advice on surviving graduate school. Of particular value are her tips for practicing for interviews, sample curriculum vitas (CVs), guidelines for graduate teachers, and strategies to tackle the dissertation process.

Peters, R. L. (2007). *Getting what you came for: The smart student's guide to earning an M.A. or a Ph.D.* (rev. ed.). New York: Farrar, Straus, and Giroux. This comprehensive resource addresses all stages of the graduate school process, from criteria for selecting a school to searching for a job. With specific regard to playing the graduate school game, see Peters's chapters on managing yourself during the program, playing politics and building your reputation, the thesis process, and social interactions with fellow students and faculty.

Walfish, S., & Hess, A. K. (Eds.). (2001). *Succeeding in graduate school: The career guide for psychology students.* Mahwah, NJ: Lawrence Erlbaum. This book addresses many of the concepts introduced in our chapter with sections on considering a career in psychology, mastering the politics of graduate school (a big part of playing the game well), the internship process, and learning skills for your career developing as a professional. Of particular value are chapters on developing mentoring relationships and dealing with the stress of a graduate program.

2

Maximizing Success in Your Graduate Training

❖

Christia Spears Brown
University of Kentucky

Self-help books frequently talk about how the key to being successful is to "visualize success." Although that may or may not be an effective strategy, it is important to know what you mean by *success*, to define what success is in any given context. As an undergraduate, success was pretty easy to define: a high grade point average. As a graduate student, success is defined more subjectively. What makes a successful graduate career for one student may not work for another student. Everyone has different goals for their graduate training, and everyone takes a slightly different path to achieve those goals. To add to the confusion, the keys to success in graduate school are usually unwritten and students are left to figure them out on their own.

One goal of this chapter (and book), therefore, is to articulate clearly what makes a successful graduate student and a successful graduate career. The second goal of this chapter is to help you maximize your success while minimizing the struggles of attending graduate school. The rest of this book will focus on the specifics of success in graduate school, such as how to write and to teach effectively. Indeed, there are very explicitly stated benchmarks, unique to each graduate program, that must be achieved in order for a student to be considered successful, such as defending your thesis and dissertation and passing your qualifying exams. In contrast, the focus of this chapter is more on those implied goals of graduate school—the ones that are critical to your success but rarely mentioned in any graduate handbook or orientation packet.

What Is Success in Graduate School?

Before discussing what makes a successful graduate student, it is important to understand how we *really* define success in graduate school. The orientation packet you received probably stated that the goal of graduate school was to develop a broad knowledge of psychology as well as an expertise in a specific area of psychology and to develop advanced research and professional skills. Indeed, graduate school is designed to help you develop an expertise in your chosen field. This is a very important goal of graduate school. However, in the pursuit of this goal, students can lose their way, following tangent after tangent and getting sidetracked in their attempts to further their knowledge base. Instead of focusing on this broad goal, I suggest there are three different, very specific goals that seem to be crucial to any graduate student's emerging success.

The first sign of a successful graduate school career is that your degree is completed in a timely fashion. For a doctoral program, that typically means 5 or 6 years. Some students hang out in graduate school for 8 or 9 years. That is never necessary. Keep in mind that graduate school is not an open-ended, indefinite time to read and think. Successful graduate students have their time frame in mind as they move through graduate school, they pay attention to deadlines, and they work with purpose.

The second sign of success in graduate school is the ability to get a job upon graduation. This seems like an obvious goal, but many students lose sight of what is necessary to achieve this goal. For academic positions, this means you should have research publications and some teaching experience. All of your work in graduate school should be geared toward meeting these objectives. In other words, you should consistently ask yourself, "Can I turn this work into a publication? Does this add to my teaching experience? Does this provide me with important knowledge or training that I may be able to use in the future?" The chair of our psychology department stated it this way: "Be very planful about how you approach your training and your career—determine your goals, figure out what training experiences will best equip you to meet those goals, and work very hard to gain those experiences and generate research products." In other words, a successful graduate school career is purposeful and goal directed (the goal being a job). To achieve that ultimate goal of getting a job, you must meet the more proximate goals of generating research publications in top journals. For a more detailed discussion regarding applying for an academic job, see Chapter 23. See Chapter 24 for a discussion of applying for clinical or other applied positions.

The third goal in striving for a successful graduate career, and one that is just as important as the others, is to meet the above two goals with your mental health intact. You should emerge on the other end of your graduate career happy, with meaningful relationships, and loving your chosen profession. Otherwise, that M.A. or Ph.D. after your name isn't really worth it. Graduate school can be a fun, rewarding, and stimulating period of your life. As you will see, by being planful, focused, and hard working, you can graduate on time, with a job, and with a wonderful experience under your belt. The rest of this chapter focuses on the best ways to achieve those goals. Also see Chapter 10, which deals with self-care issues during your time in graduate training.

What Are the Most Important Characteristics of a Successful Graduate Student?

Assuming you want to have a successful graduate career, there are specific traits you can foster in yourself to help you work toward those goals. Interestingly, in an informal poll of faculty members in which I asked them this question, not one person mentioned being smart or making good grades. Keep in mind: You made it into graduate school (congratulations!). You are smart enough to be there. That characteristic doesn't seem to be what separates successful from less successful students. Instead, faculty members' responses focused on three themes. First, many faculty members stated that they highly valued intrinsic motivation, initiative, and resourcefulness in their students. As one colleague said, "I want a 'let's get it done now, even if I have to stay late' attitude." Others mentioned that these traits led students to seek out their own funding, to enroll in writing courses to improve their writing, or to work in the lab over the weekend. Related to this, faculty members wanted students who made consistent effort, were persistent, and were always committed to and engaged in research. For example, many faculty members mentioned that they wanted their students to write every day, and that this took serious commitment. Second, many faculty members mentioned that successful graduate students were students who could ask good questions, who strived to gain independence in their thinking, and who were creative. In other words, they want students who can create interesting research projects and go beyond what others have done before. They like students who ask interesting questions in class and who see connections that others may not see. Finally, many faculty members mentioned that successful students are able to set goals and see them through in a timely fashion (as one person said, "with an emphasis on timeliness"), are able to juggle their personal lives with career objectives, and are able to set priorities and organize their activities. In other words, successful graduate students are able to manage their time and priorities.

Taken together, we begin to see a picture of what you should strive for to maximize your success in graduate school. You should want to finish graduate school in a timely fashion, with the ability to get a job and with your sanity intact. To do this, you should work hard by taking initiative and showing resourcefulness, you should strive for independent creative thinking, and you should manage your goals and priorities well. Sounds easy enough, right? This kind of success is attainable by anyone. Unfortunately, many students fall short of these aspirations. Below are some specific tips to help make those abstract traits and objectives more easily within reach.

What Are the Most Important "Dos" to Being Successful in Graduate School?

Manage your time. Most importantly, manage your time well. If you have been accepted into a graduate program—which means you had a high undergraduate GPA, high GRE scores, and a well-written essay—you are smart enough to succeed in graduate school (although you may need to repeat this to yourself over the next few years). Success will largely depend on time management. Why is time management so important? My undergraduate professor (and editor of this book) once gave me advice about graduate school that I have repeated to my own students many, many times. He said, "The work in graduate school isn't really more difficult than the work you do here [as an undergraduate]. There is just a lot more of it." That proved to be true for me as a graduate student and has been confirmed by the graduate students who work with me. Graduate school is difficult because there is a lot of work to do. Thus, managing that workload is key. The main challenge to managing your time well is that there are going to be multiple and mutually exclusive demands on your time. You will have several classes, each with heavy reading requirements each week. You will have to work on your thesis, as well as the work assigned by your advisor. You may also have to coordinate these assignments with duties from a teaching or research assistantship. Juggling these demands involves two skills: prioritizing and planning.

In terms of prioritizing, it is important to remember that coursework is not the only or even the most important thing you are working on. Unlike your undergraduate program, in which your most important goal was a high GPA, your most important goal now is ultimately to get a job. For most people, that means you must conduct research (or help your advisor conduct research) that can be published in research journals. This is critical to getting a job, even positions that will not involve conducting research (such as a clinical position or a teaching position at a small undergraduate college). Thus, in most doctoral psychology programs, doing research is more highly valued than doing your coursework. Don't misunderstand: You must also do well in your courses. Most programs require you make As or the occasional B to stay in good standing. You should also keep in mind that attending classes is critically important not only for learning material and participating in class discussions but also for establishing relationships with professors and earning their respect. The key, however, is to devote just enough time to classes to do well, but no more. More time should always be spent conducting research. So you should learn how to read the assigned reading for your class quickly, taking only one night instead of one week; you should stop tinkering with your term paper once it gets to the A level instead of pushing for the A+; and, if possible, you should gear your term papers in class toward your own area of research so your reading for class overlaps with your other research as much as possible. If two classes require very similar papers, ask the professors if you can turn in similar papers for each class. It is a constant balancing act, but not keeping these priorities is a common way that students who excelled in their undergraduate programs fail to progress in their graduate programs.

Planning is another skill that helps students juggle the multiple demands on their time. One great way to manage your time effectively is to have a detailed planner or calendar. This will be the most valuable money you will ever spend. You should spend time at the beginning of each semester or quarter, and again each week, accounting for all of your time. Be specific. Write down when you are going to read for class, when you are going to study, when you are going to be in meetings. Most importantly, assign yourself time every day to write. If you have larger chunks of time, devote those to writing the more complex parts of your papers. For example, a typical Monday: 9:00–11:00 am, Statistics; 11:00–12:00, Statistics homework; 1:00–2:00, proctor an exam for my teaching assistantship; 2:00–4:00, work on Introduction of thesis. By putting your writing time into your planner, you make it a priority and respect that time, making it as valuable as your time in class. Furthermore, that writing time should be protected—no e-mailing, no Web surfing, no students dropping by. This can be harder than you think, particularly if you have family responsibilities. But treat writing time just as you would class time and you will be pleasantly surprised how much you can get written.

You should also use your planner to make deadlines for yourself, and keep the deadlines. Another common way graduate students struggle in graduate school is by falling behind on the many small deadlines, eventually adding years to their graduate careers. As a graduate student, you must make your own deadlines and find your own discipline to stick to those deadlines. Give yourself coursework deadlines, such as what day you will start writing class X's term paper. Even more importantly, give yourself broader deadlines. You should write down which component of your thesis should be done by October, which by December, and so forth. Work out a timeline for all your major projects and plan accordingly. Use that longer timeline to work out your daily goals.

Work hard. Another important "do" for success in graduate school, to directly quote my colleague (and head of the social psychology area), is "Work your butt off." You should always be doing something, as there will always be something to do. Even when you have no looming deadline and you think you have nothing to do, make sure you are writing, reading (especially new journal articles), thinking about possible research ideas, or coding data. As a graduate student, I made a habit of always having research articles with me to read whenever downtime presented itself—waiting for the bus, at the doctor's office, or before class started. Keep in mind when you work best and be sure to fill up those times first. For example, during the middle of the day, I can stay pretty focused. So if I have unexpected downtime at 1:00 p.m., I try to catch up on reading journal articles or grading a paper. I know that I will also have downtime at 8:00 p.m., but by then, I am going to be much more interested in watching television with my family and unwinding (just as important for keeping the mental health intact). In other words, make sure your day is filled with doing something—anything—to move you toward your goals. Then, when it is time to unwind, you can completely relax because you know you were productive that day.

In addition to working hard on what someone tells you to do, take initiative. Bring research ideas to your advisor, propose a new grant application, or find funding sources for yourself. As one colleague stated, "Assuming they are smart enough to get in, I think the individual difference that has the biggest impact in determining grad school outcomes is how hard a student works. The people putting in 70-hour weeks get a lot more publications and end up with better jobs than the ones who are nowhere to be found on Friday afternoons and take weeks of vacation during the summer." No one can keep up 70-hour workweeks all the time, but remember that graduate school is a finite period of time. Hard work now will lead to a big payoff later.

Related to this idea, be visible. Some students disappear at home or the library, only to emerge 3 months later with a thesis in hand. Graduate school doesn't work this way. First, you should be in contact with your advisor regularly, getting feedback on ideas, outlines, and drafts of your paper. Second, you not only need to work hard, you also need to make sure others *know* you are working hard. You should regularly be working in your lab office or stopping by to see if your advisor needs helps working on anything. Basically, be around. Keep in mind that graduate school success is often subjective, and perceptions are important.

Keep negative feedback in perspective. Another important key to being successful in graduate school is to learn to cope with constructive criticism and negative feedback. Most students who begin graduate school are used to earning very high grades and receiving positive feedback on their work as undergraduates. Your strong academic background got you into graduate school. For many students, it is difficult to cope with the negative feedback that is a part of academia. For example, many students are upset when they turn in the first draft of their thesis to their advisor and it is returned covered in corrections. Similarly, it is hard to submit your first paper to a journal only to have it harshly rejected. It is important to keep in mind that negative feedback is the nature of graduate school and academia; it is not personal. Your advisor has probably gotten so used to it that he or she will not think to focus on the many things you are doing right. Don't be discouraged. The quickest way to improve is to be told what needs to be improved upon. Know that your advisor had the same experience as a new graduate student. If you submit papers to journals, anticipate bad reviews and brace yourself. I frequently let my own new students read the very bad reviews of papers I have submitted to journals in the past. I remind them that everyone gets harsh feedback, and yet the papers eventually got published. In other words, the criticism helped me revise and improve and wasn't a reflection of my eventual abilities.

Persevere (and then celebrate). Just as important as taking the criticism in stride, continue to persevere, and celebrate the small victories. In graduate school, as in life, things don't always work out. Your thesis may not work as expected; your ideal committee member may back out at the last minute; your most important paper may be accidentally deleted from your computer. These types of things will no doubt happen at some point. The key to success in graduate school is to persevere despite the obstacles. My own graduate advisor, a highly respected researcher on children's gender and racial attitudes, once spent 12 years getting a single paper published. She would revise and resubmit, and get negative reviews. She would again revise and resubmit, and get additional negative reviews. She would again revise and resubmit. She had to deal with a lot of criticism but kept working on it until it was published. That paper is now a highly regarded publication cited by many other researchers in her field. Similarly, a successful colleague down the hall impresses the graduate students with his 20 publications a year. Students have made comments to him about how fantastic it is that he never gets his papers rejected. He then laughs and informs them that for every one publication he has, he has three rejections. In other words, he actually gets more rejection letters than anyone. He just perseveres and, undaunted, continues to send out new papers.

With all of your perseverance, you will have successes. Some will be small—turning in the first draft of your thesis to your advisor on time—and some will be big—successfully defending your thesis in front of your committee. Because you will be spending plenty of time working hard and coping with criticism (see above), celebrate those successes. Not every celebration needs to be extravagant, but treating yourself to a fancy coffee at the coffee shop, buying yourself a new book, or taking the night off when you normally work can do wonders for keeping your motivation and morale high. Graduate school is a marathon, not a sprint. You have to stay motivated to keep going despite the obstacles and long hours. It is important to embrace the positive moments and enjoy them.

Celebrating your successes can sometimes be a challenge because you are entering a profession in which the successes are not always easy to mark. You won't be making a big sale or getting a new customer; you will not have a profit margin at the end of the year. Our successes are often less obvious. For example, it can be easy to overlook that you successfully taught an undergraduate student the value of experimental design or that you wrote a letter of recommendation that helped a student get a prized internship. But these are successes nonetheless. So when you have a success, pay attention! At a minimum, pat yourself on the back. Take a moment to refuel. Even today, I take my family out to dinner when I have a paper published. Indeed, it is less about celebrating the actual publication and more about rewarding myself for persevering through three rounds of negative reviews. I know a new set of negative reviews will be coming soon, and I want to savor and enjoy the good moments.

Seek out others. Finally, as quickly as you can, make contacts with the professors in your department. If there are faculty members in other departments doing similar research, make a point to meet with them as well. Send them an e-mail and introduce yourself. Faculty are more than willing to set up a 30-minute meeting with you. Having relationships with faculty members is important for several reasons. They will be good sources for letters of recommendation for fellowships, they can be possible committee members, and they may have the answers to your questions about research or data analysis. This will also help you become familiar with other labs and open up paths for future collaborations.

Seeking the advice and support of faculty members is also important if things begin to get overwhelming. If this happens, first seek the advice of your advisor. This is helpful because he or she can help you get the support you need. You are likely new to the area and may not know all of the available resources. This is also helpful because it lets your advisor know that you are struggling, not just slacking off and being irresponsible. If your advisor is part of the problem, seek the advice of another faculty member you trust or the chair of the department. Remember that the faculty members in your department highly value the graduate students. They took great efforts to select you from a large group of applicants. They want you to be successful, and they believe that you can be. If you are struggling, seek their help or advice. Importantly, seek their help early, before you are years behind deadlines, have alienated your advisor, and have come to hate graduate school.

What Are the Most Important "Don'ts" to Being Successful in Graduate School?

Don't get overburdened. As there are things to do, there are also things to avoid on the path to success. First, do not take on more projects than you can handle. As you get acclimated to graduate school, you will notice many opportunities for research and group activities. Graduate students who share an office with you will have great ideas about new research projects you can collaborate on together. You will receive e-mails about the Graduate Student Council needing a new treasurer. You will want to actually do the project you proposed in one of your class term papers. These are all excellent ideas—in theory. After all, you were heavily involved in extracurricular activities as an undergraduate. You spent 10 hours a week volunteering the summer before graduate school. Plus, if research is valued, isn't doing extra research projects a good thing? The answer is no. It may seem like you will have time to spare, as you are only taking two or three classes and you have 2 years to write one thesis. However, as you will quickly learn, that extra free time is an illusion. In reality, your days will be very busy with your existing commitments.

To better understand the importance of time constraints, pretend you are a typical graduate student in social psychology enrolled in your second semester of graduate school. You recently read about the department's need for a graduate student representative, and your officemate wants to collaborate on a new project idea that you two would do on the side. Both are great ideas. But, before you write that IRB application or nominate yourself to the council, think through your schedule. For example, you are taking three classes: the Statistics course required for all first-year students (meets Tuesdays and Thursdays from 9:30 to 11:00), the Social Psychology core course required for social psychology students (meets Wednesdays from 12:00 to 3:00), and an additional core course in Cognitive Psychology (meets Tuesdays from 1:00 to 4:00). You are the teaching assistant for Introductory Psychology, which meets Mondays, Wednesdays, and Fridays from 9:00 to 10:00. Because you are a teaching assistant, you must also hold office hours, which you hold Mondays from 11:00 to 2:00. Your department also requires that you attend the weekly colloquium series held Fridays from 12:00 to 1:30; you have a weekly meeting with your advisor on Mondays from 2:00 to 3:00; and you have lab meetings on Fridays from 2:00 to 3:30. You are also collecting data for your thesis, which means you are administering questionnaires to participants in the subject pool from 12:00 to 5:00 on Thursdays. Every evening after dinner, you spend 2 to 3 hours reading for class, writing a term paper, or working on your thesis. This schedule is conservative and assumes you only attend one weekly colloquium, are not supervising undergraduate research assistants, and do not have to help your advisor with other writing assignments. As is hopefully obvious, this schedule leaves very little room for anything extra. Remember, you may have a family that needs attention, and your friends will occasionally want to see you!

One trick that seems to be used by successful graduate students is to think about graduate school as a full-time job (one that easily takes 50 hours a week to do the work required of you) and *not* an extension of undergrad life. Thinking about graduate school as a full-time job is helpful because it reminds you that taking on extra commitments means adding hours into an already full schedule. It will cut into meal times, time with family, and much-needed time off. It is also helpful because it keeps you from feeling overwhelmed by your schedule. Most people, including your friends from high school or college, work that many hours per week in regular jobs. Students tend to take on too many extra commitments and then feel overwhelmed and fall behind, because they try to fit an undergraduate template (in which you filled your extra free time during the day with extracurricular activities) onto their graduate school life. Graduate school is much more similar to your chosen profession (i.e., balancing research, teaching, and possibly clinical hours) than it is to your life as an undergraduate. This is purposeful; we are training graduate students to be professionals. This will require you to shift your identity, however, and make the hard decisions about what you are able to commit to and when you need to say "No!"

Don't procrastinate. Yes, the thesis is due 2 years from now. Faculty set that deadline for a reason; it takes 2 years to do! One way to keep from procrastinating is to break the larger projects into smaller chunks and set deadlines for those smaller chunks. Put those smaller deadlines into your planner and stick to them. For example, in your first semester, you should develop a thesis topic and an outline and establish your thesis committee. Early in your second semester, you should give a first draft of your thesis proposal to your advisor and submit your project to the IRB. During your second semester, you should defend your thesis proposal to your committee, obtain IRB approval, and begin the process of data collection. Early in your third semester, you should complete data collection and begin analyzing your results. During your third semester, you should write a rough draft of your final thesis. During your fourth semester, you should refine and defend your thesis. Even those smaller chunks can be broken down further. For example, your planner should say, "Monday: Write consent form for IRB," or "Tuesday and Wednesday: Write Methods section of proposal." In other words, there is a lot to do, so start now.

Don't take too much vacation. Don't assume summer break means you can take 3 months off. Again, that was your life as an undergraduate; it is not your life now. Summers are ideal times to get a lot of work done without also having to juggle coursework. You can collect all the data you need for your thesis in one summer. Or you can spend the summer analyzing the data you already collected. In addition, summers are a great time to get teaching experience as either a teaching assistant or an instructor. Even if you take an outside job, you should spend some time writing every day. This doesn't mean that you can never take a vacation or take a week off. But treat those breaks just like vacation days you would have accrued at a job, not like summer breaks from high school where you can lounge by the pool all summer. Remember that working through the summers in graduate school adds up to an extra year of work (i.e., 3 months of work across four summers), and most people agree that finishing school in 5 years is preferable to 6.

Don't compare yourself to others. If you do (and sometimes it is hard not to), find an appropriate comparison. My students in developmental psychology, who spend an entire year individually interviewing 200 third graders at their elementary schools, often compare themselves to our social psychology graduate students, who can run 200 undergraduate subject pool participants in one week of mass testing. No wonder the students sometimes feel inadequate and behind. This is not an appropriate comparison. Also, the student who collects and analyzes her own data shouldn't compare her progress to the student who analyzed her advisor's already-collected data. Find students who conduct similar research to you before you decide that you are doomed to failure. Better yet, set your own benchmarks and deadlines. As parents around the world say, "Be true to yourself." That applies here as well.

Conclusions and Summary

Graduate school is a wonderful time to learn how to conduct research, to teach, and to think like a psychologist. It can also be an incredibly stressful period in which you have to shift your identity from that of a student to that of an independent researcher/instructor. You will have to think independently, manage many demands on your time, and conduct top-quality research. You will also have to adapt to a culture in which critiques are handed out much more often than praise. Despite this, most Ph.D.s look back fondly on graduate school as a time of fruitful exploration of ideas and collaboration. Following the tips in this book is a good first step to ensuring that you, too, emerge from graduate school with both a job and wonderful nostalgia. To summarize:

- DO manage your time well. Prioritize those things that will ultimately help you get a job. Keep a detailed planner with deadlines that you actually adhere to. By prioritizing your writing and research and sticking to a detailed timeline, you will move through graduate school quickly and have an excellent job waiting for you at the end.
- DO work hard, remembering that there is always something new that needs to be written, read, or completed. Remember that people are looking to see if you are working hard.
- DO keep the negative feedback in perspective. It is not a negative reflection of your abilities, but it should be used to improve your work.
- DO stay motivated despite criticism. Persevere even though you get discouraged. You will eventually have successes. Then, fully celebrate the successes to help fuel that motivation.
- DO seek out others for feedback, and reach out for help when you need it. There are many people who will be supportive and advocate for you. But they won't know you are struggling unless you seek them out.

But . . .

- DON'T overburden yourself with commitments that don't help you achieve your goal of getting a job. Your schedule is incredibly full, even if you don't realize it yet. Treat graduate school like a full-time job and recognize that any extracurricular activities will eat into your time off.
- DON'T procrastinate. Projects take a long time, but if you work a little at a time, you will complete them when expected.
- DON'T stop working just because it is summer. Summer, without the rush of your normal schedule, can be an incredibly productive time of year. Take advantage of it.
- DON'T compare yourself to others. We only seem to find the students who make us feel bad about our performance and progress.

❖ Suggestions for Further Exploration

Darley, J. M., Zanna, M. P., & Roediger, H. L. (2003). *The compleat academic: A career guide.* Washington, DC: American Psychological Association. Although this is a book less about graduate school and more about life after graduate school, it serves as a good model for balancing the many demands of graduate school.

Silvia, P. J. (2007). *How to write a lot: A practical guide to productive academic writing.* Washington, DC: American Psychological Association. Read this book early in graduate school, and it will help you quickly make progress.

3

Setting Your Path ❖

Begin With Your Dissertation in Mind

Daniel P. Corts
Augustana College

Holly E. Tatum
Randolph College

Before you even begin graduate school, you are faced with some serious decisions: Where do I apply? What type of degree is right for me? How do I pay for it all? For some of these decisions, you may benefit from thoughtful undergraduate advisors, or perhaps friends and family have graduate school experiences that can guide you. Ultimately, however, you will find yourself in graduate school and you are going to have to make some tough decisions: decisions about classes to take, which research projects to work on, what graduate faculty to work for and who to avoid. Unless your undergraduate advisor just left the very same graduate school you are now enrolled in, you have to come up with the answers largely by yourself.

Research suggests that the most successful students are the ones that have a sense of direction and those who can find their own path from start to finish (Gardner, 2009). The goal of this chapter is to give a single piece of advice: When in doubt, keep your dissertation in mind. This works because the dissertation is the end point of your graduate training, so it can help you make more informed decisions—and fewer wrong turns—along the way.

The advice you will find in this chapter comes from two main sources. First, we have asked a number of Ph.D.s—all working in academia—to respond to the title of this chapter. We asked, "What does 'Begin with your dissertation in mind' mean to you?" The answers actually provide the structure for the chapter, and they have been paraphrased in the text. In addition, there is a small but important social science literature on the graduate school experience relating to the dissertation. We have culled what we find most useful from this literature to flesh out what we have learned from the narratives.

When and Where the Dissertation Can Guide You

A typical graduate program includes the following requirements: coursework for the first 2 or possibly 3 years, a research or clinical practicum, a predissertation project or master's thesis (if you do not already have a master's degree), comprehensive exams or an integrative paper, a dissertation proposal, and final defense. The dissertation process can take up to 2 or sometimes 3 years. It requires that you set up a dissertation committee including your major advisor, several other faculty in your department, and often one person outside your department. In addition, you may also be assigned a teaching or research assistantship as part of your financial aid package. A Ph.D. program in clinical or counseling psychology also requires an additional year-long predoctoral internship. This is all in addition to many of the weekly activities of a graduate student described in Chapter 2—lab meetings, departmental colloquia, supervising undergraduate research assistants, data collection, and possibly even teaching your own course.

Keeping the dissertation in mind can guide many of the early decisions you are required to make, such as course selection, choosing an advisor, and even deciding which research projects to work on. But why the dissertation? Hypothetically, one could just as easily set sights on the oral exams, the comprehensive finals, or the total credit hours required and use any of these as an endpoint. So why the dissertation and not comprehensives? Estimates suggest that 50% of those who enter doctoral programs do not complete their degrees (Council of Graduate Schools, 2004), nor do 15 to 25% of those who make it to candidacy (see Lovitts, 2008). Failure to complete the degree is rarely a problem of completing classes; the problem is completing the dissertation.

Selecting Courses

Graduate school course selections are guided by multiple sources of influence. Some classes are rather obvious—they are assigned to you by virtue of the program you have entered. Other classes are purely elective, meaning you get to choose whatever interests you. Still others fall in between, as was the case for P.D.'s statistics sequence, which was a requirement, but with several available alternatives. P.D. was interested in completing a dual program in which his psychology dissertation would perform double duty, serving as a master's thesis in the statistics department. Here's how he describes his dilemma:

> *The first day of orientation, they had us sign up for the first-year sequence of statistics. Everyone had to complete a year of stats, the question was where: Should we take the stats courses offered by the Psychology Department or the Statistics Department? Since I was a psychology student,*

it first seemed to make more sense to register for the stats sequence in my home department. However, I was planning on the joint program in statistics and psychology, and this meant using my dissertation in psychology as a master's thesis in stats. This fact made my decision for me because the Statistics Department would only count the Statistics Department's first-year sequence towards the joint degree.

—P.D.

So in this case, knowing something about his dissertation helped P.D. get off on the right track by choosing the appropriate course. Granted, P.D.'s situation was probably rare, and you may not find yourself in the exact same situation. However, you most likely will be required to choose a few elective courses to complete, and you may even need to go beyond the required number of electives. It is these types of courses that are most relevant to our discussion because the dissertation can help you make the decisions.

So just how does one choose courses? If you keep your potential dissertation topics in mind, there are a few suggestions that can help. For starters—and perhaps most obviously—a dissertation topic can lead you to content areas in other departments. If you are a psychologist studying language, check out the graduate courses offered in speech pathology or philosophy. If you are interested in health psychology, explore classes in biology or public health. Work with your advisor to identify some potentially interesting areas, and you are likely to find some fascinating and rewarding classes to take. A less obvious benefit is that the right course selection can lead you to potential dissertation committee members. This was the case for P.D., whose course choice led him to a statistics professor that joined the dissertation committee. These are just a couple of the benefits of choosing courses with the dissertation in mind.

Developing Research Skills

Research and statistics courses should be taken early on in your graduate career, specifically in the first year. The timing, quality, and quantity of research coursework influences dissertation preparation, writing, and completion time (Cuetara & LeCapitaine, 2001). However, a significant proportion of graduate students feel that their coursework did not adequately prepare them for their dissertation (Golde & Dore, 2001). Therefore, developing the necessary skills to complete independent research is an integral part of your graduate training, and it may take place outside of class. In research conducted among counseling psychology programs, those graduate students who had research experience prior to the dissertation reported feeling more prepared to conduct their dissertation research and lower negative affect such as depression and anxiety during the dissertation process (Cuetara & LeCapitaine, 2001). In a longitudinal study of graduate students from different disciplines, participants reported that their research experiences provided the skills and abilities to design, carry out, and write up research for publication (Austin, 2002). If you have not completed a master's thesis prior to entering a Ph.D. program, then you will likely be required to conduct a predissertation project or a master's thesis before beginning your dissertation. Look at this as an opportunity to practice for a larger and more comprehensive dissertation project. It will also give you experience with your advisor as a research mentor. See Chapter 14 for specific advice about developing your research skills.

To put this advice into context, consider what happened to a friend of ours, S.C., a graduate student who thought he had plenty of research experience. Unfortunately, it did not prepare him for his dissertation project:

> *I spent most of my first three years working on projects that were tangential to what I had in mind for my dissertation. I thought it was great preparation because I was able to read almost all the relevant literature. I thought I was way ahead of the pack until it came time for my dissertation proposal meeting. I had the research question in mind and a hypothesis to go with it, but I was less certain about the specifics of the methodology and I was totally clueless as to how I would analyze the data. None of the work I had done up to that point had adequately prepared me for my proposal. I wound up falling behind because I had to go back to the literature to learn the methods and statistics before I could finish my proposal. Luckily, it didn't set me too far back, but I do wish I had better prepared myself.*

> —S.C.

S.C.'s experience illustrates the vital importance of exposure to research prior to finalizing your dissertation topic. Keep in mind that in psychology, graduate students are more likely to receive teaching assistantships than research assistantships (Austin, 2002). Get involved in research projects—you can ask to become involved as soon as you start. If your advisor does not have a current or ongoing project, then ask other graduate students. Join another research lab or research team and offer to help run subjects or code and enter data. Ask to sit in on research or lab meetings. Offer to proofread or edit submissions for conferences or journal publications for your peers or advisor. If there are no projects available, get together with a peer or two and put together your own research project on a topic of interest.

Even if you do not know what your dissertation topic will be, it is important to be prepared for a variety of possible statistical analyses, including learning additional software programs. Because of this, we suggest you go beyond the basic required methods courses and take additional research and/or statistics courses to improve and hone your research skills. Often these courses are offered outside of the psychology department, such as in statistics, sociology, or business.

Finding an Advisor

S.C.'s story brings up an important point—make sure you find an advisor who will prepare you for your dissertation work. It is important to find someone who meets your needs—not only with regard to your area of interest but also your personality and work habits. If you need lots of feedback, make sure that you choose someone who is willing to provide it and is accessible. Sometimes, finding the right advisor might actually mean changing your advisor. As a graduate student, it can be a stressful experience to decide to leave an advisor. However, as H.T. describes, it may be just the right move to make you successful:

> *I switched dissertation advisors after completing a Psychometrics class with a professor who was enthusiastic, energetic, and supportive. He had multiple graduate students working with him on various projects and was excited to include me in his research. It was the first time that I felt someone was going to make sure that I finished. He provided the structure and push that I needed to get my work done. We emailed or talked on the phone almost daily during the data collection and analysis phase. Although my topic was not in the original area of psychology I had planned, I am glad to have chosen him as my advisor.*
>
> —H.T.

As you can tell from H.T.'s experience, dissertation advisors come in all shapes and sizes, and it might be best to consider your options before committing to one. Having an advisor who is enthusiastic about your project can mean the difference between getting sound, prompt feedback on your progress versus a sluggish or even resistant response from someone who views supervising you as a chore. In fact, in graduate departments with a shorter time to degree and high completion rates, advisor involvement has been identified as a major factor contributing to student success (deValero, 2001). Be sure to read Chapter 20, which provides a more in-depth discussion of choosing and working with a major professor.

Preparing for the Challenges of the Dissertation

We now turn to some of the challenges you will face. Once you start on your dissertation, you will find a whole new collection of obstacles. You will be expected to write like a professional, to persevere through data collection and revisions, and to do so on your own. To help you through this process, we would like to share a bit of research and personal experience with you in this section.

Scholarly writing. Writing in and of itself is typically not taught in graduate school. It is assumed by most graduate faculty that you can both articulate an argument and write in a scholarly manner. Unfortunately, undergraduate students vary in how much they are prepared for graduate work. In fact, graduate students may have little to no experience with scholarly writing before entering graduate school (Caffarella & Barnett, 2000). In response to the lack of preparation, faculty are developing writing programs to cultivate these skills before the dissertation work. One such program, the Scholarly Writing Program, included three main areas of focus—content, process, and critiquing (Caffarella & Barnett, 2000). The critiquing aspect of the program included feedback from both professors and peers on multiple drafts of a manuscript. Programs such as these may be offered in your department or in another related department. You may also want to explore the types of workshops offered at regional and national conferences—some of which may relate to scholarly writing, such as those focused on getting publications. It may be beneficial either to seek out specific programs or courses that focus on writing or to engage in some of these activities early in your graduate program. Suggestions for writing experiences include those mentioned earlier—get involved in ongoing research, proofread or edit others' work, and offer to help review submissions for conferences or publication. Any coauthoring experiences you can glean will give you practice in both honing your writing skills and responding to feedback. In addition, when submitting written work in classes, ask for feedback. Your professors may vary on how much they offer, but usually if you ask for additional feedback, you can get it. Ask for clarification or to see examples of what your professor considers good scholarly writing. See Chapter 11 for a more in-depth look at developing your writing skills.

Isolation. Unlike students in the physical and medical sciences who often work in research teams, graduate students in the humanities, social sciences, and psychology tend to work individually with some guidance from their faculty mentors or advisors (Austin, 2002). Because of this, graduate students in psychology may experience more isolation while conducting their dissertation research. Unlike your peers in the biochemistry department, for example, who are working in more structured research labs with other graduate students, you may be the only graduate student working on a research topic or project. Developing strong peer relationships may be integral to your success in graduate school. These relationships will likely form early on when you begin your classes. After your coursework is over, you may be essentially on your own to complete the requirements of the program. Graduate students often rely on the social support from their peers to help deal with challenges in teaching and research, as well as problems that arise while completing the dissertation and comprehensive exams. Because most students are working on their own in the later stages of the program, it is important to create a peer group or cohort that meets on a regular basis to discuss these issues. Not only can you meet to talk and discuss, but you could also meet to work on statistical problems or data analysis, share resources, collaborate on presentations, or brainstorm about research ideas. It is not only important to maintain regular contact with your peers, it is also imperative to keep in close contact with your advisor throughout the problem formulation, proposal, implementation, and writing stages. Be sure to choose an advisor who is accessible and present. Losing contact with your major advisor or leaving to take a job before finishing your dissertation will almost certainly prolong your degree completion. Again, Chapter 20 has excellent suggestions on these issues.

Perseverance. The last and probably the most demanding component of the graduate school experience is the perseverance required to complete what often feels like an overwhelming task. Writing a dissertation requires a level of self-regulation that challenges even the most self-disciplined students. There are not a lot of experiences that can prepare you for this part of the process. However, there are strategies that graduate students can develop and practice early in their training before starting the dissertation.

There will be many projects and papers throughout your graduate coursework. You may be given an assignment on the first day of class that is not due until the end of the semester. You may not be given any structure or guidance on how to complete the task. And, unlike many undergraduate assignments, you cannot pull an all-nighter and succeed. You need to learn how to develop a timeline for the work. Learn to break down larger papers into sections and pace yourself. You may spend the greatest proportion of your time just collecting the resources needed to complete the project. You may also underestimate the time required to complete the task, especially if it involves collecting data.

This is when it's time to start applying some of that psychological research to yourself. Setting timelines with your advisor is a great way to stay on track. Also, contingency contracting is another way to get others involved in your progress. J.S. came up with a brilliant idea to keep her motivated.

> *I really wanted to complete my integrative review paper. No one would hold me to a real deadline. So, I took matters into my own hands and decided to give myself a deadline. I wrote a check to an organization that I do not support. I gave the check to my boyfriend and told him to put it in the mail if I was not finished by my self-imposed deadline. As a poor graduate student, this really gave me the motivation to finish it on time.*
>
> —J.S.

We are here to tell you that incentives worked for us, and there is research that supports the claim as well (e.g., Garcia, Malott, & Brethower, 1988). It doesn't have to be expensive; for one of us (DPC), a completed dissertation chapter meant a weekend off for a camping trip in the mountains. Incidentally, completed chapters still mean a reward for us.

In summarizing her qualitative work on who is successful in graduate school, Lovitts (2008) surmised that the *distinguished completers*—those students who are able to make the transition to independent research—are described as those who

> display intense intellectual curiosity, are willing to work hard, take the initiative, and have the power to persevere in the face of apparent failure. They are motivated by a strong intrinsic interest in their research and are passionately committed to their projects. They also have good advisors and are willing and able to seek out and take advice from them. (p. 320)

Chapter 2 deals in more depth with similar issues.

Choosing a Dissertation Topic

Our advice in this chapter is based on the premise that the dissertation can serve as a decision-making tool. Unfortunately, it overlooks perhaps the biggest decision you will make in graduate school: What will be your dissertation topic? Graduate students often suffer great angst while choosing the perfect subject to study. It is imperative to choose a topic of high personal interest that will support your academic and career goals. You may spend at least 1 to 2 years working on your dissertation, so the topic should sustain your interest and passion over the long, arduous journey. Furthermore, if you are headed to academia, your dissertation may serve as a springboard for an entire research program in your future. In the academic job search, your dissertation topic may define you, and therefore, you should choose carefully and take time to consider both the topic and the advisor who will best serve you.

Reviewing all the topics we have touched on in this chapter, you will see that there are pros and cons to choosing to work on part of your advisor's research as your dissertation topic. Certainly your advisor can provide resources that will support your research, including funding, equipment, training, research assistants, and laboratory space. You will likely have access to the research tools and methodologies that are being utilized in that line of inquiry. And you will have an advisor who is familiar (if not an expert) with the topic. All of these factors may facilitate your progress. Furthermore, working in an active research lab helps students avoid the isolation that often accompanies dissertation writing (see below). On the other hand, you may not be thrilled with the topic or you may want to work on the research problem from a different angle. So you might want to consider the advice of J.R., who had to choose between a ready-made dissertation topic that was less than thrilling and the topic that led her to graduate study in the first place.

> *My advisor had a lot of experience with dissertations and that definitely worked in my favor. He essentially handed me a topic and said that I was welcome to try this simple, ready-made research project, but then he warned me that the simplest projects always took the longest. It seemed paradoxical until he explained: Even the simple projects require a year, and the students who take these run out of steam in just a couple of months. A really good topic is a puzzle that you can't stop working on. The idea is that you'll work harder, but you'll be so engaged that you won't mind at all. Those are the projects that work.*
>
> —J.R.

For J.R., choosing a dissertation topic meant that she had to understand a paradox: The easiest projects are sometimes the toughest to complete, whereas the more challenging topics are sometimes, somehow, less demanding. According to J.R. it is easier to understand this paradox once you find yourself hard at work. Students who try to take the easy topic often are not as interested, so they have to force themselves to set aside work time and to sit and concentrate. On the other hand, if you are really excited about a project, it doesn't matter if it is challenging—you will live and breathe the topic, and you will look forward to those moments when you can actually sit down and write!

So where do these dissertation ideas come from? Reading, reading, and reading. To formulate a well-defined research question, you must first become familiar with the topic. A key strategy is to choose classes where research assignments or papers may serve as predissertation preparation, where you might start working on the background or literature review. Gordon (2003) suggested that one of the biggest dissertation hang-ups is the fragmented nature in which graduate work is conducted. Students divide their time between classes, research, teaching, and additional requirements and are then asked to come up with a dissertation topic. He suggested keeping notes throughout all aspects of the graduate program (e.g., coursework, research, or comprehensive exams) will help you generate possible research topics and problems.

Conclusion

When you begin your graduate program, begin with your dissertation in mind. It may seem a long way off, but it is never too early to start preparing for the challenge. You will need to know the research methodology and analytical tools when the time comes, so take advantage of the coursework and laboratory experiences of the first few years to prepare. You will also have the chance to meet people who can help you—choosing advisors and committee members with your dissertation in mind will ensure that you have access to the expertise and support you need. And remember that you will need to persevere through a year or two of intense work, often in isolation, so before you begin, it is important to make sure you are passionate about the topic.

❖ References

Austin, A. E. (2002). Preparing the next generation of faculty: Graduate school as socialization to the academic career. *Journal of Higher Education, 73,* 94–122.

Caffarella, R. S., & Barnett, B. G. (2000). Teaching doctoral students to become scholarly writers: The importance of giving and receiving techniques. *Studies in Higher Education, 25,* 39–53.

Council of Graduate Schools. (2004). *Ph.D. completion and attrition: Policy, numbers, leadership, and next steps.* Washington, DC: Council of Graduate Schools.

Cuetara, J., & LeCapitaine, J. (2001). The relationship between dissertation writing experiences and doctoral training environments. *Education, 112,* 233–241.

deValero, Y. F. (2001). Departmental factors affecting time-to-degree and completion rates of doctoral students at one land grant research institution. *Journal of Higher Education, 72,* 341–367.

Garcia, M. E., Malott, R. W., & Brethower, D. (1988). A system of thesis and dissertation supervision: Helping graduate students succeed. *Teaching of Psychology, 15,* 186–191.

Gardner, S. K. (2009). Conceptualizing success in doctoral education: Perspectives of faculty in seven disciplines. *Review of Higher Education, 32,* 383–406.

Golde, C. M., & Dore, T. M. (2001). *At cross purposes: What the experiences of today's doctoral students reveal about doctoral education.* Madison: Wisconsin Center for Education Research.

Gordon, P. J. (2003). Advising to avoid or to cope with dissertation hang-ups. *Academy of Management Learning and Education, 2,* 181–187.

Lovitts, B. E. (2008). The transition to independent researcher: Who makes it, who doesn't, and why. *Journal of Higher Education, 79,* 296–325.

❖ Suggestions for Further Exploration

Bolker, J. (1998). *Writing your dissertation in fifteen minutes a day: A guide to starting, revising, and finishing your doctoral thesis.* New York: Henry Holt and Company. Joan Bolker, Ed.D., is a psychologist and a writing counselor. Her psychological training is quite helpful when it comes to identifying reasons people struggle with the dissertation and how to address those problems.

Fitzpatrick, J., Secrist, J., & Wright, D. J. (1998). *Secrets for a successful dissertation.* Thousand Oaks, CA: Sage Publications. This book is an easy read—like getting advice from a friend. It provides a lot of clear, concise, and easy-to-use tips on completing your dissertation.

4

Relationship Issues ❖

Peers, Faculty, and Families

Susan R. Burns
Morningside College

The letter arrives, and with much trepidation because you have been waiting for what seems like forever to receive it, you open it, and with tears of joy and a huge sigh of relief, you become part of the club. What club? The club of students accepted into graduate school. As you have learned from other chapters in this book, and perhaps from your experiences in graduate school thus far, there are lots of things you can do to increase the likelihood of success in your graduate studies. Certainly, your academic coursework in your undergraduate training prepared you for this moment, right? Yes, of course! However, have you considered the issues beyond your coursework that affect your success in graduate school? The purpose of this chapter is to help you navigate issues beyond academics in graduate school: relationships. Why the need for such a chapter, you ask? If you have not learned already from undergraduate experiences or the graduate experiences you have had to this point, relationships (of many kinds) can make or break your success in graduate school.

Even prior to Bloom and Bell (1979), who described graduate school "superstars" (i.e., students who not only survive graduate school but thrive in their graduate training), faculty and students alike have been interested in discovering what it takes to make the most of their graduate training. Bloom and Bell found that these students had more than just the expected strong GPAs and GRE scores, they had five additional characteristics that increased their academic prosperity: visibility, hard work, reflection of the graduate program's values, attachment to a professor, and the "W" factor. The "W" factor, according to Bloom and Bell, includes personal attributes such as being easy to teach, not complaining, and receiving feedback well.

With a desire to update Bloom and Bell's (1979) findings and perhaps consider other characteristics that may describe graduate student superstars, Grover, Leftwich, Backhus, Fairchild, and Weaver (2006) surveyed a total of 248 faculty from graduate schools from terminal master's to doctoral programs. Similar to Bloom and Bell, Grover and colleagues found support for the five characteristics previously identified as promoting graduate school success. However, different from Bloom and Bell, Grover and colleagues asked faculty to rank the top six qualities of students who had obtained "graduate stardom." These qualities included: "(a) intelligence; (b) strong work ethic; (c) motivation; (d) dedication, determination, and persistence; (e) critical thinking; and (f) creativity" (p. 272).

Although Bloom and Bell (1979) and Grover and colleagues (2006) give us an idea of what personal characteristics and behaviors help with graduate school success, what these authors fail to mention is how having these superstar characteristics may also help students navigate the important relationships that affect success in graduate school. There are relationships within the graduate program that you will need to give attention to (e.g., with your peers, your advisor, your professors) and relationships outside of your graduate program (e.g., with significant others and/or family) that can considerably impact your success in graduate school.

Finding a Guide: The Importance of Peer Mentors

If you were to go hiking in a terrain that you have never hiked before, you would likely hire a guide to assist with the outing. Graduate school is no different. Having a guide or, more importantly, a mentor to help you navigate the experience is extremely helpful. There are several options for guides in graduate school terrain. Your peers, especially graduate students a year or two ahead of you in the program, can help you understand the politics of your program. Trust me, all programs have politics. What is it like to work with Professor X? How do you best study for the quizzes in Professor Y's class? What should you *not* do in a research meeting with Professor Z? These are all questions that you will likely have in your early stages of graduate school. Having a graduate student mentor can be invaluable. Some programs have graduate student organizations that have formal mentoring programs whereby second- or third-year students are assigned new student protégés. Having had a graduate student mentor and having been a graduate student mentor, I was grateful to get, and to give when it was my turn, the "inside scoop." These graduate student organizations also serve as a great source for camaraderie beyond their academic benefits. Because you are spending much of your time in classes with these individuals, these colleagues will become your greatest competitors, but also your strongest allies. Connect with your peers. The bonds you form with them can be beneficial personally and professionally.

Advisor: Friend or Foe?

As a part of most graduate programs, you will be assigned an advisor. That advisor may be assigned to you based upon the program in which you were accepted or the interests you have or may even be the person with whom you said you would like to work with in your application materials. Regardless of who that person is, his/her role as an advisor is slightly different than the role of an undergraduate advisor. Yes, he or she will very likely help you select your courses, but unlike your undergraduate advisor, this may also be the person who supervises your research and/or practicum/ internship experiences. Graduate students work very closely with their advisors and, in the ideal world, will ultimately see this person as more than an advisor, rather, as a mentor. What do graduate students want from a mentor? According to Perlmutter (2008), graduate students romanticize the ideal mentor as someone who

> is respected within the field and has contacts; can help you with publications and jobs; is knowledgeable about the university and its politics and policies; takes the time to help with your studies and your career; does not exploit you; is not a disinterested observer of your career but cares about you as a person and is supportive—like a coach cheering you on. (C1)

If you can find a mentor with all of these characteristics, you have hit the jackpot and will have very few worries navigating the sometimes-rough terrain of graduate school. However, not all students will be so lucky, and even if you find an outstanding mentor, he/she is human and will have up days and down days that affect his/ her behaviors toward you. To make the most of the advisor/student relationship, graduate students should learn the personality and behavioral mannerisms of their advisors. Again, your peers can be very useful in helping you better understand nuances in the relationship with your advisor.

Notably, mentoring is not a one-way street. Protégés should do their part to increase the success of the relationship.

Doing Your Part as a Protégé

Perlmutter (2008) offered suggestions for what protégés can do to "hold up their end of the bargain." Student protégés need to accept their mentors' imperfections; not be passive about asking for help; establish clear communication; understand appropriate boundaries of the relationship; accept criticism; and accept the appropriate level of independence. Again, the characteristics of superstars described by Bloom and Bell (1979) and Grover and colleagues (2006) parallel Perlmutter's (2008) suggested desirable protégé behaviors.

Feist-Price (1994) described challenges that may be faced when the mentor/ protégé relationship is cross-gendered. Some adversities of cross-gendered mentoring relationships described by Feist-Price include a difficulty developing trust and confidence, which may in turn hamper the ability to develop meaningful communication between the pair. Additionally, this author described the challenges of overcoming stereotypical roles. Men and women are often bound by societal gender roles that can negatively influence the power dynamic in a mentoring association. In cross-gendered mentoring relations, Feist-Price notes that there are limitations of role modeling. Women and men face some problems that are unique to their specific sex. Even more important in the gender pairing, some students and mentors face intimacy and sexuality concerns. This author suggests that the potential for these concerns can be a source of anxiety. The final challenge mentioned by Feist-Price is peer resentment. For example, if a male mentor has several male protégés and one female protégé, the men may misperceive the relationship between the mentor and female protégé as one that receives special treatment or attention. This misperception can lead to troubles within the peer group.

For cross-gender mentoring connections to be successful, Feist-Price (1994) recommends necessary conditions including: development of mentoring goals, cooperation of the agency (e.g., graduate program), autonomous selection process (i.e., nonforced connections), commitment to the relationship by the mentor, and the ability for the protégé to withdraw from the relationship. Finally, Feist-Price noted that there should be continued evaluation of the association.

Because I completed a terminal master's degree in experimental psychology at one institution and then went on for a Ph.D. at a different university, I had the opportunity to work with two different advisors/mentors, both of whom were the opposite gender of me. These advisors had *very* different personalities, mannerisms, and student–advisor relationship styles. What I learned with my first graduate advisor did not necessarily help me with my second; however, what was very useful was, as previously mentioned, asking my peers who had the same advisor how to best work with this professor. Without their insight and guidance, I am not sure that I would have been as successful as I was in my graduate studies. Your advisor, especially if he or she is your research mentor as well, has an enormous impact on your ability to progress through the program. Not understanding how to best relate to that individual can end or extend the time spent in your graduate experience, even if you are a good student. The relationship you build with your graduate advisor/mentor does not (should not) end upon completion of your degree. This person will also be a key player who will be writing recommendations, serving as a reference, and possibly helping you connect with prospective employers. Damaged or strained relationships with your advisor can not only hurt you during your graduate studies, but beyond as well. I was fortunate to have found a very strong mentor in one of my advisors and a very good reference from both; however, I worked very hard for both of those individuals and attempted to be the graduate student superstar as previously described. The effort I put into those relationships continues to benefit me today.

Departmental Connections Beyond the Advisor

There are other relationships within the academic setting that students should be conscientious of during their graduate training. Just as the advising/mentoring relationship can significantly impact your success in graduate school, each professor you have will have an influence on your continued success in your graduate training. Each semester in many graduate programs, advisors, instructors, and the professors who supervise teaching and/or research assistants evaluate students' performance. Once again, the "superstar" characteristics previously described can be great assets for ensuring success. Even more importantly, the departmental administrative assistant can be a very useful resource. Don't abuse him or her! Common curtsey will serve you well with interacting with this person. Faculty and department chairs will be the first to tell you that the departmental administrative assistant "runs the place!"

Family Relationships

Clearly relationships within the graduate program have a direct impact on graduate students' success, but relationships outside of the program, too, can greatly impact the outcome of graduate training. I have already discussed the importance of your peers for social support, but your family can additionally be a great source of backing. In referring to family, I first mean your parents, those who raised you, your siblings, and so forth. If you are the first in your family to pursue postsecondary education, you may have to be patient with your family's inability to fully understand the complexity of what you are experiencing. I was not only the first in my family to pursue graduate training but also the first (and only) to study psychology. My graduate training was largely in experimental psychology (personality/social psychology with an emphasis in child development), but even with lengthy conversations, much of my family persisted in believing that I was going to "analyze" them or could fix their problems. Although my family may not have understood exactly what I was studying, they could listen to my frustration and celebrate my successes.

Honey, I'm . . . in Graduate School!

Family for me, as well, during graduate school meant a husband and the addition of three children to our home. When I found out I was pregnant with my first child at the end of the completion of my master's degree, I was unsure how my advisor/mentor and my professors would react. Quite honestly, like many other women who become pregnant during their graduate program, I kept my pregnancy a secret at first, expecting negative reactions. Williams (2004), in a piece for *The Chronicle of Higher Education*, agrees, stating that "many graduate student mothers remain 'in the closet'" (p. 12). Williams also notes that even if a student's graduate advisor is supportive, he/she might run into problems with other members of the department.

I was pleasantly surprised at the support and encouragement my mentor and professors gave me. I do believe, however, part of the reason they were so supportive was because I had already proven myself in the program, and they all knew how determined I was to complete my master's degree and to further pursue a Ph.D. When I moved on to a Ph.D. program (now with a child in tow), I had to prove myself once again. The Bloom and Bell (1979) attributes become even more important when a student has to prove him- or herself. Although I was dividing my time as a student and wife/mother, I made sure that I was very visible in the program, I worked extremely hard, attempted to reflect the values of the program, proved myself as a strong researcher, student, and teaching assistant, and embodied the "W" factor (i.e., easy to teach, not complaining, and receiving feedback well). How, you ask, did I do all of these things and sustain my family relationships (including the addition of two more children during my Ph.D.)? I married well. What I mean by "marrying well" is that without my husband's support, it would have been extremely difficult to be a superstar.

What about men who have families? Surprisingly (or not, depending upon your perspective), there is not as much research or discussion of the challenges and rewards that men face when having a family during their graduate training. Perhaps why this should not be surprising is that although we have come a long way with regard to gender equality and expectations of men's involvement of the rearing of their children, there still persists the notion—and reality, in some instances—that women are the primary caregivers to their children and that their academic and career endeavors are most affected by the having and raising of children. However, for "grad dads," I would argue that the same principles for managing the responsibilities of family life and graduate school apply to men as they do to women: organization, visibility, hard work, demonstrated effort, demonstrated success, and the previously described characteristics of Bloom and Bell (1979) and Grover and colleagues (2006).

Relationships with significant others during graduate school can be blessings but additional stressors as well. Finding the right person and the right balance between focus on academics and focus on family can help you have successful relationships beyond your graduate program.

Conclusion

Rather than focusing on "what not to do" with regard to relationships in graduate school, I would simply ask you to consider the opposite of the points discussed in this chapter on how to successfully navigate relationships in graduate school. The pitfalls to avoid generally consist of behaviors that alienate and/or distract you from the success of your graduate training. You can have a 4.0 GPA and off-the-charts GRE scores, but if you do not know how to work well with a diverse group of others, then settling in and succeeding in graduate school will be a challenge. Nevertheless, with the personal and professional support that can be found in peers, advisors/mentors, professors, and family, not only can you find success in graduate school, you will also have many supporters to celebrate your success with upon the completion of your studies.

❖ References

Bloom, L. J., & Bell, P. A. (1979). Making it in graduate school: Some reflections about the superstars. *Teaching of Psychology, 6,* 231–232.

Feist-Price, S. (1994). Cross-gender mentoring relationships: Critical issues. *Journal of Rehabilitation, 60,* 13–17.

Grover, C. A., Leftwich, M. J. T., Backhaus, A. L., Fairchild, J. A., & Weaver, K. A. (2006). Qualities of superstar graduate students. *Teaching of Psychology, 33,* 247–275.

Perlmutter, D. (2008). Are You a Good Protégé? *Chronicle of Higher Education, 54*(32), C1–C4.

Williams, J. C. (2004). Singing the grad-school baby blues. *Chronicle of Higher Education, 50*(33), C2–C3.

❖ Suggestions for Further Exploration

McCune, P. (2010). *How to get the mentoring you want: A guide for graduate students*. The Regents of the University of Michigan. Retrieved from http://www.rackham.umich.edu/downloads/publications/mentoring.pdf. Although written primarily for graduate students at the Rackham Graduate School, University of Michigan, this handbook includes several insightful chapters that inform students in any program on issues from why mentors are important to what to do if problems arise.

Packard, E. (2007). Words to the wise: Get the most out of your graduate program with advice from these students. *gradPSYCH*. Retrieved from: http://www.apa.org/gradpsych/2007/11/cover-wise.aspx. This brief article from an American Psychological Association (APA) publication, *gradPSYCH*, gives very practical suggestions for how students can succeed in graduate school. Readers should note that several of these entries provide helpful suggestions for relationships with peers, faculty, and families.

Schlosser, L. Z., Knox, S., Moskovitz, A. R., & Hill, C. E. (2003). A qualitative examination of graduate advising relationships: The advisee perspective. *Journal of Counseling Psychology, 50*, 178–188. DOI: 10.1037/0022-167.50.2.178. This qualitative research gives an insightful glimpse into 16 third-year counseling psychology Ph.D. students' experiences with their graduate advisors. Through semistructured interviews, researchers learned about positive and negative experiences students had with their advisors. Findings are presented in terms of themes revealed through content analysis.

5

When Things Don't Go According to Plan ❖

Shifting Areas, Programs, or Schools

Christina M. Leclerc
State University of New York at Oswego

Jonathan B. Banks
University of North Texas

You've been successful and gained a coveted spot in a graduate program you thought would be a great fit for your research interests and career goals. Maybe you've moved to a new part of the country, made new friends, and spent some time figuring out how to be a graduate student in your new department. Here's the rub: Your graduate program is not what you thought it would be and you are having second thoughts. Take, for example, a first-year graduate student who has entered a developmental graduate program, a mere 3 months ago, straight from her under-graduate degree. Based on her undergraduate coursework and her favorite profes-sor's opinion, she applied only to developmental programs across the nation with faculty members whose research examined the cognitive development of toddlers. After a lot of research and soul searching, she now believes counseling psychology would be a better fit for her interests and abilities. Of course, swimming in her head is all of the advice she has heard from the more experienced graduate students in the department, along with the rumors and rumblings she has acquired from her recent trolls of the Internet. She has heard it is never a good idea to quit a program before finishing with at least a master's degree, as it might indicate to future graduate admis-sions committees and employers a lack of commitment, which could be construed as either a liability or a glaring character flaw depending on the situation and the individuals on the committee. On one hand, if she was certain developmental psychology was the right path at one point, how can a potential new graduate department possibly believe she is certain counseling psychology is really the right path now? On the other hand, is it worth the work and time investment of another year and a half or more to complete the master's degree, especially if it's in an area that doesn't contain much potential for skill transfer (i.e., a master's degree in developmental psychology may not result in many transferable skills that could be used toward a degree in counseling psychology). So does she leave before the semester has finished and hope no future graduate programs look too deeply into her educational background? Does she finish the semester, leave the program, and work on gaining more experience related to counseling psychology?

What about a different example student, one who may be more similar to the vast majority of graduate students who find themselves less than pleased with their experiences in graduate school? This student is into his third year of his developmental graduate program and has already completed work toward his master's degree. Life as a graduate student is not what he dreamed of, he has cold and infrequent interactions with his research mentor, and his research interests are starting to diverge somewhat from the work being conducted in his mentor's lab. Although he hasn't yet thought seriously of quitting the graduate program, the thought has crossed his mind. Perhaps if he had a nicer advisor, he might be more motivated to complete the work toward his degree? Perhaps if the research program in the lab was more in line with his interests, he might be more willing to put in the effort?

At this stage, our example graduate students have a number of options, depending on the severity of their concerns and the direction of their future career plans. A change could be as simple as shifting your dissertation research topic a bit further away from the research program of your graduate advisor, or it could be as drastic as finishing the semester and leaving graduate school for a while in order to figure out what area is a better fit for your future studies. Each option has its own considerations, hurdles, pitfalls, and benefits, so it's important to carefully assess each before making a final decision.

Changing Research Topics

The simplest way to make a change in the trajectory of your graduate education is to shift your research topic a bit. Assuming your shift is fairly minor, no major changes should be required (e.g., changes in mentors or programs). If a change in research goals is a simple extension of what you have already been working on with your research mentor, then you may simply add a new topic to your current projects and continue. Say, for example, your graduate research mentor examines the social cognitive development of older adults. A dissertation topic that examines the emotional influences on the cognitive development of older adults would be more than appropriate, assuming you have done a significant amount of foundational reading and pilot research in the area. Although it is certainly wise to stick closer to the lab research program for your master's level work, a shift toward a more independent area may be perfectly acceptable, if not encouraged, for your dissertation-level research. Shifts such as these may open up potential for a good deal of professional growth and collaboration for both you and your research mentor. If, however, your potential new research topic diverges significantly enough, you may be unable to find a common research link between your current program or mentor and your future goals. In this case, a more significant change may be necessary.

Changing Advisors/Mentors

Theoretically, before you applied to graduate programs, you carefully examined the type of research being conducted in the departments and the specific research interests of the faculty members as well. Even if you had thoroughly read your advisor's work, contacted him or her via e-mail, made a campus visit, and met with the individual in person, there is still a chance that a good matching mentor relationship was just not found. During interviews, both you and your potential advisor put your best impressions forward, and many times, graduate school applicants are so eager to gain a spot in a program that they may not have been completely clear on the direction of their research interests during the application process. It's possible your interest level in the research program conducted by your advisor is moderate but not a passion of yours. Interest in research may be misconstrued as passion during the stress-filled interview process. Whatever the reason, it may be that your concerns about your graduate program are primarily the result of a poor personal or professional connection between you and your mentor.

Changing advisors is possible, but it is a situation that must be handled with the utmost care and respect. Murray Law (2005) indicated that many students who are interested in changing advisors may often feel like they are about to commit political suicide; however, the practice is fairly common in many psychology programs. One of the main considerations, according to Murray Law (2005), is whether the switch is for personal or professional reasons; switching is more acceptable and makes more practical sense when your research or clinical interests change and working with a new mentor would foster your new interests. What is less acceptable and can be more problematic is if your desire to change mentors is the result of a real or perceived personal problem between advisor and advisee. Although it may be difficult to stick with a challenging mentor, the intellectual growth that person may offer may be worth the sacrifice (Chamberlain, 2005).

If you are indeed committed to switching mentors, Murray Law (2005) advised the first logical step is to test the political waters of the department by asking advice of more advanced graduate students who may be able to help you navigate a change in mentor without burning bridges. Next, said Chamberlain (2005), is to meet with your department chair, who can not only offer you insight into the proper departmental guidelines but may also offer some advice about the best way to end the professional relationship with your advisor gracefully. Additionally, according to Chamberlain, you should be sure to initiate and formalize a relationship with a new advisor before you cut ties with your original one. The best way to do this is to read some background research from some of the other faculty members in the department, meet with faculty who might offer a better professional fit in terms of research or practice goals, and ask more advanced graduate students about other faculty members' mentoring styles. The most important thing to keep in mind, said

Chamberlain (2005), is to be careful never to speak poorly of your current mentor. Word spreads, and the academic arena is a small world. A burnt bridge with a previous mentor may result in closed doors in the future.

The final step is to politely inform your current mentor of your intention to make a change. Chamberlain (2005) suggested you give notice, just as you would with a job, to keep the conversation professional, and be sure to indicate your decision is based on changes that have occurred in your research and career interests.

Changing Programs

If, after careful consideration, you simply aren't able to find a way to make your personal and professional goals fit into your current graduate program, then a change in program is in order. This is a major move that requires careful consideration and even more careful planning. DeAngelis (2007) suggested the first step you make is to plan ahead and think carefully. She suggested listing the pros and cons of leaving and getting input from trusted family, colleagues, and fellow graduate students who you know will keep your search quiet.

The decision to change graduate programs after starting graduate school may be difficult to make whether you are a first-year graduate student or several years into your program. The decision to change programs is important because it has repercussions beyond the years in graduate school and extends well into your professional career. Although leaving a program you are dissatisfied with may seem like a bad idea if it will set you back several years in your training, the benefits of enjoying the new area may result in a much happier career.

There are several important factors that may help to determine if changing programs is the correct decision for you. The first factor to consider is to attempt to understand why you are unhappy in your current program or why you feel that changing programs is a good decision for you. Staying motivated and maintaining a positive attitude can be difficult at times during graduate school (desJardins, 1994, 1995). Class work, research, teaching duties, and family or other life stress can easily make it difficult to stay focused. If the motivation to change programs is due to feeling overwhelmed or other typical graduate school-related stress, then it may be likely that changing programs will not alleviate the stress. However, if you find your current program is not as interesting an area of research as you thought it was prior to starting, then perhaps changing programs is the best decision. See Chapter 10 of this volume for suggestions on self-care and stress management.

Many students may enter graduate programs without a full understanding of that area of psychology. Although undergraduate advisors may try to help undergraduates attempt to define their interests by encouraging them to take classes in their areas of interest or become involved in research in that area, it may not always be possible to do so. Therefore, sometimes students may enter a graduate program they think is the area of psychology that most interests them only to discover that it is not actually as interesting as they thought. It is important not to make that mistake the second time around when looking for a new program. Many times, while in your current program, you may be able to take graduate classes in the area you are considering transferring to. If you are unable to take any classes in the area you are considering, then you should talk to faculty members in the area you are contemplating. Contacting faculty in the area you are interested in transferring to can also serve as a valuable step in deciding what schools you would be interested in applying to and whom you would be interested in having as an advisor (desJardins, 1994, 1995). Discussing research topics, career goals, and specifics of the new area of psychology with faculty and current graduate students in that area can give you a good idea as to what to expect for graduate training and your career. Before you transfer to the new program, make sure you are truly interested in that area and not just looking for "greener pastures."

Once you have determined the reason you are interested in changing programs is not due to burnout in your current program or general frustration with graduate school, it is important to consider what changing programs may require. If you are joining a new program within your current department, then it is possible any requirements that are determined by the university or graduate school may remain the same. However, the requirements of the specific program may change dramatically. Before you consider changing programs you should familiarize yourself with the requirements of the new program and determine how many of the courses you have already taken may be applied to the required coursework in the new program.

Changing programs may extend the time spent in school. If you have already completed the coursework for your current program or are even just a year or so into the coursework, you may be hesitant to start over and complete a whole new set of courses. This can result in a greater amount of time required for graduate school. Even if the majority of your completed coursework will transfer into your new program, you should expect to spend additional time in your new program.

In addition to the coursework that may be required by your program, it will be beneficial to spend enough time in your new program for you to be able to conduct research with your new advisor and publish the results. It is important not to underestimate the amount of time it takes from the beginning of a study until it is published. If you are changing programs and areas of research, it is critical that you establish yourself as a successful researcher in the new area before you leave graduate school if you are planning on having a career in academia. The time you spend in your new program may be determined more by the time it takes to publish work in your new area than by how long it takes to complete your coursework.

When examining the new program, it can be helpful to discuss the amount of time the new advisor recommends for completing your graduate training. This time and number of publications may vary by subdiscipline of psychology. Valla (2010) examined the number of publications for individuals who obtained faculty positions directly after graduate school or after a postdoctoral position by subdiscipline of psychology. Valla found the number of publications for individuals who obtained positions directly after receiving their Ph.D. ranged on average between 3 publications for developmental psychologists and 6 for cognitive psychologists to 12 for social psychologists. Discussing the amount of time it may take to have enough publications to become competitive in the new area with possible new advisors and other individuals in the new program may help to guide a decision about switching programs. Ultimately, enjoying the research and work you are doing is very important. If the area of your current program is not fascinating to you and the new program would be much more interesting, then changing programs may not only lead to enjoying your graduate training but also enjoying the work you will be doing for the rest of your career.

Once you have considered the reasons for changing programs, the requirements for the new program, and the length of time it will take to complete the new program, ensuring you leave your current program in the correct manner will impact the transition (DeAngelis, 2007). When you are changing programs, especially within the same department, it is essential to discuss this change with your current advisor. If you are not happy with your current program, then discussing your concerns and reasons for changing programs can be very helpful. Your current advisor may be able to provide guidance in determining if changing programs would be beneficial. Even if your advisor is not able to help you in making this decision, be upfront with him or her about your decisions prior to applying to a different program. Avoid burning any bridges when you leave your current program for two reasons. First, if you are interested in joining a different program within your department, then it is likely the faculty in the new program will be interested in talking to your current advisor about your interests in their program. If your current advisor is willing to serve as a reference for you, then it will serve as an indication to others that your reasons for leaving the program were sound. Second, although you are changing programs, the faculty in your current program will likely still be colleagues in the future. Ensuring any existing networks you have created are still in place will be helpful in the future when searching for jobs, conducting research, or for other professional activities.

Changing programs will also require you to become familiar with a new area of literature. Knowledge of the literature from the area you are currently in will be helpful in the future, but before you can start to apply that knowledge in an interdisciplinary manner, you must first know the new area. Stearns (n.d.) suggested new graduate students spend their first year in school reading widely. Reading the literature in an exhaustive manner allows you to gain an understanding of past and current topics that are active areas of interest and that help you to identify possible topics and approaches for your research. The number of required courses varies by program; if you have a lower number of required courses, then the expectation to seek out reading independently will be greater. Talking about the expected amount of independent reading with your new advisor will be helpful. In instances where a great deal of independent reading may not be required, the more independent reading you can do, the more knowledgeable you will be about your new area, and your understanding of what the best research questions may be will be improved. Knowledge of the literature from your old program of study may help you take an interdisciplinary approach to your research.

Expectations can differ greatly between programs even in the same department. As mentioned previously, the amount of independent reading and coursework expected may differ, but many other important differences may exist. Expectations such as amount of time spent on research, timeline for benchmarks of success (comprehensive exams, dissertation proposal and defense, etc.), and duration of graduate training, among others, may be in the program manual. When entering a new program, students should read the manual and make sure they understand all of the requirements. If you have any questions about the requirements, your new advisor or program director should be able to answer those questions or help you to find someone who can help answer them. Most faculty members are happy to help students with whom they are working; however, they are also busy with research, teaching, advising other students, and other responsibilities. Therefore, it is important to not come to them with questions you could find the answer to in the manual. Even the most patient advisor will become tired of answering questions that are already answered in the manual. If you can check the manual and still do not have an answer, then your advisor and program director are great resources for questions about the new program.

Changing Schools

The decision to change departments may be the result of different reasons. Many students may decide the program they are in is not the right area of psychology for them. If you are changing departments because the area of psychology you would like to pursue is not offered in your current department, then the advice given in the previous section on changing programs will be applicable for you. However, many students decide to change departments but remain in the same area of psychology. Students may decide to change departments for a variety of reasons. Regardless of the reason behind the change, the decision to leave a school as a graduate student must be handled carefully.

Prior to deciding to change departments, it is important to have an honest discussion with your current advisor. Many times, students may decide to change departments because of a lack of fit between themselves and their advisor. This lack of fit between student and advisor may be due to differing research interests, a mismatch between the amounts of time an advisor has to mentor and the amount of time a student needs, or even personality conflicts. Sterns (n.d.) advised that if you do not get along with your advisor, you should find a new one quickly. If you cannot find another advisor in your department willing to take you on as a student or you are not interested in the research being conducted by other faculty, then you will need to change departments. Even if you are having problems with your current advisor, it is best to talk to him or her about your decision to leave so he or she knows what you are planning on doing. Although your advisor may not support your decision to change departments, he or she will likely appreciate you being honest about your plans.

In dealing with your current school and prospective schools, it is important to be honest and professional in describing the reasons you are leaving your current school. If faculty at your current program have played an important role in mentoring you, then it may be beneficial for you to discuss your reasons for leaving with them as well. Talking with other trusted advisors may help you make the best decision for your future as well as maintain any professional contacts you have established.

DeAngelis (2007) suggested that when dealing with prospective schools, you should describe your current situation as a professional mismatch that would be rectified by attending the new school. Avoid blaming any problems on your current program or your current advisor. Saying anything negative about faculty in your current school will reflect negatively on you and would leave a negative impression on faculty in the prospective school. If you are staying in the same area of psychology, then the faculty at the prospective school may know faculty in your current program, and bad-mouthing their colleagues will not leave them with a favorable impression of you. It is also important that you do not fail to mention that you are currently in a program. It may seem easier not to mention to prospective schools that you are currently in a program in an attempt to avoid explaining why you are leaving, but your prospective school will find out you are currently in a program, and if you have not been upfront with this information, it will greatly decrease your chances of getting into the prospective school.

Once you have decided to change departments or schools, discussed the reasons with your advisor, and been admitted to a new school, it is important to be sure to familiarize yourself with the new department and the new requirements. Do not assume your new department works in a similar manner as your old department. Every department functions differently, and the faculty and administration in each department interact with each other and with students in different ways. Understanding the culture that exists in the new department is critical for fitting in and succeeding. One major difference that may exist between departments involves faculty–student interaction. Faculty in many departments may treat their graduate students as junior colleagues and are on a first-name basis with their students. Alternatively, other departments may remain more formal with their graduate students, and addressing faculty by their first names may violate the culture of the department. Understanding the culture within the department will ease the transition from your old department to your new one.

All departments will have positive and negative attributes. Even when you are unhappy with the department or program you are currently in and have decided to change departments, there will be positive attributes that may or may not be present in your new department. Depending on what this is, you may be able to help improve your new program by bringing in new ideas. It is critical that you understand the culture of the department before you attempt to make any suggestions, however, as some departments may not be open to any suggestions. If your new department has a graduate student association, any changes students are able to make may be best coming from the student organization. For example, if your old department had a wonderful brown bag meeting every month or every week but your new department does not, then it may be possible for the graduate student association to host a brown bag you may help lead. Understanding the culture of the department is critical before you discuss any possible suggestions with anyone.

The decision to change programs or departments can be a very daunting one, but if it is done for the correct reasons and approached carefully, then changing programs or departments may be the best decision for your future. Ensuring you understand why you are interested in making this change, being honest and professional in how you discuss the change with your current and prospective programs, and understanding the requirements of the new program will help to ensure a successful transition from your current program or department to your new one.

Applying to the New Program or School

Once you have decided to change programs or schools and have discussed this decision with your current advisor or another trusted professional advisor, undertaking the application process in the right way is critical. If you are changing programs, even within the same school, you will need to apply to the new program or school. Applying to graduate school a second time may be easier because of increased understanding of the time involved and the steps required, but it is also important to consider several factors such as possibly retaking the GRE, who to ask for letters of references, and how to include your current program in your personal statement.

Retaking the GRE may or may not be a part of applying to a new school or program. When deciding if you need to retake the GRE, consider your current GRE scores and determine if these scores are competitive enough to gain entry into the new program. The website descriptions for many graduate programs will give the average GRE scores for students that have been accepted into their programs. If the program's website does not list this information, then contact the program chair to find out what the average GRE score is for students in their program. It is also important to consider how long ago you may have taken the GRE. If you took the GRE within the last year or so and the scores are high enough to be competitive, then you will likely not be required to take them again. However, if it has been several years since you took the GRE, then it is likely you will need to take the GRE again. The program or school you are applying to will be able to tell you if your GRE scores are recent enough to be accepted or if you will need to retake them.

Letters of reference are often a very important component of your application material. Choosing the individuals you ask to write these letters should be done carefully in order to receive the strongest letters possible. If you are leaving your program or school after a semester or two, you may not have had a chance to make a strong positive impression on three faculty members who are able to write letters for you. In this case, you may end up having to ask the same individuals who wrote you letters before to do so again. If, however, you are leaving your current program on good terms with your current advisor, having him or her write you a letter could be very helpful for your application packet. If you have decided to leave your current program and your current advisor is unwilling or unable to write you a letter of reference, then you should attempt to have another faculty member in your current program do so. One benefit to most graduate courses is that they are smaller than most undergraduate courses, and as a result, faculty members get to know students better in graduate classes. If you have been able to make a good impression in these classes, it is possible they will be able to write a letter for you. A letter from a faculty member in the program you are leaving may serve as a strong indication to the programs to which you are applying that your rationale for leaving is strong and valid.

A final factor to consider when applying to a new program or school is the personal statement applicants must write. When you applied to your current program, you most likely had to write a personal statement, so you already have a draft to build upon. It would be a mistake to simply submit this original personal statement without any revisions. As discussed previously, DeAngelis (2007) advises that failing to mention you are currently in a program would be a mistake when applying. You should use your personal statement as an opportunity to include your experience in your current program and explain why you are leaving. As part of your personal statement, you can describe what you have learned from your current situation and why the program to which you are applying is the best fit for you. Letters of reference from faculty in your current program can help to support what you say in your personal statement. If possible, share your new personal statement with any faculty members who have agreed to write letters of reference.

During the application process, it may be worthwhile to discuss the applicability of the graduate work you have already completed toward your new intended degree program. The best way to do this is to contact the head of the graduate school or specific graduate program to inquire about transfer of credits. Depending on the divergence between the two areas, you may or may not reap benefits from this additional research. Although transferring credits from classes you have already completed at one school to another can be difficult to do depending on your new department, transferring as many courses as possible may help to reduce the number of classes required at the new school and allow for a greater amount of time to be spent conducting research. Graduate schools may place a limit on the number of transfer credits allowed for the university. Additionally, departments and advisors may want to limit the number of courses you may transfer into your new department so you can take those classes from them and be trained in their department. If you are attempting to transfer course credit to your new school, there are several items that may assist in approval of these transfer credits. Schools may require students to provide a great deal of information from each course. The material the school wants is designed to help them judge whether the course you completed would be equivalent to the course offered at that institution. For example, the University of North Carolina requires students to submit the published course description, course reading list, course requirements (assignments and grading criteria), transcripts showing the course, and information showing methods used to engage students in learning (University of North Carolina, 2010). It is also helpful to have any assignments completed, especially any written papers, so the individual responsible for making the decision about transfer credits may be able to review all possible information regarding the course you completed.

Conclusion

Now that we have discussed the pros and cons of the options available to our two example graduate students, let's revisit their cases and evaluate which is the best fit for each. Recall the first-year developmental psychology graduate student who has had a change of heart and is now more interested in pursuing a graduate education in counseling. Whereas her desire to make an early break from the program is understandable from a personal perspective (i.e., leaving a program she sees as not benefitting her future seems attractive in the short term), an early break may not be in her best professional interests. Perhaps a compromise situation could be found in which she completes the first year of the program in order to honor her fellowship contract and give her research mentor time to consider a replacement graduate student. In this circumstance, she may be able to complete coursework that may transfer to a new program, and she will demonstrate commitment to her obligations as well, which may work in her favor during the future application process. In her circumstances, a change in program or school sounds necessary given there is such a divergence from her current program and her intended one.

Our second example graduate student, on the other hand, has a very different situation. He has already completed 3 years of his program, which is a very significant time and effort investment. He has also earned a master's degree in his area and is presumably already well on his way toward completing the majority of his coursework and nonresearch requirements toward his Ph.D. Although he may not have a great personal relationship with his research mentor, a more important question he needs to address is whether his research mentor is providing him with an appropriate level of professional development. If his research program is progressing well and he is completing projects and submitting publications with a well-respected advisor, then a less-than-ideal personal relationship may be well worth overlooking. Additionally, because he is at such an advanced stage of his degree progress, a simple shift in research interests may be exactly what is in order. With some preparatory work and time with the new literature, a dissertation project that diverges a bit from the typical program of research in his lab may be enough to motivate him toward completing his degree program.

Whereas graduate school is never exactly as any student had envisioned, there are genuinely situations in which things really aren't working well and a change of some kind is in order. When a situation such as this arises, all of the possible options should be carefully considered before making any decisions. Be sure to weigh the pros and cons of any change or move before making any steps, however. Seek the advice of more advanced graduate students or department administrators whom you trust and who will keep your concerns confidential at least initially. Be honest with your current advisor/mentor, as burning bridges not only eliminates the potential for recommendation letters but may also lead to closed doors later in your career. Maintain a professional atmosphere about your change, do not speak poorly of your current or past program or mentor, and remember that the very best reason to make a change is based on a true mismatch between your career goals and the program in which you are currently enrolled. Finally, and perhaps most importantly, you should be honest with yourself and your future goals and plans. Graduate school is a difficult period that can be full of new challenges and situations you've never encountered. An honest look at the causes of your concerns about your current graduate program will prepare you for the next step or allow you a new perspective on your current situation.

❖ References

Chamberlin, J. (2005). Sticky situations in mentorships: Problems can crop up in mentorships, but solutions are not beyond students' reach. *gradPSYCH, 3*(1). Retrieved **July 6, 2011,** from http://www.apa.org/gradpsych/2005/01/mentor-sticky.aspx.

DeAngelis, T. (2007). Do it right the second time: Thinking of changing programs? Here's how to protect your long-term career goals and professional relationships. *gradPSYCH, 5*(3). Retrieved **July 6, 2011,** from http://www.apa.org/gradpsych/2007/09/secondtime.aspx.

desJardins, M. (1994). How to succeed in graduate school: A guide for students and advisors: Part I of II. *Crossroads: The ACM Magazine for Students, 1,* 3–9.

desJardins, M. (1995). How to succeed in graduate school: A guide for students and advisors: Part II of II. *Crossroads: The ACM Magazine for Students, 1,* 1–6.

Murray Law, B. (2005). First-year hurdles: Make the most of your initial year in graduate school. *gradPSYCH, 3*(1). Retrieved **July 6, 2011,** from http://www.apa.org/gradpsych/2005/09/hurdles.aspx.

Stearns, S. C. (n.d.). *Some modest advice for graduate students.* Retrieved **July 6, 2011,** from http://www.yale.edu/eeb/stearns/advice.htm.

University of North Carolina. (2010). *The graduate school handbook.* Retrieved **July 6, 2011,** from http://handbook.unc.edu/.

Valla, J. M. (2010). Getting hired: Publications, postdocs, and the path to professorship. *Observer, 23.* Retrieved **July 6, 2011,** from http://www.psychologicalscience.org/index .php/publications/observer/2010/september-10/getting-hired.html.

❖ Suggestions for Further Exploration

Chamberlin, J. (2005). Sticky situations in mentorships: Problems can crop up in mentor-ships, but solutions are not beyond students' reach. *gradPSYCH, 3*(1). Retrieved from http://www.apa.org/gradpsych/2005/01/mentor-sticky.aspx. This reference is a short over-view for the current graduate student in navigating some of the less optimal aspects of the political field of graduate-level mentorship relationships. Knowing how to relate or when to make the decision that the relationship is sufficiently suboptimal to require a change is a skill every graduate student should review.

DeAngelis, T. (2007). Do it right the second time: Thinking of changing programs? Here's how to protect your long-term career goals and professional relationships. *gradPSYCH, 5*(3). Retrieved from http://www.apa.org/gradpsych/2007/09/secondtime.aspx. DeAngelis provides a brief list of good suggestions for students considering switching programs.

Lord , A. R. (2003). A guide to PhD graduate school: How they keep score in the big leagues. In J. M. Darley, M. P. Zanna, & H. L. Roediger (Eds.), *The compleat academic: A career guide* (pp. 3–15). Washington DC: American Psychological Association. The first chap-ter in *The Compleat Academic* provides graduate students an understanding of what matters in graduate school and academia. If you are considering changing advisors, programs, or schools, make sure that you understand what is expected of you.

Zanna, M. P., & Darley, J. M. (2004). Mentoring: Managing the faculty–graduate student relationship. In J. M. Darley, M. P. Zanna, & H. L. Roediger III (Eds.), *The compleat academic: A career guide* (2nd ed.). Washington, DC: American Psychological Association. For a more comprehensive review of the ins and outs of the graduate-level mentoring relationship, this chapter delves into more of the theoretical intricacies of the graduate student–mentor relationship. Start here to get a detailed look at the various types of relationships that are common in the field and tips on how to best navigate a number of different scenarios.

6

Important Considerations
for Ethnic Minority
Graduate Students

Loretta N. McGregor
Arkansas State University

G. William Hill IV
Kennesaw State University

The challenges of graduate school, for minority students, are similar to those of most students in regard to learning the rules of a new environment and managing the course load. However, ethnic minority students may also wrestle with issues related to race, culture, discrimination, and isolation.

The first challenge encountered by most minority students is the realization that many colleges and universities no longer offer support programs designed to promote graduate education for minority students. Previously, affirmative action encouraged many colleges and universities to design programs to provide educational opportunities for minority students. This included graduate education. These programs often provided grants, fellowships, and other forms of support to ethnic minority students. The rationale behind the programs was simple. For many years, ethnic minority students had been denied adequate educational training opportunities. The programs were designed to compensate for the past transgressions that led to inequities among people of color (Office of Equal Opportunity, 2010). However, in 1996, the United States Fifth Circuit Court of Appeals ruled, in *Hopwood v. State of Texas,* that the University of Texas School of Law could no longer use race as part of its admissions criteria. Additionally, in 1996, Californians passed Proposition 209, which prohibited the use of race, sex, and ethnicity by public institutions when considering matters of determination and selection. Michigan also passed a similar law, called the Michigan Civil Rights Initiative, the same year. In 2003, the United States Supreme Court ruled, in *Grutter v. Bollinger,* that the University of Michigan's law school *could* use race as a factor in its admissions decision (Golden, 2003).

Although the 2003 ruling allows colleges and universities to use race as one admissions criterion, whether race is an acceptable admission criterion is still unclear to many administrators. Additionally, by 2003, the 1996 rulings and law had led many colleges and universities to change the way in which they administered support programs designed to assist minority students. Many institutions now focus on meeting the needs of students from "underrepresented populations" (Golden, 2003). The term *underrepresented* is nebulous and may include identification based on ethnicity. However, *underrepresented* also includes gender, sexual orientation, first-generation status, and low socioeconomic status (Hartig & Steigerwald, 2007; Huang, Brewster, Moradi, Goodman, Wiseman, & Martin, 2010; Poock, 2007). Although many schools no longer directly give special consideration to minority students, their needs and concerns persist. Hence, this chapter will explore challenges that are often unique to ethnic minority graduate students.

In a 2004 *American Psychologist* article, Maton and Hrabowski postulated four specific sets of factors that influence the academic success of underrepresented minority students in the sciences and engineering. In addition to the aforementioned challenge (Golden, 2003), we believe these four factors also apply to ethnic minority graduate students in psychology. The challenges identified include knowledge and skills development, academic and social integration, support and motivation, and monitoring and advising (Maton & Hrabowski, 2004). Although Maton and Hrabowski used the term *monitoring*, we chose to use the word *mentoring*. We believe the actions of monitoring described by Maton and Hrabowski are often actions performed by a mentor. We will address each of these factors in terms of how it can affect the academic success of ethnic minority graduate students. We will also offer recommendations to students as to how they can overcome each challenge.

Knowledge and Skills Development

Students who are interested in attending graduate school should begin their preparations long before they apply to a graduate program. These preparations should begin as early as the sophomore year of their undergraduate studies (Keith-Spiegel & Wiederman, 2000; Landrum & Clark, 2005). Such preparations should include taking the appropriate courses in undergraduate studies, preparing for the Graduate Record Exam (GRE), and engaging in an integrative experiential capstone activity such as a research project or an internship (Helms & Rogers, 2011; Kuther, 2006; Landrum & Clark, 2005; Landrum & Davis, 2010). The successful performance of these tasks is often facilitated by good academic advising and mentoring, which we discuss later in the chapter. Our comments regarding knowledge and skill development are general and could apply to all students. However, in this chapter, we will address some challenges that are unique to ethnic minority students.

Adequate preparation for graduate school is very important, and it is imperative that the student play a dynamic role in the process. Students must actively monitor their academic progress and work hard (commit) to meet the academic requirements for graduate school enrollment (Appleby, 2003). Keith-Spiegel and Wiederman (2000) suggest that graduate school selection committees are "impressed with no-nonsense psychology courses that teach students the fundamentals of theory and the science of behavior" (p. 75). They recommend students take courses such as statistics, learning, research methodology, and cognition. Oftentimes, these courses are exactly what many students avoid, preferring to delay enrolling because such classes are perceived as being extremely challenging. As you can guess, we do not recommend that students delay the most challenging coursework until the end of their senior year. Graduate selection committees may note on a transcript the delay in taking the most challenging courses. This could suggest a stalling technique to a graduate selection committee and result in a negative perception of a procrastinator (Appleby, 2003; Keith-Spiegel & Wiederman, 2000). However, adequate preparation involves more than taking the appropriate courses. Drew Appleby (2003) and R. Eric Landrum (2003) suggest that the appearance of a student's academic transcript plays a major role in the perceptions and decisions of a graduate school selection committee. Excessive withdrawals from courses, low grades in theory- and science-related courses, and the lack of an integrative experience may offer a negative or incomplete portrayal of a student's undergraduate educational experience. These events could signal a lack of preparation for graduate level work (Appleby, 2003; Landrum, 2003). Some minority graduate students have commented that they feel as if they must work twice as hard as nonminority students to prove their intellectual capabilities (Gay, 2004; Vasquez et al., 2006). Whether their perception is reality is difficult to assess. However, minority students who complete courses in theory and the science of behavior with excellent grades will stand out to admissions committees. Additionally, if the undergraduate curriculum allows flexibility for course selection, students should carefully choose courses that promote critical thinking, hone research skills, and allow for the integration of information from various courses across the psychology curriculum. These actions are sure to catch the attention of selection committees and, ultimately, may increase the likelihood of program acceptance for minority students.

Adequate preparation also involves adequately preparing for the Graduate Record Exam (GRE). The GRE is an admission criterion used by many graduate programs (Kuther, 2006; Landrum & Davis, 2010). In its current form, the test consists of three sections: analytical writing, verbal reasoning, and quantitative reasoning. The analytical writing section measures the student's critical thinking abilities and assesses the student's ability to write in a clear and concise manner. The verbal reasoning section is designed to assess reading comprehension, verbal reasoning, and the student's ability to analogically reason. The quantitative reasoning section is designed to measure the student's problem-solving abilities. It focuses on the basic concepts of math, algebra, geometry, and data analysis to which the student has been introduced while attending college (Educational Testing Service [ETS], 2010).

According to the Educational Testing Service (2008), the average GRE verbal score for African Americans was 394 in 2005 to 2006. That score was 11 points lower than the scores for Whites. In that same period, the average score for Hispanics was 433. Scores by students from both ethnic groups were lower than the national average of 482. During that same period, scores on the quantitative section were also lower for African Americans and Hispanics at 418 and 489, respectively. The average score for Whites on the quantitative section was 563, and the national average was 547 (ETS, 2008). As we mentioned earlier, GRE scores are given considerable attention in the admission process. Given that ethnic minority students appear to score lower on the test than their White counterparts, it is imperative that students of color begin preparing for the GRE well before they apply to graduate programs. Students have a limited window of opportunity in which they can take the GRE. Students must take the test before they apply for graduate school but not before they complete the prerequisite coursework. As mentioned earlier, the test assesses prior knowledge obtained through previously completed college coursework. Preparedness for the GRE demonstrates why students must complete the appropriate college coursework in a timely manner. Course completion influences a student's ability to prepare for the GRE and dictates when one can take the test. Furthermore, unlike the ACT or SAT, students typically do not take the GRE multiple times before applying to graduate school. First-generation ethnic minority students and those from low socioeconomic backgrounds often cannot afford to pay for multiple testing dates. Hence, it is crucial that minority students allow adequate study time in preparation for the GRE. Students may access the website of the Educational Testing Service for detailed information regarding enrollment and test dates (ETS, 2010).

The Educational Testing Service routinely releases older versions of the GRE for study purposes. It is our recommendation that the student take a practice test of the GRE before taking the actual exam. Practice tests can be obtained from the Educational Testing Service or a variety of other sources and will provide helpful information regarding a student's strengths and challenges. Once the student has identified deficit areas in his performance, he can work to improve his knowledge in those areas through studying the appropriate materials.

We also encourage minority students to engage in an integrative experiential activity such as a research project or internship. It is our experience that involvement in such an activity affords an opportunity to integrate information and skills obtained from various psychology courses. Furthermore, these experiences allow for skill and knowledge application in a controlled environment. We are not alone in our assertion. Dunn and colleagues (2010) voiced a similar opinion when they stated that all psychology departments "should ensure that students have opportunities for the application of acquired knowledge and skills" (p. 56). Additionally, Keith-Spiegel and Wiederman (2000) stated that both "research and practical experience indicate that socialization into the profession has already started" (p. 81). Minority students can develop essential networks and mentoring relationships through such integrative experiences. Students may also find same-ethnic-group professionals who can serve as mentors and assist them in traversing the maze of graduate education. These mentors may share their graduate school experiences with students and help to encourage them in their burgeoning success. We will discuss the roles of mentors in greater detail later in the chapter.

Academic and Social Isolation

Many ethnic minority students often experience a sense of academic and social isolation during their graduate training (Greene, 2002; McNeill, Horn, & Perez, 1995; Ulloa & Herrera, 2006; Vasquez et al., 2006). The feeling of isolation is often precipitated by the scarcity of other minority students enrolled in the graduate program, racism and discrimination, the paucity of minority faculty members teaching within the program, the loss of family and friends through relocation, and the assumption by some nonminority peers that a minority student is incapable of being accepted into a graduate program based on academic merit (APA, 2010; Greene, 2002; Malone & Barabino, 2008; Ulloa & Herrera, 2006; Vasquez et al., 2006).

It is not uncommon for a student of color to be the only minority in his or her classes and/or program. Several authors in the Vasquez and colleagues (2006) article noted that they were often called upon to "comment on or represent the 'minority perspective' during discussions" (p. 168). Being singled out in the classroom in such a manner only serves to magnify any feeling of isolation. There is great intragroup variation within ethnic groups, and minority students should not assume the role as "spokesperson" for their race. However, the student may choose to view questions about his or her ethnicity and culture as an opportunity to enlighten others and to share information about culture.

Ethnic minority students may also experience incidents of racism and discrimination by their peers and faculty members, resulting in a sense of aloneness and isolation. Discrimination in graduate school is often covert and may appear in the forms of hostility, isolation, neglect, coldness, indifference, and lack of sensitivity. Nonminority peers and faculty members may appear insensitive to issues related to race and ethnicity and often fail to recognize racism and discrimination against minority students when it occurs. Gay (2004) noted that students of color experience academic isolation through irrelevant curricula, lack of critical engagement by faculty members, and lack of validation and acknowledgements of contributions by their peers and faculty members.

Much of the curriculum in graduate education is Eurocentric in nature and often highlights the contributions made by European males (Gay, 2004). Contributions made by women and ethnic minorities often receive only cursory inclusion. The American Psychological Association does require clinical and counseling programs to include courses on the multicultural aspects of counseling; however, these courses are often limited in scope and duration (McNeill et al., 1995). Gay (2004) eloquently addressed the issue when she wrote:

> The formal education of students of color includes little content on and pedagogy for ethnic and cultural differences. Yet, these are the issues that they are frequently interested in pursuing in their own research, scholarship, and teaching after receiving their degrees. (p. 273)

The lack of ethnic minority content in textbooks and pedagogy in the classroom often goes unnoticed by nonminority faculty members and students. However, the absence of such material is glaringly obvious to minority students and speaks silently to the importance ascribed to them by the professor and/or the program. When these topics are present in the classroom, many minority students often feel that their professors and peers are hesitant to discuss the issues in depth. Students also complain that professors appear to fear critical engagement and make every attempt to avoid conversations that include a discussion of racial inequalities (Gay, 2004). If minority students bring issues of race and ethnicity up for discussion in class, "their mainstream peers often react to their contributions . . . with passive or silent indulgence. Then the conversation continues as if the students of color had not spoken at all . . ." (Gay, 2004, p. 274). In addition, faculty members may become hostile toward the student of color for "hijacking" the discussion and interjecting inflammatory comments. Although nonminority faculty members and peers may feel uncomfortable discussing issues of race and ethnicity in class, their inclusion in the curriculum is important and plays a vital role in eliminating feelings of isolation for minority students.

Students of color may want to discuss, privately, the lack of cultural content in the curriculum with their professors and mentors. This technique allows the department to take a systemic approach to addressing the issue. If a professor shows an interest in adding cultural materials to his or her classes, the student may volunteer to provide the professor with resources to aid in preparation. Students of color may also volunteer to personally deliver the information to the class and facilitate classroom discussion. This allows the professor to take a more passive role, and it does not expose his or her dearth of cultural knowledge to the class.

Although race relations in this country have improved over the past 40 years, the reality is that racism and discrimination continue to exist. Graduate students of color have probably experienced racism prior to their arrival in graduate school. Furthermore, many minority parents continue to educate their children about racism and discrimination and instruct them on how to handle such events. Students of color may not expect to find racism in the enlightened halls of the academy, but they should be aware that it is alive and well in some graduate programs. How a student deals with racism and discrimination will depend on the circumstances surrounding the event. We do not advise students to accept racist and demeaning remarks from their peers or faculty members. These individuals should be reported if a pattern of abuse is demonstrated. However, students must also "pick their battles carefully." As Greene (2002) wrote, "Although many students are tempted to get involved in every clash over race that occurs in their program, that will not help anyone graduate any sooner" (p. 1).

The lack of faculty members of color also contributes to the feelings of isolation experienced by minority graduate students. The dearth of ethnic minority faculty members results in fewer role models and same-ethnic-group mentors for minority students. In 2009, only 17.3% of all faculty members were from ethnic minority groups (National Center for Education Statistics [NCES], 2010). These faculty members are often overwhelmed with requests for their service and representation on various committees in addition to their responsibilities for teaching and advising. Universities often acknowledge the importance of having a diverse faculty. Yet, for a variety of reasons, most universities (with the exception of Historically Black Colleges and Universities) continue to employ a small number of faculty of color. Moreover, individuals of color who are employed by a university are routinely requested to serve on various committees in an effort to infuse diversity into the committees. Additionally, minority students who desire a same-ethnic-group mentor also seek out these professors. Furthermore, civic and nonprofit organizations also desire input from minority faculty members, who are often expected to represent the views of the minority community. Quite often, many minority faculty members feel a desire to "give back" to their communities and to pass on the mentoring and support they received during their educational training. However, given the aforementioned demands for their time, it is easy to see how faculty members of color may become overwhelmed. So students should also work to cultivate relationships with faculty members of a different race or ethnic group. Unfortunately, not all faculty members are interested in supporting and mentoring minority students. We will discuss ways in which minority students can cultivate such relationships in the section on mentoring and advising.

Minority graduate students may find it necessary to relocate for their graduate training if their program of interest is offered in another state. Gay (2004) noted that oftentimes, "the large universities graduate students of color attend are located in communities that are not ethnically, culturally and linguistically diverse" (p. 268). Given that many students relocate for graduate school, nonminorities may not understand the subtle difficulties encountered by minority students who relocate to communities that are not diverse. For instance, minority students who have special dietary needs as a result of their culture may find that local markets do not accommodate their needs. African American female students may find it difficult to locate hairstylists who are familiar with their hair-care needs. Additionally, simple tasks such as shopping for hair-care products and other beauty items, such as makeup that matches or compliments their complexions, can be a challenge. These students also experience a loss of their culture through the absence of culturally infused entertainment. The local radio stations do not play music from their favorite genres, nor do their favorite musical artists perform in concert at local venues. The local cineplex does not show movies that feature actors who look like them. These subtle deprivations of culture only serve to exacerbate the feelings of loss and isolation experienced by many ethnic minority students when they relocate for graduate school. Although these challenges may seem small, they can produce a level of persistent stress. The prolonged exposure to multiple stressors such as these can undoubtedly result in a negative influence on the academic performance of the student. In addition to these things, students of color also experience the loss of family and friends. The loss of support from one's family may result not only in social isolation but may also create a financial strain for the student (Guiffrida, 2005; Munton, 1990). Families may provide intangible support like babysitting, transportation, and other household needs. The student may find it necessary to pay for these services when he or she moves away from family and friends. However, ethnic minority students experience more than a loss of their families and networks. They can often experience a reduction in services.

Enedina Garcia-Vazquez stated that "my admission was seen as a result of affirmative action instead of ability. That is not unusual" (Vasquez et al., 2006, p. 158). As we mentioned earlier, many graduate programs no longer provide programs of support designed specifically for ethnic minority students. Therefore, it should be clear to most people that students of color who are enrolled in graduate school are there based on their academic merits. The only way graduate students of color can demonstrate their intellectual capabilities is through their performance in the classroom, laboratory, and other academic arenas and through their graduation from the program. Unfortunately, even then, some critics may never be convinced of the minority student's academic prowess.

Students can overcome social and academic isolation by becoming involved in a variety of activities offered through their departments, professional organizations, the university, and/or the community (Greene, 2002). One possibility is to become active in a research lab with a professor. Prior to applying to the graduate program, students should research the faculty members teaching within the program and become familiar with the research agenda of each professor. After entering the graduate program, the student may choose to work with an assigned professor or another professor with whom they have similar research interest. Many professors typically utilize the talents of multiple graduate students in their labs. Working with other students in a laboratory setting is a way to make new friends and to become actively engaged with peers. Some professors may engage in social activities with their graduate students. Attending a few such activities can afford the student an opportunity to bond with the professor and peers. Students do not have to attend every event but should consider attending some events (Vasquez et al., 2006). Students should consider attending scheduled colloquia or dissertation defenses that are open to the public. Attending these proceedings may provide an informal opportunity for minority students to interact with their peers and faculty members within the department while demonstrating interest and motivation to faculty.

We strongly recommend that minority graduate students become involved in professional organizations. Professional involvement includes membership in professional organizations, attending and presenting research at professional conferences, and volunteering in professional settings. Professional involvement can provide the student with multiple opportunities, enhance the student's knowledge about the discipline and area of interest, provide a network of potential connections, and assist in establishing relationships with faculty members who may eventually serve as mentors (Keith-Spiegel & Wiederman, 2000; Landrum & Davis, 2010). Professional involvement is crucial for minority students, who often experience both academic and social isolation during their graduate training. We further discuss the importance of professional involvement in the section below on academic and social integration.

There are numerous professional organizations in which minority graduate students may consider membership. Students may become involved in organizations at the local, regional, and national levels. Many departments sponsor local chapters of program-specific organizations such as the Rehabilitation Counseling Students Association and the Neuroscience Graduate Student Association. These organizations are open to all students and focus on providing discipline-specific activities at the local level that encourage professional development. Some institutions may also sponsor graduate student associations for students of color. Examples of such associations are the Black Graduate Student Association, the Hispanic Graduate Student Association, and the Latina/o Graduate Student Association. Although local organizations may be affiliate chapters of much larger national associations, some universities have their own stand-alone groups. For example, Purdue and MIT have their own Black Graduate Student Associations. These associations are sponsored by the institution and are not affiliated with any national organization. Furthermore, many of the national ethnic minority graduate student organizations host regional and national conferences. Students of color are eligible to attend the national and regional conferences if their school has an affiliate membership with the national organization. The conferences provide a venue for graduate students to present their research and to network with same-ethnic-group students. Students may develop friendships and collaborations with same-ethnic-group students from different institutions. These ties may assuage the feeling of academic isolation experienced by the students when they return to their home institutions. Students may also find same-ethnic-group mentors by becoming members of organizations designed specifically to promote the professional development of minority psychologists. The Association of Black Psychologists (ABPsi), the National Latina/Latino Psychological Association (NLPA), and the Asian American Psychological Association (AAPA) are a few examples of national associations that typically invite graduate students to become members. Membership in these professional organizations provides students with access to same-ethnic-group faculty members in their discipline. These faculty members may be willing to serve as mentors to the students. Finally, the American Psychological Association sponsors an Office for Minority Affairs and has a Committee on Ethnic Minority Affairs (CEMA). Any of these organizations can provide additional information to assist students of color.

Although we encourage ethnic minority students to become involved in professional organizations and to engage in service, we would be remiss if we did not warn them of the pitfalls. Similar to minority faculty members, ethnic minority graduate students may find a similar fate awaits them in graduate schools. They, too, will be in demand to serve as diversity representatives in various organizations and on numerous committees (Gay, 2004). Students must learn to balance school, research, service, and work (if applicable). On the surface, invitations to minority students to join numerous organizations and to serve on various committees may seem impressive. However, overcommitment of one's time to service may interfere with grades and ultimately reinforce critics' perceptions of the student's inability to perform in the classroom. Additionally, the student must understand that such invitations are often fraught with political overtones, and any decision to decline must be handled with care. If a minority student feels pressured to join a particular organization or to serve on a committee and feels he does not have the time, he may want to enlist the assistance of his mentor in cordially declining the invitation.

The formation of a peer study group is an effective way to overcome academic isolation. A study group allows students to share their collective knowledge and to gain additional insights into class material (Murray, 2001; Rovaris, 2002). Involvement in organizations is another way in which a student can overcome academic isolation. Students may choose to become involved at the local level by joining a campus or department-specific club, or they may choose to become involved in national organizations (Vasquez et al., 2006). Local organizations can assist students in building a network and support system. Ethnic minority students may find that organizations within the local community can also connect them with other minorities (Greene, 2002). The American Psychological Association of Graduate Students is a national organization that offers membership to all psychology graduate students (APA, 2010; Greene, 2002). Networks developed through membership in professional organizations and conference attendance can prove extremely beneficial for ethnic minority students. Ethnic minority students often lack exposure to accurate knowledge and are unaware of funding opportunities available for graduate education (Ulloa & Herrera, 2006). Networking could lead to the development of mentoring relationships with faculty members who could facilitate the transition from undergraduate to graduate school for minority students. Building a network of support through community service and volunteerism can also alleviate social isolation and serve to connect ethnic minority students with other minorities within the community (Rovaris, 2002). Students may want to establish connections with ethnic groups away from campus and within the community at large. Students should consider researching the community for established resources such as a synagogue, mosque, or church. There may be local organizations such as a Hispanic center or a local chapter of the NAACP. These organizations may be able to assist the student in establishing cultural ties within the community. Establishing networks within the ethnic community may help to alleviate some feelings of cultural loss and social isolation.

Support and Motivation

Early research into factors regarding attrition of college students suggested that successful adjustment to college partially depends on the student's ability to disassociate from family and friends (Tinto, 1988). Conversely, some authors have questioned whether this conventional wisdom applies to ethnic minority students (Guiffrida, 2005, 2006; Hendricks, Smith, Caplow, & Donaldson, 1996). Guiffrida (2006) noted that many minority groups in America are predisposed to collectivist values. These collectivist values encourage the maintenance of family ties between ethnic minority graduate students, their families, and long-time friends. Family members and friends often provide essential emotional and sometimes financial support to ethnic minority graduate students. These students have reported that family members' belief in their ability to succeed in graduate school, interest in their progress, and a corresponding commitment to the student's educational and professional goals provided the motivation many students need to continue their graduate studies (Hendricks et al., 1996).

Ethnic minority graduate students who relocate may find the stress of graduate school coupled with the loss of an established support system overwhelming. The loss of a familial social network as a result of relocation can result in a significant amount of stress (Munton, 1990). At the same time, minority students may also perceive that they receive little social support from their peers and professors. Because graduate programs often have a competitive and individualistic nature about them, this type of environment can be extremely stressful for ethnic minority students who already feel a sense of isolation because they may be the only minority person in the program.

We encourage ethnic minority students to actively seek and develop new friendships among their peers and faculty members within the programs. Gayle Iwamasa wrote that "It is important [for ethnic minority students] [sic] to get support. Discover who your allies are" (Vasquez et al., 2006, p. 164). Therefore, students should seek emotional support from various faculty members who are willing to assist. Minority students will also find that many of their contemporaries are open to collaboration and friendship. As mentioned earlier, some professors may engage in social activities with graduate students. Attending a few such activities can afford opportunities to bond with the professor and peers.

Students should also maintain ties with family and friends who can provide emotional support and encouragement. And, with advances in technology, it is much easier to maintain family ties across the miles with video calling, real-time video chats, and text messaging. Although maintaining a family support system is important and often beneficial, students must be careful to strike a balance between graduate school and family. Not all family members will be supportive of the student's effort to obtain a graduate degree. Enedina Garcia-Vazquez wrote that "[my] family worried that I would lose my ethnicity and become White. They worried that I would be too different from them and become fully assimilated" (Vasquez et al., 2006, p. 169). Minority graduate students can belay some of their family members' concerns by making a concerted effort to maintain their cultural identity. Kamala Greene (2002) suggested that ethnic minority students should "find the time to engage in activities that remind you of your culture. Make sure to eat the food, listen to the music, speak the language, and do the dances of your ethnic group" (p. B14). Engaging in these activities will allow family members to see that the student continues to embrace the importance of culture. Engaging in culturally related activities can also eradicate feelings of cultural isolation.

Mentoring and Advising

There is no shortage of literature that discusses the importance of mentoring in graduate school (Atkinson, Nivelle, & Casas, 1991; Brown, Davis, & McClendon, 1999; Busch, 1985; Johnson & Huwe, 2003; Johnson & Nelson, 1999; Vasquez et al., 2006). Mentors can play a variety of roles in a student's life including providing knowledge, advice, coaching, protection, counseling, and friendship (Johnson & Huwe, 2003). Rogers and Molina (2006) noted that institutions that were effective in recruiting and retaining students of color provided mentoring opportunities for the students. However, because nonminorities hold the majority of full-time faculty positions in higher education, many ethnic minority students have little or no access to minority mentors. Furthermore, Johnson and Huwe (2003) reported that minority graduate students "have less access to mentors when compared to their White counterparts" (p. 171). Previous research has suggested that protégés often prefer and actively seek to be mentored by someone who looks like them. Additionally, Blackwell (1989) suggested that many mentors seem to select protégés who are similar to them in sex, ethnicity, race, and social class. Johnson and Huwe (2003) wrote:

> It is easy to understand why racial similarity is frequently a salient factor when seeking a mentor. Perceived similarity may foster deeper trust, mutual understanding, and bonding that may be difficult to achieve in a mentorship with a racially different mentor. (p. 172)

Although minority graduate students may prefer an ethnic minority mentor, the few minority faculty members make the reality of that occurrence a rare event.

Conversely, Lee (1999) reported that minority students in her study "felt that having an African American faculty member was less important than having a mentor" in one's career field (p. 7). It is our belief that ethnic minority students can be effectively mentored by nonminority faculty members. However, both parties must understand that cross-cultural mentoring requires effortful participation. Johnson and Huwe (2003) identified four challenges that may arise in cross-cultural mentoring relationships. The challenges identified were issues of trust, issues related to power dynamics, differences in interpersonal styles, and difficulty requesting assistance. According to Johnson and Huwe, minority students may mistrust nonminority faculty members due to historical relationships between the ethnic groups. Johnson and Huwe recommend that the mentor and protégé acknowledge and openly discuss any feelings of mistrust. Students of color must develop an open dialogue with their mentors.

Many students of color are keenly aware of the power dynamics that exist between them and their mentors. Extremely demanding mentors may be perceived as engaging in historical forms of threats, humiliation, and racism. Female minority students may even perceive such actions as terrorizing. Again, effective communication between the student and the mentor may result in a resolution to such issues if the mentor has been falsely accused. But if a minority student is convinced that the mentor is racist or discriminating against him, he should immediately speak with the department chairperson and discontinue the mentoring relationship.

Johnson and Huwe (2003) also noted that minority students may experience difficulty seeking assistance from their mentors, fearing that asking for help may lead the mentors to perceive them as weak or incompetent. Asking for help is not a sign of weakness. On the contrary, not seeking assistance may be perceived by a mentor as arrogance or a sign of poor judgment. Students should select their mentors with great care, working with multiple faculty members before selecting one as a mentor. Students must also remember that a mentoring relationship requires consent by both parties and should not assume that a mentoring relationship exists without some type of confirmation. We recommend that students educate nonminority faculty members about the aspects of their culture that are important, as good mentors are interested in knowing what is important. As mentioned previously, the student must maintain open communication with the mentor. Even the most difficult conversations may result in a greater sense of trust between the student and the mentor.

Academic advising also plays a vital role in graduate student persistence (Vaquera, 2007). Faculty advisors guide students through the appropriate institutional procedures that lead to the fulfillment of degree requirements. Such procedures may include assisting with appropriate course selection, giving instructions regarding comprehensive exams, and providing information regarding internship, master's thesis, dissertation, and all other required tasks.

Although they may share common characteristics, an academic advisor is not the same as a mentor (Johnson & Nelson, 1999; Knox, Schlosser, Pruitt, & Hill, 2006). In some departments, students may be assigned an advisor, while other departments may allow students to select their academic advisors. Yet other departments may offer no formal advising for students (Helms & Rogers, 2011). A mentor may serve as an advisor, but an academic advisor is not always a mentor. It is important for minority students to maintain open communication with their advisors. Students must be proactive in seeking information regarding graduation requirements. They must understand course sequencing and routinely discuss their degree plans with their academic advisors. Like mentors, advisors should understand that some minority students may have little knowledge regarding graduate school (Ulloa & Herrera, 2006). Advisors should work diligently with minority students to make sure they understand the necessary requirements that lead to graduation; they should also ensure that these steps are completed in a timely fashion. It is important to note that ethnic minority students may perceive academic advising as a tangible sign of departmental support. Good academic advising may be perceived as a sign of positive departmental support, whereas poor academic advising may signal a lack of concern for minority students.

Discussion

In this chapter, we have discussed issues and challenges related to ethnic minority students and their graduate training. Additionally, recommendations to students and faculty members regarding ways in which these concerns may be adequately addressed have been presented. Yet one of the most significant issues affecting minority graduate students in general is the low number of minority students who attend graduate school.

The American Psychological Association reported that minority students constituted 22.1% of all graduate students enrolled in Ph.D. programs in 2003 (Maton, Kohout, Wicherski, Leary, & Vinokurov, 2006). In 2008, that number had risen only slightly to 25% (APA, 2010). Additionally, in 2008, ethnic minorities comprised 19% of all master's-level students (2010). This number declined from a total of 23% in 2003 (Maton et al., 2006). Furthermore, we mentioned earlier that in 2009, only 17.3% of all faculty members were from ethnic minority groups (NCES, 2010). According to Vasquez and colleagues (2006), "The ultimate goal of identifying barriers and strategies is to increase diversity among psychologists in the educational pipeline and in the profession" (p. 157). We agree with this assertion. We believe that faculty members should work to identify talented minority students during their undergraduate training and mentor them in preparation for graduate education. It is not enough to simply prepare the few self-identified students; faculty must make a concerted effort to increase the number of minority students in graduate programs. Such an increase in the number of minority students in graduate education could eventually influence the number of minority faculty members in higher education and the amount and type of research beneficial to improving the lives of ethnic minorities.

Further Recommendations

Faculty members must take into consideration the unique experiences of ethnic minority graduate students. Quite often, many of these students are the first persons in their family to ever attend college and graduate school (Vasquez et al., 2006). Based on the personal experiences of one author, this minority student had little knowledge of the graduate school admissions process and often learned through trial and error. Faculty members can initially assist minority undergraduate students by providing them with information about the opportunities afforded someone who completes a graduate degree. Furthermore, some minority students doubt their academic ability even when data from their transcripts and classroom performance demonstrate otherwise (Ewing, Richardson, James-Myers, & Russell, 1996). Encouragement by faculty members can often convince minority students to apply and ultimately attend graduate school. Faculty members who choose to mentor minority students should take the time to learn about the students' culture and, as we mentioned earlier, good mentors are interested in knowing what is important to their students. Learning about the student's culture and family sends a message to the student that she is important and the mentor cares about her success. Knowing that someone cares can promote success in minority students. Minority students do not require special attention to succeed in graduate school, as they enter the programs with the academic ability necessary to achieve. They simply require a fair opportunity for success.

❖ References

American Psychological Association Center for Workforce Studies. (2010). *2008–2009 master's- and doctoral-level students in U.S. and Canadian graduate departments of psychology.* Retrieved December 27, 2010, from http://www.apa.org/workforce/publications/10-grad study/reportstudents.pdf.

Appleby, D. C. (2003). What does your transcript say about you, and what can you do if it says things you don't like? *Eye on Psi Chi, 7*(2), 21–23.

Atkinson, D. R., Neville, H., & Casas, A. (1991). The mentorship of ethnic minorities in professional psychology. *Professional Psychology: Research and Practice, 22*(4), 336–338.

Blackwell, J. E. (1989). Mentoring: An action strategy for increasing minority faculty. *Academe, 75*(5), 8–14.

Brown II, M. C., Davis, G. L., & McClendon, S. A. (1999). Mentoring graduate students of color: Myths, models, and modes. *Peabody Journal of Education, 74*(2), 105–119.

Busch, J. W. (1985). Mentoring in graduate school of education: Mentors' perceptions. *American Educational Research Journal, 22*(9), 257–265.

Dunn, D. S., Brewer, C. L., Cautin, R. L., Gurung, R. A. R., Keith, K. D., McGregor, L. N., Nida, S. A., Puccio, P., & Voigt, M. J. (2010). The undergraduate psychology curriculum: Call for a core. In D. F. Halpern (Ed.), *Undergraduate education in psychology* (pp. 47–61). Washington DC: American Psychological Association.

Educational Testing Service. (2008). *School finance and the achievement gap: Funding programs that work*. Retrieved December 27, 2010, from http://www.ets.org/Media/Education_Topics/pdf/school%20finance/Nettles.pdf.

Educational Testing Service. (2010). *About the GRE General Test*. Retrieved December 27, 2010, from http://www.ets.org/gre/general/about.

Ewing, K. M., Richardson, T. Q., James-Myers, L., & Russell, R. K. (1996). The relationship between racial identity attitudes, worldview and African-American graduate students' experience of the imposter phenomenon. *Journal of Black Psychology, 22*(1), 53–66.

Gay, G. (2004). Navigating marginality en route to the professoriate: Graduate students of Color learning and living in academia. *International Journal of Qualitative Studies in Education, 17*(2), 265–288.

Golden, D. (2003). *Colleges cut back minority programs after court rulings*. Retrieved December 27, 2010, from http://online.wsj.com/public/resources/documents/golden8.htm.

Greene, K. A. I. (2002). In the minority in graduate school. *Chronicle of Higher Education, 49*(11), B14.

Guiffrida, D. A. (2005). To break away or strengthen ties to home: A complex issue for African American college students attending a predominantly White institution. *Equity & Excellence in Education, 38*(1), 49–60.

Guiffrida, D. A. (2006). Toward a cultural advancement of Tinto's theory. *Review of Higher Education, 29*(4), 451–472.

Hartig, N., & Steigerwald, F. (2007). Understanding family roles and ethics in working with first-generation college students and their families. *Family Journal, 15*(2), 159–162.

Helms, J. L., & Rogers, D. T. (2011). *Majoring in psychology: Achieving your educational and career goals*. Chichester, West Sussex, UK: Wiley-Blackwell.

Hendricks, A. D., Smith, K., Caplow, J. H., & Donaldson, J. F. (1996). A grounded theory approach to determining the factors related to the persistence of minority students in professional programs. *Innovative Higher Education, 21*(2), 113–126.

Huang, Y., Brewster, M. E., Moradi, B., Goodman, M. B., Wiseman, M. C., & Martin, A. (2010). Content analysis of literature about LGB people of color: 1998–2007. *The Counseling Psychologist, 38*(3), 363–396.

Johnson, W. B., & Huwe, J. M. (2003). *Getting mentored in graduate school*. Washington, DC: American Psychological Association.

Johnson, W. B., & Nelson, N. (1999). Mentor–protégé relationships in graduate training: Some ethical concerns. *Ethical & Behavior, 9*(3), 189–210.

Keith-Spiegel, P., & Wiederman, M. W. (2000). *The complete guide to graduate school admission: Psychology, counseling, and related professions* (2nd ed.). Mahwah, NJ: Lawrence Erlbaum Associates.

Knox, S., Schlosser, L. Z., Pruitt, N. T., & Hill, C. E. (2006). A qualitative examination of graduate advising relationships: The advisor perspective. *The Counseling Psychologist, 34*(4), 489–518.

Kuther, T. L. (2006). *The psychology major's handbook* (2nd ed.). Belmont, CA: Thomson Higher Education.

Landrum, R. E. (2003). Graduate admissions in psychology: Transcripts and the effect of withdrawals. *Teaching of Psychology, 30*(4), 323–325.

Landrum, R. E., & Clark, J. (2005). Graduate admissions criteria in psychology: An update. *Psychological Reports, 97*(2), 481–484.

Landrum, R. E., & Davis, S. F. (2010). *The psychology major: Career options and strategies for success* (4th ed.). Upper Saddle River, NJ: Prentice Hall.

Lee, W. Y. (1999). Striving toward retention: The effect of race on mentoring African American students. *Peabody Journal of Education, 74*(2), 27–43.

Malone, K. R., & Barabino, G. (2008). Narrations of race in STEM research settings: Identity formation and its discontents. *Science Education.* Retrieved December 27, 2010, from http://onlinelibrary.wiley.com/doi/10.1002/sce.20307/abstract.

Maton, K. I., & Hrabowski III, F. A. (2004). Increasing the number of African American PhDs in the sciences and engineering: A strengths-based approach. *American Psychologist, 59*(11), 547–556.

Maton, K. I., Kohout, J. L, Wicherski, M., Leary, G. E., & Vinokurov, A. (2006). Minority students of color and the psychology graduate pipeline. *American Psychologist, 61*(2), 117–131.

McNeill, B. W., Horn, K. L., & Perez, J. A. (1995). The training and supervisory needs of racial and ethnic minority students. *Journal of Multicultural Counseling and Development, 23*(4), 246–258.

Munton, A. G. (1990). Job relocation, stress and the family. *Journal of Organizational Behavior, 11*(5), 401–406.

Murray, B. (2001). How to survive grad school. *Monitor on Psychology, 32*(11), 72.

National Center for Education Statistics. (2010). *Employees in degree-granting institutions by race/ethnicity, sex, employment status, control and type of institution, and primary occupation: Fall 2007.* Retrieved December 27, 2010, from http://nces.ed.gov/programs/digest/d09/tables/dt09_246.asp.

Office of Equal Opportunity. (2010). *Affirmative action in education.* Retrieved December 27, 2010, from http://www.ncsu.edu/equal_op/AAPlan/Affirmative_Action_in_Education.pdf.

Poock, M. C. (2007). A shifting paradigm in the recruitment and retention of underrepresented graduate students. *Journal of College Student Retention: Research, Theory and Practice, 9*(2), 169–181.

Rogers, M. R., & Molina, L. E. (2006). Exemplary efforts in psychology to recruit and retain graduate students of color. *American Psychologist, 61*(2), 143–156.

Rovaris, D. J. (2002). How to apply and succeed in graduate school. *The Black Collegian, 33*(1), 94–100.

Tinto, V. (1988). Stages of student departure: Reflections on the longitudinal character of student leaving. *Journal of Higher Education, 59*(4), 138–155.

Ulloa, E. C., & Herrera, M. (2006). Strategies for multicultural student success: What about grad school? *Career Development Quarterly, 54*(4), 361–366.

Vaquera, G. (2007). Testing theories of doctoral student persistence at a Hispanic serving institution. *Journal of College Student Retention, 9*(3), 283–305.

Vasquez, M. J. T., Lott, B., Garcia-Vazquez, E., Grant, S. K., Iwamasa, G. Y., Molina, L. E., Ragsdale, B. L., & Vestal-Dowdy, E. (2006). Personal reflections: Barriers and strategies in increasing diversity in psychology. *American Psychologist, 61*(2), 157–172.

❖ Suggestions for Further Exploration

Readings

Buskist, W., & Burke, C. (2006). *Preparing for graduate study in psychology: 101 questions and answers* (2nd ed.). Malden, MA: Wiley-Blackwell.

Cross, W. T. (1991). Pathways to the professoriate: The American Indian faculty Pipeline. *Journal of American Indian Education, 30*(2), 13–24.

Kuther, T. L. (2008). *Surviving graduate school in psychology: A pocket mentor.* Washington DC: American Psychological Association.

Nettles, M. T. (1990). *Black, Hispanic, and White doctoral students: Before, during, and after enrolling in graduate school.* Princeton, NJ: Educational Testing Service.

Websites Providing Information and Resources for Ethnic Minority Graduate Students

American Psychological Association Office of Ethnic Minority Affairs (http://www.apa.org/pi/oema/index.aspx)

Asian American Graduate Student Association (http://aagsa.stanford.edu/)

The Association of Black Psychologists (http://www.abpsi.org/)

Hispanic Graduate Student Association (http://hgsauf.blogspot.com/)

National Black Graduate Student Association (http://www.goshatechnologies.com/nbgsa/site/index.html)

National Latina/o Psychological Association (http://www.nlpa.ws/)

7

Important Considerations for International and Older, Nontraditional Students ❖

G. William Hill IV
Kennesaw State University

Loretta N. McGregor
Arkansas State University

I t may seem odd to address adjustment challenges for both international and older, nontraditional students in the same chapter. Although specific situations vary somewhat, both groups face similar general issues as they adapt to graduate school. The common element for both groups is adjusting to an environment that is unfamiliar and requires lifestyle changes. For international students, these adjustments largely involve adapting to a new culture, which includes potential cultural differences in academic expectations. The challenges for older, nontraditional students often relate to personal lifestyle changes since they were last in school (e.g., marriage, children) and re-entering academe after an extended absence.

Focusing on the first year, our intent is to summarize and sensitize you to major adjustment issues common to both groups, with a focus on similarities and differences, and provide some strategies to address these adjustment issues. Our comments and suggestions are primarily global, often assuming that all international and all nontraditional students are similar. We recognize that the reality is that there are individual differences, and some of our observations and suggestions may not apply to individual students. For example, international students from cultures more similar to the United States (e.g., western, English speaking) will find their adjustment somewhat easier compared to other international students (Zhou, 2010). Adjustment for nontraditional students can depend on how long it was since they were last in school or whether they have a partner or children.

Time Management

Time management is an issue for any graduate student; the workload can be overwhelming. In addition to managing class work (e.g., reading, studying, completing assignments), graduate students have expectations for conducting research and engaging in social interactions that are important to future career development (e.g., networking with faculty and peers, attending conferences). Bloom, Karp, and Cohen (1998) note, "when a student is not in class or in the lab or field, he is likely to be in one of three places: at a talk, in the library, or at his desk" (p. 100).

Potential Pitfalls for International Students

Because of language challenges, international students can expect to allocate large blocks of time to completing class reading and writing assignments compared to their peers (Bloom, et al., 1998; Juwah, Lal, & Beloucif, 2006; Peters, 1997; Peterson, 2010). In addition to reading adjustments for class, graduate students also must participate in research projects with their major professor, which requires additional reading related to the research. Because of the fast pace of graduate school, it is easy for international students to devote a large portion of their time to reading and writing just to keep up.

The danger is leaving little or no time for other activities. Networking with professors and fellow graduate students is an important aspect of a graduate student's professional development. Not only is networking important to interactions and support during graduate school, but many professors and fellow graduate students will be long-term colleagues and collaborators. Setting aside time for networking should be a priority (Bloom et al., 1998; Gulgoz, 2001; Peters, 1997). In addition, international students need to attend to their social and personal lives. Failure to set aside personal time can be a major factor in contributing to the depression, loneliness, and isolation often experienced by international students (Bloom et al., 1998; Committee on the College Student, Group for the Advancement of Psychiatry, 2000; Gulgoz, 2001).

Potential Pitfalls for Nontraditional Students

Like international students, nontraditional students may find that studying and writing takes longer than it does for their peers. For nontraditional students, the loss of effective academic work habits and skills may contribute to additional time necessary for reading and writing. In addition, they will have the same expectations for research involvement and networking. However, many nontraditional students have a partner and/or children, which requires setting aside an important block of personal time for their families. Nontraditional students also potentially face time management challenges related to dealing with unexpected and unavoidable family-related issues (e.g., managing aging parents, illness of a child, managing childcare). Failure to address family time can be a significant contributor to stress, depression, and family stability (Committee on the College Student, Group for the Advancement of Psychiatry, 2000; Pederson & Daniels, 2001; Peters, 1997).

Some Suggested Strategies

Both international and nontraditional students can initially manage workload through careful course scheduling (Bloom et al., 1998; Peters, 1997). First, consider personal strengths and weaknesses and select courses in the first year that will provide a balance between them. If possible, consider a reduced course load in the first semester. Taking fewer courses can allow adaptation to the academic workload of graduate school and acquisition of effective study techniques for future success. Lightening the course load at the beginning also allows development of long-term time management strategies for other expectations such as research, networking, and social and family needs. In addition, a lighter load enables students to get a handle on understanding what is or is not a priority in their academic and personal lives (Peters, 1997). Nontraditional students may also want to explore whether the program offers flexible course scheduling through evening, online, or hybrid courses (Bloom et al., 1998). Because face-to-face courses can be an important opportunity for increasing one's skills in speaking English, we do not recommend that international students initially consider online courses.

After the course schedule is set, develop a plan for allocating study, research, and personal time. Using a weekly planner can help schedule and manage time. Students should make sure to dedicate time to their personal needs. It is easy to quickly feel overwhelmed by course and research obligations and ignore the importance of free time. Relaxation time with friends and family is critical to reducing stress and loneliness (Committee on the College Student, Group for the Advancement of Psychiatry, 2000; Gulgoz, 2001; Peters, 1997).

Nontraditional students with partners and children need to carefully plan for additional family-related tasks like quality time together, childcare, and division of routine household responsibilities (e.g., cleaning, cooking). Graduate school can be a stressful time for a family. Communication, both in preparations for graduate school and continuously throughout, is critical. This is a particular problem for nontraditional female students who need their husbands to assume nontraditional roles with respect to childcare and housekeeping. Prior to starting graduate school, potential reallocation of household responsibilities should be addressed. In addition, students must continuously monitor it for a partner's, children's, and the student's own satisfaction (Committee on the College Student, Group for the Advancement of Psychiatry, 2000; Pederson & Daniels, 2001; Peters, 1997).

Unexpected schedule challenges will arise that disrupt the best of planning. However, do not let these disruptions interfere with maintaining the overall balance between academic and personal responsibilities.

Relationships With Professors and Fellow Graduate Students

As noted above, networking is an important aspect of the graduate school experience. Both international and nontraditional students will find that interactions with professors and fellow students are likely to differ from those they previously experienced in academe.

Potential Pitfalls for International Students

One challenge faced by many international students is adjusting to cultural communication differences. Obviously, potential spoken language difficulties are a major contributor. Although a student may have done well on the TOFEL, nonnative-English-speaking students often struggle with speaking English in everyday conversation. Even English-speaking international students can struggle with conversation because of American slang and idioms and references to shared cultural experiences that are unfamiliar to international students (Bloom, et al., 1998; Committee on the College Student, Group for the Advancement of Psychiatry, 2000; Gulgoz, 2001; Peters, 1997; Zhou, 2010). Conversational difficulties and frustrations may lead international students to avoid interactions with American students and contribute to increased feelings of loneliness and isolation. Some international students may seek relationships with students from their home countries where available. Although this can reduce the sense of isolation, it delays their cultural adaptation and slows improvements in speaking English (Bloom et al., 1998; Peters, 1997).

Another challenge for some international students is adapting to the informality of relationships with professors (Bloom et al., 1998). Because academic culture in many other countries emphasizes a hierarchical relationship between professor and student, some international students struggle with the closer, informal relationship between professors and graduate students (e.g., using the professor's first name, a faculty–student relationship that can involve aspects like a friendship, socializing with the professor). In addition, international students may misinterpret verbal or nonverbal communications. For example, because nonverbal behaviors differ across cultures, some students may be uncomfortable with differences in the perception of appropriate personal space and touching (Peters, 1997).

Occasionally, international students may experience some prejudice and stereotyping based on their cultural backgrounds (e.g., a belief that all Asians excel at math; Committee on the College Student, Group for the Advancement of Psychiatry, 2000; Trice, 2003; Zhou, 2010). Sometimes this also exhibits itself through expectations that they should be an informative source on all things cross-cultural, especially their home culture. Unfortunately, for some international students, this increases their sense of separateness and being foreign (Zhou, 2010). International students may also struggle with experiences of prejudice as they shift from being a majority group member to a minority group member, including stereotyping and prejudice related to race or gender that is embedded in American culture. Finally, some faculty or students may assume that the admission of some students was to meet an affirmative action effort (Peters, 1997).

Potential Pitfalls for Nontraditional Students

Establishing relationships with fellow graduate students and professors is also challenging for nontraditional students. Because there is often a substantial age difference between the nontraditional student and other graduate students, it can sometimes be difficult to establish connections with younger peers. Further, nontraditional students can find it difficult to find time to socialize and engage in informal discussions because of family obligations (e.g., childcare, spending quality time with a partner; Committee on the College Student, Group for the Advancement of Psychiatry, 2000; Pederson & Daniels, 2001; Peters, 1997).

Relationships with professors can also sometimes be problematic. In some cases, professors seem to be uncomfortable with older students and may interpret a student's references to practical experience as threatening to their expertise because they may lack that experience (Committee on the College Student, Group for the Advancement of Psychiatry, 2000; Peters, 1997). Alternatively, some professors may anticipate having to make special accommodations for nontraditional students (e.g., late papers, less lab time, excusing absences) and expect less commitment because of their family obligations (Committee on the College Student, Group for the Advancement of Psychiatry, 2000; Peters, 1997). That is, many professors assume that graduate school is a full-time commitment and nontraditional students are basically part-time students.

Like international students, nontraditional students may experience some prejudice related to their age. Professors may assume that they are not career focused or have less to contribute to the discipline in the long term. In addition, like international students, some may perceive nontraditional students as an affirmative action effort (Peters, 1997).

Some Suggested Strategies

If a student perceives prejudice, she or he should not overreact. The student should start by analyzing the situation to determine whether the prejudice is real or possibly due to a misperception. Sometimes international students may perceive prejudice where it is not intentional but simply a situation related to a cultural misunderstanding (Peters, 1997; Zhou, 2010). Like many Americans, graduate students and even faculty lack direct experience with other cultures and may act in ways that reflect cultural stereotypes perpetuated by the media. Even though we are psychologists and understand individual differences and stereotyping, it does not mean that we always apply that knowledge in our everyday interactions. Similarly, students may have age-related stereotypes about nontraditional students as well as limited experience with working with an older person as a peer (Committee on the College Student, Group for the Advancement of Psychiatry, 2000; Peters, 1997).

Student feelings of prejudice that arise from experiences that seem to indicate that professors ignore them may also be a misperception; professors ignore all graduate students to some extent. So do not overreact to feelings of isolation or separateness within the program. Concentrate on being confident and friendly, continuously reaching out to fellow students and the faculty (Peters, 1997). Make it a point to build in time to engage in informal conversations about the program and personal struggles, asking for advice and assistance. Students will find that many professors understand if a student opens lines of communication and maintains them. Further, fellow students are struggling with their own stresses and feelings of isolation and can be a source of support.

In addition, both nontraditional and international students may interpret situations as reflecting prejudice because of their own feelings that they are different from other students. Remember that all students experience isolation, insecurity, and stress to some degree. However, if prejudice does happen, respond to it by discussing it with the individual. Be honest about the perception and focus on objective actions that may address it rather than being accusatory and demanding of change (Peters, 1997).

Lifestyle Changes

Lifestyle changes and adjustments are major issues to address. Nontraditional students are often giving up an established and settled lifestyle, while international students are transitioning from their home cultures. Many factors related to lifestyle changes for both groups need to be addressed prior to starting graduate school (e.g., financial issues, moving, finding housing, separation from established social support, visa issues for international students). However, our focus will be on how issues related to the relocation to graduate school continue into the first year and can provide additional sources of stress, and we will not address planning issues.

Potential Pitfalls for International Students

Obviously, the lifestyle change for international students is adapting to a new culture. In addition to the pressures of starting graduate school, they must also negotiate the challenges of using a potentially unfamiliar language in conversation, different social customs, and day-to-day life (Bloom et al., 1998; Committee on the College Student, Group for the Advancement of Psychiatry, 2000; Gulgoz, 2001; Peters, 1997; Zhou, 2010). For example, simple routines like grocery shopping or driving can be significant challenges, requiring one to change assumptions and unconscious habits associated with these activities. The degree of adaptation, however, varies across individual students. Students from cultures more similar to the United States (e.g., coming from an English-speaking or more western culture) will find adjustment somewhat easier compared to students from a more dissimilar culture (Zhou, 2010). In addition, students with prior cross-cultural experience will be at an advantage. International students also lack important social support because they have left behind all their family and friends. Because of distance and cost, international students are limited in their ability to schedule frequent visits home. Further, their stressors as graduate students may be unfamiliar to their family and friends, lessening the helpfulness of their previous social support resources. The combination of cultural adaptation and lack of social support is a major contributing factor to the loneliness and homesickness commonly experienced by international students (Bloom et al., 1998; Committee on the College Student, Group for the Advancement of Psychiatry, 2000; Gulgoz, 2001).

Potential Pitfalls for Nontraditional Students

Like international students, nontraditional students must adjust to relocation issues. If they have a partner and/or children, relocation can present significant stressors affecting their graduate school adjustment. Although nontraditional students and their partners should have considered, discussed, and agreed to lifestyle changes associated with attending graduate school prior to relocating, an abstract discussion may not totally prepare one for the realities of dealing with lifestyle changes (Committee on the College Student, Group for the Advancement of Psychiatry, 2000; Pederson & Daniels, 2001; Peters, 1997). Dealing with a probable loss in family income (the student losing her or his job; the partner finding a new job, possibly with lower pay) and increased expenses associated with graduate school (e.g., tuition, fees, professional expenses associated with professional memberships and conference attendance) become stressful realities, not abstract issues (Committee on the College Student, Group for the Advancement of Psychiatry, 2000; Pederson & Daniels, 2001). In addition, the reality of implementing plans for managing household chores and childcare can also become a challenge. Therefore, not only do new graduate students need to deal with their adjustments to school, they must also manage adjustments in their personal lives in negotiation with a partner and/or children (Committee on the College Student, Group for the Advancement of Psychiatry, 2000; Pederson & Daniels, 2001; Peters, 1997).

Nontraditional students who are also single parents face even greater challenges in managing their balance between home and school responsibilities. Without a partner to assist, they must take on sole responsibility for the household management and childcare. Therefore, if their child gets ill or childcare is unavailable (e.g., a childcare center closing because of weather or a holiday) and they still have graduate school obligations, they often face the challenge of no backup support (Committee on the College Student, Group for the Advancement of Psychiatry, 2000; Pederson & Daniels, 2001; Peters, 1997).

Loss of established social support can also be an issue for nontraditional students. When relocating, nontraditional students lose close contact with family and leave behind their friends. Although they may have a partner and/or children as potential sources of social support, challenges remain, such as allocating sufficient quality family time. Partners and children may experience a sense of being a secondary to the priority of the student's "job" as a graduate student. In addition, a partner may experience some jealousy and isolation due to the time devoted to school and studying and the new relationships with fellow graduate students and professors (Committee on the College Student, Group for the Advancement of Psychiatry, 2000; Pederson & Daniels, 2001; Peters, 1997).

Some Suggested Strategies

First and foremost, students should not let graduate school take over their lives! Studying for class and being in the lab can easily trap students into making it their primary priority. Maintain a social life outside of graduate school. As noted earlier in our discussion of time management, nontraditional students need to be proactive in setting aside personal time for themselves and their partners and/or children. Failing to do so contributes to additional stress, depression, and loneliness (Committee on the College Student, Group for the Advancement of Psychiatry, 2000; Gulgoz, 2001; Peters, 1997). Further, ongoing communication with a partner about sources of stress, concerns, and renegotiation of planned allocation of household responsibilities is essential (Committee on the College Student, Group for the Advancement of Psychiatry, 2000; Pederson & Daniels, 2001). Although international students may not have a partner and/or a child, it is just as important that they allocate time for a personal social life outside of studies.

As much as possible, both groups should attempt to maintain friend and family sources of social support. Fortunately, technology allows easier maintenance of contact with family and friends through face-to-face interactions over the Internet at little to no cost except for taking the time (e.g., Skype). In addition, where possible with respect to time and finances, plan some visits home.

Many campuses also provide multiple social support resources targeting both international and nontraditional students. Soon after arriving on campus (or even before), be proactive in investigating campus resources that provide support services specifically for international and nontraditional students (Bloom et al., 1998; Committee on the College Student, Group for the Advancement of Psychiatry, 2000; Gulgoz, 2001; Zhou, 2010). Most universities today are cognizant of the unique challenges and adjustments these students face and provide extensive support services across multiple campus units. For example, most campuses have specific offices, often in student affairs, dedicated to supporting international or nontraditional students. These offices provide information on resources and support mechanisms for students (e.g., available childcare, housing suggestions, support groups) and often assist in overall adjustment relative to the special needs of international or nontraditional students. Campus counseling centers are also important resources in helping students deal with depression or loneliness. Counseling services often provide free or low-cost short-term counseling for individuals and sometimes couples. They may also offer support groups specifically for international and nontraditional students.

Another possible social support strategy is establishing a social life outside of graduate school through participation in university and community clubs and organizations (Bloom et al., 1998; Gulgoz, 2001; Peters, 1997; Zhou, 2010). Visit the university's student affairs website and look for clubs or organizations that either support or advocate for international or nontraditional students and get involved. In addition, students may find clubs and organizations devoted to their personal interests and preferred activities (e.g., intramural sports programs, outdoors clubs). Getting involved in organizations, especially those not solely focused on a particular nationality, can be particularly helpful in helping international students enhance conversational English skills and adapt to American culture (Bloom et al., 1998; Committee on the College Student, Group for the Advancement of Psychiatry, 2000; Gulgoz, 2001).

Nontraditional students should encourage their partners to get involved in the university, which helps the partner feel more connected (Committee on the College Student, Group for the Advancement of Psychiatry, 2000). For example, many university campus events are free and may match a partner's interests (e.g., speakers, cultural events, sports events). Also, encourage a partner to investigate the possibility of auditing courses that may be of interest or attending departmental colloquia with you. Nontraditional students should also investigate whether specific clubs or organizations are available for student spouses or open to their participation. Many campus outdoor clubs provide low-cost trips (e.g., camping, skiing, and scuba diving) that are open to partner participation and both provide needed quality time together and an opportunity to make new friends.

Academic Adjustments

Both international and nontraditional students will experience significant adjustment issues with respect to the academic culture of graduate school. Some adjustments are similar to those experienced by all new graduate students (e.g., greater expectations for independent work, an emphasis on discussion over lecture in the classroom, more informality in professor–student interactions). However, nontraditional and international students bring past experiences that make these adjustments more difficult as well as having additional unique adjustment issues.

Potential Pitfalls for International Students

Although it is likely that international students had substantial experience with using technology for writing and research, one area they may be less familiar with is using online course platforms like Blackboard for accessing materials and participating in outside-of-class discussions and testing (Zhou, 2010). The use of these platforms is increasingly common, and international students may have a learning curve for using them efficiently and effectively.

Classroom experiences will present a number of adaptation challenges for international students. Unlike their probable experience as undergraduates in their home cultures, graduate classes are likely much smaller, emphasizing student–professor interaction and discussion and less formal lecturing (Bloom et al., 1998; Committee on the College Student, Group for the Advancement of Psychiatry, 2000; Gulgoz, 2001; Peters, 1997). Because of strong expectations for active participation (classes are small and you cannot hide), the passive role they may have adopted as undergraduates will not transfer. Further, there is an expectation that graduate students will exhibit independent thinking through critically evaluating and synthesizing material. This may not match their past cultural educational experiences, which may have emphasized content memorization and respect for the professor's authoritative expertise (Bloom et al., 1998; Committee on the College Student, Group for the Advancement of Psychiatry, 2000, Gulgoz, 2001; Peters, 1997). Further, classes may be more competitive, with students actively competing to impress the professor with their independent thinking and individual understanding (Bloom et al., 1998; Gulgoz, 2001).

Some international students may also struggle with adjusting to the more informal atmosphere of the American classroom. The use of humor by professors, a professor's informal appearance, eating or drinking in the classroom, and students speaking critically to the professor or interrupting to disagree may all be disconcerting to international students whose experience is very different (Gulgoz, 2001; Peters, 1997; Zhou, 2010).

Some course expectations may also represent unfamiliar territory. International students may find expectations of being on time for class and meeting deadlines for submission of assignments more rigid than their experience in the past (Bloom et al., 1998; Gulgoz, 2001). In addition, some students are not familiar with frequent course assessments that emphasize writing over multiple-choice tests and oral assessments (Bloom et al., 1998).

Language issues are a significant challenge in and out of the classroom for international students despite a student's strong TOFEL score. Because the TOFEL emphasizes an evaluation of written comprehension, international students often struggle with comprehending conversational English in the classroom and, subsequently, notetaking (Gulgoz, 2001; Peters, 1997; Trice, 2003). Lectures and discussions may proceed faster than non–English-speaking students can process. In addition, lectures often include American slang and idioms, unfamiliar jargon and terminology, and references to assumed American cultural knowledge as examples (products, TV programs), which complicates comprehension. International students are often reticent to ask for clarification so as not to look "stupid" (Zhou, 2010).

Reading assignments for class or out-of-class research can also present a challenge for international students. The reality is that it will take longer for them to read material than for their English-speaking fellow students to do so, which, as noted above, also represents a time management issue. In addition, unlike their prior academic experiences, reading expectations deemphasize memorization of content and emphasize critical analysis, integration, and synthesis of content across readings (Bloom et al., 1998; Committee on the College Student, Group for the Advancement of Psychiatry, 2000; Gulgoz, 2001; Peters, 1997).

The last language challenge relates to writing, which will be a significant component of course evaluations as well as reporting research results. International students struggle often with writing in three areas: grammar and spelling; ability to critique, analyze and synthesize material; and appropriate citation and paraphrasing skills. As noted before, some international students come from an academic culture that emphasizes simple summarization and uncritical presentation of content. These are not expectations of U.S. professors for writing assignments (Juwah et al., 2006; Trice, 2003). In addition, some international students engage in inadvertent plagiarism because of past academic and cultural experiences. Trice (2003) and Juwah et al. (2006) note international students may lack an understanding of the western concept of plagiarism, which is often related to cultural differences in the necessity to cite original sources. For example, Asian cultures deemphasize deviation from the original text, and the attribution of individual ownership of original ideas and cited text is not a cultural norm. Because the concept of individual ownership of ideas and writing is not a norm, international students often incorporate content without appropriate citation. In addition, these cultural tendencies may lead international students to perceive Internet content as public-domain material and to see no need to provide citations (Juwah et al., 2006). Be aware that professors expect all students to know appropriate American citation and paraphrasing practices and provide little to no writing instruction.

Shifting from the classroom, remember that another major expectation is research involvement outside of class. Based on the student's area of specialization and a professor's interest in accepting the student relative to research interests expressed in her or his application materials, an assignment to an academic advisor, or major professor, occurs prior to the student's arrival. Unlike classroom expectations of independence, major professors are likely to expect participation in their already-established research programs. Because international students come from a cultural expectation of deferring to the professor, they find it difficult to express their own research interests (Committee on the College Student, Group for the Advancement of Psychiatry, 2000; Gulgoz, 2001).

Potential Pitfalls for Nontraditional Students

Challenges for nontraditional students also relate to potential disconnects to their past educational experiences. Although they may be more familiar with the informality of U.S. classrooms, they may lack experience with expectations that classroom participation will be more interactive and deemphasize lecturing. Further, past educational experiences could still have emphasized memorization and uncritical analysis of course content. Therefore, like international students, they may face challenges in adjusting to participation expectations in graduate classes (Peters, 1997).

Another potentially significant challenge may include adjusting to the extensive use of technology in contemporary teaching and research. Many nontraditional students may lack technology skills compared to their younger peers who have grown up with technology as a central educational tool (Bloom et al., 1998; Peters, 1997). Even more than international students, they are likely to be unfamiliar with using online course platforms as well as word processing, spreadsheets, and data analysis programs. For example, graduate programs may expect familiarity with statistical analysis programs like SPSS, which their undergraduate program may not have taught.

Probably the greatest challenge for nontraditional students will be reestablishing effective study skills and habits (Bloom et al., 1998). Many nontraditional students may struggle with what were once routine academic tasks like reading academic material, writing, and taking notes after a long absence.

Finally, like other graduate students, the assignment of a major professor often occurs prior to their arrival on campus. Despite potential reluctance to assert individual interests, simply acquiescing to the assignment may not allow a student to develop the focus for professional development and research that will contribute to her or his long-term goals and interests.

Some Suggested Strategies

International and nontraditional students should take advantage of campus resources offering services that can provide them with study skill development, technology training, and writing (Gulgoz, 2001; Peters, 1997; Zhou, 2010). Although these resources often primarily cater to undergraduate students, they can be equally helpful to graduate students. For example, most campuses have a writing center that will offer free assistance in writing development, including reviewing paper drafts and assisting with proper citation and paraphrasing. The office of information technology services often offers training courses on software packages and using online teaching platforms used at the university. Finally, there are campus offices that offer study skill development workshops on topics like effective reading, notetaking, and time management (e.g., counseling center, international and nontraditional students support centers). Visit the websites for these various campus resource offices for workshop and training opportunities shortly after you arrive on campus and schedule time to attend early in the first semester.

Be assertive in asking for assistance from professors and fellow graduate students. Do not hesitate to meet with professors to get clarification concerning class discussions or course expectations and requirements. Consider organizing or joining a study group that can assist with understanding course reading assignments, preparing for class discussions, and studying for tests. If notetaking is a challenge, ask the professor's permission to audio record the class or ask classmates if they will share their notes (Gulgoz, 2001).

International students who struggle with understanding spoken English should consider taking ESL courses offered at their universities (Bloom et al., 1998; Peters, 1997). Another strategy to improve understanding of conversational English is to force themselves into situations that require the use of spoken English (e.g., joining clubs and organizations that include primarily English-speaking members, socializing and studying with students who do not speak your native language; Committee on the College Student, Group for the Advancement of Psychiatry, 2000; Gulgoz, 2001; Peters, 1997).

With respect to expectations for starting research in the first semester, a good strategy is to investigate your major professor's research interests through finding her or his recent publications and reading them. In addition, students might consider contacting their major professors before they arrive on campus for initial advice and reading suggestions. Depending on the length of time they have been out of school, nontraditional students should consider reading a current introductory textbook as well as advanced undergraduate textbooks in their area of specialization (Peters, 1997).

Parting Comments

Given personal and academic adjustments, the first semester of graduate school will be the most difficult. Advance planning and proactively addressing challenges as they arise are essential (Committee on the College Student, Group for the Advancement of Psychiatry, 2000; Peters, 1997). Although we have highlighted some of the most common challenges for international and nontraditional students and suggested strategies for overcoming them, each student will face individual issues unique to her or his past cultural or life experiences. We want to leave students with three general pieces of advice that can assist in a successful transition:

1. Develop and use social support resources, whether they are existing ones (e.g., family, friends) or newly established ones (e.g., fellow students, campus support resources, professors).

2. Identify and use departmental and campus resources to assist with transition challenges and help with academic success.

3. Do not let graduate school consume your life. It is essential that you establish a balance between school and a personal life.

References

Bloom, D. F., Karp, J. D., & Cohen, N. (1998). *The Ph.D. process: A student's guide to graduate school in the sciences.* New York: Oxford University Press.

Committee on the College Student, Group for the Advancement of Psychiatry. (2000). *Helping students adapt to graduate school: Making the grade.* New York: Haworth Press.

Gulgoz, S. (2001). Stresses and strategies for international students. In S. Walfish & A. K. Hess (Eds.), *Succeeding in graduate school: The career guide for psychology students* (pp. 159–170). New York: Psychology Press.

Juwah, C., Lal, D., & Beloucif, A. (2006). *Overcoming the cultural issues associated with plagiarism for international students.* Retrieved December 13, 2010, from http://www.heacademy.ac.uk/business/projects/detail/trdg/2005–06/plagiarism_bmaf.

Pederson, D. J., & Daniels, M. H. (2001). Stresses and strategies for graduate student couples. In S. Walfish & A. K. Hess (Eds.), *Succeeding in graduate school: The career guide for psychology students* (pp. 171–185). New York: Psychology Press.

Peters, R. L. (1997). *Getting what you came for: The smart student's guide to earning a master's or Ph.D.* (rev. ed.). New York: Farrar, Straus, and Giroux.

Peterson, L. (2010). *Writing needs of international students.* Retrieved December 13, 2010, from http://www.cgu.edu/pahes/949.asp.

Trice, A. G. (2003). Faculty perceptions of graduate international students: The benefits and challenges. *Journal of Studies in International Education, 7*(4), 379–403.

Zhou, Y. (2010). *Understanding of international graduate students' academic adaptation to a U.S. graduate school.* Unpublished master's thesis, Bowling Green State University, Bowling Green, OH. Retrieved December 13, 2010, from http://etd.ohiolink.edu/view.cgi?acc_num=bgsu1269127068.

Suggestions for Further Exploration

Readings

American Psychological Association. (2009). *Mastering APA style: Student's workbook and training guide* (6th ed.). Washington, DC: Author.

Buskist, W., & Burke, C. (2006). *Preparing for graduate study in psychology: 101 questions and answers* (2nd ed.). Malden, MA: Wiley-Blackwell.

Hasan, N. T., Fouad, N. A., & Williams-Nickelson, C. (Eds.). (2008). *Studying psychology in the United States: Expert guidance for international students.* Washington, DC: American Psychological Association.

Johnson, W. B., & Huwe, J. M. (2002). *Getting mentored in graduate school.* Washington, DC: American Psychological Association.

Kuther, T. L. (2008). *Surviving graduate school in psychology: A pocket mentor.* Washington, DC: American Psychological Association.

Landrum, E. (2008). *Undergraduate writing in psychology: Learning to tell the scientific story.* Washington, DC: American Psychological Association.

Leong, F., & Austin, J. T. (2005). *The psychology research handbook: A guide for graduate students and research assistants* (2nd ed.). Thousand Oaks, CA: Sage.

Meltzoff, J. (1997). *Critical thinking about research: Psychology and related fields.* Washington, DC: American Psychological Association.

Schindley, W. (2002). *Adults in college: A survival guide for nontraditional students* (rev. ed.). Mt. Pleasant, TX: Dallas Publishing.

Siebert, A., & Karr, M. (2008). *Adult student's guide to survival & success* (6th ed.). Portland, OR: Practical Psychology Press.

Silvia, P. J. (2007). *How to write a lot: A practical guide to productive academic writing.* Washington, DC: American Psychological Association.
Simon, L. (2009). *New beginnings: A reference guide for adult learners* (4th ed.). Upper Saddle River, NJ: Prentice Hall.

Websites Providing Information and Resources for Graduate Students

American Psychological Association of Graduate Students (http://www.apa.org/apags)
National Association of Graduate-Professional Students (http://www.nagps.org)

8

Graduate Students
With Special Needs

❖

Alex Watters
University of Nebraska, Omaha

Susan R. Burns
Morningside College

T o understand life for graduate students with special needs, readers first need the context of how one of your authors (AW) became a *student* with special needs. In providing brief details to the background of his story, we hope to illustrate how life can change in a moment and take a new direction with new challenges and opportunities. These challenges and opportunities need not be seen as obstacles too large to overcome on the path of personal and professional success; however, these challenges present individuals, in particular students, with additional considerations that those without special needs may not even ponder. Although this chapter will focus on Alex's personal experiences with a physical disability, we share recommendations from others' research on the topic as well.

A Life-Changing Moment: Alex's Story

Upon graduating high school, if you were to tell me that after college I would be attending graduate school, I would have thought you were crazy. It is not that I disliked school, I simply never saw myself taking that path. However, after 2 weeks at Morningside College, my world was altered drastically. I had come home for a weekend with some friends to stay at their cabin and enjoy the last few days of nice fall weather. After some time of conversation around the campfire and tossing the football around, a couple of girls and I decided we would go swimming in the lake one last time before the weather would become too cold. While the girls were inside changing, one of their little brothers and I went out on the dock to wait for them to join us. As we were approaching the end of the dock, suddenly a gust of wind came up and blew my hat into the water. I quickly slipped off my shirt and dove in to recover it. At the time, I did not necessarily pay much attention to how deep the water would be as I was nearing the end of the dock and was next to a boat hoist, but this lack of consideration was one that would forever alter my future.

I could not immediately discern what the snap sound was when I dove into the water, but I distinctly remember hearing it. I quickly realized that neither my arms nor my legs were moving and that I had better start swimming or I was going to be in some trouble. I would later be told that the water was a mere 18 inches deep and that snapping sound was my neck breaking under the weight of my body plunging into the water. While I lay there, face-down in the water, I remember thinking to myself, "Swim, you need to swim," but my body was not responding. I remember the frustration, the constant questioning, "Why am I not swimming?" Time seemed to stand still. After a few more moments, I began to better understand the gravity of the situation. I distinctly remember thinking, "This is it, if it's my time to go, it's my time to go." Then everything went black. . . . After being rescued from the water and life-flighted to an Iowa hospital, I was quickly rushed into surgery, where they discovered that my C5 vertebrae had been shattered, causing a pinch of my spinal cord. The injury left my body paralyzed from the chest down with minimal use of my arms. To remain mobile, I would be confined to a wheelchair and require a specially adapted van to get me around. My circumstances also require that someone assist me with the most basic of tasks from assisting with meals to getting dressed or going to bed.

Before breaking my neck, I had gotten a taste of what college was like and I knew I wanted to be right back where it had started. To get a feel for college courses and assure myself that I would be able to handle it because I could no longer type my papers or take notes in the normal college student fashion, I signed up for a community college course in a school that was located in a neighboring town. To say that this course was easy would be an understatement; however, looking back on it, maybe it was just the type of confidence building I needed to assure me that I would be able to go back and be successful in college.

Life as a College Student (in General) With Special Needs

Once I had the community college course under my belt, I knew I was prepared to go back to school. I wanted to start my college career where it had already begun—Morningside College. Throughout this transition period back to college and throughout my 4 years, I was assisted by a wonderful woman who became my girlfriend, assistant, notetaker, and driving force. I had met her while in rehab at Craig Hospital (Colorado), where she decided that she would like to move back to Iowa to help me in this new chapter of my life. Although her assistance throughout this time definitely made my transition easier, in no way would I say that what I went through was always enjoyable.

Although colleges and universities are legally bound to provide reasonable accommodations for students with physical and learning disabilities, many educators are not trained in how to best teach individuals with special needs. As Liebert, Lutsky, and Gottlieb (1990) suggested, little is known about how well the needs of students with disabilities are met and what educational systems can do to better meet those needs. In a survey of 106 respondents who had graduated from a high school for youth with physical disabilities located in a suburban area, Liebert and colleagues found that more than three-fourths of the students attended or were currently attending college; however, more than half said that they had difficulties adjusting to college training. Many of their respondents as well indicated the desire for "more intensive guidance counseling, especially in the areas of job placement; additional training or upgrading of job skills; more help with transportation; and more access to social and recreational programs" (p. 60).

Morningside College, where I completed my undergraduate degree, is a small private institution with approximately 1,200 full-time students and class sizes ranging from around 40 students in some of my larger courses to less than 10 in some of my seminar-style classes. Although I was confident in my ability to thrive in this type of environment, going to college with a disability, no matter how confident you are, can still be daunting. Going to a college of Morningside's size had some advantages and disadvantages. On the bright side, people definitely noticed me around campus and were both inquisitive and willing to help, but it also meant that everyone knew me or asked questions about me throughout campus. I am not shy, but at times it was overwhelming feeling like a spectacle. People tend to stare at those with disabilities, and the environment that a small college such as Morningside provided definitely fueled that more than if I had gone to a state school, for instance.

The closer I came to graduating, the more nervous I became about entering into the real world. To be honest, I enjoyed going to school and knew that someday I wanted to make the world a better place with what I chose to do with my career; however, my regular disability checks and uneasiness about entering into uncertain economic security in some ways may have played a part in my decision to attend graduate school. Having studied political science and global history, graduate school was almost a necessity to give any future career options a chance for success. I began to look for different types of careers that would interest me.

Becoming a Graduate Student With Special Needs

Although physical disabilities create unique circumstances and difficulties for some graduates students, we also want to highlight challenges graduate students with learning disabilities may experience. Paquette (1997) acknowledged students with learning disabilities may face challenges in their search for and application to graduate school. Paquette surveyed chairpersons from APA-accredited clinical and counseling psychology programs as a part of his dissertation and a larger project of developing a resource guide for applying to graduate school for those with learning disabilities. Results from his survey indicated that chairperson respondents were open to providing accommodations but not to altering the standards for admissions. Although respondents also indicated a belief that students with disabilities could successfully complete graduate-level work in psychology, they also acknowledged having limited expertise and experience working at the graduate level with students who have learning disabilities. Furthermore, many reported having very few students in their programs with learning disabilities (i.e., 40% of those who responded reported not having students with learning disabilities).

Ganschow, Coyne, Parks, and Antonoff (1999) conducted a 10-year follow-up study examining the programs available and services provided to graduate students with learning disabilities. Their original survey, which was sent out in 1985 to graduate and professional programs, included 91 questions that could be divided into eight categories: general program question, support-type programs, diagnostic evaluations, program accommodations, services, counseling, relationship with the institution's special education program, and program interface with special education, dissemination, and evaluation. In their 10-year follow-up, Ganschow and colleagues mailed surveys to the same 682 graduate and professional programs that had participated in the original research. Although many improvements had taken place in graduate and professional school programs for addressing services and programs for individuals with learning disabilities, when asked how many students with learning disabilities were enrolled in their programs, 77.1% indicated they either *could not answer* or that the question *was not applicable,* 11.9% said that they did not have any students with learning disabilities enrolled, and those remaining reported having fewer than seven students with learning disabilities enrolled. Ganschow and colleagues concluded that although there is a much greater awareness of learning disabilities and institutional services available for these students, there was no change in the interface of services, dissemination of information, and evaluation of programs. These authors suggested that there should be greater publication by graduate and professional schools of the services provided and/or acceptance of students with learning disabilities. As Khubchandani (n.d.) suggested, schools have made great strides in compliance with federal regulations set for by the Americans with Disabilities Act (ADA) of 1990; however, "negative attitudes are perhaps the single most significant barrier faced by individuals with disabilities in the educational process" (¶ 2). These negative attitudes can be experienced by students with physical or learning disabilities and may limit the extent to which students with special needs ask for the assistance necessary for success.

Attempting to pick a graduate school or program can seem like a challenge in itself, but I feel that doing so with a disability adds a whole other element. After doing some extensive searching and visiting a prospective school that I, erroneously, thought was the best fit for me, I discovered that there was a fairly new master's program being offered through Creighton University's (Omaha, NE) law school on conflict and dispute resolution. Because it was my first time applying to graduate school, the fact that I was doing so with a disability and the complications that this reality would inherently bring with it were not necessarily at the forefront of my mind. I simply wanted to go to the best school I could get into, one within easy driving distance of my parents, and one where I felt the people around me were as enthused about my program as I was. At the time, I did not give much thought to the public transportation of the city, the disability-assistance programs that I would need to transfer from Iowa-based to wherever I would be going, or who would be taking care of me once I got there. I knew that things would most definitely be changing: I no longer wanted to live on campus, so commuting became an issue; my Iowa programs were no longer going to be available; and my girlfriend who had been taking care of me throughout my undergrad was no longer going to be a part of my life. I know that I was thinking of things to remedy these circumstances, but the procrastinator in me took hold and I just prayed that everything would pan out.

Challenges to Consider on the Road to Graduate School

I realized that being accepted was just part of a long, complicated process in the transition of a disabled student moving to another city and all of the changes that would need to be made. The first was fairly obvious: where was I going to live? Living on campus at Morningside College and having people around me 24 hours a day if needed had become like a comfort blanket. I felt assured that if anything should happen, someone in the dorm would be able to come and help me. I recognized this and knew that living on my own was simply not an option at this point in time. I contemplated living in one of the dormitories on Creighton's campus but felt that I would feel out of place as a graduate student. So I began looking at other options. Conveniently, but after lengthy discussion and consideration, some good friends of mine agreed to get an apartment with me. Once it was determined that the three of us would be getting an apartment together, I knew that they were not going to be able to do everything for me, so I began looking into home health care agencies. Similar to the search for graduate schools, I consulted the Internet—what did anyone do before Google? I found a few possibilities and began contacting them to see what services I would be eligible for that they offered. This process was a little nerve-wracking for me. Up until this point, my previous girlfriend and family had been the only people that had ever done my personal care such as getting me up and dressed in the morning, helping me in the shower, and so on. I was not excited to teach my routine to numerous different people who would perform these tasks while I was at graduate school. I had been spoiled only having one or two people that needed to know my preferences on how I like my pants adjusted or how I always take a drink of water after I brush my teeth; now there was the possibility that I would have to be training a different person for every day of the week. These types of things can cloud your mind and make you more apprehensive about the future than need be, and although this process of finding an agency that was willing to provide daily caregivers was easy, the transition of government assistance from one state to another and the training of those caregivers was another story!

Challenges and Opportunities Experienced in Graduate School

Throughout my undergraduate studies, I was able to learn a valuable lesson that I think became even more valuable throughout graduate school: make connections with those around you. When I first visited Creighton to look at the graduate program as an undergraduate senior, the first person I met who was related to the program was the secretary of the department. Honestly, I feel the term *secretary* for her, like for many, is a misnomer because it does not encompass all that she does for the program. I would be remiss if I also undercredited how valuable my connection with her has been to my experience at Creighton. She was very helpful and friendly that first day, and I made sure to keep in contact with her to further that relationship. However, she is one of the many people I have reached out to and made a connection with to enhance my experience in graduate school. There are countless others who have helped me throughout my journey, such as those in the disability assistance office and my professors themselves. All of these individuals have collectively made my transition to graduate school, and success in it, all the easier. However, this is not something that comes naturally for all people.

As an outgoing person, I always love meeting new people and talking with them, but it is much more than that. I try to genuinely get to know them as a person no matter what capacity their relationship is with me. And although it is important to establish good rapport with those at the top of a graduate studies program, such as upper administrators or directors, it has been the relationships that I have made throughout my classes that made going to graduate school with a disability possible. The ways in which my fellow students have helped me are vast. Students from our program have helped drive me to school and taken notes in my classes, but by my making connections and becoming friends with them, they also have instilled in me the confidence to succeed regardless of my disability. That is why I make sure, when I am meeting a new person, to make the best impression, because you never know how that person is going to influence you or shape your experience.

The next lesson I learned from embarking on this path of going to graduate school with a disability is that you need to be prepared for things to go wrong. When people become dependent on things, whether it is technology or other people, there is a higher probability of something going wrong. For college students, the trouble lies in being too dependent on technology and not saving that year-end research paper in multiple places. A great number of students, myself included, have, at one point or another, had that punched-in-the-gut feeling when you realize that one of your projects that you have worked on for so long has magically disappeared into computer oblivion. I also have learned that for students with disabilities, in preparing for these types of things, you are often left dependent upon others for assistance. Do not get me wrong; I am forever grateful for those who have helped me along the way. There are countless persons to whom I am grateful: all the people who have been involved in getting me to where I am today: my day-to-day caretakers, my notetakers, my roommates, those who have given me a ride to class or helped me get my school materials out of my book bag. However, on multiple occasions, things just seem to go awry, and the ability to keep your cool and persevere is key if you are to survive something as stressful as graduate school. In my experience and as suggested from professionals in the field (e.g., see Olkin & Williams-Nickelson, 2004), communication is vital to success in graduate training when students have disabilities of all sorts.

Not only is communication necessary, but graduate program flexibility in process and procedure is important for students with special needs. Reeser (1992) conducted personality interviews with 14 students with learning and/or physical disabilities who were either enrolled in or were graduates of BSW/MSW programs and 12 program directors in Michigan to better understand the students' experiences with field placement practica. Reeser found that program directors agreed that students with disabilities are expected to meet the same educational outcomes and standards required by the program, but that finding placements for the students was more difficult and time consuming. Although directors indicated that most field agencies were willing to accept students with disabilities, sadly, they also reported there was a "hierarchy of acceptable disabilities" with "students with learning disabilities and other invisible handicaps [being regarded] as most desirable" (p. 103). What Reeser (1992) recommended from her findings was that there needs to be greater dialogue between instructors and students regarding students' abilities and disabilities to create the best outcome for all involved.

Similarly, Bethke (2004) surveyed 30 graduate students with learning disabilities from APA-accredited doctoral programs and found students' perseverance within a graduate program was directly linked with overall rating of satisfaction with the faculty and program. Participants also reported that self-disclosure with peers also was connected to satisfaction with peer relationships. Galdi (2008) interviewed graduate students with visual disabilities and found that although students reported experiencing many barriers (e.g., negative attitudes of professors, inaccessible course materials, and difficulties with transportation), those who were successful had psychological factors that enabled their success (e.g., altruism, perseverance, resourcefulness, resilience, and goal orientation) and supportive relationships with role models and mentors. I (AW) experienced many of these factors within my graduate program. I feel that my success and determination within this program come not only from my character but also from the relationships with the individuals around me. My ability to stay goal oriented and persevere through the difficult times can be directly attributed to my positive experiences with faculty and overall satisfaction with my program. Importantly, I made sure, when searching for graduate programs, that my views were consistent with those around me such as the professors and administrators; I felt that it was imperative to my experience that those around me be willing to assist me when needed and share a vision of my goals.

Throughout my time at graduate school, there have been instances, thankfully few, where I have faced challenges (e.g., being late to class due to a caretaker or ride not coming through, major difficulties in securing transportation to and from my internship). However, I have been taught a lesson that I think all people with disabilities or any kind of dependency must learn: Things will go wrong. I also feel, though, that with proper planning and the right connections, anyone can get through anything. After all, I may be disabled, but nothing is stopping me from reaching my goals.

Conclusion and Final Recommendations

Success in graduate school takes a multitude of qualities; we believe it takes even more to be successful as an individual with a disability. Furthermore, there are many ways in which a student with a disability can prepare him- or herself to ensure the greatest likelihood for success. Alex's experiences and research from Liebert and colleagues (1990) suggest that, in order for a student with disabilities to reach his/her full potential in graduate school, he/she must be able to vocalize his/her needs. Clarity in communication with professors, peers, and service providers helps to address and assist students with disabilities. One of the inherent attributes of disabilities is that they are all unique and individuals' needs vary tremendously. Therefore, it is vital that students be comfortable explaining their disability to many different levels of personnel within the school itself: administrators, advisers, professors, and, in some cases, their fellow students. Comfort with one's disability and the ability to vocalize needs will directly affect students' experiences within the programs and their chances of success.

Part of the communication process involves documentation. Students' provision of recent documentation that outlines accommodations appropriate for graduate education, especially in instances where a student's disability is "invisible" (e.g., various learning disabilities), will allow graduate programs to better facilitate assistance. As Olkin and Williams-Nickelson (2004) remind us, "Programs have the right to request documentation of any disability or the nature of functional limitations caused by the disability, but may choose to not exercise this right in some instances when a disability is readily visible" (p. 6). Khubchandani and Williams-Nickelson (2004) provide an outstanding resource guide for psychology graduate students with disabilities that addresses many of the specific strategies and suggestions for success. For example, the chapter written by Olkin and Williams-Nickelson (2004), labeled "strategies for program orientation and preparing for a successful experience," (beginning on p. 5), gives specific strategies for speaking with instructors (e.g., clearly explain the disability, make specific suggestions for facilitating success, talk about previous successful accommodations, discuss details about examinations, and help the instructor problem-solve issues). This resource guide has a wealth of information useful to any student with special needs preparing for graduate study.

In sum, we would urge those with disabilities who are interested in graduate school to "go for it." If my experience and supporting research have taught me anything, it is that nothing is impossible and one should always chase one's dreams. Often, living with a disability can bring many hardships and doubts; however, assistance programs are available to be utilized. With assistance and perseverance, students with disabilities, like any students, should strive to reach their fullest potential.

❖ References

Bethke, A. F. (2004). The relationship between psychology graduate schools and the experiences of graduate students with learning disabilities. *Dissertation Abstracts International, 65.*

Galdi, L. (2008). Factors that enable graduate students with visual disabilities to succeed in their educational pursuits. *Dissertation Abstracts International, 68.*

Ganschow, L., Coyne, J., Parks, A. W., & Antonoff, S. J. (1999). A 10-year follow-up survey of programs and services for students with learning disabilities in graduate and professional schools. *Journal of Learning Disabilities, 32,* 72–84.

Khubchandani, A. (n.d.). Moving beyond the ADA. Retrieved July 7, 2011, from http://www .apa.org/pi/disability/resources/beyond-ada.aspx.

Khubchandani, A., & Williams-Nickelson, C. (Eds.). (2004). *Resource guide for psychology graduate students with disabilities.* Retrieved July 7, 2011, from http://www.apa.org/pi/ disability/resources/publications/guide.pdf.

Liebert, D., Lutsky, L., & Gottlieb, A. (1990). Postsecondary experiences of young adults with severe physical disabilities. *Exceptional Children, 57,* 56–63.

Olkin R., & Williams-Nickelson, C. (2004). Strategies for program orientation and preparing for a successful experience. In A. Khubchandani & C. Williams-Nickelson (Eds.), *Resource Guide for Psychology Graduate Students with Disabilities*. Retrieved **July 7, 2011,** from http://www.apa.org/pi/disability/resources/publications/guide.pdf.

Paquette, T. (1997, November). Applying to clinical and counseling psychology programs: A guide for people with learning disabilities. *Dissertation Abstracts International Section A, 58.*

Reeser, L. (1992). Students with disabilities in practicum: What is reasonable accommodation? *Journal of Social Work Education, 28,* 98–109.

❖ Suggestions for Further Exploration

American Psychological Association. (n.d.). *Disability mentoring program.* Retrieved from http://www.apa.org/pi/disability/resources/mentoring/index.aspx. The American Psychological Association (APA) provides a mentoring service for students with disabilities whereby they are connected with an APA member psychologist who also has a disability. This mentoring program allows graduate students to have a resource who has directly experienced graduate training. This website also includes helpful information regarding tips for mentors, mentees, and additional resources regarding policy and law.

Khubchandani, A., &Williams-Nickelson, C. (Eds.). (2004). *Resource guide for psychology graduate students with disabilities.* Retrieved from http://www.apa.org/pi/disability/resources/publications/guide.pdf. Written by experts from the American Psychological Association's Committee on Disability Issues in Psychology (CDIP) and the American Psychological Association of Graduate Students (APAGS), this resource guide addresses issues from law to practical how-to pieces of advice for success in graduate programs in psychology. This highly recommended guide speaks to specific program requirements (e.g., preliminary examinations to internships) and makes recommendations for how students with disabilities can use available resources for success.

Zinkiewicz, L. (2004). *Postgraduate supervision and support in psychology.* Retrieved from http://www.psychology.heacademy.ac.uk/docs/pdf/p20040422_postgrad_sup_pro.pdf. An excellent resource that describes the varieties of support that will be beneficial in graduate school. You will find this short, readable article most helpful.

9

Important Considerations
for Online Graduate Training

*Victor A. Benassi**
University of New Hampshire

Michael J. Lee
University of New Hampshire

Are you considering applying for admission to an online graduate program in psychology? If you are, there are many factors for you to consider before you make decisions on how to proceed. What type of psychology do you want to pursue? What type of degree will you need? What type of career do you want—applied, teaching, research? Numerous resources will be helpful to you in deciding whether pursuing a graduate degree in psychology is right for you and, if so, what you need to know to make that goal a reality. For example, the American Psychological Association (APA) maintains an up-to-date webpage on "Applying to Graduate School" that includes a lot of useful information (http://apa.org/education/grad/applying.aspx).

In the United States alone, hundreds of postsecondary institutions offer some form of graduate training in psychology. Of the programs to be found in these institutions, the vast majority are presented in "traditional" on-campus formats. There is, however, a growing number of programs in professional, clinical, counseling, and other areas of psychology that are offered either exclusively or predominately online. Large numbers of students are pursuing graduate degrees from

*We thank Rachel A. Rogers and Margaret L. Murray for reading and commenting on several drafts of this chapter. Correspondence concerning this chapter should be sent to Victor A. Benassi, Department of Psychology, University of New Hampshire, Durham, NH 03824. E-mail: vab@unh.edu.

institutions that have no traditional campus setting or full-time permanent faculty, and many of these are for-profit institutions. In considering earning a graduate degree at such an institution, various factors should be weighed, some of which are the same factors that guide choices about traditional programs and others particular to online programs.

This chapter is intended for those who are considering earning an online graduate degree in a field of psychology. We use the term *online* to refer to programs that are offered entirely (or nearly entirely) online and at a distance. There is no physical campus at which students take courses, meet with faculty and other students, conduct research, and so on. The campus is *virtual*. Students interact with faculty, staff, and other students via the Internet, using electronic mail, chat rooms, and other virtual communication services. Programs typically use a courseware system for students to access course and program material, to interact with faculty and other students, to submit course assignments, to take exams, and so forth. The courseware may have been developed by the institution offering the program or be one of the commercially available ones (e.g., Blackboard©). Many programs or courses are hybrid in nature. We use the term *hybrid* to refer to programs that include the features listed above but that also include interaction with faculty, and usually other students, at a physical location (which could be a campus, space rented by the program, etc.).

In addition to the distinction between online and campus-based programs, there is sometimes a distinction to be made between for-profit (also called proprietary) and not-for-profit institutions, both of which offer online degree programs. In addition to such relatively new proprietary programs in higher education, many established universities, which operate on a not-for-profit basis, have developed online degree programs. We will consider the distinction below when we address considerations having to do with faculty.

Is an Online Graduate Program a Good Choice for You?

In progressing from an undergraduate curriculum to a graduate program, most people experience an increase in the amount of academic work they are expected to perform and also in the degree of independence and autonomy they have as they approach that academic work. For many students, the resulting freedom is clearly a positive feature of graduate education; for some, it is the cause of problems that undermine their ability to complete their program. In online programs, where "real-time" events are the exception, there will likely be an even greater degree of autonomy—especially in regard to how one schedules work on a day-to-day basis. However, it would be a mistake to assume that greater autonomy and independence for the learner mean less structure for the program or diminished work expectations. The structure of an online program might be less overt while being no less real than that of a campus-based program. Moreover, the workload might be as great, albeit distributed in a manner that is more flexible and more suited to the personal schedule and lifestyle of an individual learner. The key is finding a balance between the need for external structure and the need for the freedom to create such structure for oneself.

One last point on this topic: Once you matriculate in a graduate program in psychology, whether it be an online, hybrid, or campus-based program, your success will be based, in large part, on how well you deal with many of the issues discussed elsewhere in this book—for example, developing and maintaining positive professional relationships (Chapter 4), developing your writing (Chapter 11) and research (Chapter 14) skills.

Type of Degree and Area of Specialization

As you will learn, if you already do not know, online graduate programs in psychology are offered at the master's and doctoral levels in many areas of study. Many, perhaps most, graduate programs are offered in areas related to professional practice (most often clinical, counseling, and school psychology), but online master's and doctoral programs are available in many other areas of specialization as well (e.g., industrial/organizational psychology, media psychology, sports psychology, neuropsychology). As with any graduate program, you will need to have a clear sense of why you want to earn a graduate degree in psychology and what you want to do after you earn the degree. For example, if you think you want to become a faculty member at a traditional campus-based 4-year college or university, you will almost assuredly need to have a doctoral degree. Also, it is important to know that a hiring committee for such a position would be unlikely to look favorably upon applicants who earned their degrees online.

Educational Philosophy

Educational institutions of all kinds have statements of their philosophy on education, their purpose, their mission, and their goals for students and the institution as a whole. You will want to answer the following questions regarding any programs you are considering. Does the program have a clearly defined philosophy of education and is that philosophy appropriate for the field in which you want to study? Does the program curriculum make sense to you in terms of the stated program philosophy? As you investigate online programs, the institution's mission statement and educational philosophy might be a good place to start. Does the program's literature—online or on paper—communicate such a philosophy? How can you determine the extent to which its education and training models are aligned with this philosophy? The question of the appropriateness of the philosophy to "the science and practice of psychology" is dependent upon your view of the discipline of psychology, which makes the question an ideal lens through which you can begin to evaluate your own comfort level with the program.

If you are interested in earning a doctoral degree in psychology in an area related to professional practice, you should learn all you can about accreditation of doctoral programs in the areas related to professional practice. The APA considers, for possible accreditation, programs in clinical psychology, counseling psychology, school psychology, and other developed practice areas (American Psychological Association [APA], 2007). Accreditation is discussed in detail below.

Admission

One feature of online graduate programs in psychology that distinguishes them from most campus-based programs is their very high acceptance rate for applicants. Without citing acceptance rates of specific programs, we note that rates for most online programs are indicative of an essentially "open admissions" situation, whereas more traditional, campus-based programs range from somewhat selective to highly selective. If "selectivity" is seen as a proxy for quality (of students and programs)—and this is not necessarily the case—then most online, proprietary programs would be ranked lower than the on-campus programs. Whether the same distinction exists between on-campus and online programs at traditional higher education institutions varies from institution to institution.

The Question of Accreditation

Accreditation is a complex and critically important topic in higher education in the United States and in many other countries. Before you apply to any online or hybrid graduate program in psychology, spend time learning about the accreditation status of the institution offering the degree and, if appropriate, the accreditation status of the graduate program itself. In the United States, the gold standard for accreditation of colleges and universities is accreditation by one of six regional accrediting bodies recognized by both the Council for Higher Education Accreditation (http://www .chea.org/Directories/regional.asp) and by the U.S. Department of Education (http:// www2.ed.gov/admins/finaid/accred/accreditation_pg6.html).

It is important to understand the distinction between accreditation of a postsecondary institution and accreditation of a specific program within that institution. In psychology, for example, some graduate programs in psychology seek and receive accreditation status from the American Psychological Association (in practice areas noted above). However, many institutions that offer graduate programs in these areas are not accredited by APA (either because accreditation was not sought or it was not granted) and, in all other areas of psychology, the APA does not provide accreditation. However, there are many accreditation agencies in the United States (and elsewhere) that provide accreditation status to institutions or to specific degree programs. Be sure that you investigate carefully before you make a decision to apply to or attend an online graduate program (or any graduate program, for that matter). Talk with professors or academic administrators at your undergraduate institution for their advice on issues related to accreditation and on specific accrediting agencies.

For an example of the accreditation criteria used by APA to evaluate professional graduate programs, refer to "Guidelines and Principles for Accreditation of Programs in Professional Psychology" (APA, 2007). If you plan to matriculate in an online or hybrid program in a professional practice area, you should know that only two were accredited by APA as of 2007 (Murphy, Levant, Hall, & Glueckauf, 2007). You should refer to the most recent edition of *Graduate Study in Psychology* (APA, 2011) to check on the status of any graduate program in which you have interest.

Selecting the Right Program

Curriculum

Once you have decided which type of graduate program you want to enter and the specific degree you want to earn, you might well have to choose from among dozens of institutions that offer an online version of that program and degree. Just as you would have to do in choosing among campus-based programs offered by well-known institutions, in making your choice of an online program, you will have to distinguish between an institution's claims and the actual academic experience being offered. Here the challenge lies in gathering and evaluating information in terms of its academic accuracy rather than its marketing messages.

Most institutions make available online some information regarding the curriculum associated with a specific program. Accompanying an up-to-date list of required and elective courses, one might expect to find an overview of the program, a statement regarding the program's emphasis (e.g., research or practice), intended outcomes, information on program faculty, and a typical course of study. The typical time to degree completion for full-time and part-time students should be spelled out and course descriptions should be readily available. The kind of information you will want to gather is the type that is included in the graduate program descriptions that appear in *Graduate Study in Psychology* (APA, 2011), an annual publication of the American Psychological Association.

In our experience, it is not always easy to secure this type of information about online psychology graduate programs. When seeking information from certain institutions, you will likely have to speak with an "advisor" before being sent the information you are seeking. This person may have no direct involvement with the program you are considering and may actually be a marketing agent. Unless you want to be engaged in a general conversation about the school's offerings, it is important that you make it clear that you are requesting an electronic copy of the curriculum of the particular program in which you are interested. In order to keep the conversations with such "advisors" focused on the questions you want answered, it is a good idea to have published program information in front of you when you have a follow-up conversation about the curriculum. Be sure to write down your questions ahead of time.

To make an informed choice about an online graduate program, it would be useful to frame a set of questions that you would like addressed by someone who is directly associated with a specific academic program rather than a person who works for the larger institution. A good place to start framing your questions is with the APA Report "Principles of Good Practice in Distance Education and Their Application to Professional Education and Training in Psychology" (2002). Several of the "good practices" outlined in this report could become the basis for your evaluative questions. Before students are admitted to a program, does the institution inform them about what technologies they will need to access and what technical proficiency will be required of them? Are program related features clearly and definitively described—for example, costs and payment policies, curriculum design, timeframe of course offerings, library and other learning services, arrangements for interaction with the faculty and other students, independent learning expectations, estimated time for program completion? In addition, does the institution provide information on registration, financial aid, academic advising, academic grievance procedures, and access to library resources (including electronic databases)? Are there opportunities to interact with fellow students, both informally and in the context of collaborative learning experiences?

Even if the curriculum is clearly spelled out and well aligned with the program's objectives, pursuing a degree online can be an isolating experience if a program is not structured in a manner to provide opportunities for learning in a community. Does a program provide for frequent and substantive interaction with instructors and fellow students through e-mail, live chats, discussion forums, and so forth? Before making a multiyear commitment to an online program, you will want to investigate this feature. Ask the program representative with whom you are in communication for names of faculty and students and for their contact information. Contact these people and ask them how much informal and formal contact exists between participants and in what specific ways the program promotes contact opportunities. Just as the selection of the right on-campus program might involve a campus visit with the chance to speak with faculty and students, so too your selection of an online program should involve a visit to a *virtual* campus.

Faculty

Even before you apply to and definitely before you decide to enroll in an online graduate program, you should gather as much information as you can about the faculty who would be your teachers, advisors, and mentors. What percentage of faculty in your area of study are full-time, ongoing members of the institution? How were they selected for their positions? Who reviewed their credentials—content area specialists, administrators, or faculty out of the specialization area? Was there a formal search? During our informal examination of online psychology graduate programs, we found great variability in the ease or even possibility of learning about the faculty. You should carefully consider the qualifications of faculty and the nature and degree of their professional commitment to a graduate program, and you can do this only if you have information about them. If an institution you are considering has a strong faculty and makes a commitment to building and maintaining that faculty, there will be evidence of this fact on a program website.

Residency (On-site Components)

As noted previously, some graduate programs are offered completely online, but there are hybrid programs—especially doctoral programs—that have face-to-face residency requirements. In one such program, a third-year residency requirement involves two 2-week seminars and nine weekend seminars at campus centers in different parts of the country. Such experiences can provide valuable opportunities to work in collaborative learning communities and to be part of a professional network, but they can also be very costly and difficult to fit into one's normal schedule without significant advance planning. As with the search for information about curriculum and other academic requirements, it is important to ask clear questions and look for specific answers when it comes to such residency requirements. How much flexibility will there be over the course of one's degree program? Upon entering a program, does one commit to a series of residencies—annual or otherwise—at fixed times? Be sure to determine whether your time and residency commitments are mapped out before you start the program.

Transferring Credit

This chapter has been written with the student in mind who is considering enrolling in an online graduate degree program. However, other students may only be interested in registering for a specific course. They might, for example, be enrolled in a campus-based program and want to complete a course in an area of interest or one that might meet a requirement in their current program. In such cases, several considerations should be taken into account. If you would like the credit associated with the course to be considered for transfer to your home institution, check with your program coordinator or department chair before enrolling in the course to determine whether it can be used to meet a program requirement. Do not assume that approval will be granted. Many faculty members are reluctant to give credit for courses taken elsewhere, and we suspect this reluctance might be heightened in the case of online courses. Beyond the program level, college and university registrars pay close attention to the accreditation status of the institution from which transfer credit is being sought by students. For example, if the institution is in the United States and is not accredited by one of the six regional accrediting agencies referred to above, it is extremely unlikely that transfer credit will be accepted.

Closing Thoughts

This chapter has focused on assisting you in determining whether earning an online degree in psychology is a good choice for you. We have said very little about important considerations once you begin your academic program. That would take another chapter, and space does not permit that effort here. Take a look at the "Suggestions for Further Exploration" below for some good sources.

Making a decision to apply to and enroll in an online psychology graduate program should be made only after doing a lot of self-reflection and background investigation and after discussing the matter with one or more trusted current or former psychology professors. If they are unable to assist you, they should be able to recommend someone who could. Doing your "homework" will be well worth the effort and should put you in an excellent position to make choices that could have a profound effect on your professional future.

❖ References

American Psychological Association. (2002, June). *Principles of good practice in distance education and their application to professional education and training in psychology.* Report of the American Psychological Association Task Force on Distance Education and Training in Professional Psychology. Retrieved July 7, 2011, from http://www.apa .org/ed/resources/finalreport.doc.

American Psychological Association. (2011). *Graduate study in psychology.* Washington, DC: Author.

American Psychological Association, Commission on Accreditation. (2007). *Guidelines and principles for accreditation of programs in professional psychology.* Retrieved from http://www.apa.org/ed/accreditation/about/policies/guiding-principles.pdf.

Murphy, M. J., Levant, R. F., Hall, J. E., & Glueckauf, R. L. (2007). Distance education in professional training in psychology. *Professional Psychology: Research & Practice, 38,* 97–103. doi: 10.1037/0735–7028.38.1.97.

❖ Suggestions for Further Exploration

Chamberlin, J. (2009, November). Are online classes for you? *GradPsych, 7*(4). Retrieved from http://www.apa.org/gradpsych/2009/11/e-learn.aspx.

Shajnfeld, A. (2010). *Choosing an online psychology program.* Retrieved from http://www.onlinepsychologydegrees.com/articles/choosing-an-online-psychology-program.

10

Self-Care in Graduate School

❖

Finding Your Optimal Balance

Carolyn A. Licht
Office of Counseling and Psychological
Services, Fordham University

> *"Being a graduate student is like becoming all of the Seven Dwarves. In the beginning you're Dopey and Bashful. In the middle, you are usually sick (Sneezy), tired (Sleepy), and irritable (Grumpy). But at the end, they call you Doc, and then you're Happy."*
>
> —Ronald T. Azuma (2003), from his online guide
> (http://www.cs.unc.edu/~azuma/hitch4.html),
> *"So long and thanks for the Ph.D."*

Making the decision to attend graduate school in psychology, or any field, for that matter, is not only a daunting perspective but can also be a life-changing moment for many. Whether your journey to this goal has been a direct one from high school or you have taken a more roundabout trek out in the wilds as a member of the workforce, very little in life can adequately prepare you for the often grueling but extremely meaningful graduate experience. As arduous and scary as it was preparing for the GREs and completing graduate school applications, nothing really compares to the elation combined with the abject terror that a letter of acceptance may bring. The questions immediately start to bombard your mind: Am I smart enough, young enough, driven enough to survive? Can I financially afford graduate school? How will I juggle my significant relationships and attend school at the same time? What about my plans to start a family? Will I even be able to get a job in this economy if I put in all this time and effort? The list of questions will go on and on, and at times you will likely start to question your sanity for making the decision to pursue your Ph.D.; I mean really, couldn't you earn just as much with a lesser degree or by pursuing a completely different career choice?

But seriously, we each have our own reasons for taking this journey, and regardless of how hard it may ultimately prove to be, it is truly a worthwhile endeavor. I, myself, was among the growing number of individuals who chose to enter the field of psychology later in life, as a second career, and had to face the unique challenges of being significantly older than my cohort. This is actually not such an uncommon phenomenon anymore. According to the American Psychological Association's Center for Psychology Workforce Analysis and Research (Wicherski, Michalski, & Kohout, 2009), about 18% of psychology doctorate recipients in 2007 were between ages 35 and 44, and 10% were over age 45; however, those under age 35 still make up the largest percentage of doctoral recipients at 68%. Regardless of your age or prior life experiences, all graduate students struggle at some point to balance their academic pursuits with their personal lives and responsibilities. Sacrifice is not an unfamiliar construct for most graduate students and, in fact, most accept or even embrace it as a way of life. In your quest for academic and professional success, you may find it necessary to forfeit time, money, and even personal relationships in the name of scholastic progress. Graduate students in general are motivated to make these sacrifices based on their own desire to attain perceived success (internal factors) and by the expectations set by others (external factors)—loved ones, professors, society at large, and so forth. Hopefully, your sacrifices are also driven by your passionate commitment (Dlugos & Friedlander, 2001) to the work that you will do as a psychologist in whatever career setting you choose.

Whether your motivation is more internally or externally driven, I know from personal experience how difficult and sometimes even impossible it can be to make yourself a priority, especially in the competitive waters of academia, as well as in the early stages of establishing yourself as a professional. In hindsight, I realize now how beneficial it would have been for my current professional endeavors if I had learned how to be more flexible and balanced in my professional and personal life roles during my graduate years rather than waiting until I was out in the "real world." For the average graduate student, meeting deadlines and chipping away at degree requirements often involve working long hours at the expense of sleep, exercise, good eating habits, and leisure activities. By the time you emerge from your graduate program, you may already feel burnt out. Initiating the activities that will allow you to discover a healthy balance between your professional endeavors and personal desires should not be delayed until you are in the midst of your career and feeling even more overburdened but, rather, should ideally begin much earlier in your career development process so that you never reach that point at all. Therefore, an excellent time to cultivate and practice all the self-care skills that you will be introduced to in this chapter is during your graduate years when you are setting the foundation for your future career path and the multiple roles you ultimately will play. These are not easy lessons to learn and you are certainly not going to be offered a graduate course in this skill set. However, the sooner you can start developing and practicing self-care behaviors, the healthier and happier you will likely be in the long run. Your definition of "balance," your means of achieving it, and your ability to juggle competing responsibilities and interests will set the pace for your postgraduate years and determine the quality of your day-to-day life. Discovering your own unique balance will ensure that you not only survive graduate school, which is something akin to simply existing despite difficulty, but rather that you will have the opportunity to thrive and flourish by performing at an optimal level emotionally, behaviorally, cognitively, and physically. Therefore, my primary goal for this chapter is to drive home the point of how important *you* are in this journey. If you ignore your own needs as you focus on everyone and everything else in your life, you will soon discover that there is not enough of *you* left as a resource (Licht & Nash, 2009).

Defining Balance

> "To *acquire balance means to achieve that happy medium between the minimum and the maximum that represents your optimum. The minimum is the least you can get by with. The maximum is the most you're capable of. The optimum is the amount or degree of anything that is most favorable toward the ends you desire."*

> —Nido Qubein, motivational speaker
> and president of High Point University

We have all heard the benefits of taking a balanced approach to life, but I have grown to realize over the years that we need to first define what "balance" actually means in the context of our individual lives before we can put this notion into practice. The word *balance* evokes in many the image of equally weighted scales, like those representing the Libra zodiac sign, and that symbolize such constructs as harmony, equilibrium, equality, and justice. *The American Heritage Dictionary of the English Language* (2000) provides two definitions of balance: "a state of equilibrium or parity characterized by cancellation of all forces by equally opposing forces" and "the power and means to decide." For me, coming from a prior career as a ballet dancer, the notion of balance reminds me more of the dancer *en pointe* who maintains an utter stillness as she balances on one leg while her other leg extends from one pose to the next, creating an unequal distribution of weight around her center. This image speaks more to the relevance of the second dictionary definition that suggests that balance is not necessarily static, constant, or equally distributed but, rather, is more about discovering what works optimally for you. As a graduate student, you will not always have the power to choose how you divvy up your time and activities, but you will still be responsible for dealing with the consequences of your actions. The constant need to make decisions and to set priorities knowing that there will always be something that is not chosen or that may have both positive and negative outcomes can be extremely stressful and, at times, seem overwhelming. An important step that will allow you to better prepare for graduate school and beyond is understanding the additional challenges that you may face emotionally, financially, energetically, and so forth depending on where you decide to pursue your graduate degree and what area of psychology you choose to seek. The other chapters in this book can help guide your decision-making process (i.e., you may choose to seek a career in an academic versus a clinical setting) and provide invaluable information and advice for overcoming the obstacles that may thwart your efforts to maximize your professional and personal functioning.

The types of stressors you face as an undergraduate and graduate student, as well as how you create your balance and cope, may differ depending on where you are in your stage of life and the multiple identities, both career- and non–career-related, that you endorse (Licht & Nash, 2009). Are you a traditional student who entered college right after high school and has parental financial support for graduate school? Are you an older adult pursuing a second career in psychology who must juggle family responsibilities along with a new career? No matter what your answer, you will still need to make yourself a priority from the start if you want to maximize your ability to be passionately committed to whatever you choose to do. Even if you think you have anticipated all of the potential challenges of graduate school, you must learn to be flexible and adapt, because life tends to throw surprises at you when they are least expected or desired.

Stress and Its Consequences

Life during graduate school can be a mixture of joy, anticipation, anxiety, and frustration. All your hard work facing the myriad challenges of your graduate curricula, comprehensive exams, thesis/dissertation, and internship will eventually be rewarded with the conferring of your degree if you can survive up to that point. Of course, then you must face the daunting task of finding a job and/or having to pay back student loans. A major occupational hazard for all of us both during and after graduate school is burnout. As a graduate student, you may face a number of challenges and stressors that place you at risk for experiencing burnout and eventually, if not addressed, impaired professional competence (Barnett, Baker, Elman, & Schoener, 2007). Excessive workload with a high demand for productivity and recurring pressured deadlines, inadequate free time, financial pressures, and so forth, all over an extended period of time with few rewards and little recognition, combined with being in a position with minimal power and control, create stress; in other words, being a graduate student, or for that matter an early-career psychologist, is stressful. If ignored, this burnout at its worst can be devastating, resulting in the failure to complete your degree or having to give up on your career goals. The risk for burnout does not end with the conferring of your Ph.D., as clearly illustrated by the staggering results reported by the Occupational Safety and Health Administration (OSHA) that male psychologists have the highest suicide rate of any profession (O'Connor, 2001). Of course, I am not implying that you will end up as some extreme statistic if you enter this field; rather, the goal of this chapter is to prevent this type of negative outcome from ever happening by increasing your awareness of the potential risks and offering to help you avoid the pitfalls, many of which I made in the course of my journey, so that you can do a better job of keeping your life in balance.

How to Self-Evaluate

As you are well aware, stress is an everyday fact of life that results from your inter-actions with both external (i.e., the environment, social relationships) and internal (i.e., physiological and cognitive) factors (Davis, Eshelman, & McKay, 2000; Licht & Nash, 2009). Stress leads to psychological and physiological responses that alter or upset your personal balance in some way. When the stressors in your life, posi-tive or negative, are unrelenting, as they often are in graduate school, or when little stressors accumulate and you are unable to recuperate from any one of them, burnout can result (Barnett et al., 2007). Most graduate students possess certain personality traits that help them to persevere in their academic pursuits but can also contribute to their risk of burnout. Many graduate students, including myself then and now, exhibit perfectionistic tendencies. We are the classic overachievers who place high expectations (often unrealistic) on ourselves to excel with a very steep learning curve and no room for failure. You know the type—the ones who feel guilty when relaxing or worry about what task comes next even before finish-ing the current one. Consequently, we are also the ones who will ignore the internal alarms that signal a need for help or be reluctant to ask for help for fear we will be perceived as inadequate or unreliable. Because burnout does not happen overnight and can be difficult to fight once you are in the middle of it, the earlier you recog-nize and address the signs of impairment, the better chance you have of avoiding burnout. Recognizing your own risk for impairment and making a commitment to ongoing self-care efforts is an ethical imperative (Barnett et al., 2007) and is clearly articulated in Principle A, Beneficence and Nonmaleficence, of the American Psychological Association Ethics Code (APA, 2002): "Psychologists strive to be aware of the possible effects of their own physical and mental health on their abil-ity to help those with whom they work" (p. 1062).

The first step in identifying the signs of impairment is becoming increasingly self-aware of your physical and emotional states when you are feeling healthy. This healthy self-awareness provides a baseline level of functioning in which to compare any subtle or significant changes in your personal and professional behaviors. Some changes to be particularly conscious of that might be first signs of impairment or burnout (Barnett et al., 2007; Davis et al., 2000) include changes in your behaviors and emotional states such as becoming forgetful, feel-ing anxious, or having trouble concentrating. Feelings of frustration, hopeless-ness, irritability, lack of emotional energy, and reduced productivity are also characteristic of distress. You should ask yourself if and why you are feeling less motivation, fulfillment, or pleasure from your daily activities. Are you coming up with excuses to miss classes, requesting extensions on due dates for assign-ments, or finding yourself increasingly bored or irritated with your research endeavors?

As the state of burnout progresses, physical symptoms can develop and might include experiencing frequent colds, headaches, vague aches and pains, teeth grinding, crying jags, fatigue, insomnia, nightmares, or changes in appetite and weight. The combination of symptoms can put you at higher risk of developing depression, anxi-ety, or other psychiatric conditions (Barnett et al., 2007). Increased use of alcohol and prescription or illegal substances as a means of coping can further result in a decreased ability to effectively implement and utilize your academic and clinical skills or interact appropriately in your personal life (Barnett et al., 2007; O'Connor, 2001). If you are unable to identify these signs of stress, then you may need to rely on feedback from your graduate peers, teachers/mentors, friends, or family members. Listen to your inner voice and the voices of trusted others.

Discovering Balance Through Self-Care Activities

Self-care is a universally affirmed concept but a poorly implemented activity and a deceptively simplistic notion, particularly as it relates to the lives of graduate students, especially those entering the caregiving field of psychology (Barnett et al., 2007). It is ironic that although many of us are guided by a strong desire to work with or help others, we do so at the expense of our own personal self-care. Self-care activities must be individually defined and discovered. It is also extremely important to minimize your use of negative coping strategies (i.e., self-medication, seeking emotional gratification from high-risk activities, etc.) and engage instead in what Kramen-Kahn and Hansen (1998) termed "positive career sustaining behaviors" (p. 130). These include activities as basic as seeking diversity in your professional endeavors (i.e., those outside of your graduate curricula), taking regular breaks from school-related tasks, getting adequate rest and exercise, and having a balanced and healthy diet (Barnett et al., 2007). In the remainder of this chapter, I will highlight different activities or strategies that I routinely utilize now and I strongly believe would have been beneficial during graduate school to rejuvenate my mind, body, and spirit (see also Licht & Nash, 2009).

Time Management

Most people approach the subject of time management with one major question: "How can I get more done in less time?" Effective time-management strategies can help minimize deadline anxiety, procrastination, and work fatigue and give you more energy for renewal and more time to enjoy your daily activities. For effective time management, you will need to learn to conserve, control, and create time by being wise with how you expend energy during the hours of the day, by recognizing and setting realistic priorities, and by learning to say "no" when necessary. Davis and colleagues (2000) proposed a six-step program designed to improve your time-management skills. First, you must decide what is most worthwhile or valuable to you. The next step of effective time management involves designing and setting goals that you want to achieve given the constraints of your time and other resources. Your goals, whether they are academic, personal, or family oriented, should be consistent with your values, specific enough to be achievable, positive, and balanced across the different facets of your life. You should also remain flexible and open to adapting your goals to ongoing changes in your life. The third step in effective time management is to identify the specific steps you need to take in order to achieve each of your goals. Your action plan should include information on what resources (i.e., financial, support, etc.) you will need to achieve your goals, ways in which you will monitor your progress, the most likely reasons you might procrastinate and how to combat this tendency, and, finally, what rewards you will use to motivate yourself. This action plan leads directly into the fourth step of effective time management, which is evaluating how you spend your time; this can be done by keeping a log or diary of your daily activities for at least three typical days. This log is designed to help you break down and examine as carefully as possible the ways in which you designate your time so that later, if necessary, you can decide if you want to redistribute the amount of time you spend in each of your activities and how consistent they are with your values and goals. The fifth step is to combat your tendency to procrastinate and to determine what activities you tend to avoid and why. If you are avoiding an activity that is fundamental to achieving any of your goals, then it is essential that you change your circumstances or approach in order to increase your chances of successfully performing the relevant task. The sixth time management step is to get better organized, although this step should probably be initiated early in your decision-making process. Purchase an organizer, such as a spiral binder or hand-held computerized system, that includes a daily, weekly, and monthly calendar component, and then plug in all of your major activities and responsibilities, along with the time required for each of them. You should also schedule "nonnegotiable appointment time" for leisure and for other personal commitments; this may improve your likelihood of not forfeiting these essential activities. Finally, one of the most important time-management skills you can adopt is simply to keep everything in perspective by maintaining your sense of humor and flexibility when things do not work out as planned.

Sources of Renewal

The Mind–Body–Spirit Connection

All aspects of the self—the mind, the body, and the spirit—are interconnected. It is the balance between them that can create newfound energy and inner peace. The key to achieving this balance is to be flexible, diverse, moderate, and in harmony with your own rhythms and needs. In other words, you must become fully aware, in a nonjudgmental way, of your own thoughts, body sensations, and feelings as you experience them.

Self-Care of the Mind

Given the complementarity between your personal and professional development, for optimal functioning and continued growth, you must nurture yourself on an emotional, an intellectual, and an interpersonal level; in other words, you must honor and respect the needs of your mind. You cannot ignore your mind when it is tired or impaired by too much stress. Developing increased self-awareness and the capacity to engage in self-monitoring allows you to realistically assess your strengths and vulnerabilities and to recognize when you can intervene on your own behalf versus when you should seek support from others. Seeking support does not have to occur only in times of extreme trouble. To the contrary, developing support-seeking behaviors should be a natural part of your graduate learning experience and is an essential component of your professional development and personal growth. By seeking peer support and consultation, mentoring relationships, social networks, professional associations, individual and group supervision (for those in applied/clinical programs), and personal psychotherapy, you are not only promoting your own self-care efforts, but you are also serving as a role model and reducing the stigma experienced by others who need to seek help (Barnett et al., 2007).

Cultivate relationships. Conferring with peers, a mentor, faculty, or a supervisor, either within your academic program or at outside practicum (externship or internship) sites, can be invaluable in helping you process your graduate experiences and resolving issues of concern (Barnett et al., 2007). It can also be worthwhile to look beyond your immediate cohort or graduate class to develop these supportive relationships. I found it almost life-saving to develop peer and mentoring relationships with the graduate class ahead of my own when I found it difficult to connect with my own, much younger cohort. My relationships with this more senior cohort benefited me not only on an emotional level but also on a professional level through their sharing of knowledge and experiences. Their guidance and advice helped me to stay more focused and efficient in my academic pursuits and, with the additional support of my dissertation mentor and other faculty advisors, allowed me to complete my program in an accelerated manner so that I was conferred my degree side by side these same supportive peers. Joining peer study groups can reduce your sense of isolation and give you the opportunity to benefit from the perspectives and strategies of others. A competent and caring supervisor, mentor, or advisor can also give you feedback on your progress, offer advice on how to better structure your schedule, or help you establish realistic goals and expectations for your dissertation research and other academic goals. It takes time to develop trust with supervisory relationships, and even then it may never be easy for you to risk exposing your vulnerabilities. However, with time, you can establish a professional norm of appropriate personal self-disclosure. Another important component of creating a balance between your personal and professional roles that can be nurtured during your graduate years is the development of a support system: a network of individuals who may serve as future mentors, colleagues, supervisors, references, and friends. You may want to join professional societies such as the American Psychological Association. These types of activities can help confirm your passion for the field and may become sources for letters of recommendation or future job opportunities. They are also opportunities to develop lifelong relationships that can foster your professional and personal development.

Personal therapy. As previously highlighted, many graduate students have personality traits or vulnerabilities that place them at increased risk of distress and impairment (Barnett et al., 2007). If stress becomes overwhelming and coping strategies seem inadequate, you may want to consider seeking professional help to prevent symptoms from developing into serious diagnostic disorders. It is not uncommon for students to develop symptoms of their own, especially when they are studying all the different diagnostic criteria of various mental disorders; however, just because pseudo-symptoms may at times be triggered by reading about them does not necessarily mean that they cannot develop for real in response to stress from the day-to-day pressure of graduate school. Having the opportunity to talk to a professional who really does "get it," who understands the challenges of the graduate experience, as well as the profession of psychology in general, because of their own life experiences can be both comforting and invigorating. You will deal with your own issues and gain insight as you grow and develop into a more complete and mindful person.

Self-Care for the Body

Listening to your body helps you know what you need and teaches you that you have limitations. As important as it is to address the basic essentials of self-care, like routine dental and medical check-ups, it can be equally beneficial to regularly schedule activities that maintain or enhance your physical functioning; getting a massage, acupuncture, or a chiropractic adjustment once a month, for example, may decrease your risk of future injury simply by improving your body alignment and reducing your overall physical tension.

Sleep. You may view sleep as merely a "down time" when your brain shuts off and your body rests. In a rush to meet school, family, or other social responsibilities, you cut back on your sleep, thinking it will not be a problem, because all of these other activities seem much more important. A common myth is that people can learn to get by on little sleep (such as *less than 6 hours* a night) with no adverse consequences. Research suggests, however, that adults need at least 7 to 8 hours of sleep each night to be well rested (Owens, 2007). A number of vital tasks are carried out during sleep, helping you to maintain good health and to function at your best. While you sleep, your brain is hard at work forming the pathways necessary for learning and creating memories and new insights (Owens, 2007). Without enough sleep, you cannot focus and pay attention or respond quickly. A lack of sleep may even cause mood problems. In order to improve your sleep patterns, it is important to incorporate time to wind down from your daily activities or, at the very least, schedule some brief rest breaks throughout your day.

Exercise. Exercise is one of the simplest and most effective means of stress reduction. Indeed, if there is one form of self-care that graduate students should place at the top of their lists, it is exercise. Not only does regular exercise improve physical problems, such as high cholesterol, diabetes, high blood pressure, and the pain resulting from long hours sitting at a computer (i.e., carpal tunnel syndrome, low back pain, etc.), it also has distinct mood and cognitive advantages, including an ability to boost higher-level thinking and to combat depression and anxiety. If going to the gym sounds torturous or too expensive, there are many alternative ways to integrate exercise into your self-care routine. Walking upstairs instead of taking the elevator or riding a bike to school instead of using public transportation can not only improve your physical health but may also reduce the stress of the typical rush-hour commute.

Nutrition. Eating is one of the natural joys of life, but healthy eating is a learned skill and not something that just comes naturally. In the midst of juggling classes, research, and practicum experiences, finding time to eat at all, let alone monitoring your nutritional intake, can seem an impossible task. You might not even recall the last time you prepared a home-cooked meal and sat down at a table to eat. In fact, if your life resembles mine at times, cooking spontaneously is not an option because your main food source consists of a six-pack of Diet Coke and some hard-to-identify nonperishable items that would be ideal donations for food drives. Our fast-paced society, along with our myriad available fast-food options, further encourages us to eat on the run and denies us the time to relax when we eat. As difficult as it might be, you have the power to take charge of your eating habits, and taking charge will make a positive difference in your overall well-being. You fuel your body and mind with the proper nutrients by eating with balance and enjoying what you eat. Eating healthily does not have to take a lot of time. You can prepare a healthy meal just as quickly as an unhealthy one. It is just a matter of planning ahead, having the right foods on hand, and learning how to cook quick, healthy meals. Ask friends or classmates who eat healthfully how they manage to find time. If possible, get family members involved and ask them to help prepare meals or do other tasks. Find a cookbook or collect recipes that feature time-saving ideas. It can often be worthwhile to develop an "eating buddy" arrangement with a classmate or friend who shares a similar schedule, both as a reminder to eat and as a way to ensure a pleasurable break during the course of a stressful day.

Self-Care for the Spirit

The spiritual journey presumes a certain degree of ego strength and, hence, any movement toward genuine human development is growth in the spiritual life. It is important to acknowledge both the spiritual dimension of your career path and your own spiritual needs as a human being.

Leisure. Earning a Ph.D. can be like running a marathon: If you do not pace yourself, you either will not reach the finish line or will not be in any shape to do anything else once you do. You need to set aside "me time," even if it is only a few minutes each day, in which you focus solely on your own needs and desires. Use meditation and deep breathing exercises to relax, even if just for 5 minutes between classes or while studying as a way to refocus and refresh your energy and motivation. Leisure time allows you to enter a state of mind in which you can experience fewer demands, as well as less pressure and worry. The most important thing during such times is to enter into the moment fully, with all your being, which can turn the most ordinary experiences into something extraordinary and spiritual. In order for your leisure time to be a truly nourishing experience that promotes your physical health, it needs to be an end in itself, not a means to an end. When you relax and play, you become happier, more creative, healthier, and more resilient to life's setbacks.

Mindfulness and affirmations. Much of your stress may come from thinking about the past or worrying about the future rather than focusing on what is going on in the here and now. Mindfulness is an activity that can be done at any time; it does not require sitting or even focusing on the breath but, rather, is done by focusing your mind on what is happening in the present moment, while noticing your mind's tendency to chatter endlessly with commentary or judgment. By noticing that the mind is continually making commentary, you have the ability to carefully notice those thoughts and then decide if those thoughts have value. You are free to release a thought ("let it go") when you realize that the thought may not be concrete reality or absolute truth.

Affirmations are a way of turning negative self-talk, which leads to stress, into positive, life-affirming statements. They are always stated in the present tense—*I am, I have, I choose*—and they reflect what you wish to experience, not what you *should* or *could*. Think back to what you say when you might be getting sick or feeling tired: "I don't feel sick" or "I don't have time to be sick." What do both of these statements have in common? They are negative and focus on what you do not want to happen. More positive and effective statements are, "I feel energetic and healthy," or "I am relaxed and have plenty of time to do what needs to be done." At first it may feel silly to state over and over the exact opposite of what you are feeling. But with regular practice, you will notice a change. The inner world of your thoughts and feelings will be in line with the outer world of your experience. Your mind and body will work together to produce a positive result.

Career and Life Planning

Developing your philosophy of life, based on your guiding values and beliefs, is vital to achieving a sense of meaning and purpose for your actions and decisions and, as such, is another essential self-care activity. What are your priorities and goals, professional and personal? What do you imagine yourself doing 5 or 10 years down the road? Your career plan begins with a brave and focused look forward into your future and should be explored early in your graduate experience when you are completing the first steps on this long journey. Perhaps you would like to be a tenured professor, a respected director of a department, or a therapist with a thriving private practice. Maybe you see yourself working part-time and focusing more on having a family. Once you have determined your specific long-range career and life goals, you can begin to plan backward from them, listing the steps you will need to take to attain them and the obstacles that might need to be conquered on the way. Do not be surprised or concerned, however, if your goals change over the course of your graduate studies; be flexible and understand that your career goals should be fluid and adaptable to your changing outlook and experiences. I would have never imagined myself becoming a psychologist during my years as a professional ballet dancer, and then once I made the decision to pursue this career field, I would have never predicted that I would end up working in the types of settings or with the populations that I am now passionately committed to helping. These decisions were shaped by all my learning experiences, the diversity of which opened my eyes to the many options and possibilities. If I had stuck with my original career goal that was based more on my book knowledge rather than my lived experiences, I would have ended up being very disappointed and frustrated with the outcome of all my hard work. Although it can be helpful to seek the advice and perspectives of others who have chosen similar career paths, it is important to recognize that your happiness and sense of fulfillment will ultimately be based on your own heart and passions, not the motivations of others. A major benefit of an appropriate match between your philosophy of life and your chosen profession is that you will dramatically improve your chances of avoiding burnout and the other impairments that can plague so many psychologists.

Conclusion

It takes a special person to pursue a graduate-level education and to choose a career in the field of psychology; the years of schooling are long and demanding, but the rewards and opportunities for growth are great. Looking back at my own graduate experience, I recall how isolating and overwhelming the process could be. I entered graduate school with the primary goal of survival, of earning my Ph.D. as quickly and flawlessly as possible no matter the consequences to my personal life. In retrospect, although I am proud of my accomplishments, I wish that I could have developed stronger self-care skills and taken a more balanced approach to life from the start, so that I could have prevented hardships from occurring in the first place rather than having to learn these skills as a form of intervention after the fact. You will learn quickly, as I did, that if you cannot take care of yourself, you will be unable to care for others. Your life is made up of many vital areas aside from graduate school, including your health, family, interpersonal, spiritual, and so forth. Finding balance does not necessarily mean spending an equal amount of time pursuing each area but, rather, discovering the optimal division of time and energy for each that gives you a sense of fulfillment and completeness. The goal of graduate school should not be just to survive but, rather, to thrive and to mindfully experience the journey as a reward all in itself. Strive to develop your own identity and style, and feel passion for the work that you do and for the *you* that you are.

❖ References

American Heritage Dictionary of the English Language (4th ed.). (2000). Boston, MA: Houghton Mifflin.

American Psychological Association. (2002). Ethical principles of psychologists and code of conduct. *American Psychologist, 57,* 1060–1073.

Barnett, J. E., Baker, E. K., Elman, N. S., & Schoener, G. R. (2007). In pursuit of wellness: The self-care imperative. *Professional Psychology: Research and Practice, 38,* 603–612.

Davis, M., Eshelman, E. R., & McKay, M. (2000). *The relaxation and stress reduction workbook* (5th ed.). Oakland, CA: New Harbinger Publications.

Dlugos, R. F., & Friedlander, M. L. (2001). Passionately committed psychotherapists: A qualitative study of their experiences. *Professional Psychology: Research and Practice, 32,* 298–304.

Kramen-Kahn, B., & Hansen, D. (1998). Rafting the rapids: Occupational hazards, rewards, and coping strategies of psychologists. *Professional Psychology: Research and Practice, 29,* 130–134.

Licht, C. A., & Nash, D. (2009). Creating balance as a new professional: Caring for others by caring for yourself. In S. F. Davis, P. J. Giordano, & C. A. Licht (Eds.), *Your career in psychology: Putting your graduate degree to work.* Malden, MA: Wiley-Blackwell.

O'Connor, M. F. (2001). On the etiology and effective management of professional distress and impairment among psychologists. *Professional Psychology: Research and Practice, 32,* 345–350.

Owens, J. A. (2007). Sleep loss and fatigue in healthcare professionals. *Journal of Perinatal and Neonatal Nursing, 21,* 92–100.

Wicherski, M., Michalski, D., & Kohout, J. (2009). *2007 Doctorate employment survey.* Washington, DC: American Psychological Association.

Suggestions for Further Exploration

❖

Christensen, A. (1999). *The American Yoga Association's easy does it yoga*. New York: Simon and Schuster. Easy-to-use illustrated guide introducing the basics of gentle yoga exercise, breathing, and meditation that can be used for personal self-care or in your professional endeavors to promote renewed physical and emotional wellness.

Davis, M., Eshelman, E. R., & McKay, M. (2000). *The relaxation and stress reduction workbook* (5th ed.). Oakland, CA: New Harbinger Publications. This workbook is designed to teach you stress management and relaxation techniques. Exercises are included to increase your awareness of your personal reaction to stress and to build your sense of control and mastery over the stressors in your life.

Norcross, J. C., & Guy, J. D. (2007). *Leaving it at the office: A guide to psychotherapist self-care*. New York: Guilford Press. This guide addresses the real-world struggles that psychotherapists face in balancing their professional and personal lives and emphasizes the importance of tending to one's physical, emotional, and spiritual needs. It describes and illustrates 12 self-care strategies that are grounded in the authors' extensive research and clinical experience.

Recognition for Learning. http://recognitionforlearning.ca/learner/contacts.php. This website provides links to the websites of organizations and educational institutions that provide prior learning experience services.

SECTION II

Developing and Maturing

After a relatively short period of settling in to graduate school, you will soon be involved in a range of experiences that will likely be new for you. Hopefully, you have established good habits of time management, productive work, effective study habits, reasonable self-care, and superb departmental citizenship. Now, as you develop and mature in graduate school, you must turn your attention to building the many skills that will allow you to excel in graduate school and create a strong foundation for your professional activities after graduate training. This section of the book focuses on skill development. Becoming an effective writer, teacher, clinician, counselor, researcher, and presenter are all central in your graduate training experiences. In addition, you can add to your repertoire excellence in preparing for comprehensive exams, oral exams, and grant writing. You will find in this section of the book a wealth of sound advice and practical suggestions for maturing and developing in all of these important domains.

11

Effective Writing

❖

Did You Mean to Say That?

Bernard C. Beins
Ithaca College

Your writing should reflect what you think. This apparently simple statement summarizes succinctly what this chapter is all about and what writing is all about.

Once you understand this principle, writing becomes easier. But doing it well will probably never actually be easy because thoughts are complex, nuanced, and multidimensional, so expressing them effectively in a series of linear sentences is difficult. In addition, a single word can take a multitude of meanings, so you may need to ponder your choice of wording in order to be confident that the reader will interpret your writing in the way that you intend. Furthermore, facts that you want to convey are not always clear and unambiguous; rather, they are often merely translucent, reflecting the subtleties of context as much as an objective truth.

Mark Twain said in a letter to George Bainton that "the difference between the almost right word and the right word is really a large matter—'tis the difference between the lightning-bug and the lightning" (Bainton, 1891, pp. 87–88). Is this statement true? Has anything of importance ever really been called into question or led to controversy because of poor wording?

The answer to this question is a definitive "yes." Consider the second amendment to the United States Constitution. This amendment has the following wording: "A well regulated Militia, being necessary to the security of a free State, the right of the people to keep and bear Arms, shall not be infringed." The actual meaning of these words is not entirely clear; the ambiguity has led to appeals to the Supreme Court, which seems to have decided the cases based on personal beliefs of justices rather than on legal principles. What is the problem? The wording is not grammatical, and the various clauses have an uncertain relation to one another.

It is unlikely that your writing will have as monumental an effect as the second amendment to the Constitution. But others will see the words you write as reflecting your thought processes. If your writing is not cogent, people will conclude that your ideas are not cogent. And if they have to fight through your choice of words and your syntax, the impact of your writing will suffer.

Fortunately, it is possible to write with clarity and precision while simultaneously showing the excitement you have for your ideas. Psychologists have pointed out that William James was a clear and effective writer. Joseph Jastrow wrote well and extensively for popular magazines in the early decades of the twentieth century. More recently, I recall from my graduate student days hearing that one of the reasons that Ulric Neisser's (1967) *Cognitive Psychology* was so influential was because it was so well written. You are not William James, Joseph Jastrow, or Ulric Neisser. Still, you can develop solid writing skills. This chapter is meant to help you down that path.

Read Widely

Effective writing develops and unfolds over time. One of the most useful strategies in preparation for good writing is to be a constant reader. The more widely you read, the more exposure you have to both good and poor writing. You can learn to recognize what constitutes each and why a particular piece of writing is good or poor. It may help to pay specific attention to prose that seems either crystal clear or entirely opaque and to identify what it is about the writing that stands out positively or negatively.

As a psychology graduate student, you probably spend much of your reading time with the psychological literature that appears in professional journals and books. Unfortunately, this may not be the best strategy in looking for guidance on your own writing. Eight decades ago, the committee that created the first document on APA style recognized that at least some psychologists had meager writing skills, recommending that "the writer who is incompetent in spelling, grammar, or syntax should seek help" (Bentley et al., 1929, p. 58). Science writing in general has often had the reputation of being uninteresting. Author Bill Bryson (2003) commented that the science he read as a student was "always at least a long-distance phone call from the frankly interesting" (p. 5).

Bruner's (1942) assessment of psychologists' questionable writing skill has echoed over the decades. She noted that scientific writing does not have to be dull; however, in many cases, it is exactly that. An editorial assistant at APA, Bruner asserted somewhat sardonically that

> Sometimes in my more desperate moments, indeed, I have even succumbed to a conviction that authors are engaged wilfully [sic] and with malice in suppressing every vestige of spontaneity and emphasis in what they are writing. . . .The knowledge that he is "reporting an experiment" freezes the pen of many an author; thereafter, in a mistaken attempt to achieve the workmanlike and to avoid frivolity, he succeeds in becoming merely dull. (pp. 52–53)

One of the values of reading widely, including materials outside of psychology, is that such reading can enhance effective use of vocabulary. Seeing how authors use words in different contexts helps to develop an awareness of better word selection and use (Wolsey, 2010). The more you read and the more you pay attention to the mechanics and style of your own writing, the better prepared you will be to communicate effectively.

An enhanced vocabulary is associated in and of itself with better writing. Dunsmuir and Blatchford (2004) found among elementary-aged students that one of the predictors of writing effectiveness was vocabulary. Generalizations from 10-year-olds to college or graduate students and to professional psychologists might be tenuous, but there is enough indirect evidence (e.g., Wolsey, 2010) to believe that even in (or after) higher education, vocabulary size and writing skill will be significantly correlated.

A different aspect of reading widely is to gain as much knowledge about your topic as you can. The more you know about it, the greater the likelihood that you will have a sense of important issues and how they relate to one another. In fact, it may be a mistake to begin a writing project without a reasonably well-developed idea of the flow of your ideas. By approaching a set of subtopics in your writing independently, you risk failing to connect them in important ways because of the lack of a useful overview. This lack of connection among ideas is one failure that distinguishes novices from proficient, expert writers.

Related to the idea of connections, one point not to forget is that you should spend a great deal of time thinking before you write. It sometimes appears that beginning writers miss this seemingly obvious point. Another fact of writing that is obvious to experienced authors is that revision is a necessary facet of all writing. The trick is to know what you want to say, then to say it, and finally, to revise it so that you have actually said what you wanted to say.

Prepare, Think, Write, and Revise

Writing takes time, both in anticipation of the writing and when you actually compose your text. It will virtually always require revision, too. The better your preparation, though, the easier the writing and revising will be. In this section of the chapter, I will describe some research on the differences between novice and expert writers so that you can plan and execute your writing more like an experienced author. The generation of effective writing style is a developmental process, so you should expect it to take time and practice.

Prepare

Depending on the nature of your writing, your first step will differ. If you need to generate a topic on your own, you have a universe of ideas from which to select. As such, your initial theme might be too broad for a single-focus paper. Or you may select a topic that is too narrow and about which you would be able to locate too little background information. As such, you can engage in *preresearch* that involves generating possible topics that you can broaden or narrow as needed.

If somebody assigns a topic about which you must write, you have one step fewer to complete than if you have to generate your own theme; you may not have to engage in preresearch. Instead, you work on the second step, known as *preliminary research*, in which you determine the specific focus of your topic. The third step in moving toward a final theme is called *focused research* in which you identify a variety of sources of information. As you move through each step, you alter your scope of ideas to a single theme and progress from general sources of information to more scholarly and detailed work (Beins & Beins, 2008).

Where can you get information to start your writing project? For professional writing, professional sources are an obvious choice: books, book chapters, and peer-reviewed journal articles. However, an additional but controversial source of information is Wikipedia. There is significant opposition to student use of this online encyclopedia (e.g., Jaschik, 2007), although it is generally as accurate as *Encyclopedia Britannica* on scientific topics (Giles, 2005). Even with the opposition and with some institutions' policies that students may not cite Wikipedia in their papers, students use the online encyclopedia regularly. It appears that students have a good sense of appropriate use. That is, they often use it as a starting point and identify appropriate scholarly references listed in the Wikipedia entry and use it in combination with other sources (Head & Eisenberg, 2010).

Interestingly, in its entry on stereotype threat, Wikipedia correctly points out that in the seminal Steele and Aronson (1995) research, scores of students on the dependent variable were adjusted by using SAT scores as a covariate. This is far from a trivial issue: Removing stereotype threat did not equalize the actual scores across groups; it was only when the researchers statistically adjusted the scores on the basis of SAT results that equality of groups appeared. (The interpretation of the results of using the covariate is itself controversial [Helms, 2005; Sackett, Hardison, & Cullen, 2004], but that is a different matter.) Introductory psychology textbooks invariably overlook this important detail. Some peer-reviewed research includes the use of a covariate without mentioning that the original research did so (e.g., Johns, Schmader, & Martens, 2005), but some make no mention of the use of a covariate at all (e.g., Inzlicht & Kang, 2010). Thus, the use of Wikipedia might actually provide a better starting point than high-quality peer-reviewed journal articles.

The important element in evaluating sources involves the content, not the superficial aspects of information delivery. For example, some people assume that a website whose URL ends in *.org* is more credible than one that ends in *.com*. But the website www.martinlutherking.org is operated by a neo-Nazi group, and the website www.stanleymilgram.com was created by the scholar Thomas Blass.

Another facet associated with trust in one's sources is whether you rely on primary or secondary sources. As a general rule, citing an original source is preferable to relying on secondary sources. When you have the primary source of information in front of you, you know exactly what the author said and, presumably, what that person meant.

One boon to scholars regarding primary sources is the availability of older books on the Internet. For example, if you are interested in the work of Sigmund Freud on dreams, you can access his 1921 book *Dream psychology: Psychoanalysis for beginners* through Google books (http://books.google.com). There is a myriad of complete historical volumes for scholars or other interested readers to view, including such luminaries as Hugo Münsterberg, Carl Jung, William McDougall, Edward Lee Thorndike, Francis Galton, and others. (Interlibrary loan is also a convenient way to obtain books that are not available locally. College, university, and public libraries all offer this service to patrons.)

In contrast, you could rely on somebody's interpretation of a primary source. The problem here is that the second person will be conveying only part of the original author's work; the missing information might be more important for your focus than what is presented. Or the second writer might misinterpret the ideas of the primary author. Not all primary sources are easily accessible, so you might need to use a secondary source on occasion, but you should do so cautiously. (And you should never cite an original source if you have not actually read it.)

As Madigan, Johnson, and Linton (1995) pointed out, in psychology, writers are permitted to paraphrase and reinterpret another author's work to support new ideas because the data are the most important elements driving a discussion. This tradition in psychology means that a secondary source may alter the emphasis relative to the primary source. In the humanities, an author's language is very important, so other writers tend not to paraphrase. These traditions result in the use of paraphrase in psychology and the use of direct quotation in the humanities. One consequence of these differing traditions is that when students take writing courses taught by faculty with a background in the humanities, the emerging writing skills do not align with those of psychology. So novices in psychology may need to abandon the approaches they learned in those writing classes.

Another important element to writing is to rely on multiple sources. For virtually any manuscript you write, there will be numerous sources that relate to your topic. The more you know about the topic, the more cogent the arguments you can create. By citing different sources, you will see how critics have responded to an argument and how subsequent writers have developed the ideas further. Your credibility as an author may also be enhanced by presenting all sides of a controversial argument because the reader will know that you are not ignoring important ideas.

The most useful source for finding publications related to your topic may be PsycINFO®, the database provided by APA for publications going back to 1892. However, even Wikipedia can be useful. If you were writing about stereotype threat, you could find nearly 2,500 entries in PsycINFO that contain the phrase *stereotype threat*. Obviously, this is more than you would want to read, and many of them would likely be unrelated to a narrow investigation of stereotype threat, but most professionally written materials will appear in the database.

On the other hand, the Wikipedia article on stereotype threat lists only about two dozen citations, but the sources include such prestigious publications as *Psychological Science, Journal of Personality and Social Psychology,* and *Journal of Experimental Social Psychology.* It could be a good place to start. Once again, it is important to note that the credibility of the source is the important issue, which is something that you need to assess using your own critical assessment.

Think

The issue of adequacy of sources notwithstanding, in talking with my students about the papers they write, I have discovered that one recurring matter involves the fact that when they begin a project, they do not have a good sense of what the final product should look like. That is, they may have a topic assigned to them, but because they have not generated it themselves, they have little sense of the scope of the project or how to approach the task. When they are writing on a topic of their choice, limited background in the area may also lead to an uncertainty about the focus of the writing.

If you are unsure about the point of your writing, it is hard to focus on a single, coherent message. The result can be something like a stream-of-consciousness essay that flows from one idea to another without a unifying theme. Although this approach may generate an interesting literary essay, it will not be appropriate for scientific writing, which needs to be rhetorically clear and straightforward: You are making an argument that has to be convincing.

In the development of a manuscript, experts and novices take different approaches to creating their focus, which can affect the effectiveness of the writing. According to Hayes and Flower (1986), writers in general try to figure out what the end product will be like; then they construct a set of goals to achieve that end.

Experts produce more elaborate networks of goals, and they connect those goals in more complex ways than novices do. Thus, effective communication is not merely a matter of explicit knowledge of a topic. Rather, cogent writing involves connecting ideas in thoughtful networks. Development of the links among ideas requires time spent thinking about the concepts and their relationships before the writer puts pen to paper. Writers would do well to treat the statement of "putting pen to paper" as more than mere metaphor. Research has revealed that when research participants write in longhand, the result is better writing and more thorough development of ideas compared to participants who type directly into the computer (Haas, 1989; Ransdell & Levy, 1994). Writing is a slower process than keyboarding (at least for efficient typists), which may allow more time for an idea to emerge and may affect how one expresses an idea.

Once you develop a sense of your arguments, you need to identify your audience. Much writing by students takes the form that psychological professionals produce. But this is not the only audience for which you may write. For example, you might create a manuscript designed for people in another discipline. A divergence in type of knowledge is not the only difference between scholars in psychology and other areas, like the humanities. Writers from a given background constitute a language or discourse community with traditions that differ from those in other communities (Bizzell, 1992). Knowledge of the community involves understanding not only what information is conveyed but also how. That is, the way we write represents our worldview.

Scholars of discourse communities recognize elements of style that are important in conveying nuances in a message. As Bizzell (1992) proclaimed, "Producing text within a discourse community, then, cannot take place unless the writer can define her goals in terms of the community's interpretive conventions" (p. 89). Similarly, in Magnifico's (2010) discussion of audience, she stated that "the writer might use her own preferences as a surrogate for those of a larger audience, imagining someone with her own characteristics as a piece's ideal reader" (p. 170).

You may have noticed that both of these direct quotations use *her* to represent the generic writer; it seems unlikely that the authors were commenting on a process that involves only female writers. Contemporary style dictates against using the masculine pronoun (i.e., *he*) generically; the use of *her* generically represents a statement that is part of the message that the author conveys.

Within psychology, Madigan and colleagues (1995) have noted that writing conveys both the content and the tradition of the discipline. So your final written product involves not only what you know but also how you think and express your thoughts. For example, Madigan and company pointed out that psychologists seldom personalize their disagreements with others. Writers do not attack the individual (called an *ad hominem* attack); rather, psychologists focus on the validity of the data or the conclusions. In contrast to psychology, they stated that in the field of literary criticism, personal attacks would not be considered unacceptable.

Consequently, writers new to psychology (or to any discipline) have to navigate through the content, which involves explicit knowledge. But they also have to fathom the tacit knowledge in the culture of the discipline. Rawson, Quinlan, Cooper, Fewtrell, and Matlow (2005) have reported the same phenomenon in the health professions.

As Elton (2010) has pointed out, experienced writers make use of tacit knowledge without necessarily being aware of it. Because they are unaware, it may be quite difficult for them to inform beginning writers of what is implicit. So the question emerges about how one can acquire the tacit knowledge.

The answer to this question is related to the first major point of this chapter: Read widely, and read a lot of psychology. A robust body of empirical research has revealed that people acquire complex knowledge without knowing either that they have acquired it or what that knowledge is (e.g., Reber, 1967, 1969). In the context of writing, experienced academics can recognize the flow and structure of professional writing without really being able to verbalize what it is they are picking up on (Elton, 2010).

This intuitive approach appears to reflect exposure to the structure of knowledge (and writing) and a dawning comfort over time about the way information "should be" structured. As Reber (1989) suggested,

> To have an intuitive sense of what is right and proper, to have a vague feeling of the goal of an extended process of thought, to "get the point" without really being able to verbalize what it is that one has gotten, is to have gone through an implicit learning experience and have built up the requisite representative knowledge base to allow for such judgment. (p. 233)

Expert writers attend to purpose, type of discourse, and audience simultaneously, reflecting on the storehouse of implicit and explicit knowledge as a whole. As such, awareness of content alone may not be sufficient to guarantee effective communication (Magnifico, 2010).

The fact that successful writing within a discipline involves tacit and overt knowledge has implications for the process of learning to write for your audience. The generic academic writing course may instill a sense of grammar and focus, but many elements of communication may be specific to one's discipline (Elton, 2010). So writers with only basic writing skill need to work on changing their style over time and to pay constant attention to the effectiveness of their communication.

If you intend to write for a broader audience, awareness of the expectations of readers is critical. In writing for a lay audience, for instance, you need to capture their attention right away, perhaps within a sentence or two (Sommer, 2006). The question of whether you should write for a nonacademic audience has spurred debate, with some questioning whether academic colleagues will recognize the value (or even the appropriateness) of publishing outside of disciplinary journals (e.g., Sommer, 2009). Nonetheless, some career positions will require such writing.

In contrast to readers of popular writing, psychologists reading professional literature are used to wading through dense, nearly impenetrable prose in order to ferret out useful information. Still, for maximal effect in your writing, you should avoid what Clark (1953) lamented more than half a century ago as "the increasing dullness in most of the articles" (p. 747).

Identifying your audience will affect the way you express your ideas. As a general principle, in writing for psychologists whose orientation is toward well-specified behaviors and objective measurements, it is best to provide careful and detailed descriptions of observable behaviors (Magen & Magen, 2010).

Write and Revise

As you will see in this section of the chapter, I will devote relatively little space to the actual process of writing because good writing begins with reading to acquire a sense of disciplinary style, thoughtful planning, and development of a focus and an audience. These elements are necessary before any actual writing occurs. If you have gone through these preliminary steps, the writing itself will follow organically from your well-developed ideas.

An outline or a concept map, which is a graphic representation showing a semantic network of related ideas, may be helpful in your structuring of a manuscript, but either is likely to be a scant version of your actual prose. Kaufer, Hayes, and Flower (1986, cited in Hayes & Flower, 1986) reported that even for people creating quite detailed outlines, the ideas in the outline were expanded by a factor of eight in the manuscript.

After you have finished the preparatory, conceptual work of developing and connecting concepts, the actual process of writing begins. Hayes and Flower (1986) noted that novice and experienced writers compose sentences the same way, basically left to right. The difference between these two types of writers lay in (a) the length of the writing, with experienced writers generating more than half again as much text as novices, and (b) longer sentence fragments on the part of experienced writers. Hayes and Flower speculated that the ability to work in larger units may contribute to more effective writing.

Another factor differentiating novices from experts seems to be a constant awareness of the audience. Experts use their knowledge of the putative audience to narrow their focus (Magnifico, 2010). A third difference involves the awareness of what Magnifico called *genre schemata*. That is, novices are solving different problems than experts are. Novices are trying to figure out how to narrowly represent overt knowledge in text, whereas experts maintain awareness of the purpose of the writing. Magnifico suggested that novices become experts by practice, exposure to appropriate writing, and a growing awareness of how they write.

A greater understanding of your own writing will make revision more effective. Novices often attend to more superficial aspects of their prose, such as wording. Experts are attuned to multiple dimensions, including the goals of the text, whether the current version achieves the goals, and how to create a better version (Hayes & Flower, 19986). With the greater scope of attention by experts, it is not surprising that they spend significantly more time revising their work than novices do.

As the present discussion implies, improving your writing takes time, awareness of the process, and patience. Students may have had years of direct instruction in writing, but it is actually not clear how effective such instruction is. When Dermer, Lopez, and Messling (2009) provided explicit training on how to produce concise writing, the effect was temporary and the training did not help them recognize when their own writing was wordy.

Unfortunately, the limitations in your own writing can be difficult to discern (e.g., Dermer et al., 2009), so getting another person to read and respond to your prose can be helpful because that other person will not have the same blind spots and biases that you have; as such, that person will be able to provide useful feedback to you in your revision. Similarly, you may gain insight into how others interpret what you have written, which can prompt you to greater clarity in your work (Yang, 2010). In addition, Ransdell and Levy (1994) revealed that when writers aimed their work at an unfamiliar audience, their use of the language improved. This ability to assess your own writing by adopting the perspective of somebody else might help you determine if you have achieved your communication goals.

Unfortunately, the research literature is somewhat mixed regarding the use of others' reviews in improving writing. For example, Covill (2010) reported that peer reviewing does not lead to better writing, although it may spur student writers to begin revising early, and it may improve the writers' attitudes. Dunn (1996) and Cathey (2007) stated that students whose writing was reviewed by other students claimed that peer review benefitted their writing. However, Dunn did not measure improvement, and Cathey stated that the students' writing scores did not change as a function of peer review.

On the other hand, Cho and Shunn (2007) and Fallahi, Wood, Austad, and Fallahi (2006) both reported improvements with peer review by students. Interestingly, Cho and Shunn noted that review by an expert (i.e., an instructor) exerted a negative effect on the quality of the writing. Their conclusion was that the perspectives of the novice writer and of the instructor were sufficiently different as to lead to an uncomfortable mixture of the student's perspective and that of the instructor in the revision. Their conclusion hints at the importance of the implicit aspects of writing, with the instructor having a better-developed sense of the general flow of professional writing.

A variant on this strategy of finding a naive reader to assess your work is to set your own writing aside for a few days or longer (if you have the luxury of time), then to reread your manuscript. What was fresh and clear when you wrote it may be less so upon a later reading. When you are writing, you have access to your complete set of thoughts on a topic, some of which you do not express because, at that point, they seem so obvious. As such, you think that what you have written expresses your ideas sufficiently. Rereading your work later with a more naïve eye may alert you to deficiencies that you failed to spot while you were writing.

Ethical Writing

Ethical Principles and Standards

In your writing, you should strive to behave ethically. The American Psychological Association (APA) has developed a set of ethical standards and principles that relate to written work. There are multiple facets of ethics that are relevant here, but the two principles of integrity and justice are paramount. The *principles* are aspirational;

that is, they are general goals. In contrast, ethical *standards* are specific points that APA considers enforceable. If psychologists violate these principles or standards, they may face professional sanctions.

The standards that are important here include boundaries of competence, avoidance of false or deceptive statements, reporting research results, duplicate publication of data, and publication credit. APA has addressed these issues explicitly in its *Ethical Principles of Psychologists and Code of Conduct* (APA, 2010). Although the standards pertain to a wide variety of professional activities, I will relate them to the writing process.

Essentially, the standards mandate that, as a writer, you not exceed the boundaries of your competence. In the context of writing, you should not be writing for publication in areas in which you have too limited expertise to convey information accurately. Similarly, you should not make false or deceptive statements; the purpose of professional writing is to develop ideas coherently and with integrity. Deceptive writing may win arguments in the short run, but it is unethical. This point is true for reporting research results, but it is also valid for any conclusions you draw.

When you publish work based on data, you should not republish it as new information in a different forum. You can present such work in a different publication ethically if you acknowledge that you are drawing on previously published material.

Finally, with respect to the standards, writers need to consider the issue of potential coauthorship. It is inappropriate to claim coauthorship for work to which you did not contribute substantially; it is also unethical for another person to attribute authorship to you if you did not participate significantly in a project. Likewise, first authorship generally recognizes that the person was the most important contributor to a project. Authorship is not a courtesy accorded to a person; it should reflect the role of the individual in producing the work.

Plagiarism

Plagiarism is one of the most serious breaches of conduct that a writer can commit. It involves taking credit for the work of others and can be troublesome both professionally and legally (e.g., in copyright infringement). In developing your ideas, you must let your readers know where those ideas originated if they are not yours.

Any time you have presented an idea that originated with somebody else, you need to cite the originator of the idea. So if you have forgotten where you came across an idea and do not cite a source, you may still be plagiarizing, even if it is unintentional. Useful references regarding what constitutes plagiarism are available (e.g., Examples of Plagiarism, 2004); they are helpful because the issue is not always straightforward. However, in general, if you use somebody else's words, you need to put them within quotation marks and cite the source; if you paraphrase somebody else's words, you do not need to use quotation marks, but you still need to say where you got the ideas.

The one exception about citing sources involves common knowledge. Generally, if you cite information that you would expect to be general knowledge by your audience, you do not need to cite the source. So, for instance, if you discuss psychologist George Miller's admonition to "give psychology away" for a readership of psychologists, you would not cite the source in which his idea appeared. But if you were writing for nonpsychologists, you would cite the article in *Psychology Today* in which Millers's statement appeared because you would not expect them to know about Miller's statement. It is not always clear what constitutes common knowledge, so a conservative approach is probably reasonable, citing sources whenever you think that the audience might not know the reference to which you allude.

An issue that relates to plagiarism that generates some controversy is so-called *self-plagiarism,* which refers to using your own previously published words in a new publication. The important issue here is that writers not try to pass old ideas off as new. A number of scientists appear to believe that reusing material from previous methodology sections of papers and even from an introduction section is not problematic as long as the research described in an article is new (e.g., Akst, 2010). If you are thinking of reusing material from previous work, it is best to check with the person or organization about policies related to potential self-plagiarism.

Finally, many people regularly draw material from the Internet for presentations, and there may be a temptation to use that material (e.g., pictures, graphs) in one's own work. Just because you can access material on the Internet does not mean that you are free to use it. It may be in the public domain, as with material produced by the government, but it might be copyrighted by a person or organization, in which case you may not use it without permission. This may be an issue not only of plagiarism but also of copyright infringement.

Copyright laws are complex, but the general principle is that if you change the wording of text substantially or if you take data and represent them in a novel way, it is not a copyright violation: People can copyright the expression of their ideas, but not the ideas themselves. However, even when you just paraphrase another author, you still need to cite the source of the information. Fortunately for the psychology community, APA has a very gracious policy concerning use of its copyrighted material and permits use of materials from its journals without having to pay copyright fees or to seek permission from authors. Permission is not required for (a) a maximum of three figures or tables from a journal article or book chapter, (b) single text extracts of less than 400 words, or (c) series of text extracts that total less than 800 words (APA Copyright and Permissions Information, 2010). APA does require that you cite the source of the material and indicate that APA owns the copyright to it.

The Mechanics of Writing

Entire books have been written about how to write well and how to use APA style (e.g., Beins & Beins, 2008). The presentation here will be too abbreviated to cover the same ground in detail, but I will highlight some important issues in writing effectively, starting at the level of the word and moving to larger elements.

Using the Right Vocabulary

English is a very nuanced language, so the use of a particular word often conveys a meaning that is absent when a different word is used. So if you are discussing material possessions among people who have a lot of money, it makes a difference whether you use the adjective *affluent* (wealthy) or *opulent* (lavishly wealthy). At the other end of the spectrum, people with little money and no job may qualify for *welfare* (with a negative connotation) or *public assistance* (with a neutral connotation).

The more you read, the better your vocabulary will become, but as your vocabulary grows, you should make sure that you know not only the denotation (dictionary definition) of a word you might use but also its connotation (the associations that go beyond the denotation).

I once encountered a person who wanted to describe the very end of a process and, to emphasize his point, wrote about a *penultimate* decision, thinking that this word would emphasize the finality of the process more than *ultimate* would. Unfortunately, *penultimate* refers to something that is not yet at the end, so the actual message was in contradiction to the intent. In choosing your words, a dictionary and a thesaurus will both come in handy, but do not simply lift a word from a thesaurus because, although it might be related to your ideas, it might have a distinctly different flavor to what you intend to convey. A word-processing program like Word® has a built-in thesaurus; you should be careful in using it. For example, as a synonym for *happy,* it lists *blissful,* which would be an inappropriate word in many cases.

Another issue in word choice is that, as a rule, simpler is better. Your job in writing is to communicate. Using language that is complex and wording that is obscure does not facilitate communication. As your writing style emerges, you will find ways to express yourself with your own unique style, but it should not be at the expense of understandability.

Grammar

Most students regard grammatical rules as an inconvenience. In reality, though, "grammar is not just a series of unfortunate rules that you are supposed to learn. Rather, grammar is what enables us to communicate effectively" (Beins & Beins, 2008, p. 71).

The grammatical structure of your writing greatly influences how easy it is to read. To achieve the greatest impact in your writing, one of the easier strategies is to make sure you use active-voice verbs; failure to do so is a hallmark of the novice writer. Passive-voice verbs are quite characteristic of dull writing; in addition, they may hide important information. For example, when things go wrong, politicians are prone to make statements like "mistakes were made." This is a good example of a passive-voice verb. It is not clear who made the mistakes, so the politician can acknowledge the mistakes but not take any responsibility for them. A better approach, in terms of communicating, is to say "I made mistakes" (which politicians avoid saying). Structures using active-voice verbs lead to more powerful sentences.

You may not have learned basic grammatical principles directly, so you may not know the difference between active- and passive-voice verbs. Essentially, active voice sentences have a sequence that is structured to present information about who did something, what they did, and what the object of their action was (if there was an object).

It is tempting in writing an APA-style research report to say that *The participants were instructed to complete the personality inventory by a person of the opposite sex.* It would be more forceful (and more compact) to say that *A person of the opposite sex instructed participants to complete the personality inventory.* Passive-voice verbs probably occur as much as they do because people write sentences from left to right and are less apt to revise the beginning of a sentence than the end. If the writer is thinking of the object of an action, that is the first word in the sentence, and a passive-voice verb may come naturally.

In addition, older writing styles, like early versions of APA style, cautioned writers not to use the pronouns *I* or *me*. So authors would not say *I administered the inventory*. Rather, they would say *The subjects were administered the survey by the experimenter*, which uses twice as many words. Fortunately for the sake of writing style, this stricture has disappeared.

Further, better writers show economy of expression. That is, they do not use unnecessary words; instead, they reserve lengthier expressions for situations in which they really do need more words. For example, instead of saying *each and every person,* you can simply say *every person*. Or in describing the actions of research participants, you do not need to say *the participants were asked to complete the personality inventory*. Instead, merely say that *the participants completed the personality inventory*. It is always a good idea to revise your work with an eye toward reducing the number of extraneous words.

Another problem in some writing is the lack of transitions across sentences and paragraphs. When you are creating your narrative stream, it is bad form to conclude your discussion of an idea, then to begin a new idea without providing a transition to the new idea. It helps the reader if you make the flow of information clear to the reader. If there is no connection between ideas, it might be prudent to create a new section with its own heading.

In fact, psychologists regularly indicate the beginning of a new idea by creating a new section. Madigan and colleagues (1995) compared the writing of psychologists, historians, and scholars in modern languages; they discovered that psychologists use about three times as many headings as historians and five times as many as the modern language scholars. When you do not create a new section to your writing, you help readers when you let them know how a new idea relates to what you have just discussed. Beins and Beins (2008, p. 74, Figure 7.1) have listed 86 different words and phrases that express transitions when you want to add information, show contrast, reveal elaboration of a point, emphasize, and others.

Expressing Your Ideas

Professional writing says something about you as a professional. If you want people to take your writing seriously, you need to write in the manner that psychologists accept as standard. The way you express your ideas has much the same impact as the way you dress. Both say something about you. And in both instances, it is quite easy to convey a message you do not want to.

Psychological writing tends to be fairly formal. So writers typically do not use contractions (e.g., *don't* rather than *do not*). In addition, abbreviations used in instant messaging or emoticons (i.e., smiley faces) convey an informality that does not comport with the seriousness of your message.

Similarly, in psychology, writers use so-called hedge words (as in *to hedge your bets*); these words indicate a level of uncertainty. Madigan and colleagues (1995) provided 32 ways to hedge in drawing a conclusion, including phrases like *our suggestion is* or *it appears to be* (p. 432). This type of wording implies that the knowledge is provisional—later work might invalidate it, so the author does not want to go out on a limb. Some sources, such as Wikipedia, refer to these as *weasel words,* which they do not regard favorably. Nonetheless, that is the style of psychology.

In summary, writing well takes time, thought, patience, and experience. There are many different ways to express any single idea. The important point is that, when you express your ideas, you select the most useful words, embed them in clear and coherent sentences, draw connections to ideas in other parts of your manuscript, and structure the entire package in a format that other psychologists will recognize as suitably professional. Once you have done all this, you will be in the position to revise it so that it truly expresses what you intend.

❖ References

Akst, J. (2010). When is self-plagiarism OK? *The Scientist.* Retrieved November 12, 2010, from http://www.the-scientist.com/blog/display/57676/.

American Psychological Association. (2010). *Ethical principles of psychologists and code of conduct.* Retrieved from http://www.apa.org/ethics/code/index.aspx.

APA copyright and permissions information (2010). Retrieved from http://www.apa.org/about/contact/copyright/index.aspx.

Bainton, G. (Ed.). (1891). *The art of authorship: Literary reminiscences, methods of work, and advice to young beginners.* New York: D. Appleton & Co. Retrieved from http://books.google.com/books.

Beins, B. C., & Beins, A. M. (2008). *Effective writing in psychology: Papers, posters, and presentations.* Boston, MA: Blackwell.

Bentley, M., Peerenboom, C. A., Hodge, F. W., Passano, E. B., Warren, H. C., & Washburn, M. F. (1929). Instructions in regard to preparation of manuscript. *Psychological Bulletin, 26,* 57–63. doi:10.1037/h0071487.

Bizzell, P. (1992). *Academic discourse and critical consciousness.* Pittsburgh, PA: University of Pittsburgh Press. Retrieved from http://books.google.com.

Bruner, K. F. (1942). Of psychological writing: Being some valedictory remarks on style. *Journal of Abnormal and Social Psychology, 37,* 52–70. doi:10.1037/h0062165.

Bryson, B. (2003). *A short history of nearly everything.* New York, NY: Broadway Books.

Cathey, C. (2007). Power of peer review: An online collaborative learning assignment in social psychology. *Teaching of Psychology, 34,* 97–99.

Cho, K., & Shunn, C. D. (2007). Scaffolded writing and rewriting in the discipline: A Web-based reciprocal *peer review* system. *Computers and Education, 48,* 409–426. Retrieved from http://www.sciencedirect.com.

Clark, W. H. (1953). Psychological writing. *American Psychologist, 8,* 747–748. doi:10.1037/h0053468.

Covill, A. E. (2010). Comparing peer review and self-review as ways to improve college students' writing. *Journal of Literacy Research, 42,* 199–226. doi:10.1080/10862961003796207.

Dermer, M. L., Lopez, S. L., & Messling, P. A., III. (2009). Fluency training a writing skill: Editing for concision. *Psychological Record, 59,* 3–20. doi:10.1348/0007099041552323.

Dunn, D. S. (1996). Collaborative writing in a statistics and research methods course. *Teaching of Psychology, 23,* 38–40. doi:10.1207/s15328023top2301_8.

Dunsmuir, S., & Blatchford, P. (2004). Predictors of writing competence in 4- to 7-year-old children. *British Journal of Educational Psychology, 74,* 461–483.

Elton, L. (2010). Academic writing and tacit knowledge. *Teaching in Higher Education, 15,* 151–160. doi:10.1080/13562511003619979.

Examples of plagiarism, and of appropriate uses of others' words and ideas (2004). Retrieved from http://www.indiana.edu/~wts/pamphlets/plagiarism.pdf.

Fallahi, C. R., Wood, R. M., Austad, C. S., & Fallahi, H. (2006). A program for improving undergraduate psychology students' basic writing skills. *Teaching of Psychology, 33,* 171–175. doi:10.1207/s15328023top3303_3.

Freud, S. (1921). *Dream psychology: Psychoanalysis for beginners.* New York, NY: James A. McCann Company. Retrieved from http://www.books.google.com.

Giles, J. (2005). Internet encyclopaedias go head to head. *Nature, 438,* 900–901. doi: 10.1038/438900a.

Haas, C. (1989). Does the medium make a difference? Two studies of writing with pen and paper and with computers. *Human-Computer Interaction, 4,* 149–169. doi:10.1207/s15327051hci0402_3

Hayes, J. R., & Flower, L. S. (1986). Writing research and the writer. *American Psychologist. Special Issue: Psychological Science and Education, 41,* 1106–1113. doi:10.1037/0003-066X.41.10.1106.

Head, A. J., & Eisenberg, M. B. (2010, March 1). How today's students use *Wikipedia* for course-related research. *First Monday, 15*(3). Retrieved from http://www.uic.edu/htbin/cgiwrap/bin/ojs/index.php/fm/article/view/2830/2476.

Helms, J. E. (2005). Stereotype threat might explain the black-white test-score difference. *American Psychologist, 60,* 269–270. doi:10.1037/0003–066X.60.3.269.

Inzlicht, M., & Kang, S. K. (2010). Stereotype threat spillover: How coping with threats to social identity affects aggression, eating, decision making, and attention. *Journal of Personality and Social Psychology, 99,* 467–481. doi:10.1037/a0018951.

Jaschik, S. (2007, January 26). A stand against Wikipedia. *Inside Higher Ed.* Retrieved from http://www.insidehighered.com/news/2007/01/26/wiki.

Johns, M., Schmader, T., & Martens, A. (2005). Knowing is half the battle: Teaching stereotype threat as a means of improving women's math performance. *Psychological Science, 16,* 175–179.

Madigan, R., Johnson, S., & Linton, P. (1995). The language of psychology: APA style as epistemology. *American Psychologist, 50,* 428–436. doi:10.1037/0003-066X.50.6.428.

Magen, R. H., & Magen, J. G. (2010). Revisiting Aunt Fanny: Evaluating professional writing. *Social Work Education, 29,* 792–809. doi:10.1080/02615471003599327.

Magnifico, A. M. (2010). Writing for whom? Cognition, motivation, and a writer's audience. *Educational Psychologist, 45,* 167–184. doi:10.1080/00461520.2010.493470.

Neisser, U. (1967). *Cognitive psychology.* New York: Appleton-Century-Crofts.

Ransdell, S. E., & Levy, C. M. (1994). Writing as process and product: The impact of tool, genre, audience knowledge, and writer expertise. *Computers in Human Behavior, 10,* 511–527. doi:10.1016/0747–5632(94)90044-2.

Rawson, R. E., Quinlan, K. M., Cooper, B. J., Fewtrell, C., & Matlow, J. R. (2005). Writing-skills development in the health professions. *Teaching and Learning in Medicine, 17,* 233–239. doi: DOI: 10.1207/s15328015tlm1703_6.

Reber, A. S. (1967). Implicit learning of artificial grammars. *Journal of Verbal Learning and Verbal Behavior, 77,* 317–327. doi:10.1016/S0022–5371(67)80149-X.

Reber, A. S. (1969). Transfer of syntactic structure in synthetic languages. *Journal of Experimental Psychology, 81,* 115–119. doi: 10.1037/h0027454.

Reber, A. S. (1989). Implicit learning and tacit knowledge. *Journal of Experimental Psychology: General, 118,* 219–235. doi:10.1037/0096-3445.118.3.219.

Sackett, P. R., Hardison, C. M., & Cullen, M. J. (2004). On interpreting stereotype threat as accounting for African American–White differences on cognitive tests. *American Psychologist, 59,* 7–13.

Sommer, R. (2006). Dual dissemination: Writing for colleagues and the public. *American Psychologist, 61,* 955–958. doi:10.1037/0003–066X.61.9.955.

Sommer, R. (2009). Dissemination in action research. *Action Research, 7,* 227–236. doi:10.1177/1476750308097028.

Steele, C. M., & Aronson, J. (1995). Stereotype threat and the intellectual test performance of African Americans. *Journal of Personality and Social Psychology, 69,* 797–811. doi:10.1037/0022-3514.69.5.797

Wolsey, T. D. (2010). Complexity in student writing: The relationship between the task and vocabulary uptake. *Literacy Research and Instruction, 49,* 194–208. doi:10.1080/19388070902947360.

Yang, Y. (2010). Students' reflection on online self-correction and peer review to improve writing. *Computers & Education, 55,* 1202–1210. doi:10.1016/j.compedu.2010.05.017.

❖ Suggestions for Further Exploration

Beins, B. C., & Beins, A. M. (2008). *Effective writing in psychology: Papers, posters, and presentations.* Boston, MA: Blackwell. This volume gives very helpful guidance regarding development of ideas and creating a compelling manuscript. It also provides help in developing oral and poster presentations.

Florey, K. B. (2007). *Sister Bernadette's barking dog: The quirky history and lost art of diagramming sentences.* Orlando, FL: Harcourt. This nonacademic volume provides an easy-to-digest wealth of information on sentence structure and how elements of a sentence relate to one another.

Truss, L. (2003). *Eats, shoots and leaves: The zero tolerance approach to punctuation.* New York: Gotham Books. This entertaining, nonacademic book illustrates how easy it is to fall prey to common errors in writing and how to avoid them.

12

Developing Your Teaching Skills ❖

Robert Bubb
Auburn University

William Buskist
Auburn University

I n his classic book, *Teaching Tips,* Bill McKeachie (Svinicki & McKeachie, 2011) described good teaching as easy for some and not so easy for others. He also noted that, regardless of one's ability, "good teaching consists of learnable skills" (p. 333). Much like playing a sport or a musical instrument, experience and practice provide opportunities to develop and hone teaching skills. Indeed, improving teaching skills is not a passive process; it requires concerted and sustained action. You must be motivated, and just as importantly, you must dedicate considerable time to working at becoming a good teacher. In this chapter, we describe the basic skills that comprise good teaching, offer suggestions to improve these skills, and recommend resources to enhance your teaching effectiveness.

At its most fundamental level, good teaching consists of a combination of professional communication and interpersonal skills. Professional communication skills focus on teaching technique, and interpersonal skills involve developing rapport with students. Research directed at understanding the qualities and behaviors of excellent teachers consistently shows that these two factors are essential to effective teaching (e.g., Buskist, Sikorski, Buckley, & Saville, 2002; Keeley, Smith, & Buskist, 2006; Lowman, 1995). If we view teaching as a form of leadership (Norr & Crittenden, 1975), then a professional communication and interpersonal skill orientation should not be surprising. Both orientations are heavily supported in leadership theory literature with the presence of both orientations being superior to either alone in influencing the quality of leadership performance (Aamodt, 2007). As such, integration of both orientations will lead you to be a more effective teacher and classroom leader.

Your level of professional communication and interpersonal skills will combine to give you a unique teaching style. As you obtain more experience teaching, your style will continue to develop and mature. Your teaching style will also be shaped by personal factors, such as your goals and ambitions as an academic, as well as your interaction with students. In fact, one of the best ways to improve your style of teaching is to seek and implement useful feedback from your students.

Keep in mind that teaching takes many forms, all of which depend on both effective communication and interpersonal skills in order to attract and maintain student attention, keep students engaged in the learning process, and inspire them for further learning. Thus, these two skill sets are important to effective teaching regardless of whether you lecture, use active learning techniques, or use some combination of them in your teaching.

Developing Your
Professional Communication Skills

Professional communication skills center on conveying knowledge to students so that they "get it." To the extent that students understand course content and develop corresponding skill sets in any given course, we say that their teachers are effective or good. Effective teachers are knowledgeable and stay up to date in the subject matter, are well prepared, successfully communicate information to students, create supportive learning environments, and have high standards for students' academic achievement (Keeley et al., 2006).

Be Knowledgeable and Up to Date

Students expect their teachers to be experts in the subject matter, and so do college and university administrators. Teachers demonstrate their expertise by accurately answering student questions, using clear examples, and not reading directly from their lecture notes or off their PowerPoint slides (Keeley et al., 2006). Teachers who read their notes from behind a podium or verbatim off of their PowerPoint slides convey both unfamiliarity with course content and a lack of confidence in their ability to teach that material to students.

In developing your lesson plans, research your topic extensively, but then be highly selective of which aspects of your topic to present. Remember, class time is finite, and you cannot possibly cover every aspect of the subject matter. Rather, you should choose those aspects that are most difficult for students to understand, most applicable to the key points you wish your students to learn regarding the subject matter, and most representative of how those aspects relate to everyday life.

As Svinicki and McKeachie (2011) noted, failing to stay up to date in the subject matter is both unprofessional and unethical. A cornerstone of higher education is sharing with students cutting-edge information that enhances their understanding of both the theoretical and practical elements of the subject matter. You can become—and stay—up to date in your subject matter by (a) reading current journal articles in the area, (b) attending both research and teaching conferences, (c) selecting a current textbook for the course, and (d) talking to faculty and graduate student colleagues about recent developments in your field. You can develop ideas about how to present this information in engaging ways by staying current with print and electronic news sources that suggest ideas for connecting aspects of your subject area with current events and students' everyday lives. Connecting course material with current events is an excellent strategy for capturing your students' attention during class.

Be Prepared

A lack of course preparation is the most common ethical violation committed by instructors (Tabachnick, Keith-Spiegel, & Pope, 1991). Being prepared to teach is much more than creating a set of notes or PowerPoint slides for class. Indeed, being well prepared begins well before the beginning of the academic term when you develop or refine your overall goals for the course. Once these goals have been established, you next typically create specific student learning objectives (SLOs) for each aspect of the subject matter you will address throughout the course. Once you have selected your SLOs, you can then start to tailor lectures and class presentations, assignments and projects, and exams and other assessments of student learning to meet those objectives (Davis, 2009).

When preparing for any given class period, select the SLOs you wish to incorporate into your class presentation and then carefully pull together and integrate up-to-date information, including graphics or audio-visual materials that will help your students learn. A good rule of thumb is to try to make no more than two or three major points during class, and then use explanations, demonstrations, and other course activities to help students understand those points.

As you prepare your class presentation, try to anticipate student questions and plan specific points in your presentation to stop and pose questions, develop discussion, or insert a demonstration. If a student asks you a question to which you do not know the answer, say "I don't know," and then do your best to find the answer and bring it with you to the next class or drop your students an e-mail that provides it. There is no harm in admitting that you don't know everything about your subject matter. It is certainly more ethical and less potentially embarrassing than to lie to your students about the answer only to have them discover later that you really don't know your subject area very well. The latter is also guaranteed to give you zero credibility with your students.

Be an Effective Communicator

Being knowledgeable about your subject matter is one thing. Effectively communicating that information to your students is another. To communicate effectively with your students, you must not only know your subject matter but also convey it in a clear, coherent, and compelling way.

Effective communication begins simply with speaking in a loud, clear voice using notes and other materials that are organized logically and sprinkled with helpful examples or class demonstrations. It also involves using unambiguous language and giving students ample time to hear what you are saying, think about it, and write it in their notes. Students need time to hear, understand, and take notes about what is being said. Thus, you will find it beneficial to pause frequently during class to allow your students to catch up with you. Likewise, you will find that providing interim summaries during class time will allow your students to rehear the material and fill in any gaps in their notes. An excellent tool for providing interim summaries is to allow students to contribute to the process. For example, after having lectured or engaged in discussion with students for 15 to 20 minutes, ask a student or two to summarize the main points or arguments so far in the class period. Engaging students in active learning exercises such as this one helps them to become engaged in the process of learning during class rather than just sitting passively and taking notes.

An excellent way to begin a class is to start with a compelling question or a controversial event in everyday life that is relevant to your topic. This strategy is often successful in capturing students' attention at the beginning of class (Davis, 2009; Svinicki & McKeachie, 2011). Many teachers find that they can maintain their students' attention by involving them in class discussion or other activities that require student participation for the remainder of the class period (Fink, 2003; Weimer, 2002).

One of the best ways to generate class discussion and interest is to pose questions to the class. However, not all teacher-generated questions are created equal: Vague questions such as "Do you understand?" or "Is that clear?" are not helpful in generating lively discussion. Questions like these often provoke affirmative head nodding but little commentary, because most students are not brave enough to admit out loud that they do not understand the material. Instead, pose clear, specific questions that do not have simple "yes" or "no" answers. Thus, questions such as "How does classical conditioning affect what people feel and think?" or "Can someone provide an example of the fundamental attribution error?" will provide plenty of room for student commentary and, in some cases, even healthy debate. Remember, too, to pause for a short while (15 to 20 seconds) after posing questions to give students ample time to think about an answer. Better yet, ask students to write out their answers to your questions before you call on them or ask them voluntarily to respond. We often use the "think-pair-share strategy": We pose a question and ask students to write their response to it in the margin of their notes or on a scrap of paper. Next, we ask students to form pairs and discuss each other's answers to the question. Finally, we call the class together and ask students to share with the entire class the major points they covered during the paired discussion. In our experience, we have found that giving students time to write out an answer to a question posed in class increases their willingness to participate and enhances the overall quality of the discussion.

Finally, effective communicators simplify complex information in such a way that students are able to understand it clearly. These teachers do three things particularly well in achieving this remarkable feat. First, they use simple terms and avoid jargon. When they cannot avoid jargon, they define terms clearly. Second, they provide plenty of examples to help students understand course topics, including asking them to generate examples to double-check if students truly can apply what they are learning. Third, and perhaps most important, these teachers do not cram as much information as possible into the class period. Because they understand that humans are limited in their abilities to process large amounts of information, they spend more time in class prompting their students to think about the subject matter than trying to cover every detail of it. After all, facts and figures within any discipline change rapidly. What is more important, at least from the standpoint of effective teaching, is that students develop the thinking skills necessary to understand, evaluate, and synthesize that information for future use. In short, effective communicators put learning, not teaching, at the center of the class.

Be Mindful of What Your
Students Know—and Do Not Know

An important part of being an effective communicator is knowing your audience—your students—and their current level of understanding of the subject matter. After all, if your students already have an excellent grasp of particular aspects of the topic, there is no need to use precious class time to cover them. But how do you know what your students understand? One effective and low-stakes tool for assessing student knowledge is the CAT or classroom assessment technique (Angelo & Cross, 1993). CATs are brief assessment activities that teachers assign, primarily at the end of a class, to help them learn what aspects of the class material students had difficulty understanding. Typically, a teacher will pose a question such as "What was the most important point of today's lecture?" or "What was the most difficult concept for you to understand during class today?" Students write out their answers on a blank piece of paper that they turn in anonymously to the teacher. The teacher spends some time after class reading students' answers and then determines what concepts students do not understand well. At the beginning of the next class, the teacher then reviews this difficult concept, perhaps by using different wording to describe it and different examples to help illustrate it. Thus, teachers who are effective communicators seek to understand what their students do and do not comprehend and then take steps to help them better understand especially difficult material.

Developing Your Interpersonal Skills

Within the context of teaching, a teacher's interpersonal skills can powerfully influence the student–teacher relationship. Fostering a warm and supportive classroom atmosphere that encourages students to learn the subject matter and relate it to their lives helps inspire them to learn for learning's sake and increases the likelihood that they will engage in prolearning behaviors such as attending class, paying attention, taking notes, and enjoying both the subject matter and the professor (Benson, Cohen, & Buskist, 2005; Wilson, Ryan, & Pugh, 2010; Wilson & Taylor, 2001). What qualities and specific behaviors lead to the development of a strong and positive student–teacher relationship? Buskist and colleagues have attempted to answer this question by studying the habits and practices of excellent teachers (e.g., Buskist et al., 2002; Keeley et al., 2006; Schaeffer, Epting, Zinn, & Buskist, 2003). Their research suggests several key qualities and behaviors that contribute to student–teacher rapport: encouragement and caring, enthusiasm, open-mindedness, realistic expectations, and understanding.

Be Encouraging and Caring

You can encourage and show you care for your students by praising them when they perform well and offering to help students who struggle (Keeley et al., 2006). A simple way to encourage and care for your students is to send a congratulatory e-mail after each exam to students who received an A and a supportive e-mail to students who received a poor grade. Let your A students know that you noticed their efforts and appreciate their hard work. Invite students who performed poorly on the exam to drop by and see you during your office hours to talk about their study habits and exam performance (Buskist & Howard, 2009, 2010).

Be Enthusiastic About Your Teaching

Teachers show their enthusiasm for teaching when they demonstrate through both words and deeds that they are genuinely happy to be in the classroom and share their love of the subject matter with their students. Behaviors that reflect enthusiasm include smiling during class and using appropriate hand gestures, facial expressions that reflect excitement or interest, and voice level and inflection to underscore key points (Buskist et al., 2002). Enthusiasm is such a key element of effective teaching that it led master teacher Charles Brewer (2002) to admonish all would-be teachers to "develop a passion that approaches religious fervor" (p. 504). Enthusiastic teachers also show their excitement for teaching by preparing class sessions that engage their students mentally and emotionally by making class engaging and surprising. An effective way to keep class interesting is to vary your presentation delivery. For example, rather than offering students 50 minutes of straight lecture, break it up by including occasional group work, problems to solve, active learning activities, or brief video clips.

Be Understanding, Flexible, and Open Minded

Life happens. Sometimes forces beyond students' control affect their class performance. Cars break down, dogs eat homework, and relatives pass away. Some students must work to help pay for school, which often creates at least an occasional conflict with examinations. Students fall ill, sleep through alarms, or can't find a parking spot. They may be members of athletic teams or campus groups that require them to miss class due to travel. Open-minded teachers understand that students must sometimes miss class or an examination. Depending on the legitimacy of the excuse, you may give students more time to complete coursework, be available outside office hours and class times, or spend extra time explaining difficult concepts in and out of class. Most of the time, students just want you to take the time to listen to them, understand their (legitimate) situation, and not judge them as bad students. However, be assured that some students will have no hesitation in lying to you about why they missed a class or were late with an assignment. There is no one single, hard-and-fast rule for determining which students are being honest and which ones are lying. The method we rely on to help keep all students honest is simply checking up on all students' excuses. For example, if a student turns in an excuse from a doctor, we call that doctor's office to confirm that the student in question was seen by the doctor on the day(s) covered by the excuse. We do not ask the reason for the student's visit to the doctor—that would violate the student's privacy rights. If the doctor's office confirms the excuse, the student is in the clear; but if the doctor's office does not, then we call the student into the office and have a discussion with him or her regarding the discrepancy.

You can also demonstrate open-mindedness by listening to and heeding student feedback about your course. A simple way to generate student input is to ask students to tell you, anonymously and in writing, about things they like about your course and what aspects of the course might make their learning experience better or more enjoyable. Not all student suggestions need to be implemented, but any legitimate suggestions should be considered. Asking for and obtaining student feedback 3 or 4 weeks into the semester allows enough time for you to make any necessary adjustments to the course or schedule and gives students the impression that you are genuinely concerned with students' learning.

Be Realistic and Fair in Your Expectations of Students

Students have more going on in their lives than just your course. They may be taking several other classes, working part-time, participating in academic and non-academic extracurricular activities, balancing social relationships, and learning to live on their own for the first time. Thus, students expect, and reasonably so, an appropriate workload and fair testing policy.

Being realistic means that teachers provide an appropriate level of work for their students given the specific nature of the course (e. g., upper-division courses generally require more reading and more rigorous learning experiences and testing than introductory courses). Realistic teachers thus balance the need to cover content with the limited time resources of the academic term. For example, as much as teachers might want to assign a traditional textbook plus several supplementary readings (other texts, journal articles, etc.), they recognize that the human brain can only process a limited amount of information in a given time frame and so strive to strike a balance between covering the subject matter and spending time engaging students in activities that promote a deeper understanding of the content that is covered.

Being fair means three things. First, teachers do not include material on examinations that they did not cover in class or in the assigned reading. Second, teachers write clear, coherent, and relevant test questions. And third, teachers eliminate questions that turn out to be, for lack of a better phrase, poor questions. Poor test questions may include those that are unnecessarily confusing, have multiple correct answers, or are answered correctly by students at a less-than-chance level. If your institution has an assessment resource center, then psychometric properties such as question discrimination can be useful in determining excellent and poor questions. In some cases when poor questions are administered, the teachers gives the whole class the points they would have otherwise earned for getting those questions correct, and in other cases, teachers simply calculate grades based on the total number of questions answered correctly out of the new number of questions that the teacher actually kept for that particular examination.

Developing and Refining Your Teaching Style Through Assessment

Your unique combination of professional communication skills and interpersonal skills interact to form your teaching style. Teaching style centers on *how* you teach rather than on *what* you teach, although in some cases, your subject matter may set boundaries for some aspects of your teaching style. Both your professional communication and interpersonal skills can be improved through feedback that you collect from self-assessment, your students, and your peers. In a study of national award-winning teachers of psychology, Buskist (2002) found that master teachers constantly sought feedback to improve their teaching.

Self-Assessment

Self-assessment of teaching is a process in which teachers individually reflect on their teaching goals, the methods they use to achieve these goals, and the extent to which they have accomplished these goals. Such reflection is prompted by the teacher's personal desire to improve as a teacher (i.e., formative assessment) and not by outside forces such as departmental policies where the aim is to evaluate teaching for purposes of salary increase or promotion (i.e., summative assessment). For some teachers, reflection involves keeping a log or journal in which they describe particularly significant teaching experiences and then record their thinking about and emotional reactions to these incidents. The purpose of the teaching log is to take the time to develop insight into one's teaching in an effort to learn what steps might be taken to improve it further.

At the heart of self-assessment is the statement of teaching philosophy, which is a short (1–2 pages) summary of your basic beliefs, values, and ideals related to teaching and learning (Korn, in press). The purpose of creating this document is to reflect over these beliefs, values, and ideals and how they translate into what you do as a teacher to help your students learn. The statement of teaching philosophy allows one to step back from the day-to-day efforts involved in teaching to examine the bigger picture of what teaching actually means and the factors that forcefully impact that picture. Although the statement's primary purpose is for self-reflection, it is often required by many institutions as part of the job application or as part of the dossier required for annual review, tenure, or promotion.

Another useful form of self-assessment is to take time after each class period to reflect over what went well in your class and what you might improve. Making a short list of pros and cons can be helpful to you in understanding what you can do on a daily basis both to maintain your teaching strengths (pros) and to develop a plan to address areas in need of improvement (cons). In developing such a plan, you may find it helpful to consult the teaching literature for tried and true approaches to teaching well (e.g., Bain, 2004; Buskist & Benassi, in press; Buskist & Davis, 2006; Davis, 2009; Forsyth, 2003; Goss Lucas & Bernstein, 2005; Korn & Sikorski, 2010; Svinicki & McKeachie, 2011). In addition to these books, there are several excellent journals that publish empirical research and theory on college and university teaching (e.g., *International Journal on the Scholarship of Teaching and Learning, Journal on Excellence in College Teaching, New Directions in Teaching and Learning,* and *Teaching of Psychology*).

Student Evaluation

You are no doubt familiar with student evaluations—paper-and-pencil or online surveys aimed at gathering student opinion regarding their learning experiences in any given class. Although there has been and still remains controversy regarding the validity of student evaluations as a measure of teaching effectiveness (e.g., McKeachie, 1997), there is general agreement that these evaluations can be of some value in helping faculty and graduate students identify their strengths and weaknesses as teachers.

Because student learning is affected one way or another by your teaching on a weekly basis, students are in a unique position to provide constructive criticism on those aspects of your teaching that benefit their learning and those aspects that impair it. Typically, student evaluations are conducted at the end of the semester, which means that it is too late to use any of their feedback to improve their experience in your class. To avoid this unfortunate problem, you should ask your students to provide you formative feedback earlier in the semester, perhaps at mid-semester, if not earlier. Having early formative feedback may allow you to adjust your teaching to improve not only their learning experiences but also their enjoyment of the course.

You should request both quantitative and qualitative feedback. Numbers alone cannot tell you how you can improve your teaching. Numbers merely indicate the extent to which you are doing well in a particular aspect of teaching; they cannot tell you *how* to improve your teaching. For that, you need to ask for written student commentary. The good news is that you really only need to ask three questions: First, what aspects of the course are going well? Second, what aspects of the course might be improved, And third, what suggestions do students have for improving them?

After you've gathered the answers to these questions, sort them into two piles (*what to keep doing in your teaching* and *what to potentially change in your teaching*) and then take some time to think about them in the solitude of your office or home. Based on these reflections, develop a plan that focuses on retaining or enhancing your existing teaching strengths and improving other aspects of your teaching. If, after reading and reflecting over the student evaluations, you find you have several areas in need of improvement, target only the one or two areas that you think will provide the most immediate and largest improvement in your teaching. Once you've made these decisions, you are ready to go back to your class, thank your students for taking the time to provide feedback, and share with them the things that you plan to improve or change about the course and your teaching. Of course, some things you cannot change or don't feel that you should change. That is okay, but you should share your rationale regarding these issues with your students. In our teaching, we have found that students often feel more positive about central aspects of their courses if teachers take time to explain their rationale for the choices they make in designing a course.

In reading through your evaluations, you may encounter two very interesting things. First, you will receive some negative feedback—and some students show little tact in expressing their discontent—and second, some of the comments you receive (good, bad, or in between) will be contradictory.

Negative statements can be hurtful, but you must learn not to take them personally or too seriously. In one instance, I (WB) received an evaluation that stated: "Dr. Buskist is by far the worst teacher I've ever had. I have learned nothing from him whatsoever. I think I should get my tuition refunded for having wasted my time in his class." Needless to say, I was taken aback when I read this comment, and I felt bad that the student reacted to my class this way. However, I didn't dwell on it too long—it was the only strongly negative comment out of more than 200 comments that I received for this class that semester—all the rest where either very positive or constructively critical.

When some evaluations for a course contradict other evaluations, then you must decide, given your goals and student learning outcomes for the class, which evaluations offer a more accurate assessment of your class or which offer better advice for improving the class. For example, if some students say that they really learned from and enjoyed a particular learning activity that you used in the class, but another group of students said the exact opposite, then you must call into question the nature of the activity and whether you can improve it to make it a more effective and enjoyable learning experience. Chances are that you can modify the activity to accomplish both. If not, then perhaps you might explore substituting a new activity for this one.

Peer Evaluation

One of the most effective forms of gathering feedback about your teaching is to ask a peer or a faculty development specialist to observe you teach. A peer might be a fellow graduate student who has classroom teaching experience and a reputation for being an effective teacher or a faculty member in your department with the same reputation. A faculty development specialist is a faculty member who has had training in pedagogical methods and who is an expert at teaching. Faculty development specialists generally work in teaching and learning centers, which are common at many college and universities.

Whereas peers can generally provide you feedback about the substance or content of your teaching, faculty development specialists can provide you feedback about your teaching strategies and the many variables that impact student understanding of the subject matter. Thus, you may consider asking both a peer and a faculty development specialist to observe your teaching. You may find peers to be less intimidating than faculty development specialists. However, they also may be more lenient and less forthright and honest with their evaluations because they have a social relationship with you that they wish to protect. Faculty development specialists are more likely to give honest and constructively critical feedback because they don't know you personally. Another advantage of seeking help from faculty development specialists is that they generally have extensive knowledge of the teaching and learning literature and can point you to useful resources in regard to any aspect of your teaching. These resources may include information to help you write and refine your statement of teaching philosophy or create a teaching portfolio to document your effectiveness as a teacher (Seldin, 2004).

Common Mistakes Made by Graduate Student Teachers

Teaching is a complicated and messy business. To be sure, even the best teachers sometimes struggle with getting their teaching right day in and day out. For new teachers, particularly graduate students, teaching can be an especially daunting task. Graduate students often worry that they will not be effective teachers, and for good reason—they have little or no experience that has prepared them to teach well at the college and university level (Goss Lucas, in press). And as mistakes go, new graduate students make their fair share. In fact, Buskist (2000) observed new psychology graduate student teaching assistants over several years and discovered that many of them tended to make the same or similar mistakes in their first semester of teaching. He also offered suggestions for addressing each type of mistake. Table 12.1 summarizes these mistakes and how to correct them.

Table 12.1 Common Mistakes Made by Graduate Student Teachers (Adapted from Buskist, 2000)

Mistake	Potential Solution
Starting the class cold	Get to class early and "chit-chat" with students, review material from last class by posing questions about it.
Reviewing graded materials at start of class	Save the last 10 to 15 minutes of class to review graded materials.
Projecting weak presence	Speak loudly, make eye contact with all students, use appropriate hand gestures, smile during class.
Weakly integrating major points	Link major points together through examples, demonstrations, and logical transitions.
Relying too heavily on notes	Use only minimal notes or PowerPoint slides—avoid using too many slides or cramming too much information on them.
Talking with back turned on class	Speak only while facing students.
Giving ambiguous demonstrations	Describe key features of the point being made, demonstrate those key features, and then summarize those points to drive them home.
Posing vague questions	Ask specific questions rather than questions such as "Does everyone understand?" or "Does that make sense?"
Not reinforcing student participation	Thank individual students for participating or otherwise acknowledge their questions and comments.
Not repeating students' questions or comments	Even in small rooms, make it a practice to repeat all student questions and comments to ensure other students heard them.

Because classroom teaching is live, occurs in real time, and necessarily involves interacting with other people, what unfolds in the classroom is to a large extent unpredictable. Thus, you will find that it is impossible to anticipate how to handle many mistakes that you will make as a teacher. Accept the fact that you will make mistakes and that these mistakes will be public. There is not an excellent teacher who didn't make mistakes, and some of them stupid ones at that, when learning how to teach. But because they desired to excel as teachers, they were patient with themselves and worked hard to correct those mistakes—they did not allow mistakes to deter them from their quest to fulfill their potential as teachers. As you will discover in your teaching career, although you will continue to improve as a teacher, you will still make mistakes, at least occasionally. Even the best teachers—including those who have been teaching for decades—still goof up every now and then.

When you make a mistake, stay calm, react to it with reason, and, where appropriate, inject a bit of good humor. Even with experience, you will never feel comfortable making mistakes in class, but you will find yourself getting better and better at reducing their likelihood and responding quickly and appropriately to correct them.

Conclusion

Because teaching is as much a craft as it is a profession, it often takes sustained effort over many years to become a truly outstanding teacher. Individuals who become outstanding teachers focus on a single question to guide their skill development: How can I become a more effective teacher? The answers to this question are as unique as the individuals who pose it, and thus what makes one teacher outstanding may not be what makes another teacher outstanding. However, what all outstanding teachers have in common is that they ask themselves the question and then spend a good share of their professional lives seeking answers. Their search for answers to this question inevitably leads them to develop effective communication and interpersonal skills, although, again, the exact ways in which outstanding teachers develop these skills vary from teacher to teacher. Very often, as we've suggested in this chapter, these answers lead teachers to adopt teaching methodologies other than the straight lecture. Although some teachers still lecture for the entire class period, many others supplement their lecture with in-class active learning techniques, and still others have abandoned the lecture altogether in favor of using these techniques exclusively in their teaching.

Thus, although this chapter provides a starting point for you to learn about good teaching and how to discover ways to become an even better teacher, it only scratches the surface of what is possible along these lines. We urge you to follow the suggestions we have offered in this chapter for improving your teaching skills and for avoiding common mistakes that new graduate students make in their first months of teaching. Don't stop there, though. We hope your earnest attempt to answer the question "How can I become a more effective teacher?" will lead you to immerse yourself in the vast literature on effective college and university teaching and to experiment with new methods and techniques of teaching that you discover there. We urge you to visit the classroom of faculty with reputations as excellent teachers and observe what they do that makes them so effective at helping students learn. Take time to talk to others about good teaching and seek advice at every turn on how to develop your pedagogical prowess. Join the Society for the Teaching of Psychology (STP; http://teachpsych.org/), which exists for the singular purpose of improving the quality of instruction for all teachers of psychology. Read *Teaching of Psychology*, which is published by STP and is one of the premier disciplinary journals on teaching at the college and university level. Read STP's collection of e-books on teaching (http://teachpsych.org/resources/e-books/index.php). Attend conferences on the teaching of psychology, such as the National Institute on the Teaching of Psychology (NITOP; http://www.nitop.org/) or regional teaching of psychology conferences (see the STP website for details). If you are willing to do all these things, we can confidently make you this promise: You *will* become a better teacher, and perhaps even an excellent one.

❖ References

Aamodt, M. G. (2007). *Industrial and organizational psychology: An applied approach* (5th ed.). Belmont, CA: Thomson Wadsworth.

Angelo, T. A., & Cross, K. P. (1993). *Classroom assessment techniques* (2nd ed.). San Francisco: Jossey-Bass.

Bain, K. (2004). *What the best college teachers do.* Cambridge, MA: Harvard University Press.

Benson, T. A., Cohen, A. L., & Buskist, W. (2005). Rapport: Its relation to student attitudes and behaviors toward teachers and classes. *Teaching of Psychology, 32,* 236–238.

Brewer, C. L. (2002). Reflections on an academic career: From which side of the looking glass? In S. F. Davis & W. Buskist (Eds.), *The teaching of psychology: Essays in honor of Wilbert McKeachie and Charles L. Brewer* (pp. 499–507). Mahwah, NJ: Erlbaum.

Buskist, W. (2000). Common mistakes made by graduate teaching assistants and suggestions for correcting them. *Teaching of Psychology, 27,* 280–282.

Buskist, W. (2002). Effective teaching: Perspectives and insights from Division Two's 2- and 4-year awardees. *Teaching of Psychology, 29,* 188–193.

Buskist, W., & Benassi, V. (Eds.). (in press). *Effective college and university teaching: Strategies and tactics for the new professoriate.* Thousand Oaks, CA: Sage.

Buskist, W., & Davis, S. F. (2006). *Handbook of the teaching of psychology.* Malden, MA: Blackwell.

Buskist, W., & Howard, C. (2009). Helping failing students part 1: The actively failing student. *APS Observer, 22,* 27–28, 37–38.

Buskist, W., & Howard, C. (2010). Helping failing students part 2: The passively failing student. *APS Observer, 23,* 41–44.

Buskist, W., Sikorski, J., Buckley, T., & Saville, B. K. (2002). Elements of master teaching. In S. F. Davis & W. Buskist (Eds.), *The teaching of psychology: Essays in honor of Wilbert J. McKeachie and Charles L. Brewer* (pp. 27–39). Mahwah, NJ: Erlbaum.

Davis, B. G. (2009). *Tools for teaching* (2nd ed.). San Francisco: Jossey-Bass.

Fink, L. D. (2003). *Creating significant learning experiences: An integrated approach to designing college courses.* San Francisco: Jossey-Bass.

Forsyth, D. R. (2003). *The professor's guide to teaching: Psychological principles and practices.* Washington, DC: American Psychological Association.

Goss Lucas, S. (in press). Allaying graduate student fears about teaching. In W. Buskist & V. Benassi (Eds.), *Preparing the new professoriate: Strategies and tactics for developing effective college and university teachers.* Thousand Oaks, CA: Sage.

Goss Lucas, S., & Bernstein, D. A. (2005). *Teaching psychology: A step-by-step guide.* Mahwah, NJ: Erlbaum.

Keeley, J., Smith, D., & Buskist, W. (2006). The Teacher Behaviors Checklist: Factor analysis of its utility for evaluating teaching. *Teaching of Psychology, 33,* 84–90.

Korn, J. (in press). Writing and developing your philosophy of teaching. In W. Buskist & V. Benassi (Eds.), *Preparing the new professoriate: Strategies and tactics for developing effective college and university teachers.* Thousand Oaks, CA: Sage.

Korn, J. H., & Sikorski, J. (2010). *A guide for beginning teachers of psychology.* Retrieved from the Society for the Teaching of Psychology website: http://teachpsych.org/resources/e-books/guide2010/index.php.

Lowman, J. (1995). *Mastering the techniques of teaching* (2nd ed.). San Francisco: Jossey-Bass.

McKeachie, W. J. (1997). Student ratings: The validity of use. *American Psychologist, 52,* 1218–1225.

Norr, J. L., & Crittenden, K. S. (1975). Evaluating college teaching as leadership. *Higher Education, 4,* 335–350.

Schaeffer, G., Epting, K., Zinn, T., & Buskist, W. (2003). Student and faculty perceptions of effective teaching: A successful replication. *Teaching of Psychology, 30,* 133–136.

Seldin, P. (2004). *The teaching portfolio: A practical guide to improved performance and promotion/tenure decisions* (3rd ed.). Boston: Anker.

Svinicki, M., & McKeachie, W. J. (2011). *McKeachie's teaching tips: Strategies, research, and theory for college and university teachers* (13th ed.). Belmont, CA: Wadsworth.

Tabachnick, B., Keith-Spiegel, P., & Pope, K. (1991). Ethics of teaching: Beliefs and behaviors of psychologists as educators. *American Psychologist, 46,* 506–515.

Weimer, M. (2002). *Learner-centered teaching: Five keys to practice.* San Francisco: Jossey-Bass.

Wilson, J. H., Ryan, R. G., & Pugh, J. L. (2010). Professor–student rapport predicts student outcomes. *Teaching of Psychology, 37,* 246–251.

Wilson, J. H., & Taylor, K. W. (2001). Professor immediacy as behaviors associated with liking students. *Teaching of Psychology, 28,* 136–138.

❖ Suggestions for Further Exploration

Buskist, W., & Benassi, V. (Eds.). (in press). *Effective college and university teaching: Strategies and tactics for the new professoriate.* Thousand Oaks, CA: Sage. This book contains 23 chapters written by some of psychology's top teacher-scholars. Each chapter blends theory and research to create a practical guide for preparing graduate students and new faculty for becoming effective teachers.

Buskist, W., & Groccia, J. E. (Eds.). (in press). *Evidence-based teaching. New Directions in Teaching and Learning.* San Francisco: Jossey-Bass. This book provides an overview of 10 self-contained semester-long systems of teaching and learning and the empirical data that support their effectiveness. The book also provides detailed instructions for implementing each of these systems.

Davis, B. G. (2009). *Tools for teaching* (2nd ed.). San Francisco: Jossey-Bass. This book covers all aspects of teaching. It features 46 to-the-point chapters on teaching strategies and techniques. It is a concise, practical, how-to book on teaching and contains an abundance of tips for first-time as well as experienced teachers.

Gurung, R. A. R., & Schwartz, B. M. (2009). *Optimizing teaching and learning: Practicing pedagogical research.* Malden, MA: Wiley-Blackwell. This book focuses on using empirically verified techniques for teaching. The book reviews and critiques different pedagogical practices and offers suggestions for improving one's teaching by understanding and implementing these proven practices.

Korn, J. H., & Sikorski, J. (2010). *A guide for beginning teachers of psychology.* Retrievable from the Society for the Teaching of Psychology website: http://teachpsych.org/resources/e-books/guide2010/index.php. This book is the Society for the Teaching of Psychology's newest e-book and is free. It is downloadable either as a whole book or on a chapter-by-chapter basis. Korn and Sikorski offer easy-to-follow and practical tips for improving one's teaching across every aspect of instruction.

Svinicki, M., & McKeachie, W. J. (2011). *McKeachie's teaching tips: Strategies, research, and theory for college and university teachers* (13th ed.). Belmont, CA: Wadsworth. This classic book covers all aspects of teaching from preparing to teach one's first class to thinking about how to prepare students to become lifelong learners. The book has been updated continually since the first edition was published in 1951 and is current right up to the latest developments in teaching technologies, including electronic technologies.

13

Developing Your Clinical and Counseling Skills

❖

Radha G. Carlson
Central Regional Hospital and
University of North Carolina at Chapel Hill

One of the joys and stressors of being a clinical or counseling psychologist is the ability to wear many different hats. Depending on the specifics of your program, the expectations of a graduate student in this field are much more complex than in other areas, as you're likely being trained to be both a researcher and a clinician (and a teacher and a supervisor and a consultant, etc.). Luckily, once you have your degree, you can focus on perfecting certain skills. This chapter is about how to develop your clinical and counseling skills during your graduate training.

As with most things, there is no one right way to develop your clinical skills. But, in general, you will want to approach your clinical training in a smart, methodical manner. One mistake graduate students can make is just to go with the flow and do what their program tells them to do, taking practicum placements that are convenient and learning only through what is taught in classes and in supervision. It is very easy to take this passive approach to your clinical training, but you must take a more active role to get the most out of your time as a trainee. Since psychologists can wear so many hats, many of you may plan never to wear your clinician hat after you earn your degree. Even so, developing your clinical skills is an important part of your graduate training and is especially important for matching with your desired internship program, which is a necessary step toward your degree. The following 10 strategies may help you on the path of becoming an active participant in your journey to becoming a competent and versatile clinician.

Strategy #1: Fully Accept Your Anxieties and Insecurities About Being a Clinician

The idea of being in a therapist's chair for the first time can be an anxiety-provoking concept. What happens if I can't think of anything to say? What if I can't help them? What do I do if they ask me a personal question? Considering that you have made it to grad school, you are probably used to succeeding and receiving concrete feedback that you are doing well. With therapy, it is an entirely different ballgame. There are often no right or wrong answers (except when it comes to certain ethical decisions such as do not sleep with your clients), and determining your success as a clinician is much more complex than receiving an A on an exam. Your clients sometimes will give you positive feedback, sometimes will be mad at you, and sometimes will no-show for appointments. It is important to reflect on the motivations behind clients' attitudes toward therapy, but resist the temptation to use those reactions as a barometer for your clinical skills. Instead, remind yourself to take a broader view of the progress that is being made, and realize that no matter how skilled you are, some days you and your client will feel like things are easily moving forward and other days will feel stuck. Being self-reflective regarding your counseling skills is essential, but being overly self-focused can interfere with your ability to attend to the person in front of you. Thus, once you are able to fully embrace your insecurities as a therapist and thereby become less self-conscious, you will be better able to be fully present with your client.

As you continue to develop your clinical skills, it is important to progressively push your comfort zone if you want to make the most of your training experiences. Once you feel comfortable and competent in one domain (e.g., individual therapy with depression), it can be tempting to seek out additional experiences in the same area. However, growth comes only through learning new things, which requires some level of anxiety. The benefit of being a trainee is that you can experiment with new skills and new populations with the safety of close supervision. Take advantage of this unique time in your career to broaden your knowledge now, which will ultimately make you more confident, competent, and versatile once you are an independent psychologist. Sometimes doing the type of work that makes you the most uncomfortable leads to the most powerful learning experiences. Of course, the idea is to gain mastery of skills before moving on to the next one and thus build upon a strong foundation.

To sum up this strategy, it is important to embrace your anxieties and limitations while on the journey to confidence and competence. It is expected you will feel like a fish out of water at first, but rest assured that as you tap into your natural interpersonal strengths, you will become more and more comfortable in the role of a clinician. Trust in yourself and allow yourself to go through this natural progression without becoming too comfortable once you feel like you know what you are doing.

Strategy #2: Decide What Type of Clinical Training You Want: Specialized or Generalized

Some programs do not have a lot of options for practicum placements, whereas others have a plethora. If you do have the luxury of choosing your placements, try to think carefully about what type of training you want. To some extent, you won't know what you like and what you are good at until you do it, but it is still best to have a master plan in mind when deciding the type of clinical experiences you want. For example, would you like to specialize in one type of population (e.g., adults with severe mental illness), or would you prefer to focus on a more generalized approach and try to get a range of experiences across diagnoses, age groups, and settings?

There are two main reasons why you should decide on the more "expert" versus "Jack-of-all-trades" approach early on. One, it will help you shape your experiences so you become the psychologist you want to be. Two, it will help you immensely when you apply for internships (and then jobs) at the end of your graduate training. You are much more likely to land the internship position you want if you are able to paint a coherent picture of how your prior experiences relate to your future career goals. Whether you are thinking long-term about what types of clinical work you want to be prepared for after your degree or more short-term about the best way to finish your degree, having a game plan for choosing practicum experiences is important.

When choosing clinical experiences, here are some things you should consider:

• Specialization: The key to developing a specialization is to still get a variety of experiences within your area. Specialization does not mean being a one-note clinician. Individual therapy, group therapy, family therapy, assessment, and intake interviews are all ways to achieve different competencies within the population in which you are interested. As mentioned previously, you want to challenge yourself consistently to learn new skills. Even if you want to work with a specific group of people, there are still plenty of ways to challenge yourself to become more diverse by seeking out different types of clinical responsibilities or different varieties of clients within your particular interests. Aside from focusing on a certain population, you may decide you want to specialize in a certain type of clinical work. For example, if you want to develop an expertise in neuropsychological assessments, it will be important to focus on getting assessment experience across a range of populations rather than across a range of treatment modalities (e.g., assessments with patients with traumatic brain injury, with geriatric populations, with people with severe mental illnesses). Another way to develop diversity within a concentration is by working with clients from all different backgrounds in terms of race, ethnicity, age, education, or income. For example, if you want to develop a specialty doing interpersonal therapy (IPT) for depression, therapy with a wealthy middle-aged Caucasian woman with depression may be very different than therapy with a first-generation American Hispanic teenager with depression.

• Generalization: The challenge to taking a more generalized approach is to get a wide range of experiences while still developing a cohesive story. A hodge-podge of placements that do not have a connecting theme can make you look like you do not have focus rather than like you are trying to become a versatile psychologist. The key to creating a generalized approach is to develop another unifying theme besides a particular population or domain of clinical work. There are many ways to do this, but it requires a bit more creativity than the more specialized approach. One way to reach this goal is through developing a clear theoretical orientation. Perhaps you are interested in learning to do therapy from a cognitive behavioral perspective with clients from a variety of age groups and diagnoses. In this example, even if you have seemingly unrelated experiences (e.g., conducting group therapy with cancer patients, doing individual therapy with prisoners, and doing couples therapy and assessments with children in a general outpatient clinic), you can paint a comprehensive picture of having a well-developed method of approaching clients in any situation from a solid theoretical orientation that makes you seem grounded yet versatile.

• Quality of placements: If you are still not sure which placements to seek out even after considering the factors listed above, another strategy is to choose the placements that have the highest quality of training. The best source of information on this topic is often more senior students who have direct experience with the different sites. Ask about the specific clinical experiences they were able to get (what disorders, what type of clinical responsibilities), but these may not be the most important factors to consider. The quality of supervision can sometimes be even more important than other factors. Having good supervisors is crucial for developing solid clinical and counseling skills, and a strong supervisor–supervisee relationship can provide a fertile environment for rich personal development as a clinician. Throughout your graduate experience, you will also want to consider who will write your letters of recommendation for internship, postdoc, and/or job applications. To write a strong letter, supervisors need to have a clear picture of your clinical skills as well as be able to speak to your skills within supervision (e.g., ability to reflect on countertransference, openness to feedback). The faculty in your program will be able to give you some information about different supervisors, but past practicum students will likely be able to give you the most useful perspective about what it is like to work with particular supervisors. Other factors you may want to consider include the number of face-to-face hours you will get at a site (some sites have high no-show rates, which means you may not be guaranteed a certain number of hours each week), stressors specific to the site (e.g., length of commute, difficulty finding physical space for therapy, cumbersome paperwork, strained relationships between disciplines), and the reputation of the site within the community. The more information you can gather before you choose a site, the better.

Strategy #3: Figure Out What Theoretical Orientation Fits Your Style Best

There are important reasons why you want to develop a solid theoretical orientation. Most importantly, it will drive how you conceptualize your clients' presenting problems and then determine what type of therapy you offer them. Aside from determining your interactions with your clients, it can also determine the fit between you and your training sites. Some theoretical orientations can be complementary and add to each other, but others can differ greatly. When applying for internships, one of the essays you will write will be about your theoretical orientation. If you have a firm CBT orientation, for example, it is less likely that you will be a good fit with a site that is distinctly psychoanalytic in its approaches. It can be a good learning experience to dabble in different theoretical orientations, but if a site approaches clients from a perspective that is not consistent with your worldview, your training experience and the quality of treatment you provide your clients are likely to be compromised.

So how do you go about choosing your theoretical orientation(s)? Some programs make developing a theoretical orientation a focal point across training experiences, whereas others leave the topic more for individual development. Fortunately, there are many avenues to developing your theoretical orientation. A starting place is taking a class on different clinical theories and treatments. You can also be introduced to cutting-edge treatments and orientations by going to psychology conferences and workshops. These experiences will mainly give you the vocabulary to explore theories in greater depth with your clinical supervisors.

The primary way of developing your theoretical orientation will be discussing your clinical work in supervision and experimenting with different ways of thinking about your clients. It is also of utmost importance to supplement your supervision and clinical work with readings that are related to the type of client you are seeing. Read, read, and read some more! If you are seeing a client with borderline personality disorder (BPD), try reading books about BPD from different theoretical orientations to see which approach(es) make the most sense for you and your client. For example, you could read *Cognitive-Behavioral Treatment of Borderline Personality Disorder* by Linehan (1993) for a dialectical behavioral therapy (DBT) approach. You can also read the chapter on BPD in *Cognitive Therapy of Personality Disorders* by Beck, Freeman, Davis, and associates (2004) for a more pure cognitive behavioral therapy approach. For a different perspective, you could also read *Psychodynamic Psychotherapy of Borderline Patients* by Kernberg, Selzer, Koenigsberg, Carr, and Appelbaum (1989). These books are just a small sampling of how you can research different approaches to the same disorder and thus develop your case conceptualization and treatment skills by using what works for you and your client.

Trainees sometimes make the mistake of thinking they have to pick one and only one theoretical orientation. However, even if you are limited to only one type of therapy (sometimes required by training programs or site policy), you can still experiment with different ways of conceptualizing a particular case. For example, if you are leading a DBT group and are constricted to using the DBT handouts in your implementation of the therapy, you may not be able to experiment with treatments from other perspectives. However, you can still discuss with your supervisor how you might think of the development of the clients' presenting problem from a psychodynamic perspective. Thus, your conceptualization skills can develop in different ways from your clinical skills. This approach to developing a theoretical orientation can also ensure that your client receives consistent treatment, and in this case empirically based treatment, even when you are exploring varied ways of thinking.

Strategy #4: Seek Out Resources (Books, Workshops, etc.) to Supplement Your Program's Training

In addition to reading books about specific approaches to specific disorders, it is also important to your development as a clinician to do supplemental reading that is broader. You are already doing this to some degree, as you are reading this book! Supplemental reading outside of assigned reading from your program can help you develop your professional identity and help with more specific goals such as building an overarching theoretical orientation. As a starting place for thinking about your development as a therapist, I recommend *The Gift of Therapy: An Open*

Letter to a New Generation of Therapists and Their Patients by Irvin Yalom (2002). The book provides guidance on more general themes ranging from topics like note keeping to developing a strong therapeutic relationship with your client to talking about sensitive topics like death with your clients. Although Yalom can be described as an existential psychologist, the advice in this book can be applied across theoretical orientations.

There are many methods for discovering helpful books. I was browsing the psychology section at a bookstore and picked up the Yalom book mentioned above, and then I recommended it to just about everyone in my graduate cohort (I am currently on my third copy of the book from lending it out so much that it was lost by other students). Although I lucked out at the bookstore, a more reliable way of discovering helpful resources is by consulting with your supervisors and peers. Starting a clinician book club with your fellow graduate students can be a good way to get social support that provides both emotional and informational support outside of your typical training experiences. A fellow graduate student in my program started a weekly mindfulness peer group for therapists in training, where we met to discuss ways to improve as therapists by using mindfulness techniques from the book *Mindfulness and the Therapeutic Relationship* by Hick and Bien (2008). Not only were we able to discuss the points in the book, we were also able to practice some of the mindfulness meditation techniques in the group together. This is just one example of how you can creatively develop learning opportunities outside of formal program-sanctioned experiences.

Throughout your clinical training, you may want to buy copies or keep a list of books, treatment manuals, and handouts that are used at your various practicum placements. It is never too early to start adding to your clinical toolbox, and this will make it easier to build upon your skills rather than reinvent the wheel with every new client. There are also plenty of wonderful resources online. Division 12 (Society of Clinical Psychology) of the American Psychological Association provides updated information on research-supported psychological treatments, including information on the level of support for different therapies and resources for obtaining clinical materials (http://www.PsychologicalTreatments.org). For free therapy materials, several government organizations provide free and easy access to a range of materials. The Substance Abuse and Mental Health Services Administration (SAMHSA) has great materials online that you can order (for free, but shipping charges may apply) or download, including videos, client workbooks, and treatment manuals (http://store.samhsa.gov/home). SAMHSA has another website for its National Registry of Evidence-based Programs and Practices (http://www.nrepp.samhsa.gov). This website allows researchers and developers to submit information on interventions that have demonstrated positive behavioral outcomes in at least one study and for which implementation materials are ready for public use.

As mentioned in a previous strategy, going to psychology conferences and workshops is also a useful tool for supplementing your program's training. Going to and presenting at conferences is often given as advice for furthering a research career. Conferences are definitely meant for this purpose, but psychology conferences often have very useful presentations on the development and evaluations of cutting-edge treatments as well as more basic science to help foster understanding of the etiology of different disorders. You may not notice this immediately as a student, but many conferences provide continuing education credits, which are required for maintaining licensure. Thus, depending on the conference, there may be many psychologists for whom research is not a primary focus of their career. Having this mix of psychologists in one setting is the perfect opportunity for observing how research and clinical work coexist and inform each other.

Strategy #5: Don't Go It Alone. Consult, Consult, Consult

"Consult, consult, consult" is a general rule for your entire career, not just during your early training experiences. Helping people with their mental health is a huge responsibility, and we owe it to them to provide the best, most ethical care possible. This ranges from learning a new type of therapy to referring a client to someone with more experience in a particular area to figuring out if you need to report abuse or have someone hospitalized. When in doubt (and even when not in doubt, particularly during early training experiences), do not make ethical decisions by yourself. As a psychology trainee, you should never feel like you are alone when making tough clinical decisions. You are surrounded by sources of support, even if it sometimes feels hard to reach out and ask for it. Your direct supervisor is the obvious primary source of consultation but certainly not your only option. Seeking your own personal therapy is a wonderful way to explore difficult issues and countertransference reactions that are sparked by your clinical training, which you may not feel comfortable sharing with your supervisor (or may not be appropriate for the setting). Peers in your clinical program can also be invaluable resources, as they are likely having the same challenges, fears, and struggles as you are. Referencing Strategy #1, realize that clinical work is hard, and the learning curve can be pretty steep, so embrace your insecurities and seek the social support of others that are in the same situation as you. Just remember to always respect the confidentiality of your clients when seeking support or consultation from others.

When it comes to first developing your clinical skills, "consult, consult, consult" does not apply just to ethical decisions or tough decisions but can also refer to general social support from your colleagues and more casual types of consultation about how to approach a certain case. I have had many discussions with peers and supervisors based on even the smallest details, such as how to phrase a certain point, how to position chairs for group therapy, or whether therapists change the way they dress based on the types of clients they are seeing that day. Being a student affords you the opportunity to be a sponge for soaking up how different clinicians approach all sorts of different issues, not just the big-hitting questions of therapy approaches or ethical dilemmas. Consult, consult, consult on pretty much everything so you can make the most informed decisions possible.

Strategy #6: Seek Out High-quality Supervisors

The definition of an ideal supervisor differs from person to person. It may also differ depending on the specific point in your professional development. When you are first starting out, you will likely benefit from someone who is very supportive and provides very close supervision. As you become more independent, you will likely benefit from someone who allows you more freedom and creativity in your clinical work. Thus, there is no single answer for what characteristics define high-quality supervisors. In general though, seeking out supervisors who are supportive and knowledgeable and challenge you to grow is a good bet. If you find someone with these traits, it can provide a rich environment for your development as a clinician.

On the flip side, an absent, critical, and/or unreasonable supervisor can practically ruin an otherwise good clinical opportunity. Sometimes institutions choose people to supervise based on necessity rather than on their desire and abilities to provide good supervision. If you cannot avoid being assigned to this type of supervisor, it can be even more important to follow the other strategies listed in this chapter. Seek support and guidance from others. Do outside reading. Seek clinical experiences through other avenues. Accept your anxieties and follow your gut. Above all, look at the situation as a potential learning experience rather than as an obstacle. This will likely not be the last time you are required to work with someone who is less than ideal. Take the opportunity to hone your interpersonal and problem-solving skills, which will aid you in your future professional relationships. The experience may also benefit your future clinical work, as you will be better equipped to help clients who are themselves struggling with difficult work situations.

To increase your chances of getting the right supervisor for your needs, ask senior graduate students about their experiences. If several trainees give glowing reviews of one particular supervisor, chances are you will also have a good experience with that person. Take negative reviews with a grain of salt, though, as one person's negative experience may be specific to her or his situation or personality style. If multiple people had similar problems, you may want to think through your placement choice carefully. Some sites may have several options for supervisors, though, so if you are having difficulties with a given supervisor, you may want to speak up to try to repair the situation or switch supervisors so you can find a better match.

The quality of supervision does not rely just on the characteristics of your supervisor. If you are having difficulties in supervision, ask yourself what you can do to improve the situation. Are you becoming too defensive? Are you avoiding talking about your weaknesses? To get the most out of supervision, you have to be open and take risks by revealing what makes a particular case difficult for you. You do not want to treat your supervisor as a personal therapist, but you do want to treat him or her like a mentor. It can be difficult to open up about your weaknesses, because supervisors often give evaluations of your clinical skills that become part of your academic record. Finding a balance between being confident while still being open to growth is key.

Strategy #7: Look for Clinical Experiences Outside of Practicum

Depending on the resources and stipulations in your department, standard practicum placements are not the only way to develop your clinical skills or accrue hours for internship applications. If available, working as an interviewer, assessor, or therapist for a clinical research study is a wonderful way to get extra hours and experience. One of the benefits of this type of work is that you will get experience with using treatment manuals and a structured protocol, something that is not always available in your typical practicum setting. This is beneficial for learning how to implement treatment manuals in the future, which is an important part of providing empirically based treatment to your future clients. If you would like research to be a primary part of your future career, doing part of your clinical or counseling work in the context of a research study is a wonderful way to integrate these two facets of your professional development. If your program allows it, students can often get experience providing clinical services for a research study outside of their primary research lab.

In addition to clinical research, some programs also have senior graduate students provide peer supervision or mentorship to beginning graduate student therapists. This is a great way to learn supervision skills and solidify your own case conceptualization and clinical skills. Hours spent supervising other students can also usually be counted as face-to-face hours for internship applications.

Strategy #8: Eliminate Your Clinical Blind Spots

Clinical psychologists are trusted to do a lot of different things: provide individual therapy, conduct group therapy, work with people of any age, testify as expert witnesses in court, be knowledgeable about psychological research, conduct all types of assessments (cognitive, personality, emotional functioning, etc.), work with families, educate communities, consult with other professionals, supervise trainees, and a whole long list of other responsibilities. If you spend your entire graduate career just getting experience with individual therapy with adults, you are really short-changing yourself, your clients, and your future as a psychologist. In fact, part of your responsibility as a developing clinician is to identify your clinical blind spots and do your best to eliminate them.

If you are lucky, you will have supervisors who will force you to grow by assigning you clients that fill a certain training need, even if you protest. I once had a supervisor that wanted me to get experience with a certain diagnostic category. I argued that I wanted to specialize with a different population, so why did I need to get experience with something that did not interest me as much? My supervisor's answer? Unless you hang a sign over your door saying "No [blindspot] clients allowed," you won't always be able to choose who you see, so you better develop the skills now. Because this supervisor pushed me when I needed to be pushed, I am now a more competent clinician who can help a broader range of people. When you are a student, it is easier to expand your competencies because you are under close supervision. Once you are independently practicing, it may be more ethical to refer a client to someone else if you are not able to seek additional supervision for help with developing new skills. Take advantage of resources available as a student, and lay the foundations for being a well-rounded psychologist while the opportunities are easily accessible.

Blind spots can be something obvious, such as inexperience with a certain type of work, or something more subtle yet pervasive, such as failing to notice nonverbal cues from your clients. Others can sometimes see your omissions better than you can, which makes supervision techniques such as reviewing videotapes of therapy sessions so useful. We only know what we know, so discussing our recollections of a therapy session in supervision can leave out a lot of important information. While listening to tapes of therapy sessions, supervisors can pick up on client comments that you could have questioned further but didn't or subtle changes in tone of voice that you missed. Blind spots can be easily left unnoticed if some form of direct supervision is not utilized.

I personally have had the most blind spots revealed while coleading group therapy sessions with my supervisors and other trainees. Being able to witness, directly and in the moment, how other therapists conduct the sessions has been enlightening for me. Each therapist may pick up on different cues from the client and comment on different things that the client says. Processing the session afterwards with your coleader can further reveal different observations and thought processes regarding which direction to take therapy. Through this method of learning, I have become more aware of my own biases and patterns in therapy and how I tend to notice and follow certain themes but avoid others. I have to constantly challenge myself to look for my blind spots and pay more attention to those areas rather than stay in the groove that is more natural for me.

Strategy #9: Seek Diverse Clients

Becoming a well-rounded psychologist does not just mean getting experiences with a variety of disorders and with different clinical domains. It also means seeking out a diversity of clients. In fact, getting experience with diversity is so important that one of your four essays for internship applications will focus on this topic. When someone mentions diversity, the first characteristic that often pops into his or her head is ethnicity or race. However, there are many other factors that you can look for when seeking diverse clients, including: sexual orientation, gender, language, age, diagnosis, region of the country, nationality, income, living situation, career, family makeup, physical illness or disabilities, education level, religion, and hobbies or interests, just to name a few. Mere exposure to diverse clients does not make you culturally sensitive, though, so use supervision well to establish competence in these areas.

There are several reasons you should seek out clients from diverse backgrounds. First, you will maximize your competence in working with a variety of individuals. Second, you will learn more about who you are as a person and as a clinician as you are forced to look at the world through the perspective of your clients and experience sometimes unexpected countertransference toward clients. Sometimes trainees (and seasoned professionals) will be surprised by their own reactions and difficulties when working with someone who has fundamentally different values and beliefs about the world. It is important to explore these issues early on in your career so you are better able to work through them later as you continue to encounter them.

Getting resources on how to work with different cultural groups can be difficult. The American Psychological Association (APA) has several divisions that provide information on multicultural psychology, and each division's website can be a good place to start when doing background research for deciding how to best approach a particular case. Division 45 focuses on ethnic minorities; Division 44 provides guidelines for the treatment of lesbian, gay, bisexual, and transgender clients; and Division 35 is for the psychology of women. Several divisions of APA have worked together to create guidelines for multicultural counseling proficiency (APA, 2003). Often, though, your clients are the best persons for teaching you about their culture, and it is important not to make assumptions or generalizations about clients based on information you have read about a particular group.

Strategy #10: Follow Your Gut

It is important to develop specific skills, but it is also important to develop your identity as a therapist and to use your natural style to make the specific techniques more effective. Strategy #1 was to fully accept your anxieties and insecurities about being a clinician. Beginning students often worry about saying the right or wrong thing or doing the right or wrong therapy. In the end, one of the things that will most help you with diminishing that anxiety is realizing that your most powerful clinical tool is what you have worked your lifetime to fine tune: your instincts and your natural ability to relate to other human beings. Paying attention to your "clinical gut" can lead you to sometimes surprising insight with your clients. In some ways, having a good clinical gut is a natural ability or a skill that you do not necessarily develop, but being able to tap into your intuition and trust your instinct does take practice. This strategy does not mean to just follow your assumptions and believe that you are always right. Instead, this strategy is more focused on using your clinical gut to develop hypotheses and take calculated risks.

Summary

This chapter can be summed up with the following advice: Try to get the best experiences possible by thinking through your choices ahead of time and using the resources around and within you to develop into a competent clinical or counseling psychologist. The specifics of your journey will depend on your goals and the opportunities you can find within your program. Regardless of your particular choices, it is important to balance mastering specific skills with pushing yourself to go beyond your comfort zone. To help you prepare for developing specific clinical and counseling skills, ideas for further reading are provided in the Suggestions for Further Exploration section that follows.

❖ References

American Psychological Association. (2003). Guidelines on multicultural education, training, research, practice, and organizational change for psychologists. *American Psychologist, 58,* 377–402. doi: 10.1037/0003–066X.58.5.377.

Beck, A. T., Freeman, A., Davis, D. D., & Associates. (2004). *Cognitive therapy of personality disorders* (2nd ed.). New York: Guilford Press.

Hick, S. F., & Bien, T. (Eds.). (2008). *Mindfulness and the therapeutic relationship.* New York: Guilford Press.

Kernberg, O. T., Selzer, M. A., Koenigsberg, H. W., Carr, A. C., & Appelbaum, A. H. (1989). *Psychodynamic psychotherapy of borderline patients.* New York: Basic Books.

Linehan, M. (1993). *Cognitive-behavioral treatment of borderline personality disorder.* New York: Guilford Press.

Yalom, I. D. (2002). *The gift of therapy: An open letter to a new generation of therapists and their patients.* New York: HarperCollins.

❖ Suggestions for Further Exploration

Barlow, D. H. (2007). *Clinical handbook of psychological disorders: A step-by-step treatment manual* (4th ed.). New York: Guilford. After beginning clinicians have developed their basic skills with the book listed below, they can use this book to develop more advanced clinical techniques. This book provides information on empirically based treatments and assessments for different disorders. It presents a mixture of both the research support as well as the more practical how-to for implementing the interventions.

Ivey, A. E., & Ivey, M. B. (2009). *Intentional interviewing and counseling: Facilitating client development in a multicultural society* (7th ed.). Pacific Grove, VA: Brooks/Cole—Thomas Learning. This book provides tips on the basic fundamentals of interviewing and doing individual therapy with clients. It is particularly useful for beginning clinicians who have never seen a client yet. Topics covered include everything from basic listening skills and asking open-ended questions to larger issues of ethics and multicultural competence.

14

Developing Your Research Skills

Regan A. R. Gurung
University of Wisconsin–Green Bay

Research is at the very foundation of science, and being a good research scientist is fundamental to being a successful psychologist. Whether you are aiming for a career as a clinician seeing clients on a daily basis, an academic career teaching in a college or university, or particularly if you are considering a research-based career, you have to be well versed in the scientific process. Practicing clinicians need to be able to evaluate evidence-based treatments and new developments in the field. Good teachers need to be able to incorporate the latest findings into their classes. The bottom line: having strong research skills is one of the most marketable and functional skill sets you can have. In this chapter, I first overview the main ways of gathering knowledge, then highlight the importance of research skills in the field of psychology. I then discuss some of the ways you can develop your research skills and enumerate some critical habits to foster to enhance your research acumen.

Ways to Knowledge: Scientific Research

There are many ways to gather knowledge, and methods of inquiry vary across disciplines. Disciplines such as English and history take the hermeneutical approach, in which interpretation is important and textual meaning is constructed through a blend of understanding and explanation (Donald, 2002). In the social sciences, the scientific method rules supreme. The scientific method consists of universal standards for knowledge claims, common ownership of information, integrity in gathering and interpreting data, and organized skepticism (Krathwohl, 1985). Science insists on empirical demonstrations, uses objective methods, replicates findings, and uses an explicit playbook in communicating knowledge (i.e., publication in peer-reviewed scholarly outlets). Knowing how to conduct scientific research is a part of all psychology graduate training programs. Whether you are working toward a master's degree, a degree in professional psychology (i.e., Psy.D.) or a traditional doctorate (i.e., Ph.D.), knowing how to do research is important.

Research Is an Essential Skill

A good indicator of the importance of research is the fact that research skills are a key learning outcome of the undergraduate psychology major (see APA, 2005, 2007; Dunn et al., 2010). Research is also a central part of what it means to think like a psychologist (Peden & Wilson VanVoorhis, 2009). Your research skills will be important in many parts of your career as you conduct your own scholarly research and later mentor your own graduate students and undergraduate research assistants.

The relevant content objectives from the National Standards are listed in Table 14.1. The National Standards are among the most explicit statements of objectives for research knowledge. The APA guidelines for the psychology major similarly include explicit goals for research (e.g., Goal 2 under Learning Goal I, APA, 2007, pp. 9–10). The suggested learning outcomes for this goal are shown in Table 14.2 and again provide a nice reference point for you to assess where you stand.

Table 14.1

CONTENT STANDARD IA-3: Research strategies used by psychologists to explore behavior and mental processes

Students are able to (performance standards):

IA-3.1 Describe the elements of an experiment.
IA-3.2 Explain the importance of sampling and random assignment in psychological research.

Students may indicate this by (performance indicators):

a. Identifying examples of representative and biased samples in research designs
b. Specifying how random assignment permits causal inferences
c. Explaining the importance of being able to generalize results of research
d. Describing how sample selection (e.g., representation of gender, ethnicity, age) influences results

IA-3.3 Describe and compare quantitative and qualitative research strategies.

Students may indicate this by (performance indicators):

a. Explaining the characteristics of surveys, naturalistic observation, case studies, longitudinal studies, cross-sectional research, and experiments
b. Identifying the suitability of a given method for testing a given hypothesis
c. Specifying the populations to which a particular research result may be generalized

CONTENT STANDARD IA-4: Purposes and basic concepts of statistics

Students are able to (performance standards):

IA-4.1 Define descriptive statistics and explain how they are used by behavioral scientists.

Students may indicate this by (performance indicators):

a. Providing examples of situations in which descriptive statistics can be used to organize and analyze information
b. Explaining how statistical analysis can add value to the interpretation of behavior
c. Citing a statistical finding to strengthen an argument

IA-4.2 Explain and describe measures of central tendency and variability.

Students may indicate this by (performance indicators):

a. Calculating the mean, median, and mode for a set of data
b. Explaining the characteristics of a normal distribution
c. Providing examples of psychological variables that tend to be normally distributed
d. Applying the concepts of variability, such as range and standard deviation, to supplement information about central tendency in a normal distribution

IA-4.3 Describe the concept of correlation and explain how it is used in psychology.

Students may indicate this by (performance indicators):

a. Differentiating between positive, negative, and zero correlations
b. Identifying and providing examples of how correlations can be used to predict future behavior or performance
c. Explaining the difference between correlation and causation

IA-4.4 Recognize how inferential statistics are used in psychological research.

Students may indicate this by (performance indicators):

a. Recognizing the basic process that psychologists use to draw statistical inferences
b. Defining statistical significance as a statement of probability
c. Recognizing limitations in interpretation of statistical significance

CONTENT STANDARD IA-5: Ethical issues in research with human and other animals that are important to psychologists

Students are able to (performance standards):

IA-5.1 Identify ethical issues in psychological research.

Students may indicate this by (performance indicators):

a. Discussing ethical issues in psychological research
b. Identifying historical examples of research that may have departed from contemporary ethical standards
c. Acknowledging the importance of adhering to APA and government ethical standards and procedures (i.e., Institutional Review Boards) for working with humans and other animals
d. Explaining the use and value of humans and other animals in behavioral research, including their ethical treatment

CONTENT STANDARD IA-6: Development of psychology as an empirical science

Students are able to (performance standards):

IA-6.1 Discuss psychology's roots in philosophy and natural science.

Students may indicate this by (performance indicators):

a. Describing the form psychology took before the 20th century (e.g., Aristotle, Locke)

(Continued)

Table 14.1 (Continued)

   b. Summarizing some 19th century scientific research findings (e.g., Helmholtz, Weber, and Fechner)
   c. Analyzing how philosophical issues become psychological when tested empirically

IA-6.2 Describe the emergence of experimental psychology.

Students may indicate this by (performance indicators):

   a. Defining psychophysics and describing its impact on empirical psychology
   b. Identifying Wilhelm Wundt's contributions to experimental psychology
   c. Comparing philosophical argument with the empirical method

IA-6.3 Recognize the diversity of psychological theories in the 20th and 21st centuries.

Students may indicate this by (performance indicators):

   a. Describing the 20th and 21st centuries "schools" of psychology (e.g., behaviorism, Gestalt psychology, psychoanalysis, humanistic psychology, cognitive psychology)
   b. Showing how different theories of psychology produce different explanations of a particular behavior (e.g., truancy, altruism)
   c. Explaining the growing influence of new approaches to psychology (e.g., positive psychology, behavioral genetics, or the study and practice of psychology at the beginning of the 21st century)

IA-6.4 Describe psychology's increasing inclusiveness of diverse interests and constituents.

Students may indicate this by (performance indicators):

   a. Comparing the diverse topics that generate contemporary research with early research emphases
   b. Identifying how research biases have influenced research design and scope
   c. Exploring reasons why psychology had more limited participation from women and ethnic minorities in its early stages
   d. Highlighting contributions by ethnic minority psychologists
   e. Describing historical events and processes affecting the experiences and opportunities of minority groups

---

Unfortunately, not all graduate students will have had the same preparation at the undergraduate level. Tomcho and colleagues (2009) analyzed course syllabi and faculty self-reported coverage of both research methods and statistics course learning objectives to assess the concordance with APA's learning objectives and found course syllabi generally contained appropriate research methods and statistics content. Instructors' self-reports, though, did not always match syllabi. Although only 9% of research methods syllabi included the expressly stated goal of distinguishing the nature of designs that permit causal inferences from those that do not, instructors on average self-reported 80% of course time devoted to this topic.

Psychology is a science, although most undergraduates do not fully understand what this means. In a large survey of psychology majors, Holmes and Beins (2009) showed that over time, students' knowledge of scientific thinking increased, whereas their tendency to see psychology as a science did not. Students reported greater interest in practitioner activities than scientific ones, and these divergent interests were associated

Table 14.2   APA Undergraduate Guidelines

GOAL 2: Research Methods in Psychology

Understand and apply basic research methods in psychology, including research design, data analysis, and interpretation.

Suggested Learning Outcomes

2.1 Describe the basic characteristics of the science of psychology.

2.2 Explain different research methods used by psychologists.

    a. Describe how various research designs address different types of questions and hypotheses

    b. Articulate strengths and limitations of various research designs, including distinguishing between qualitative and quantitative methods

    c. Distinguish the nature of designs that permit causal inferences from those that do not

    d. Describe how the values system of the researcher can influence research design and decisions

2.3 Evaluate the appropriateness of conclusions derived from psychological research.

    a. Interpret basic statistical results

    b. Distinguish between statistical significance and practical significance

    c. Describe effect size and confidence intervals

    d. Evaluate the validity of conclusions presented in research reports

2.4 Design and conduct basic studies to address psychological questions using appropriate research methods.

    a. Locate and use relevant databases, research, and theory to plan, conduct, and interpret results of research studies

    b. Formulate testable research hypotheses, based on operational definitions of variables

    c. Use reliable and valid measures of variables of interest

    d. Select and apply appropriate methods to maximize internal and external validity and reduce the plausibility of alternative explanations

    e. Collect, analyze, interpret, and report data using appropriate statistical strategies to address different types of research questions and hypotheses

    f. Recognize that theoretical and sociocultural contexts as well as personal biases may shape research questions, design, data collection, analysis, and interpretation

2.5 Follow the APA Ethics Code in the treatment of human and nonhuman participants in the design, data collection, interpretation, and reporting of psychological research.

2.6 Generalize research conclusions appropriately based on the parameters of particular research methods.

    a. Exercise caution in predicting behavior based on limitations of single studies

    b. Recognize the limitations of applying normative conclusions to individuals

    c. Acknowledge that research results may have unanticipated societal consequences

    d. Recognize that individual differences and sociocultural contexts may influence the applicability of research findings

with differential ways of thinking and of viewing the field of psychology. Psychology majors should graduate with a good sense that research is important. Virtually all psychology programs in a major survey of departments in the United States showed that students are required to learn statistics or research methods (Perlman & McCann, 1999; Stoloff et al., 2010). In fact, research methods is one of the only courses, next to the introductory course, that is uniformly required (98% of institutions surveyed, Stoloff et al., 2010). Overall, students can expect seven courses that offer research experiences in the typical psychology curriculum (Perlman & McCann, 2005). This knowledge is important for you to keep in mind as you hone your own research skills and then foster research skills in others as you teach and mentor.

Whether you take research methods as an undergraduate or in graduate school, you are often faced with the question of what topic to research. In graduate school, the answer and the results of what you decide can play a major role in your future career. What should you pick?

What Should You Do Research On?

Fortunately, you do not have to pay allegiance to your application personal statement for the rest of your academic life. You may find that your research interests change during your graduate training. Expose yourself to as many different topics as possible and take as wide a range of classes/seminars as possible. Even if you think you have settled on a dissertation topic from day one (see Locke, Spirduso & Silverman, 1993), take classes in related areas and topics. It also will help to know what other departmental faculty in your research area are doing. Take a class from them, arrange readings, or even try and work on a project with them if it interests you and if they are accommodating. Allow yourself time to get a good, strong background in your area and a sense of what is out there.

Let me be idealistic for a moment. Perhaps one of the biggest contributions you can make to a field is to derive a theory that has great heuristic value, ties together many unexplained phenomena, and provides for pragmatic applications that can change lives for the better (e.g., Higgins, 2004; Pendry, Driscoll, & Field, 2007; Van Orden, Witte, Selby, Bender, & Joiner, 2008). Theory plays an extremely important part in research and science in general (Kruglanski & Higgins, 2004). Theoretical work in psychology benefits from a well-developed understanding of the prior empirical and theoretical work on a problem and from informed intuitions (Cacioppo, 2004). Because psychology is so integral a part of life and is so personal, anyone new to psychology arrives with many intuitions, prior beliefs, and naive theories about processes and behavior based on unsystematic experiences and observations. These intuitions can hinder or foster theoretical progress (Cacioppo, 2004). Theory creation calls for both random variation and flexibility and critical selection processes (tightening), not unlike evolution (Fiedler, 2004). Learning how to develop theory is, therefore, a critical research skill to develop, and the best way to do it is by looking at models of theory development (Fiedler, 2004; Fiske, 2004; McGuire, 2004; Taylor et al., 2000; Uchino, Thoman, & Byerly, 2010) and practice. There are a number of good guides out there. For example, Jaccard and Jacoby (2010) provide hands-on tools for generating ideas and translating them into formal theories with examples drawn from multiple social science disciplines and research settings.

The basic research process is relatively common across areas of psychology. You start with an interesting phenomenon, formulate research questions, decide on a methodological approach to use, assess your success in answering your research questions, and then either revise your study and try again or publish your findings (Sansone, Morf, & Panter, 2003.) In an undergraduate research class, you were probably given a list of possible ideas. Perhaps you looked through some journals to inspire your research ideas. Most graduate students include some semblance of a research plan in their personal statements for graduate school. Although exact numbers are hard to come by, I would not be surprised if most graduate students go on to research careers working on topics somewhat removed from what they waxed eloquently about in their application statements. So where do good research ideas come from?

There are many ways to answer this question. The easy ones: Good research ideas come from personal passions or interests. Good research ideas come from recognition of what is missing in existing literature. Good research ideas come from the real world, from recognizing problems that need to be solved. There are many examples, such as Stanley Milgram's interest in obedience from his noticing the atrocities of the Holocaust and Elizabeth Loftus's interest in repressed memories relating to personal incidents of memory distortion. Ask yourself, "Is there any real-world value to what you are doing or want to do?" It is one thing to do some research because it is interesting to you, but to spend time and money on it, it is a good idea to think about whether your findings will change the human condition. If that sounds too lofty, remember that few people's research changes life as we know it. That said, it should not be an immense leap from your research to a real-world application. Will your work advance theory? Is it a common issue? The social psychologist Robert Cialdini commented that "if there is evidence that the effect occurs regularly and powerfully in multiple environments, it is simply more worthy of examination" (Crandall & Schaller, 2002, p. 22).

It is telling to listen to what established researchers have to say on this point. Some years ago, the editors of *Dialogue,* the newsletter of the Society for Personality and Social Psychology (SPSP, Division 8 of APA) asked prominent researchers how they knew what research ideas to pursue. The answers (Crandall & Schaller, 2002) were compelling though perhaps disheartening (to those looking for a sure answer). In general, researchers had trouble putting the answer in words. Some answered that "it sort of feels right" (Mahzarin Banaji, Galen Bodenhausen, Shelley Taylor). Others used their own excitement to guide them—if it was exciting, it was research worth doing (Marilynn Brewer, Brenda Major)—or others invoked their own curiosity (Elliot Aronson). If your research does not excite you, it is probably a good idea to find another topic. On this note, Anthony Greenwald provides some very specific advice. I remember a class I took with him in graduate school, and he made us write the title and abstract of our experimental research projects within the first week of the research methods class. In his view, if you cannot write the title and abstract or if you can write them but you do not find them compelling, then stop before you start. This is advice he wished he had had when he started his career (Crandall & Schaller, 2002), and now you have it. Believe me, it is good advice to practice. I have found it useful and effective, as it makes you think about your research in a way in which you are rarely trained. You are essentially starting to write before you think you are ready to start, and it pays off (Boice, 2000).

When Should You Try Something New?

When you find something to do research on, how do you know when to stop? You could spend a successful career if your results are significant, but what if you are not getting anywhere? In graduate school, your cohort will often be too gentle or kind to tell you to stop, and even faculty mentors may have trouble knowing which ideas are more valuable than others or deserving of continued effort in the face of null results. If you lose interest in the problem you are studying, if you continually fail to get a study to work, or if the magnitude of your effect size is weak, it is a good idea to move on to other topics of research. This is difficult to do when you are early in your career (still in graduate school), but sometimes it is better to move on and not be swayed by the sunk cost of time and effort.

An Overview of Research Skills

As you can probably guess, a full description of the main research skills you will need is beyond the scope of this chapter, but I will give you an overview of what you should know and what you will get from a research methods course.

At its core, research consists of testing hypotheses, and there are three distinct approaches to hypothesis testing (validation, falsification, and qualification). The development and nature of the experimental paradigm began a little over 80 years ago with the work of Fisher, who first formalized essential elements of research, including the manipulation of independent and dependent variables, randomization (including both random selection and random assignment), and statistical testing (Pelham & Harton, 2006). Other essential characteristics of research you need to be familiar with are validity, reliability, and measurement scales as they apply to psychological research. Validity and reliability are crucial to both experimental and passive observational research (naturalistic research that does not involve the manipulation of variables).

The most commonly used nonexperimental designs include case studies or single-participant designs, single-variable studies whose purpose is to describe the state of the world (epidemiological research, research on public opinion, and research on judgment and decision making), archival research, surveys, and interview research. The form of research that affords the most control is the true experiment, in which the researcher uses random assignment and thus has control over all of the independent variables of interest. True experiments are further broken down into one-way designs and factorial designs. In some studies, such as repeated measures designs, researchers hold some control over individual differences by exposing participants to more than one level of an independent variable. Of course, you cannot always manipulate variables (e.g., exposure to carcinogenic cigarette smoke), so psychologists also conduct quasi-experiments in which they study naturally occurring differences (e.g., smokers and nonsmokers). This is the tip of the iceberg in terms of research methods terminology, representing some of the most common elements of research design. You can familiarize yourself with many of these terms, issues, and research skills by reading peer-reviewed scholarly articles published in journals in your field. A research methods class is an essential foundation, but reading journal articles is what keeps your research mind sharp.

Building Research Skills Vicariously: Reading Journals

The best way to sharpen both your research acumen and your statistical prowess is to read the journals in your field. In this day and age, you need not have a stack by your bedside, but you can have pdf files on your laptop (or iPad or other digital reading device). The important thing is to make time in your weekly schedule to read articles. The first step in any research endeavor is to know what has been done on the same topic, and reading the research literature is a critical part of your research skills training. Every university library worth its salt will provide free journal access to many, if not all, journals. Take the time to subscribe to alerts at the critical journals you aspire to publish in for your area (e.g., *Journal of Personality and Social Psychology* for social psychologists, *Health Psychology* for health psychologists, *The Counseling Psychologist* for counseling psychologists, and so on).

You should be reading for ideas for research and examples of research designs, and also for practice with statistical analyses. At the most basic level, exposing yourself to the published literature in the field and, in particular, in your area of study nicely prepares you for the eventuality of publishing your research in those outlets. Once you identify the key journals you should be reading (start with the flagship journal of your American Psychological Association division or the Association for Psychological Science, and then look at the sources of articles in the reference list of an article you found interesting or relevant), it is a good idea to sign up for electronic alerts. Sometimes called RSS feeds (really simple syndication), almost every journal or psychological society has a way for you to get the table of contents of the most recent publications sent right to your e-mail account. You can look over the content and dig deeper into a particular article if you see something relevant. The regular e-mail alerts are also a nice reminder for you to keep abreast of recent publications.

While on the topic of journal articles and electronic media, here is a key tangent regarding increasing your reading efficiency. It pays to have a good way to organize your articles. Once upon a time, faculty would trudge over to the library, find the issue of the journal they were interested in, make a photocopy of the article they wanted, and then read and mark up their copy. Although some folks still do this, it is much more efficient to use an all-electronic format. Once you get an electronic alert of a new journal issue being published, you can often get a pdf file of the article (mostly through your home university library subscription). Save the file either on your computer hard drive or university server, or, even better, in the "cloud." Cloud computing, essentially the use of servers at various sites that you can access from a variety of devices, enables you to save your article pdfs for later use. Two very common places to save such pdfs are Google Docs and Dropbox, which are both free. No more stacks of paper and file cabinets full of articles needed. Furthermore, you can often search for terms or information across your documents.

An article published on something you are interested in can be a goldmine of information. The introduction should provide you with a wealth of relevant citations together with an immediate sense of how up to date you are on your topic of interest. If you are keeping up with the literature, you should recognize many of the citations in the article. With consistent reading, you should run into the usual suspects in terms of citations. It is a great feeling to read an article hot off the press and recognize most of the research discussed in the introduction section. Of course, this also gives you a good "to read" list.

The Method section of an article provides a nice opportunity to test your own research skills and your knowledge of the subject area. Once you are cognizant of the hypotheses being tested from the Introduction section, you can now see one way (the authors') of testing the hypotheses. Reading and understanding a variety of designs gives you the basic building blocks for when you want to design your own study. If you can understand *what* exactly researchers did (i.e., their research design), you will be in a better position to evaluate the results and critique the methodology. It is always a fun exercise to see if you can come up with better ways to test the hypotheses. It is a lot easier to critique someone else's work than your own.

The Discussion section provides you with great fodder for future research. Most good articles have a strong Limitations section as well as a Future Directions section. Not only will you be able to generate a number of your own future directions, but it will also be useful to ponder those outlined by the authors. Ask yourself if you agree with what the authors propose as next steps. Do the suggestions lead directly from the findings discussed in the article? Such mental exercises will make you a more robust researcher.

One special tip: Do not wait until journals come out to read current research. Hot off the press is good. Before it hits the press is even better. Contact researchers in the field whose work you follow and ask if they have preprints of their articles, manuscripts accepted for publication that are in line to be released. Talk to faculty of your institution or your mentors and see if you can review manuscripts. You could review a manuscript your mentor is reviewing and see if you both caught the same issues. You should also consider contacting journal editors and volunteering to be a manuscript reviewer. Sometimes faculty mentors ask their graduate students to review articles that they do not have time to review themselves. In either case, try and review manuscripts. Not only does this give you practice in identifying good (and bad) research, it also exposes you to research before it is published, giving you a head start.

Building a Research Skills Library

Beyond reading journal articles, it will also be prudent to invest in building a research library stocked with resources to help you do research. Research methods have changed over time (Smith & Davis, 2003), and it is good to have resources that expose you to the wide array of possible methods and designs. Articles provide good models, but they do not provide enough guidance. Furthermore, although the best place to begin to build your research skills is a research methods class, it always helps to have some good references in hand.

The first best reference you will have is your textbook from your research methods class. This will often provide you with the key reminders you need about the main forms of research. You will also find that researchers tend to use a small set of research methods and statistics—those that they were trained with, those that their advisors used, or those with which the majority of work in their fields are conducted. Social psychologists, for example, love to use 2×2 designs and multivariate analyses of variance (MANOVA) to test for group differences, multiple regressions to predict variance, or structural equation modeling to test for relationships between designs. These are all good statistical methods that nicely map on to research methods (e.g., the MANOVA is great for basic experimental research). Make sure that you first learn about as many forms of research design as possible so your research plans are not constricted by your research methods knowledge. Some basic books that serve as good introductions to doing research and are good references are by Babbie (2010) and Dunn and colleagues (2010). You may also benefit from reading about theory construction and factors surrounding theory building (see the special issue of the journal *Personality and Social Psychology Review,* Kruglanski & Higgins, 2004).

Together with strong research skills, it is important to have good references to guide your statistics. One of the most readable books on statistics is by Field (2009), who not only gives you the basics behind the major statistical methods you will use but also provides the commands and results tables from the most commonly used statistical package (SPSS, the Statistical Package for the Social Sciences). Research and statistical skills are intertwined.

Statistical Knowledge Is Essential

Being comfortable with statistics goes hand in hand with having strong research skills. Many schools yoke research methods classes with statistics classes and also require students to take statistics before methods. The reason for this pairing is simple. Different types of research designs need different statistical methods. Sometimes poor research design requires complex statistical methods to clean things up. For example, you may discover you did not measure for third or extraneous variables, or some control variables actually varied across conditions. You may have grossly unequal sample sizes. Any of these issues can be somewhat rectified by appropriate statistical tests. Conversely, the cleaner the research design, the cleaner the statistics needed, whether quantitative or qualitative.

Quantitative analyses form the backbone of research in the natural and social sciences, though both these areas also incorporate qualitative methodologies, which are often critical to theory building and preliminary explorations. You should be well informed about both to be prepared for what your research will need. One of the main drawbacks of quantitative analyses is that they sometimes make it easy to forget about theory. Researchers are sometimes so excited to have numbers to play with that the theory that guided the research in the first place takes second place to the emerging patterns in the numbers (there is a time and a method for letting the data shape your theory). Indeed, quantitative researchers do collect numerical information and use statistical analyses to determine whether there are relationships between the numbers, but this does not have to be as cold or difficult a process as it sounds. Furthermore, qualitative researchers do "process data" as well. Qualitative data processing brings order to observations and often involves coding, classifying, or categorizing the observations. In contrast to quantitative analyses in which a standardized unit (e.g., a score on a questionnaire or scale) is used, coding in qualitative analyses focuses on the concept as the organizing principle. There is a nice middle ground where one can do quantitative analyses on what started out as a qualitative investigation.

Qualitative analyses often involve closer connections among theory, data collection, and analyses and are most distinguishable from quantitative research by not always being driven by a formal hypothesis about how variables are related. For example, you do not have to assume that a given method of instruction is better than another or that certain classroom factors will facilitate learning more than others. Instead, the main goal is to describe the situation or process in as rich detail as possible and to explore possible reasons why certain outcomes may take place. Like an undercover cop, the qualitative researcher often immerses herself in the setting. Hypotheses and theory then emerge from these observations. An example is the Grounded Theory Method (e.g., Urquhart, Lehmann, & Myers, 2010) of qualitative analysis. This theory stresses the importance of building theory using an inductive basis using observations to reveal patterns in behavior and then builds theory from the ground up without preconceptions.

A Note on Collaboration

Research is an enterprise often best undertaken in collaboration. Whereas generating research ideas may be an exciting independent activity, it helps to get feedback on your research ideas and even to work with others who may have expertise that you do not. If your statistical skills are not as strong as you would like, it is beneficial to collaborate with a statistician. More importantly, it may be prudent for you to collaborate with someone with research know-how in areas outside your own but that relate to your research ideas. In one of my favorite examples of collaboration, a group of colleagues at UCLA pooled their collective expertise to develop a brand new theory of stress, the Tend-and-Befriend Theory (Taylor, et al., 2000). The paper involved individuals skilled in evolutionary psychology, health psychology, physiology, close relationships, social support, and animal behavior. Individually, none would have been able to write what is now a modern classic in health psychology. Together, the paper is an interdisciplinary symphony uncovering a major new form of stress response.

Some collaborations take place naturally. In graduate school, you will probably work directly with one or more mentors on their research or variations on their research themes. As a junior faculty member, you will probably develop your own independent research. Do not leave your mentoring relationships behind. Nurture your research relationships as your interests warrant, but not at the expense of other projects (Zacks & Roediger, 2004). In fact, in graduate school, you should try to collaborate on as many articles as you can. Even getting research exposure— proofreading drafts, looking at grant proposals your advisor is working on, reviewing manuscripts—will go a long way toward building your own research skills. These forms of collaborations, sometimes implicit (e.g., you may get thanked in an author note for your work reviewing a paper), sometimes explicit (e.g., you get to be a coauthor of a paper), are absolutely essential to develop. The key here is you have to take the initiative and ask. You cannot afford to wait until something comes your way. In some graduate schools, faculty mentors are very cognizant of cultivating their graduate students. In other schools, it may not occur to the faculty mentor to think about it. Publishing in high-tier journals and garnering million-dollar research grants is difficult to do on the first shot. The more practice and exposure to these processes you can get, the better off you will be. Better still, if you go into an academic career, being able to foster strong collaborations and have many papers in the pipeline, as it were, will go a long way toward tenure and promotion.

Conclusion

Most graduate programs have structured courses that methodically help you learn what it means to be a competent academic: how to do valid research, learn the important theories in your area, successfully obtain research grants, review manuscripts, and learn the basic elements of teaching. The chapters in this book provide a wonderful list of tips to guide you through the process and make sure you know what you should be getting out of graduate school. Take a critical look at the structure of your own graduate program (i.e., consult graduate handbooks, course catalogues, upper-level students), and if the program is deficient in any of the key areas described in this chapter (and this book), take the initiative to get what you need. I list some key resources for you to enhance your research skills at the end of this chapter. Mobilize yourself.

Some of the key tips for enhancing your research skills are: Make time to read journal articles in your area, work on being comfortable with statistics, and collaborate with your cohort and faculty. Armed with these basic reminders and this book, you are ready to embark on the exciting adventure of doing research. Enjoy the ride.

❖ References

American Psychological Association. (2005). *National Standards for the Teaching of High School Psychology*. Washington, DC: Author. Retrieved from www.apa.org/education/k12/national-standards.aspx.

American Psychological Association. (2007). *APA guidelines for the undergraduate psychology major.* Washington, DC: Author. Retrieved from www.apa.org/ed/resources.html.

Babbie, E. R. (2010). *The basics of social research* (5th ed.). Belmont, CA: Wadsworth.

Boice, R. (2000). *Advice for new faculty members: Nihil nimus.* Boston: Allyn & Bacon.

Cacioppo, J. T. (2004). Common sense, intuition, and theory in personality and social psychology. *Personality and Social Psychology Review, 8*(2), 114–122. doi:10.1207/s15327957pspr0802_4.

Crandall, C., & Schaller, M. (Eds.). (2002). *Dialogue: The newsletter of the society for personality and social psychology, 17*(2), 12–15.

Donald, J. G. (2002). *Learning to think: Disciplinary perspectives.* San Francisco: Jossey-Bass.

Dunn, D., Brewer, C., Cautin, R., Gurung, R. A. R., et al. (2010). Curriculum. In D. F. Halpern (Ed.), *Undergraduate education in psychology: A blueprint for the future of the discipline.* Washington, DC: American Psychological Association.

Fiedler, K. (2004). Tools, toys, truisms, and theories: Some thoughts on the creative cycle of theory formation. *Personality and Social Psychology Review, 8*(2), 123–131. doi:10.1207/s15327957pspr0802_5.

Field, A. (2009). *Discovering statistics using SPSS* (3rd ed.). London: Sage.

Fiske, S. T. (2004). Mind the gap: In praise of informal sources of formal theory. *Personality and Social Psychology Review, 8*(2), 132–137. doi:10.1207/s15327957pspr0802_6.

Higgins, E. (2004). Making a theory useful: Lessons handed down. *Personality and Social Psychology Review, 8*(2), 138–145. doi:10.1207/s15327957pspr0802_7.

Holmes, J., & Beins, B. (2009). Psychology is a science: At least some students think so. *Teaching of Psychology, 36*(1), 5–11. doi:10.1080/00986280802529350.

Jaccard, J., & Jacoby, J. (2010). *Theory construction and model-building skills: A practical guide for social scientists.* New York: Guilford.

Krathwohl, D. K. (1985). *Social and behavioral science research.* San Francisco: Jossey-Bass.

Kruglanski, A., & Higgins, E. (2004). Theory construction in social personality psychology: Personal experiences and lessons learned. *Personality and Social Psychology Review, 8*(2), 96–97. doi:10.1207/s15327957pspr0802_1.

Locke, L. F., Spirduso, W. W., & Silverman, S. J. (1993). *Proposals that work: A guide for planning dissertations and grant proposals* (3rd ed.). Newbury Park, CA: Sage.

McGuire, W. J. (2004). A perspectivist approach to theory construction. *Personality and Social Psychology Review, 8*(2), 173–182. doi:10.1207/s15327957pspr0802_11.

Peden, B. F., & Wilson VanVoorhis, C. R. (2009). Developing habits of the mind, hand, and heart in psychology undergraduates. In R. A. R. Gurung, N. L. Chick, & A. Haynie (Eds.), *Exploring signature pedagogies: Approaches to teaching disciplinary habits of mind.* Sterling, VA: Stylus.

Pelham, B. W., & Harton, B. (2006). *Conducting research in psychology: Measuring the weight of smoke* (3rd ed.). Belmont, CA: Wadsworth.

Pendry, L. F., Driscoll, D. M., & Field, S. T. (2007). Diversity training: Putting theory into practice. *Journal of Occupational and Organizational Psychology, 80*(1), 27–50. doi:10.1348/096317906X118397.

Perlman, B., & McCann, L. I. (1999). The most frequently listed courses in the undergraduate psychology curriculum. *Teaching of Psychology, 26*(3), 177.

Perlman, B., & McCann, L. (2005). Undergraduate research experiences in psychology: A national study of courses and curricula. *Teaching of Psychology, 32*(1), 5–14. doi:10.1207/s15328023top3201_2.

Sansone, C., Morf, C., & Panter, A. (2004). *The Sage handbook of methods in social psychology.* Thousand Oaks, CA: Sage.

Smith, R., & Davis, S. (2003). The changing face of research methods. *Handbook of research methods in experimental psychology* (pp. 106–126). Malden: Blackwell. doi:10.1002/9780470756973.ch6.

Stoloff, M., McCarthy, M., Keller, L., Varfolomeeva, V., Lynch, J., Makara, K., et al. (2010). The undergraduate psychology major: An examination of structure and sequence. *Teaching of Psychology, 37*(1), 4–15. doi:10.1080/00986280903426274.

Taylor, S. E., Klein, L. C., Lewis, B., Gruenwald, T., Gurung, R. A. R., & Updegraff, J. (2000). The female stress response: Tend and befriend not fight or flight. *Psychological Review, 107,* 411–429.

Tomcho, T., Rice, D., Foels, R., Folmsbee, L., Vladescu, J., Lissman, R., et al. (2009). APA's learning objectives for research methods and statistics in practice: A multimethod analysis. *Teaching of Psychology, 36*(2), 84–89. doi:10.1080/00986280902739693.

Uchino, B. N., Thoman, D., & Byerly, S. (2010). Inference patterns in theoretical social psychology: Looking back as we move forward. *Social and Personality Psychology Compass, 4*(6), 417–427. doi:10.1111/j.1751-9004.2010.00272.x.

Urquhart, C., Lehmann, H., & Myers, M. D. (2010). Putting the theory back into grounded theory: Guidelines for grounded theory studies in information systems. *Information Systems Journal, 20*(4), 357–381. doi:10.1111/j.1365-2575.2009.00328.x.

Van Orden, K. A., Witte, T. K., Selby, E. A., Bender, T. W., & Joiner, T. r. (2008). Suicidal behavior in youth. In J. Z. Abela, B. L. Hankin, J. Z. Abela, B. L. Hankin (Eds.), *Handbook of depression in children and adolescents* (pp. 441–465). New York: Guilford.

Zacks, J. M., & Roediger, H. L.(2004). Setting up your lab and beginning a program of research. In J. M. Darley, Zanna, M. P., & H. L. Roediger III (Eds.), *The compleat academic: A career guide* (2nd ed.;pp. 135–152). Washington, DC: American Psychological Association.

❖ Suggestions for Further Exploration

Babbie, E. (2010). *The basics of social research* (5th ed.). San Francisco: Cengage. One of the most widely adopted research methods books that is a good resource and refresher course for all you should have learned in a college methods/statistics class.

Darley, J. M., Zanna, M. P., & Roediger III, H. L. (Eds.). (2004). *The compleat academic: A career guide* (2nd ed.). Washington, DC: American Psychological Association. An indispensible guide for any academic psychologist. It covers every aspect of the academic life from doing research, setting up a lab, getting grants, and managing your time to being productive.

Dunn, D. (2010). *The practical researcher: A student guide to conducting psychological research* (2nd ed.). Malden, MA: Wiley-Blackwell. This book provides many ways to be an efficient and organized researcher. It has detailed suggestions for how best to generate ideas and to organize the different steps of your research endeavors.

Field, A. (2009). *Discovering statistics using SPSS*. Thousand Oaks, CA: Sage. This is one of the best-written guides out there that covers both how to use SPSS and to do a large number of statistical analyses. Funny, detailed, robust.

Pelham, B. W., & Blanton, H. (2006). *Conducting research in psychology: Measuring the weight of smoke*. San Francisco: Wadsworth. A readable introduction to research methodology with relevant examples and a useful instructor's manual you can use if you are teaching or a teaching assistant for research methods.

Tashakkori, A., & Teddlie, C. (2010). *Sage handbook of mixed methods in social and behavioral research*. Thousand Oaks, CA: Sage. A resource for complex research methods that nicely outlines a wide variety of intricate and very effective research designs.

15

Developing Your Presentation Skills

❖

Lonnie Yandell
Belmont University

As your role changes from primarily that of student to teacher or researcher, you will increasingly find it necessary to speak to different groups of people in a public setting. Whether you make a presentation at a teaching or research conference, a workshop, a job interview, or for a guest lecture, an important part of your professional growth will be your development as a public speaker. Most of us are not naturally skilled at public speaking, and for many of us, it is our number one fear. However, public speaking is a skill that can be developed, and like most complex skills, it requires practice and extensive experience to master. But as one trade book on public speaking has suggested, we don't all have to be world-class speakers (Walker, 2010). Just giving a pretty good presentation is a good place to start, although the stakes are clearly higher in some situations (e.g., a job talk) than in others (e.g., a talk in front of your graduate student peers). In this chapter, I present important ideas concerning presentation skills in general and offer some suggestions of things to do and things to avoid in your presentation preparation and delivery. I then discuss issues that are related to two very common presentation tasks for professional psychologists, the research talk and a poster presentation. Please also consult Chapter 18, Skill Development for Oral Presentations and Examinations, which deals with oral exam presentations and also offers excellent suggestions for dealing with public speaking anxiety.

Good Public Speaking Is Like Good Teaching

Great speakers, like great teachers, have the ability to make complicated things seem simple. Unfortunately, we often learn how to speak publicly much the same way we learn how to teach, by emulating others. Although this is not necessarily a bad way to learn, both teaching and speaking are complicated activities that do not have a simple or a set method that always works. It is helpful if you take the attitude of a teacher rather than a lecturer when delivering a talk (Garmston & Wellman, 1992). A good teacher tries to connect with the learner. It is important to help students expand their mental models with new information. In order to do this, the teacher needs to know something about what the student already knows regarding the subject being taught. In Chapter 12 of this book, Bubb and Buskist suggest some great ways to discover what your students already know so that you can fashion your teaching accordingly. The teacher should help students connect their experiences with the new information that you present. Good teachers try to build a scaffold between what the students know and what the teacher wants them to learn. This principle holds true for any public presentation. Unfortunately, for most public presentations, you do not have the luxury of assessing the knowledge of your audience or adjusting your presentation to fit the audience's knowledge level. Therefore, you must connect almost immediately with your audience.

Hoff (1992) suggested that the first 90 seconds are the most important part of a presentation. You must immediately connect with your audience. Audiences, including students, have short attention spans. Standing behind a lectern reading a prepared script is guaranteed to anesthetize the most enthusiastic audience. Develop many lively, short segments that maintain attention. Consider inserting some type of audience participation, whether it be simply asking questions of the audience or actually interacting with specific members of the audience. Always maintain eye contact with the audience if possible and work on ways to demonstrate your point rather than just stating it.

The overarching goal of any talk is to communicate with, or teach, an audience. Therefore, it is always important to "know your audience" and keep this in mind as you prepare the talk. It is important to consider both the personality of the speaker or teacher and the characteristics of the audience or students. We have all sat through talks that either did not provide enough background information or proceeded so fast as to make it incomprehensible. Other speakers have presented so much information or at such a slow pace that we spent more time fighting sleep than understanding the talk. Try to develop a relationship with the audience by being sensitive to their needs. I work at a predominately undergraduate institution, and over the years, numerous speakers have delivered talks to our students. Unfortunately, some of the speakers have delivered talks not oriented to the students but instead either to the professionals or the faculty in their field, even though the primary audience was undergraduates. Although the information they presented had the potential to be interesting to the students, because it was presented at an inappropriately complicated level, students found the talks boring and frustrating. The talks that were well received by our students almost always were seen as great learning experiences.

As all speakers soon find out, you cannot "wing" a lecture and hope to do well. This is also true of a speech. You must prepare! Always practice your talk and, ideally, deliver it to someone you can trust to give you candid feedback. Do not read your speech, and do not try to memorize what you will say. Instead, use notes, in large type, that can help remind you of the order of your ideas and major points you want to stress. You should tell stories and provide plenty of examples. Regardless of the audience's expertise, it is important always to talk to the audience and not to your notes, to your slides, or to the floor. Work at making eye contact with individuals in the audience. Talk to the audience members in the back of the room to make sure you can be heard. If you want to be heard, you must enunciate your words clearly, speak with enough volume, and speak at a comfortably slow pace. If possible, move around, use gestures, and in general do not be afraid to show your passion for your topic. If you are not well prepared, do not bring attention to this fact and do not apologize. This will make your lack of preparation seem worse. These are all important suggestions for both teachers and public speakers.

Everyone gets nervous when getting ready to deliver a speech, whether a veteran or a novice. Nervousness is unavoidable, and so it is best to accept it and not fight it. There are a few pointers to manage your nervousness. Develop a warm-up routine. A brisk walk, a splash of water to the face, or talking out loud in a private space so that you don't alarm anyone can warm you up. Of course, the more you have practiced your speech, the more manageable your nervousness is likely to be. One interesting suggestion is to audiotape your presentation and listen to it a number of times before you give it (Hoff, 1992). Listening to the audio recording a number of times will help your memory and confidence. You also can check the timing of the presentation with the audio recording.

Just as important as speakers knowing their audience, they must also know themselves. Whether you are an introvert or an extrovert can affect how you choose to develop a talk. Think about your personal strengths and areas that may not be as strong. Speakers should always strive to be interesting, but this can be achieved in many ways. One way is to be personable, which means you convey to the audience that you are aware of and care about their thoughts and feelings. Before the start of your talk, you can also informally speak with audience members who are present. This behavior shows you are personable and may help both you and them feel more at ease. Humor is another great way to facilitate interest, but humor must be treated carefully. My daughters, in a way only your own offspring can do, have candidly informed me that I can't tell a joke. With this self-knowledge, I choose humor for a talk very carefully and try to get ample feedback from friends (*not* my daughters) before I use humor in a talk.

For most presentations, the audience is given the opportunity to ask questions, either during or, most often, following your presentation. Dealing with questions is always important and can even be the most important aspect of a presentation such as a job talk (see Chapter 23). Remember that the questions you receive are an indication of the audience's interest in your talk. Listen carefully to the question asked. If you do not understand the question, ask for clarification. You may want to repeat the question to make sure you have understood it correctly. If you do not know the answer, then say so. Try to anticipate questions that are likely and have responses prepared ahead of time. Many times questions are really suggestions, and if you can recognize this, then acknowledge the suggestion and promise to act on it if you can. Remember not to respond defensively, as this will alienate not only the questioner but the entire audience.

Physical Tools

When preparing a public presentation, you should carefully consider the physical tools you will use. Will you be using visual aids, such as a computer with PowerPoint, slide projector, overhead projector, flip charts, or other props; or will you give what has been referred to as a "naked talk" (Young, 2009)? Although visuals, when used properly, can add interest and order to a presentation, they can also be used so poorly as to wreck the entire talk. A good rule of thumb is that if all you have is text to present, visual aids should *not* be used.

Using a computer to project PowerPoint slides is the default method of presentation in academics, as it has been for years in business. Many professional academic conferences are informing presenters that laptops and projection systems are routinely provided, but overhead projectors are not available. At a recent teaching conference, a prominent speaker commented at the beginning of her talk that she was using PowerPoint because "everyone at my school does." PowerPoint has become the Velveeta cheese of presentation methods. I borrow this clever analogy from Ludy Benjamin (2002). Benjamin noted that most consumer surveys identify various types of gourmet cheese as the most favorite type of cheese. Rarely is Velveeta cheese mentioned as a favorite, but it is by far the best selling cheese. Benjamin applied this analogy to teaching using the lecture method. Although the lecture method may be criticized, it is by far the most often used method in college teaching. I think it also applies concerning the use of PowerPoint for presentations. Although there is ample criticism of the use of PowerPoint for teaching and other types of presentations, PowerPoint is probably the most popular type of presentation method.

PowerPoint can be used to "teach" by facilitating interest and order. The key to PowerPoint is in the effective use of graphics, not text. A series of bulleted text slides is sure to "dull down" your talk and lead to the awful "death by PowerPoint." Instead, use text sparingly, never using full sentences but only important words or short phrases. Normally use at least 24-point text. If you do not have room on a slide, first consider cutting some text and then, if necessary, add another slide. Always use a consistent style, including fonts, bullets, and background. Rarely will "clip art" from a presentation package serve to improve a presentation. Instead, use graphics to organize and explain rather than just to represent or decorate (Leavitt, n.d.). Graphics that are specific and relevant to the points you are trying to make should help you communicate your important ideas.

Even with the most compelling graphic material, your commentary should be the focus of the presentation. You should not let PowerPoint overshadow you as the presenter. You can help the audience select the relevant information, organize it, and integrate it into your overall goals of the talk. Tying an attention-grabbing graphic with a personal and relevant story is an excellent way to interest and involve your audience. Graphics are a great way to "teach" your audience. Using simple "builds" with complex graphics can allow you to control what the audience is attending to and allow you to guide and interpret a more complex image. For example, you may want to show only one portion of a graphic and explain what it represents. Then arrange for additional portions to appear and talk about each as they appear. Be very careful about using distracting animation. Having an image sweep in from the top with an audible "swish" can be distracting and irritating. Simple "appear" and "disappear" is usually more effective.

Only use technology that you are comfortable with and that you have practiced using. Most graduate students have used PowerPoint; however, there are always new tips or tricks that improve your use of this powerful program (see Daniel, 2011, for more excellent tips for using PowerPoint). Laser pointers are very simple to use, but they should only be used when needed to point out information on a slide. Video clips can be very engaging when used appropriately. However, using video is fraught with possible technical difficulties, and you should be well practiced with this technique before you use it (see Cleveland, 2011, for more hints on the use of video). As with any new technology, make sure any video clip has a subsidiary role to your oral presentation and that you are well versed in using it.

One modern truism is that if you use technology, it will eventually break down at the most inopportune time. There is no way to completely avoid this, but you can prepare. Try to have a backup plan or plans. Bring spare parts to any equipment you will use, such as extra bulbs for a projector or an additional laser pointer. If at all possible, practice with the equipment you will actually use. Keep in mind too that not all computers are compatible. If you prepare a PowerPoint talk on a Mac, be sure it formats properly on a PC if the presentation system uses a PC. Be prepared to give a "naked" talk. But above all, try not to show your panic when something goes wrong. Although some people will notice if your laptop freezes in a presentation, most will not notice as long as you can calmly restart it while you continue to elaborate on an issue or ask a question. Showing panic will alert everyone to your feelings and distract them from your talk.

Should you use handouts for a talk? There are arguments for and against this practice. Although handouts do allow you to provide the audience with information they can refer to later, they can detract from your talk by distracting the audience from what you are saying. A good compromise is to distribute handouts after you have delivered your talk or offer to send an electronic copy of your PowerPoint to those who are interested. This way, your audience can take away information but not be distracted from your talk.

So far I have discussed pointers for any type of presentation. There are two specific types of presentations you are very likely to encounter: the research talk and a poster presentation. I now turn to these presentation tasks.

The Research Talk

One of the most common types of presentations you will give is a scientific talk, which is usually a description of a research study, or a review of many studies. This type of talk is often required at a professional conference, as part of the interview process for a job, or as a guest lecture. Scientific talks have a reputation of being boring because they are too complicated, contain too much information, or are presented at an information level much beyond the audience. Giving a clear, concise, and interesting scientific talk can greatly enhance your image as a scientist.

One key to developing a good scientific talk is to structure the talk in a way that is easy to follow and slowly guides the audience logically through your story of the research process. To introduce the topic, you should start out with rather broad statements that most people, whether they are familiar with your topic or not, can relate to. An anecdote or very brief illustration that introduces your subject matter in a way that others can easily understand can gradually draw your audience into the research story you will tell. Then provide your listeners with just enough information for them to understand your main question, which may be in the form of a hypothesis or thesis statement. This is not the place to impress your audience with your extensive knowledge about the topic. Just provide the audience with the necessary information to understand why your main question is relevant. Audiences do not have the luxury of going back over ideas they may have missed or slowing down to consider a new idea like they would if they were reading the talk. You do not want to put them under too much cognitive load or they may become confused and discouraged, in which case they may become bored and disinterested. For this first section of the talk, start out broad and then narrow the topic using relevant information to lead to your specific main question or hypothesis.

Your audience now should be interested in how you approached answering your main question. Now you present your methodology. Here it is very important to provide enough information for the audience to understand your method, but not so much that they become overwhelmed. Keep in mind what the overall purpose of the method is and focus on communicating that purpose. If you are successful in presenting the method clearly, it is much easier to explain your findings. When you present your data, make an explicit effort to relate each finding to a hypothesis. Your data should lead directly to the main point of your talk. What do you want the audience to remember about your research? What findings have you contributed to this topic's research literature? This is your take-home message.

It is usually best to rely on graphical presentations for presenting data. A useful graph can be the most important part of a successful research presentation. For a graphic to add to the presentation, it must be carefully created and effectively presented. In my teaching experience, I have found that students will spend a significant amount of time carefully constructing a beautiful graph and then nervously flash it quickly to the audience with little explanation. They will often immediately read the means of the groups pictured and move to the next slide. The audience is not sure what the graph meant and will have a hard time understanding the most important part of the research. I have to impress upon my students the importance of slowing down, explaining the structure of the graph before relating the values, and allowing the audience time to digest the meaning of the data. Once you have commented on the structure of the graph and related the main values, you can then provide a "spin" to remind the audience how this finding relates to your main question. It is better to present just the most important data with time to understand it than to present more peripheral data too quickly. Of course, if you have more time than the typical 15-minute research presentation, you may be able to go into more detail. Such would be the case in a job talk with a 50-minute format. The method and results sections of your talk have to be very specific and oriented to your main question so the audience can follow your story. Once this is accomplished, you are now ready to drive home your main take-home message. You can then relate your findings back to the information you reviewed in the introduction. Again, only discuss the information that is directly related to your main question. End the talk with future plans for research and prospects for further developments in the areas you have covered. This is often the most neglected part of a research talk. Try to end strong and give the audience some idea of how this research is likely to proceed in the future.

Often the most anxiety-producing portion of a research talk is the question-and-answer period that follows. This is a time of uncertainty for which the speaker cannot plan ahead, and it is difficult to practice for this part of the talk, but some simple suggestions can help you prepare. It is important to keep to the point. Some audience questions will be off topic, and sometimes your answers may drift from the talk topic. It is best to stay on task and remind the audience of the focus of the talk and offer to talk at a later time to the person asking the off-topic question. It is also very important to listen carefully to the question. When you are nervous, it is easy to miss the meaning of a question. It is helpful to repeat the question to make sure everyone heard it and to allow the person asking it to correct you if you misunderstood. Try to keep your answers brief and avoid being perceived as defensive. It is certainly better to say "I don't know" than it is to be perceived as trying to fake an answer. Sometimes a question is actually not a question at all, but a suggestion or position the questioner wants to advocate. It is best to acknowledge the comment and move on to the next question. Keep in mind that the job talk is a higher-stakes presentation. For example, at a job talk, which will be longer, you should probably treat every question with respect even if it is off topic—the questioner may be on the search committee! I refer you to Chapter 23 in this book for a more detailed discussion of the job talk.

Poster Presentations

A poster presentation is a popular way to present research at conferences. It is also a great way to meet face to face with your audience and discuss your research in a more personal manner. There are two main aspects to a poster presentation: the actual physical poster and the presenter. Keep this in mind when creating the poster. The poster itself is not meant to stand alone; the presenter should have a major role. Create the poster to grab attention and to focus the reader on the most important aspects of the research. Remember that poster sessions usually contain a large group of posters on similar topics, and only the ones that quickly and easily attract attention (while staying professional) will be read. For this reason, I suggest that you not use extensive text, especially pages or even paragraphs of text. In fact, some of the most effective posters do not use any sentences at all. Often only key words or phrases convey enough information for a reader to follow the general outlines of your research. Of course, you are also there to answer questions or to add information the reader might not understand.

Your poster should also feature graphics of your findings. The most important information from your research should be illustrated graphically in the middle of your poster. Just as marketers put the best-selling items at eye level in a grocery store, your main take-home message should be displayed prominently on your poster. Only include an abstract if it is required by the conference, and do not include a reference list. Generally, a conference will provide specific suggestions for the poster layout, such as at least 24-point font and three or four columns that go from top to bottom and left to right. Try to give your poster a pleasing overall symmetrical balance for the layout and make sure the title is big enough to be read from several feet away.

You must also carefully consider how you will print and transport the actual poster. There was a time when you could print out a number of 8 1/2 by 11-inch sheets of paper and paste them on cardboard for your poster. With the availability of computer software to produce professional-looking posters, using this paper method is not advisable. Although you can use professional graphic software such as Adobe Photoshop, these programs are often not readily available and are costly. PowerPoint has become a very popular means of creating posters because of its availability, low cost, and ease of use. There are a number of both commercial and noncommercial websites (you can just search for "PowerPoint poster template" on the Web) where you can download a PowerPoint poster template, copy and paste your content into a template, and then further customize the design.

Most of the commercial sites offer a service through which you can upload your PowerPoint poster file, and they will print it for a reasonable price and mail it back to you. This may be necessary if you do not have a poster printer (36 inches at least) available. Most popular poster sizes are 36 by 48 inches. These are best transported in a cardboard tube that can be found at most office supply stores. I also suggest carrying the poster if you are flying to a conference to make sure the poster arrives with you unharmed. Another alternative is to have the PowerPoint files printed by a commercial printer. If you are familiar with your destination city and have enough time, you can take your file on a flash drive and have it printed in the destination city. For many, this alternative should only be used as a backup method should something happen to the poster you are carrying.

The author of the poster should remain with the poster during the entire poster session. Well before your session, try to visit the room where your poster will be presented. Although most conferences will provide you with pushpins to mount your poster, it is best to bring some pushpins along and perhaps some tape to mend any unforeseen accidents. Do not read the poster to the viewer. Prepare a quick, one- or two-sentence overview of your poster and be sure to point to the take-home message on the slide. You should be appropriately dressed and attentive to the audience that passes by your poster. A friendly manner can attract people to your poster as much as attractive graphics. The poster session is set up to allow you to interact with persons who are interested in your research. Avoid spending too much time in an exclusive conversation with any one person. However, this is a great place to network with fellow researchers, potential collaborators, and even future employers. You can put contact information on the poster, but even better is to bring business cards to make available. A handout, such as an abstract or one-page copy of your poster, is good to have available. A one-page image of your poster is easy to print using PowerPoint. Be sure to include contact information on your handouts.

Summary

Public presentations are great opportunities for psychological professionals to showcase their teaching and research knowledge. Although most of us are not naturally gifted at speaking, it is a skill that can be developed. Treating your talk as a teaching situation will help you make a meaningful connection with your audience. Making an effort to know your audience and your own strengths and weaknesses can help you prepare an effective talk. Public presentations require preparation if you want to increase the chance it will be successful. There is no substitute for practice, and frank feedback is invaluable. Prepare and practice with the physical tools you will be using, whether you use cutting-edge technology or just handouts and a lectern. Use technology that is appropriate for your content and comfortable for you to use. Remember that although only a few of us can be fantastic speakers, almost anyone can deliver an organized and interesting talk with adequate preparation and practice.

References

Benjamin, L. T. Jr. (2002). Lecturing. In S. F. Davis & W. Buskist (Eds.), *The teaching of psychology: Essays in honor of Wilbert J. McKeachie and Charles L. Brewer* (pp. 57–67). Mahwah, NJ: Lawrence Erlbaum.

Cleveland, M. (2011). A practical guide to using YouTube in the classroom. In D. S. Dunn, J. H. Wilson, J. Freeman, & J. R. Stowell (Eds.), *Best practices for technology-enhanced teaching and learning connecting to psychology and the social sciences* (pp. 197–206). New York: Oxford University Press.

Daniel D. B. (2011). A practical guide to using YouTube in the classroom. In D. S. Dunn, J. H. Wilson, J. Freeman, & J. R. Stowell (Eds.), *Best practices for technology-enhanced teaching and learning connecting to psychology and the social sciences* (pp. 87–104). New York: Oxford University Press.

Garmston, R. J., & Wellman, B. M. (1992). *How to make presentations that teach and transform*. Alexandria, VA: Association for Supervision and Curriculum Development.

Hoff, R. (1992). *"I can see you naked."* Kansas City, MO: Andrews and McMeel.

Leavitt, M. (n.d.). *Learning from visuals: How well-designed and well-used visuals can help students learn, An academic review*. Wiley Faculty Network. Retrieved October 21, 2010, from http://wfn.wiley.com/pg/file/wfn1/read/82368/learning-from-visuals-whitepaper.

Walker, T. J. (2010). *How to give a pretty good presentation: A speaking survival guide for the rest of us*. Hoboken, NJ: John Wiley and Sons.

Young, J. R. (2009, July 20). When computers leave classrooms, so does boredom. *Chronicle of Higher Education*. Retrieved from http://chronicle.com.

Suggestions for Further Exploration

Berk, R. A. (2003). *Professors are from Mars, students are from Snickers: How to write humor in the classroom and in professional presentations*. Sterling, VA: Stylus. This funny book from a funny teacher and scholar has a chapter on including humor in your professional presentations as well as your classroom.

Garmston, R. J., & Wellman, B. M. (1992). *How to make presentations that teach and transform*. Alexandria, VA: Association for Supervision and Curriculum Development. This guide takes a definite teaching angle to public presentations and provides some great advice.

Hoff, R. (1992). *"I can see you naked."* Kansas City, MO: Andrews and McMeel. This is one of the best books on making presentations and is fun to read.

Kosslyn, S. M. (2007). *Clear and to the point: 8 psychological principles for compelling PowerPoint presentations*. New York: Oxford University Press. This book is one of the best for developing an understanding of psychological principles for developing useful graphical presentations. A very helpful handbook, especially for using PowerPoint.

Leavitt, M. (n.d.). *Learning from visuals: How well-designed and well-used visuals can help students learn, An academic review.* Wiley Faculty Network. Retrieved October 21, 2010, from   http://wfn.wiley.com/pg/file/wfn1/read/82368/learning-from-visuals-whitepaper. This white paper from a teacher at Arizona State University has many great ideas about how graphics can be used to teach.

Morgan, S., & Whitener, B. (2006). *Speaking about science: A manual for creating clear presentations.* New York: Cambridge University Press. This is one of the few manuals for presentations that is specifically oriented to scientific presentations. This is a very thorough and insightful guide.

Nicalo, A. A. M., & Pexman, P. M. (2003). *Displaying your findings: A practical guide for creating figures, posters, and presentations.* Washington, DC: American Psychological Association. This informative book has a chapter on poster presentations and a chapter on slides and overheads for research presentations.

Walker, T. J. (2010). *How to give a pretty good presentation: A speaking survival guide for the rest of us.* Hoboken, NJ: John Wiley and Sons. This is a guidebook for all types of professionals. I like it because it has many simple and practical hints on how to efficiently prepare and deliver a talk.

16

Success in Externships and Internships

Erica Chin
New York-Presbyterian Hospital-Morgan
Stanley Children's Hospital of New York;
Columbia University Medical Center

Laurie Reider Lewis
Columbia University Medical Center

Of the many moments in the lengthy journey through a psychology doctoral program, few moments are as dramatic as the one in which you discover if and where you have matched for internship. For the psychologist-to-be, the year-long predoctoral internship, which is exclusively devoted to engaging in supervised clinical work and is a requirement, along with dissertation, to earn your doctorate, represents a culmination of multiple years of coursework, practica, and research. It is the capstone of a graduate career in psychology.

In many respects, the internship application and match process can be as exhilarating, thought provoking, and intense as the process of applying to college or graduate school. While you are moving through this process, it will surely be the talk of the lunch table among your friends, the dinner table with your family at home, and the thoughts that spin around your head as you walk through the day. Many psychology students are concerned about the increased competition to secure an internship placement. According to the Association of Psychology Pre-doctoral and Internship Center (APPIC), in 2009, approximately 24% of psychology students who participated in the match process were not placed, the highest nonmatch number to date. However, this also means that 76% of students do achieve a match, and this chapter aims to assist you in successfully navigating this process.

Nevertheless, the predoctoral internship is actually one of the final steps of your journey through graduate school. Arriving at that point is the result of hard work, thoughtful reflection, and strategic planning. Your internship application will contain rich information about you: your educational background, your research interests, your work and personal history. It will also summarize the quantity and quality of your years spent thus far in applied settings conducting supervised clinical work as a doctoral student in psychology. These experiences, gained through your externships, will speak volumes about who you are as a candidate, what your interests and competencies are, and how prepared you are to embark on the next stage of formal clinical training.

You will eventually tire of explaining the different meanings of the terms *internships*, *externships*, and *practica* to your friends and family, but as a psychologist-in-training, your understanding of these terms is essential to building a solid training foundation. Both externships and internships provide hands-on experiences for the development of skills required as a psychologist. Externships and other applied work experiences, often referred to as practica, occur on a part-time basis in conjunction with other requirements, such as coursework and research during graduate school. In contrast, an internship is, in essence, a full-time job. Furthermore, an internship is usually a salaried position that is accompanied by greater demands for independence, initiative, and clinical decision-making, as well as participation in additional training activities such as research and didactics. Externships and the internship work together to provide you with a practical and theoretical knowledge base as well as a web of professional connections that will influence your career as a psychologist for years beyond graduate school.

The purpose of this chapter is to speak about the practical and logistical aspects, or the "nuts and bolts," of externships and internships. More importantly, this chapter encourages you to construct these experiences through a careful assessment of who you are and what you wish to achieve from your practical training experiences in graduate school. In so doing, may you enjoy the journey of your graduate career in psychology as well as the destination.

Getting Started: The Self-Evaluation Process

Just as you begin a road trip with a map of a route that reflects the purpose of your adventure as well as your personal traveling style, your journey through graduate school will be richer and more productive if you first evaluate who you are and what you want out of the experience. Although variables such as individual and career goals and areas of interest may evolve over the course of your personal and professional development, you can only make current decisions based on what you know of yourself and of your situation in the present moment and what you think you may want for the future. Furthermore, self-evaluation, in and of itself, is a core skill of competence as a psychologist to be nurtured and practiced over the course of your graduate training and beyond.

Thus, before embarking on the process of selecting clinical training sites, consider the following questions: (a) What are my professional goals? (b) What type of clinical work am I genuinely interested in? (c) What skills do I wish to develop through my graduate training experiences? (d) How will any hands-on experiences complement and supplement my coursework? And, (e) What are my strengths and weaknesses as I currently understand them?

Let's explore these questions in greater depth:

What are my professional goals?

By asking yourself this, you can help yourself to clarify other critical, guiding aspects of your personal and professional identity such as:

(a) What values do you endeavor to bring to your work as a psychologist? (b) What do you hope to contribute to the field and practice of psychology? (c) What lessons do you wish to learn through your work? And, (d) Where do you see yourself in 5, 10, and 15+ years?

In other words: What do you want to do and what will it take to get there? Moreover, how will what you do as a psychologist mirror who you wish to be? These questions highlight the importance of alignment between self and profession.

Ideally, clear personal and professional goals that are *specific, attainable, and measurable* will corroborate your answers to these questions as well as ultimately enable you to communicate to others what your training needs are. This, in turn, will facilitate a thoughtful, purposeful process of selecting rewarding clinical training experiences. Alternatively stated, the better you can answer the question "Who am I?" the easier it will be to answer the question "Where should I go?"

A current fourth-year student in a clinical Ph.D. program summed up these ideas when she explained how she has carefully selected her externships, research projects, and dissertation based on her long-term goal of becoming a psychologist who specializes in the treatment and research of posttraumatic stress disorder. This personal and professional mission was fueled by a family member's impairing experience with the condition.

What type of clinical work am I genuinely interested in?

This question is closely tied to the former about professional goals, and as with many questions, this one generates areas for further inquiry. For example, you may now ask yourself: (a) What population(s) am I interested in working with (e.g., children, adolescents, adults)? (b) Are there any specialized areas of clinical work that especially appeal to me (e.g., consultation liaison, neuropsychological assessment, forensics, geropsychology)? And, (c) In what type of environment would I like to work (e.g., an urban training hospital, college counseling center, community mental health center, veterans' administration medical center, corrections-related facility, private practice, school-based clinic)?

These can be very difficult questions to answer given that many psychology doctoral students are capable of succeeding in a wide range of contexts. By choosing to pursue one avenue of psychology or setting versus another, there is a natural emotional process involved in letting something go. This is one of the wisdoms of career choice—in the pursuit of one thing, you may have to give up another.

If you have defined specific populations of interest and/or a specialty area that complements your larger personal and professional goals, outline the steps necessary to achieve competency in those areas. A current intern in a child-clinical program always knew he wanted to treat youth and families. Throughout graduate school, he sought out training opportunities that fit with this greater goal. For example, he gained experience conducting therapy with young and school-aged children, adolescents, and families in community mental health settings as well as hospitals and schools. He also ensured that he rotated through at least one external-izing and internalizing disorder clinic given that these are the disorders considered to be the bread and butter of clinical child practice, while also gaining expertise in cognitive-behavioral interventions. In addition, he balanced his psychotherapy experiences with training in psycho-educational, psychological, and neuropsycho-logical assessment in order to understand how learning, communication and lan-guage, and neuropsychological disorders affect the emotional and cognitive development of children. This example illustrates the notion that there are benefits to steering yourself toward a committed specialization versus being a jack of all trades as noted in Chapter 13 (Developing Your Clinical and Counseling Skills).

For some, as is the case with this student, it is easier to define professional goals and a focus for training experiences. For others, it may not be. For those for whom this is the case, engaging in a formal self-evaluation process, perhaps with the assis-tance of a supervisor, graduate advisor, or mentor, can be helpful. But the remarks of one faculty member in a clinical psychology department who trains between six and eight students yearly in a university-based outpatient clinic are important to bear in mind as well: "I have seen enough students achieve career goals through so many multiple pathways that I'm convinced there is no one 'right way' to choose training experiences . . . there's no single or small set of requirements to succeed."

What skills do I wish to develop through my graduate training experiences?

As you make an effort to incorporate your interests into applying for training sites, remain mindful of developing a varied set of core clinical skills or competencies. These competencies will ultimately be your tools of the trade in the field and practice of psychology and will be one of the defining features of your identity as a psychologist.

So, what competencies do you wish to develop? Diagnostic interviewing? Neuropsychological assessment? Clinical research? Expertise in a specific therapeutic modality? Given the multifaceted roles and responsibilities of psychologists, it is likely that your answer will touch upon various skill sets and areas of competence. Furthermore, take note of how the competencies that you wish to foster are likely to be closely tied to your personal and professional goals and interests.

Some helpful suggestions about which aspects of clinical expertise to focus on are also borne out in the literature on this topic area, which further illustrates how the interaction between professional goals, interests, and the development of competen-cies can guide your decision-making process. When Kaslow, Pate, and Thorn (2005) surveyed practicum site coordinators, academic training directors, and internship directors with regard to the types of experiences deemed most valuable as part of the preinternship practicum experience, competencies in psychological assessment in addition to psychotherapy were highly valued. With the exception of school psy-chology academic training directors, who rated psycho-educational testing of pri-mary importance followed by cognitive and objective personality assessment, the top three assessment experiences ranked were diagnostic, cognitive, and objective personality. At the time of this survey, neuropsychology, projective personality, and health psychology assessment experiences were considered less critical. Nevertheless, if your interests lie in working in a medical or consultation setting, developing skill sets in these assessment areas may be more of a priority for you.

In regard to types of clinical interventions, seven different service modalities were also ranked for importance during practicum training—individual, family, couples, groups, schools, community, and organizational intervention (Kaslow et al., 2005). Individual-level intervention was rated most highly, followed by family-level intervention for medical school sites and community mental health center training directors. The ratings of university counseling centers and VA medical centers differed somewhat in that group interventions were ranked second to individual interventions, which makes sense given the needs of the clients served by that setting.

Ratings for experience with various theoretical orientations were examined as well. Competencies in conducting cognitive-behavioral, cognitive, and behavioral therapies were rated more highly than other orientations, while skills in delivering existential/humanistic and psychodynamic therapies were judged less important. It should be noted that anecdotal evidence may differ on this topic depending on your geographical region; for instance, the New York City Metro area has a number of training sites that remain primarily psychodynamic in orientation.

Be sure to check out the APA Assessment of Competency Benchmarks website (go to http://www.psychtrainingcouncils.org/documents.html and click on the Assessment of Competency Benchmarks link) as you track the development of your core competencies.

How will any hands-on experiences complement and supplement my coursework?

Your coursework is another important foundation of your graduate training experience. However, it is through your applied experience, gained through clinical and/or research externships, that you bridge the theoretical knowledge gathered throughout your course of study about areas relevant to the practice and research of psychology to the actual work of psychology itself. In turn, the knowledge obtained through your externships informs your formal studies, allowing you to consolidate what you are learning, thinking about, and doing at all levels. Through this integration of reflection and action, your identity as a psychologist will begin to emerge.

Thus, it will serve you well to consider how your externships fit with your formal coursework, particularly as you advance in your graduate studies and are likely to have greater flexibility with respect to both the classes and training experiences that you select. When this aspect is considered along with your short- and long-term personal and professional goals, interests, and desired skill set or competency areas, you will be guided by an even clearer rationale for externship selection.

An early-career psychologist described the basis through which he chose externships by discussing how his professional goals and interests lay in the field of forensics. While his formal coursework provided him with theoretical and practical foundations, it was general and broad. If he wanted to position himself strongly for a forensic internship, he needed to be very strategic about selecting externships and research opportunities relevant to the field of forensic psychology so as to demonstrate committed interests in the area and to develop skills accordingly.

What are my strengths and weaknesses and how do I understand them at the current time?

Given the various choices that you are required to make over the course of your graduate and professional career, the quest to "know thyself" as a psychology graduate student assumes different forms, a journey that will hopefully continue even after you earn your degree and one that results in a constant process of self-evaluation. A clear understanding of your strengths and weaknesses—and whether or not they are able to be either capitalized upon and modified or are more constant and a result of enduring temperament and personality traits—is also important when considering practica experiences.

One recent graduate of a doctoral program recalled how her early clinical experiences revealed her strength in building rapport with patients but highlighted weaknesses in diagnostic interviewing and disposition planning. Consequently, she procured an externship in a psychiatric emergency room, where she could learn, develop, and hone skills under close clinical supervision essential to her identified areas of weakness while also capitalizing on her strength of connecting to patients in acute crisis. Another graduate noted how his introverted nature led him to feel more comfortable and effective working in individual rather than group modalities. While he sought experiences conducting group therapy that challenged him beyond his comfort zone, he ultimately did not feel as effective or gratified in his work. He also found that involvement in clinical research and writing activities, through which he excelled, closely matched his temperamental style and work preferences, while also allowing him to engage in meaningful endeavors that coincided with his overarching professional goals and interests.

In sum, self-evaluation is an ongoing process that informs your formation as a psychologist. Keep in mind that you can always edit and redefine your goals, interests, skills, strengths, and weaknesses as you progress through your program and gain new experiences.

Identifying Mentors and Quality Supervision

You are not alone in the process of self-evaluation and professional development. As the spouse of one psychology graduate student joked, "It takes a village to raise a psychologist." Peers, graduate advisors, clinical department chairs, professors, mentors, and clinical supervisors represent an extensive social network from which you can draw in order to gain personal and professional support, practical guidance, sound advice, instruction, constructive feedback, and valuable insight about navigating the world of externships and internships, and about your professional development as a whole. You are not trained as a psychologist in the abstract, you are trained by people, and like other art forms, the practice of psychology is enhanced by solid and constructive apprenticeship. The importance of quality supervision cannot be stressed enough in clinical and counseling training. Additional comments on quality supervision may be found in Chapter 13.

One current postdoc remarked, "The mentors that I learned the most from listened well, took a genuine interest in my overall development as a psychologist, and helped me to find my own style and approach rather than supervising in a more removed, academic manner. I also liked when supervisors were specific and practical in questions and recommendations, and it helped when I was prepared with specific questions and scenarios." When it came to dealing with negative supervision experiences, this same psychologist noted that she "had to seek supervision elsewhere from peers and other mentors" if addressing concerns directly with her supervisor remained unproductive. Ultimately, do not hesitate to advocate for what you need from supervision, but also be willing to participate actively in your own learning process. As one externship supervisor explained, "I really get frustrated when students come to supervision and haven't even thought about their cases—they show up just hoping the supervisor will give them the answers."

On a practical level, the professional relationships that you make in graduate school can also facilitate postdoctoral job opportunities, so do not hesitate to network and to seek out those who can benefit your growth in ways that complement who you are and wish to be. Doing so also demonstrates that you are open to feedback. One training director of a hospital-based internship emphasized this point by commenting how trainees "must be open to learning and have the mindset that being a psychologist is an experience of lifelong learning—you can always benefit from someone else's experience and knowledge to expand your own perspective."

Stages of Training

Prior to Internship

When looking ahead to the entirety of graduate school, it feels as though it will take forever to finish and that there is all the time in the world to partake in various training experiences. In reality, multiple graduate program requirements and personal responsibilities render time more limited. You will have approximately three to four externship opportunities and 1 year of internship; your externships will be the primary base by which your clinical experiences will be measured for internship. It follows, then, that these clinical training experiences as a whole will further influence future postdoctoral opportunities and choices. Therefore, it is important to have a sense of urgency early in your training about the experiences that you select so you do not have a sense of emergency later in your graduate career for not having taken advantage of available opportunities.

A number of variables influence externship selection. First, there is some variability in the opportunities available to different graduate students. The clinical externship process is partly dictated by the specific graduate program and discipline that you belong to. For example, school psychology programs may require that their students spend at least 1 year of fieldwork experience at a predetermined school district. Likewise, some clinical and/or counseling psychology programs may have an in-house university-based clinic or counseling center by which practica are assigned in the second or third year of graduate training. Alternatively, there are programs that encourage students to apply to outside agencies such as community mental health centers, college counseling centers, inpatient facilities, residential programs, and private practices for externship credit. Consult your program's training director and/or department chair as well as peers and supervisors for guidance on the practical aspects of applying for externship such as how many externships are required, how to locate sites, and how to apply.

Second, geography may play a role in what externships you choose and/or have access to. For example, it may be easier to apply to a range of sites if you are close to a major metropolitan area with a host of hospitals, community mental health clinics, and schools to choose from. Third, other factors such as resources available to commute to sites, competing roles and responsibilities, and affiliations or fixed obligations as in the case of funded positions, for example, may come into play. Fourth, there is always the goodness of fit between you and the site to consider in addition to other goals. As one former doctoral student put it, "My goal for training was to learn as much as possible so that I could be an effective therapist with my clients . . . there are so many ways to do that . . . good training is one that equips you with a lot of tools, based on good research and proven technique, but also encourages you to find your own voice and to think about the individual client, beyond the technique and methodology so that you are genuine and real with your clients and they feel understood." She adds, ". . . a training program can be really strong on providing tools for practicing, but it should also convey an attitude and approach towards the work we do that reflects an individualized, sensitive approach."

If you are unsure of a specific population or area of interest, apply to generalist sites for externship that will provide you with rotations in different areas of clinical practice such as in inpatient and outpatient settings and with different populations. If you do find yourself undecided about a specialty, securing high-quality generalist practica early in your training allows you to focus on developing core competencies before dabbling in as many specialties as possible. This helps you to avoid the pitfalls of having a scattered and random listing of subspecialty experiences to the detriment of developing a cohesive set of competencies and of appearing unfocused and uncommitted to your training. Again, there is no single path to success and no magic formula for later acquiring the internship of your choice. One training director states, "I like trainees who have sought out varied experiences during grad school in terms of settings in which they have externed and theoretical orientations to which they have been exposed and received training." She also recommends that students gain exposure to evidence-based treatment approaches.

If you anticipate that you will apply to a general psychology internship, it is wise to seek out at least one inpatient site as well as an outpatient short- and long-term therapy setting for your earlier externship training experiences. Inpatient settings provide a key opportunity to evaluate the acute presentation of a patient's illness, conduct a detailed initial intake interview, assess the course of illness, make a DSM-IV clinical diagnosis, and formulate a disposition. When applying to outpatient settings, look for exposure to both brief and extended individual psychotherapy experiences, family therapy, and group therapy. Lastly, as an applicant for psychology internship, aim to have at least 10 integrated assessment reports completed during your externship training years. Note that an integrated report generally includes a history, an interview, and at least two tests from one or more of the following categories: intellectual, cognitive, personality, and/or neuropsychological assessment.

Finally, in anticipation of eventually having to report your training hours in your internship application, track every client hour you spend according to intervention type (e.g., individual, group, and family therapy; assessment), demographic type (e.g., age, race, sex, sexual orientation, ethnicity), and setting (e.g., community mental health outpatient, inpatient, residential, college counseling), while always keeping your curriculum vitae (CV) up to date. The importance of doing this as you proceed through graduate school cannot be overstated; while it may seem like administrative trivia, "tracking as you go" will save you a tremendous amount of time, effort, confusion, and anxiety when you are chin-deep in the taxing process of completing your internship applications.

Internship

As previously stated, for the majority of trainees, the predoctoral internship represents the pinnacle of many years of coursework and externships, heralding an intensive period of consolidating what has been learned thus far and marking the opportunity to refine clinical skills. It also signals the completion of one of the final requirements for earning a doctoral degree, hence opening the door to a life beyond graduate school. That being said, merely securing an internship is not enough, as the quality of your internship experience is of great importance (Oehlert, Sumerall, Lopez, & Merkley, 2002).

The process of preparing and applying for internship is a task to be taken seriously. As noted at the beginning of the chapter, there are concerns about increased competition to secure an internship placement. These concerns are rooted in statistics (Keilin, Baker, McCutcheon, & Peranson, 2007) that show that between 1999 and 2007, the number of internship applicants increased by 18%, whereas the number of positions offered increased by 9.6%. And, again, there are statistics that show that about a quarter of the 3,958 psychology students who participated in the match process were not placed in 2009 (APPIC).

If these statistics are daunting, do not despair! You can optimize your chances of matching successfully by committing yourself to ongoing thoughtful self-evaluation, strengthening core clinical competencies through the selection of relevant training opportunities, earning glowing recommendations from your supervisors and graduate faculty, and presenting yourself well during interviews. The internship match process is aptly named since it culminates in a match or best fit between your own and your training site's goals. Rodolfa and colleagues (1999) demonstrated this by examining inclusion and exclusion criteria in intern applicant selection and found that the fit between applicant goals and site opportunities was the primary inclusion variable. On the other hand, exclusion variables included a poor fit between goals and site opportunities, lack of APA accreditation of the applicant's program, incomplete doctoral course work, and incomplete comprehensive exams. Lopez, Oehlert, and Moberly (1996) surveyed 115 directors of APA-accredited internships regarding their selection criteria and found that clinical experience, letters of recommendation, and interview outcome were the top three. So, again, make the most of your clinical training by planning for the best possible match between your professional goals and your training sites.

Application Timeline

A common question among psychology students is when is the best time to apply for internship. There are many important personal as well as academic factors that influence this decision such as: (a) Completion of academic prerequisites such as coursework and comprehensive exams per doctoral program requirements; (b) dissertation progress; (c) financial and family issues related to the need to complete graduate school and/or a need or desire to relocate for internship; and (d) the feeling of being ready to apply, defined as having enough experiences to be a competitive candidate and/or being able to articulate the best match between personal goals and training site characteristics.

In regard to dissertation progress, a frequently debated question among prospective applicants is, "How much of my dissertation needs be completed before starting internship?" Perhaps one of the best pieces of advice the authors received during graduate training was that "a good dissertation is a done dissertation." Even though defending a dissertation prior to the start of internship is not always a practical reality for many students, those who have completed dissertation proposals were significantly more likely to obtain internship interviews than those who had not defended proposals (Callahan, Collins, & Klonoff, 2010).

Ultimately, there is no hard and fast rule about when it is ideal to defend your dissertation unless your program prescribes otherwise. However, here are some pros to completing your dissertation prior to the start of or during internship: (a) Having your dissertation completed enables you to focus your time and energy on often demanding internship responsibilities; (b) most jobs and postdoctoral positions ("postdocs") become available near the conclusion of your internship year—having all of your academic and training requirements behind you can make you a more compelling candidate; (c) the sooner you earn your doctorate upon completing internship, the sooner you begin to accrue licensure hours through a job or postdoc; and (d) if you are considering a career in clinical research or academia, a completed, potentially publishable dissertation may be a significant asset as well as a springboard into a specialty area.

As far as the actual match, the timeline is fixed per the Association of Psychology Postdoctoral and Internship Centers (APPIC) guidelines. It occurs once a year and is conducted electronically. Information about internship sites, application procedures, and the match process can be accessed through APPIC's website (www.appic.org). Your doctoral program will also likely provide you with guidance about the process. However, given that many applications for internship are due in early November, it is recommended that you begin the process in the summer prior to when you apply.

Although doctoral programs may differ in their recommendations, and students vary in their personal style in approaching the process, here is a general outline of when and how to proceed:

June/Early Summer: Department Endorsement

The first practical step in preparing for internship is to meet with your program's director of clinical training and/or department chair with the purpose of reviewing your academic progress and confirming that your faculty gives you the green light to apply. At the most basic level, this typically means that you have completed your coursework, comprehensive exams, and, perhaps, successfully proposed your dissertation. Your director of clinical training and/or department chair will need to write a brief letter endorsing your readiness for internship as part of your application, so keep in mind that it is in your best interest to ensure that he/she can speak to your personal strengths and areas for continued development and growth.

June/July: Review Potential Site Materials and Requisites

Next, consult with the APPIC directory of internship sites through www.appic .org. Create an exhaustive list of sites that interest you, noting the contact information for training directors, application due dates, and requested supplemental materials. If you are able to relocate, group potential sites by geographic regions and evaluate the likelihood that you can eventually move or afford to travel (financially and time-wise) far for interviews. Then begin to request materials directly from different sites and review internship websites as well as program brochures so you can better assess each site's training goals and clinical opportunities and how they fit your goals for internship.

Remember, the process is about a match. Ask yourself, "Does the program match my personal and professional goals?" A useful list of personal and professional criteria with which to weigh and evaluate sites may be found in the article "A Decision-Making Technique for Choosing a Psychology Internship" (Stewart & Stewart, 1996). Although different criteria may be weighted more or less by each candidate, salient questions are: (a) Does the site match your professional interests? (b) Does the program offer a specialized rotation in a specialty you would like to have more exposure to? (c) What is the amount and quality of supervision? (d) What is the stipend? (e) What level of health insurance coverage is provided? (f) What is the cost of living in the geographic area? (g) What are your subjective feelings about the site? (h) What is the reputation of the site? And, (i) How many interns are hired by the site or find work elsewhere upon completion of their internship? A formal list like this can also help you to generate and incorporate your own criteria into the selection process.

Another common question that students ask is, "How many sites should I apply to?" The results of a 1999 APPIC survey revealed that while applying to five or more sites increases your odds of matching successfully, applying to 25 or more sites actually decreases your odds of matching. Pincus and Otis (2008) note, though, that these numbers may reflect the possibility that less competitive candidates applied to a greater number of sites. As of the most recent 2009 APPIC survey, the average number of sites applied to is about 15. In addition to your interest in certain sites, when arriving at a number appropriate for you, keep in mind practical matters like your ability to submit quality applications to all sites since the more applications you have to submit, the greater the work required to do so. Also consider the monetary, time, and labor cost involved in attending internship interviews and the need to attend to competing personal and professional responsibilities while engaging in the internship application process.

As you narrow down your list, create a spreadsheet of sites, complete with training director information, addresses, deadlines, and supplemental application requirements (e.g., a sample testing report or case write-up, supplemental essays). A student shared a strategy she used to organize internship-related paperwork: "I had a large binder where I organized each site's brochure, drafts of my essays, testing reports, etc." Another used a file box with separate hanging folders for each site for the same purpose. Ultimately, use what works for you.

June: Update and Review Your CV

The summer is an opportune time to review your CV and to think about information that you would like to include in a sample cover letter. Your CV and cover letter are the vehicles by which you will have the first opportunity to display who you are as a candidate by highlighting your academic credentials, graduate training and work experiences, and employment history. It also provides you the chance to spotlight your special skills, awards earned, and publications. However, a note of caution: Be accurate and truthful about how you represent yourself in your vitae. Abstain from embellishing it in ways that open the door to future embarrassment. An example is provided by those who tout language proficiencies as a way to gain a competitive edge; it is unfortunate to hear stories of candidates who have reported fluency in Spanish, for example, only to be caught out during an internship interview conducted in Spanish.

Reach out to peers, clinical supervisors, and graduate advisors for samples of CVs, and have them review your completed version to ensure quality. There are a number of written resources on crafting strong CVs. Generally, though, your CV should include the following information:

- *Education*: Highlight your bachelor's, master's, and doctoral work. This section can also include your dissertation topic or title.
- *Clinical experiences*: Include previous externships as well as relevant job experience (e.g., milieu specialist on an inpatient unit or residential facility), and provide a brief description of your responsibilities and role. If you utilized a specific type of therapy or empirically supported treatment, list it. Research experiences such as involvement in projects and grants (e.g., research assistant, project coordinator) may be included in this section, or they can be addressed in a separate section titled as such.
- *Publications*: List book chapters to which you have contributed as well as articles published in peer-reviewed journals.
- *Presentations and posters*: Indicate professional conferences attended and presented at as well as any community presentations you have conducted.
- *Awards, advanced training, and/or membership in professional organizations*: Do not hesitate to share your accomplishments and affiliations!

July: Essays

In addition to updating and reviewing your CV, the summer is an ideal time to start writing your draft essays and sample case reports. Be mindful of the word limit on the essays and plan on writing a number of drafts and revisions. Again, call upon peers, supervisors, and advisors to provide constructive feedback on your materials. The best essays communicate an applicant's experience, goals, and rationale for why he or she is a good match for the site in a concise, humble, and vivid manner. Your writing samples, along with CV, are the primary avenue by which internship sites will initially evaluate you as a match for their program. Your professional goals, personality, and skills should clearly shine through your essays, CV, and writing samples. As one training director states, "Strong internship applications are those that distinguish themselves in the applicant's ability to write about their work and experiences in a way that conveys a deeper understanding of the work that they are doing rather than expresses stock explanations of a treatment orientation or why cultural issues are important. It is sort of an intangible quality that comes through in the essays."

Typical APPIC essays include an autobiographical statement, an essay asking candidates to describe their theoretical orientation and approach to case conceptualization, experiences with diverse populations, and research interests. Aim to have your autobiographical statement reveal a sense of your personality without sharing uncomfortable personal information.

August: Letters of Recommendation

The quality of your letters of recommendation plays a significant role in your strength as a candidate. In general, you will need at least three recommendation letters, although some sites ask for additional letters as part of their supplemental information requirements. When requesting letters from previous supervisors and faculty, ask them directly if they are able to write you a strong letter of recommendation that can capture your personal and professional strengths and characteristics. If faced with the choice, it is better to receive a thoughtful and detailed recommendation from a faculty member who knows you well than a brief, lukewarm letter of recommendation from a faculty member from a well-named institution. By requesting letters early in the application process, you demonstrate respect for the demands placed on your recommenders' schedules as well as ensure that you receive letters back in time to submit them along with your application. One intern recommends that in addition to talking with your recommenders in detail about your qualifications, goals, and internship application process, provide them with an updated CV, a list of the internship sites to which you are applying, appropriately addressed and stamped envelopes as needed, and any other necessary paperwork in a folder with your name and important deadlines on it.

August: Register Through APPIC

By the end of the summer, you will have to register and start your APPIC application online through the APPIC website. Hopefully, you have tracked your clinical hours to date, as well as the number of patients you have seen, by intervention, setting, and demographic type. Do not become anxious about the quantity of your hours, as the quality of your hours is ultimately more important to training directors. This is substantiated by the results of an APPIC survey of training directors (2009), which demonstrated that the specific number of hours a candidate possesses is not considered to be one of the most important aspects of a candidate's application. This survey showed that the median number of doctoral intervention hours was 539, a number that does not represent the necessary hours to match for internship but, rather, just the median number of hours among the sample of intern applicants; the median number of doctoral assessment hours equaled 152.

Be accurate when reporting assessment experiences as well. For instance, when recording testing experience, verify what defines a full battery rather than counting every test you have ever administered as a full battery, which is likely misleading and inaccurate. In 2009, the median number of integrated assessment reports among applicants was seven adult and five child/adolescent cases (APPIC). Again, use these numbers as references only and focus your energy on communicating the quality and type of your clinical experiences in the most aboveboard fashion.

November/December: Submission of Applications and Initiation of Interview Process

By late autumn, your applications have been submitted and the waiting begins for interview invitations. Internship interviews vary greatly by site. Some sites will have a more traditional one-on-one series of interviews with different faculty members and current interns, while others may conduct group interviews or "fish bowl" observations of candidates participating in small-group discussions. Consider asking a peer or supervisor to practice interviewing with you and give you feedback. A few mock interviews will help you formulate some of your answers out loud and will also assist in decreasing some of your anxiety. Be sure to review your site's materials prior to the interview. You will want to clearly communicate what aspects of the site are a good match for your training goals as well as areas in which you feel you will be able to contribute to the team and institution. Bring extra copies of your CV and be prepared to summarize different experiences in an organized and thoughtful manner. Remember that you are also evaluating each interview site as a best fit for you. Despite the pressure to match, take the time to find out more about the site and the satisfaction of the current interns. Preparing a set of questions about the site that you wish to ask at the time of the interview will prove helpful with this process.

December/January: Interviews, Interviews, Interviews!

During this period, holiday festivities become overshadowed by intense involvement in interview-related activities: preparing for them by reviewing site materials and rehearsing interview questions, attending them, reflecting on them, and managing an array of feelings elicited by the process as a whole. The time commitment alone can be overwhelming. One former student reflected on how challenging it was to balance what felt like a relentless interview schedule with ongoing academic, job, and family responsibilities. While she was excited by the prospect of approaching the end of the application process and by getting a feel for the sites firsthand, it was also very stressful and exhausting because she didn't get much down time and there was still anxiety about the ultimate outcome of match.

Although self-care is critically important throughout your graduate career, it is particularly necessary at this juncture to attend to your physical and psychological needs. A current fifth-year doctoral student who recently went through the internship application process shared how she prioritized self-care in order to remain calm and confident in spite of the demands of the task. "I made sure to exercise, hung out with friends on the weekends, and went to weekly therapy sessions . . . My best advice is to be strategic and don't be afraid to ask for help! I found that almost everyone I asked was more than happy to help me."

Another recent graduate recalled how he utilized cognitive restructuring techniques to address thoughts of self-doubt and catastrophic beliefs. He replaced thoughts like "I am not as strong as the other candidates with whom I am interviewing" and "I am never going to match" with cognitions such as "I have developed a strong set of clinical skills in therapy and testing by benefitting from as many training opportunities as I could during my graduate training thus far" and "I will ultimately end up at the best internship training site for me, and will take advantage of the opportunities offered there." These reframing activities resulted in a decrease in physical feelings of anxiety (e.g., upset stomach and shortness of breath), particularly the night before interviews, as well as an increase in feelings of optimism and confidence.

A training director provides a word of caution, though, about prospective turnoffs during the interview process. She warns against "a preoccupation with expected workload and benefits packages. It is also a turnoff when the trainee, in an attempt to demonstrate competence, appears too confident for their level of training and experience."

Many students speak about the anxiety, anger, self-doubt, competition, and jealousy that arise between peers during the application process in general and during the interview period in particular. Each person's approach to managing these feelings and the competitive realities of the process is unique; for example, some avoid interacting with peers during this period in order to avoid complicated feelings and/or uncomfortable situations—such as a friend being invited to interview at your top site from which you have not yet heard—while some select a few choice friends in or out of their program in whom to confide about their experiences. There is no right or wrong way to deal with this, although the better approach is clearly the one that creates the least amount of internal and external conflict for you and for those whom you care about. At the very least, expect that you and others are likely to experience some or all of these uncomfortable feelings at one point or another during the process to varying degrees, all of which are normal.

February: Match Time

You have spent countless hours toiling over every word in your CV, essays, case summaries, and testing reports. You have obsessed over whether you have enough hours listed in your APPIC application. You have consulted with peers, supervisors, advisors, and therapists about everything under the sun about internship. You have fretted about every aspect of your interview performance from your appearance to your answers. You have worried about your strength as a candidate. You have survived an unremitting schedule of work and interviews. Congratulations, you are now ready to rank . . . and to be ranked!

In the world of predoctoral internship protocol, February is a crucial month, ushered in by the act of rank-ordering your sites and shepherded out by the discovery of the first phase of match results. The rank-order process is straightforward. First, you rank your preferred sites from highest to lowest, while internship sites rank preferred applicants from highest to lowest. Then both parties submit those lists to APPIC electronically, thereby formally jumpstarting the match process. This 3-week process is administered by computer on behalf of APPIC by National Matching Services Inc., which uses an algorithm to place prospective interns based on a literal match between applicant and site preferences depending on how each site and applicant orders the other.

How you rank your sites will depend on a number of subjective factors but will generally reflect which site you think best suits your professional goals and, perhaps simply, which site feels better to you. Some students recommend quantifying factors, like reputation, quality and quantity of supervision, and types of rotations, that are important to you in a prospective site by assigning each factor a numerical value and then summing it up to arrive at an overall site value. So, hypothetically, if you prioritize quality of rotations and setting as critical variables, you may rank Site A as follows: Quality of rotations = 2/5 and Setting = 3/5, and Site B like this: Quality of rotations = 4/5 and Setting = 3/5. According to this formula, you would rank Site B higher. However, sometimes one site just feels like a better fit even if it might fall a point or two below on a quantitative ranking scale, and this may weigh more heavily in your final ranking. In such cases, one need not remind a psychologist-to-be about the role of qualitative interpretation of data.

Once your list is submitted, the next step is to wait for Phase I Match Day to find out whether you have matched and where. This occurs at the end of February. Any applicants who are not placed during Phase I are eligible to participate in Phase II, during which time positions that remain unfilled during Phase I remain available for prospective interns. During Phase II, which occurs over the course of March, applicants resubmit applications to available sites and interview accordingly. Applicants and sites then submit rank order lists at the end of the month, and Match results are released a week later. If there are any applicants and sites that remain unmatched at this juncture, then each can proceed to the clearinghouse, the final stage in the Match process.

Depending on the outcome of Match, you will surely experience a range of feelings. Joy, relief, excitement, sadness, disappointment, embarrassment, anxiety, frustration, and anger are common emotions named. If your feelings are more negative, it may be an important time to draw upon your network of personal and professional support to help you manage your feelings, as well as engage in self-care practices, so that you may move forward in the most productive way possible.

February/March: The Start of Internship

The time between finding out about Match and actually beginning your internship may feel like the calm before the storm of sorts, but it represents an important transition period on your journey toward completion of graduate school. It is often a time of good-byes—good-byes to clients, to supervisors, to professors, to fellow students, to the structure and lifestyle of graduate school, and maybe even to a home. It can also be a time of completion, a wrapping up of coursework, of externships, of projects, and of relationships, as well as a time to deal with feelings about progressing towards internship. Furthermore, it is a chance to reflect upon all that you have accomplished thus far.

Ultimately, though, now that your externships are done and your internship opportunity is in front of you, it is a time for looking ahead—to new experiences, to yet-to-be-discovered personal and professional opportunities, and to interpersonal connections—and to feel proud of all of the steps that you have already taken on this journey of a thousand miles.

❖ References

2009 APPIC match statistics, match report from the APPIC Board of Directors (2010). Retrieved November 1, 2010, from http://www.appic.org/match/5_2_2_1_11_match_about_statistics_general_2009.html.

Callahan, J. L., Collins, F. L., & Klonoff, E. A. (2010). An examination of applicant characteristics of successfully matched interns: Is the glass half full or half empty and leaking miserably? *Journal of Clinical Psychology, 66*, 1–16.

Kaslow, N., Pate, W. E., & Thorn, B. (2005). Special section: Practicum training—academic and internship directors' perspectives on practicum experiences: Implications of training. *Professional Psychology: Research and Practice, 36*, 307–316.

Keilin, W. G., Baker, J., McCutcheon, S., & Peranson, E. (2007). A growing bottleneck: The internship supply demand imbalance in 2007 and its impact on psychology training. *Training and Education in Professional Psychology, 14*, 229–237.

Lopez, S. J., Oehlert, M. E., & Moberly, R. L. (1996). Selection criteria for American Psychological Association accredited internship programs: A survey of training directors. *Professional Psychology: Research and Practice, 27*, 518–520.

Oehlert, M. E., Sumeral, S. W., Lopez, S. J., & Merkley, K. B. (2002). Internship placement data: Is non-placement the only concern? *Journal of Clinical Psychology, 58, 10*, 1323–1326.

Pincus, D. B., & Otis, J. (2008). The clinical psychology internship guide. Retrieved November 11, 2010, from http://www.psychzone.com/files/Pincus%20Otis%20Internship%20Manual%202008.pdf.

Rodolfa, E. R., Vielle, R., Russell, P., Nijer, S., Nguyen, D. Q., & Mendoz, M. (1999). Internship selection: Inclusion and exclusion criteria. *Professional Psychology: Research and Practice, 30*, 415–419.

Stewart, A. E., & Stewart, E. A. (1996). A decision-making technique for choosing a psychology internship. *Professional Psychology: Research and Practice, 27*, 521–526.

❖ Suggestions for Further Exploration

American Psychological Association. http://apa.org/education/grad/index.aspx. In addition to providing the latest news about the field of psychology, the official website of the American Psychological Association contains relevant resources for graduate and post-doctoral students including but not limited to topics such as mentoring and self-care, career development, and dissertations and research. By clicking on the internships link (http://apa.org/education/grad/internship.aspx), you will discover a wealth of information about the subject.

Williams-Nickelson, C., Prinstein, M. J., & Keilin, W. G. (2008). *Internships in psychology: The APAGS workbook for writing successful applications and finding the right fit* (2nd ed.). Washington, DC: American Psychological Association. An exceedingly practical guide recommended by students and training directors alike, this resource can be purchased directly through the APA website at a discounted rate for affiliates. This helpful workbook offers step-by-step advice on managing various aspects of the internship application process.

17

Preparing for Comprehensive Exams

Valerie M. Gonsalves
Fulton State Hospital

Leah Skovran Georges
University of Nebraska–Lincoln

Matthew T. Huss
Creighton University

"If I fail, at least I can pursue my lifelong dream to become a circus performer/
nature photographer/actor/business owner/insert your career of choice here."
We have all had these thoughts at one time or another, and the impending milestone
of comprehensive exams is certainly one of those times in graduate school. As the
comprehensive exam approaches, we consider the worst possible outcome: *failure*.
Fret not; with adequate knowledge, preparation, and time, every graduate student
is capable of passing comprehensive exams (comps). Graduate programs are not in
the habit of admitting students who do not have the basic skills necessary to succeed, so they expect you to succeed. The goal of this chapter is to outline expectations, preparation strategies, and approaches to recovery for comps in order to help
you along the way to success.

What Are Comprehensive Exams: Comps, Quals, Prelims?

Comprehensive exam formats vary greatly from school to school. Typically, schools require either oral or written comprehensive exams, though some schools require both (Bourg, 1986). Bourg researched 24 professional psychology programs and discovered that comprehensive exams are designed to cover one or more of the following content areas: research design and statistics, clinical/intervention, assessment, general psychology, and professional/ethical means. Of course, this survey was of practice-oriented professional programs, and comprehensive exams in experimental/nonclinical programs in psychology do not focus on some of these areas. Furthermore, comprehensive exams vary, being specifically tailored to a student's area of interest, or they can be composed of both student-specific and general discipline questions. For example, some programs may ask questions about a broad array of psychologically relevant topics, whereas other programs may ask questions about specified content areas and others about a narrow body of literature relevant to a specific line of research.

Purpose of Comprehensive Exams

Why do comprehensive exams exist? Besides removing 5 years from an otherwise healthy individual's life, what purpose do they serve? Historically, the exam was administered for entrance, advance standing, and graduation and consisted of oral demonstration of knowledge and synthesis of the doctrines and philosophies relevant to the field (Manus et al., 1992). Today, the comprehensive exam has become a rite of passage so students can feel as if they have earned a degree. It is seen as a hurdle that everyone must overcome, in part, because everyone else before faced it.

For some, the primary purpose of evaluation is demonstration of integration of knowledge (Anderson, Krauskopf, Rogers, & Neal, 1984). Manus, Bowden, and Dowd (1992) evaluated counseling programs and found that the majority of programs identified "the purpose and philosophy of comprehensive examinations was an integration and synthesis of knowledge as well as an assessment of basic skills and abilities" (p. 681). Although it seems that there is a generally agreed-upon purpose to comprehensive exams, there are idiographic differences as well. Programs identify specific purposes they believe the examinations hold, and there is variability in these intended purposes. Some graduate programs are similar to the University of Wisconsin–Madison and believe that "by passing the preliminary exams the student demonstrates his or her competence to begin dissertation research" (University of Wisconsin–Madison Department of Psychology, n.d.). The fact that nearly all programs require the comprehensive exam be passed prior to beginning dissertation research is in keeping with this purpose. However, others are like the University of California–Los Angeles graduate program that points out that the purpose of the comprehensive exam is not to determine whether the student should be allowed to continue in a doctoral program but, rather, to identify areas that may need improvement in order to prepare one completely for candidacy (University of California,

Los Angeles, 2010, p. 71). That is to say, if it is unlikely that a student will meet all the requirements and earn a doctoral degree, these students are identified early in their training and encouraged to perform additional work to meet those requirements.

Furthermore, the true purpose and the resulting format of content exams may be dependent on your mentor or committee. Some advisors will take a developmental approach, tailoring the assessment to your specific career goals, and others will take more of the traditional assessment approach, examining the depth and breadth of conceptual knowledge broadly related to the field. If you are at the point where you are preparing for your comprehensive exam and have spoken at length about preparation with your advisor, it is more important to focus on strengthening your breadth and depth of knowledge in the appropriate areas than it is to focus on your future in the program. Said differently, spend more time preparing based on the feedback your advisor has given you and less time worrying about passing.

Choosing Your Committee

One of the first steps in preparing for your comprehensive exams is frequently the selection or identification of an oversight committee. In some programs, this committee is specific to your comprehensive exam. In other programs, this committee is a carryover from your master's thesis or overall doctoral candidacy. Furthermore, committee members may serve different roles. Some members may serve primary functions and other secondary, even very secondary functions. Whatever the format, make sure you are clear about the procedures of your specific department or program. Some programs allow you to choose the faculty members that make up your committee. If your program happens to do so, you may want to spend some time carefully selecting committee members. Your advisor will chair your committee in almost all cases. Choosing the other members depends on what your goal is. For example, if you are writing a paper that will likely be published, then it may be wise to include faculty members who are highly successful scholars, as they may be able to provide valuable hints that will improve the likelihood that your paper will be appealing to a journal. If you are writing a grant, you may wish to choose faculty from other departments, as grant agencies may look more favorably on proposals that span several disciplines.

If you are choosing your committee members, try to pinpoint their exact roles on the committee as you are developing the group. It may help if you express this directly to people when you ask them to join the committee. If they know in what area you are looking for guidance, they can tailor their feedback to it. For example, if you want someone to give you specific feedback on your application of a theory or on your methodology, be sure to ask him or her for this feedback so you are getting the most out of your committee experience.

It is also important to keep in mind that not all committee members are going to have a specific purpose; sometimes, unfortunately, they are simply fulfilling a job requirement to help you meet your department requirements. You may end up with someone whose interests do not match up well with yours despite your best efforts. We know of one student who approached five faculty members who declined to participate on her committee because of conflicting academic appointments, sabbatical, or being too busy to take on another task. In that case, she ended up with a committee member who did not necessarily have expertise in her proposed area of research, but this faculty member was available, participated, read the proposal, and provided feedback. We encourage balance when choosing your committee members. You need to weigh who will make a fabulous contribution against who has less-relevant expertise but will have the time and energy to meaningfully participate.

Options and Choices for Format

Various approaches have been used in conducting content examinations. In some cases, your program specifies the precise format. In other situations, it is agreed upon by a committee you select prior to completing your comprehensive exams, and in other cases, the graduate student has some input in the format. The exam may take the format of an essay, objective, or oral exam. Alternatively, the committee may desire to examine a writing sample, perhaps in the form of a literature review, grant proposal, or portfolio. Some clinical psychology programs assess the student's clinical skills in the form of an oral presentation. Programs may select a combination of exam types to evaluate the skills determined to be the most important.

If your program requires an exam, this may be in the form of written essays, objective questions, or oral presentations. An essay exam can be either proctored or take-home and can vary a good deal in terms of the questions and material based on your specific program. The essay exam may be a single question that requires a well-thought-out, detailed answer, or it may be a series of essay questions spread out over the course of a few hours or even several days of testing. Some schools provide students with a reading list and require the student to have a comprehensive overview of many different areas. Some schools provide little direction and test students on any material covered throughout their graduate training up to that point. Other schools focus the exam to specifically cover material surrounding the student's research interests. The benefit of the essay exam is that it allows the student to convey knowledge of the information in his or her own words and style. However, it is tempting for students to attempt to demonstrate the depth and breadth of their knowledge by writing too much or by including information that is not directly relevant to the question asked. It is important to clarify the question asked and be sure that this question is answered when reviewing your work. Often, you may have prepared a lot of information that you will not have an opportunity to present in your answer. That is okay! This information is likely directly relevant to your career and may be useful in other areas if not on the comprehensive examination.

In a similar manner, some programs may require the student to take an objective test, which will likely include multiple-choice and short-answer questions. It is possible that essay questions may appear on the exam as well. If your program requires an objective test, most likely it will cover a wider array of information than exams of other formats. The benefit of this test is that it allows for relatively objective evaluation procedures. However, this test does not allow for much explanation of answers, which may limit your opportunity to showcase the range of your knowledge.

Another method of examination is the oral exam. This exam can also vary in content but usually involves presenting information to a panel of faculty members. Other graduate students may or may not be allowed to be present for the exam. For students at the University of Washington–Seattle, the oral exam is the most common format chosen. According to the graduate student handbook, students are required to consult their committee members about the nature of the exam, including the breadth and depth of the exam and the materials that will be covered (Department of Psychology, University of Washington, 2009, p. 27). The committee members can assist in forming a reading list. An oral exam may be given in conjunction with or instead of an objective or written exam. The purpose of an oral examination is to assess the student's ability to communicate about a specialized topic area with others both inside and outside the field of study. Again, oral exams may take place over several hours or several exam sessions over a few days. The benefit of the oral exam is that it allows for thorough explanation of the information learned, and it allows for more spontaneous formulation of answers, which may be a format desirable to some students. Alternatively, for students with a fear of speaking in public or who prefer to take time in formulating their answers and do not think quickly on their feet, this type of exam may be very stressful. In addition, because the answers are not recorded, it may be difficult to review during the evaluation and feedback process. If there is a point of contention regarding the evaluation, students may find it more difficult to reconstruct their answers to discuss an area of concern.

In addition to more traditional exam formats, many programs allow students to write a paper on a specific topic and allow this paper to meet the requirements for a comprehensive examination. Papers take several different formats. Some schools allow students who have a peer-reviewed publication to submit this work as evidence of mastery and allow this publication to meet the requirements of the program. Other schools require a comprehensive literature review in the area relevant to the student's dissertation or proposed field of research. Many students eventually submit this literature review for publication or conference presentation, but many schools only require that the paper be written and not necessarily published in order to satisfy the requirement. It is not uncommon for a literature review to be accompanied by an oral defense of the review. As above, the oral defense typically takes place in front of a committee. It includes a presentation of the material by the student and time for questions and answers from the committee. Often, only select members of the committee will have read drafts of the paper, and feedback from the whole committee is obtained at the defense. The benefit of a paper is that it allows for specificity and depth that some other formats may not incorporate. In addition, the paper often serves as the introduction to a dissertation or turns into a publication, so it performs double duty of meeting a requirement and benefitting the student in some other way. Further, the student typically picks the topic and likely has a vested interest in the topic of choice. However, a paper can be frustrating, as it may undergo many iterations before it is approved. This experience can be difficult for students who are anxious to finish their requirements and are stymied by waiting for approval from their readers. As advisors and committee members often have competing or more pressing projects to attend to, the student's paper may take a while to complete. Frequently, programs do not have specific deadlines for the completion of these papers, which may leave the student stuck in a holding pattern.

Programs also allow students to meet the comprehensive exam requirement by preparing a grant proposal. A solid grant proposal requires an extensive literature review, the development of an interesting and novel research project, and a solid presentation of methodology and research design. Though some programs require the full proposal to be submitted, other programs may consider the completion of the literature review and research proposal sufficient for passage. Preparing a grant proposal can be a particularly useful method of completing a comprehensive examination, especially if the student is preparing for a career in academia, because it allows the student to learn the skill of grant writing while fulfilling a program requirement. Much like the paper, it allows the student to complete two large tasks by completing only one project. Writing a grant is a rather lengthy process and requires communication with several departments within a university structure, so the student must make sure to allocate sufficient time. Further, a grant proposal frequently requires Institutional Review Board approval prior to submission, which means the student may have to complete additional tasks prior to completing the requirement for passage of the comprehensive exams. The good news is that this is often the foundation for the dissertation, and if the grant proposal is an alternative selected, the student may be in good position for completion of the dissertation regardless of whether the grant is funded, since the methodology for a project has already been identified.

A less common but interesting alternative to traditional forms of assessment is the development of a portfolio. Cobia and colleagues (2005) highlight the following seven areas as domains to be included in the portfolio: teaching, supervision, counseling, research, leadership, professional issues, and inter/intrapersonal functioning. In many ways, a portfolio can seem like a vita except, typically, only certain areas are highlighted, and these areas may be discussed in more detail than on a vita. There can be opportunities for both specific and general lines of inquiry. For example, students may be asked to answer general questions about research methodology and also include information about their own specific lines of research. Some of the benefits of a portfolio include allowing for assessment of students over time in the context of actual practice and allowing students to comment on their own growth and performance (Wolf, 1991, as cited in Cobia et al., 2005). Because of the nature of this assessment, students begin preparing a portfolio from virtually their first day of graduate school. The portfolio is beneficial because it allows the student to show not only knowledge learned but also professional growth. In addition, it may be tailored and used when a student applies for a job, as it shows breadth of experience throughout a graduate career. Furthermore, portfolios allow for ongoing evaluation, as programs may elect to review the document at the end of each semester or at specific points throughout one's graduate career. However, compiling a portfolio requires a lot of time and advance planning. If a student is expected to start thinking about the portfolio during the first semester of graduate school, this may be overwhelming, and students who do not plan well may fall behind in their compilation of the project. In addition, because of the volume of work produced during graduate training, students may have difficulty selecting the few pieces that show progression or highlight their best work.

Clinical psychology programs present the opportunity for a unique comprehensive exam. These programs may require you to demonstrate mastery of certain clinical skills in order to pass your comprehensive exam. For example, you may be required to present a specific case, discussing assessment, case conceptualization, interventions utilized, and methods for monitoring progress. In addition, the committee may wish to evaluate your clinical skills by viewing a video recording or listening to an audio recording of the session. It may be important to cite the research that you reviewed in formulating your interventions. Further, as the exam typically takes place midway through training, the committee may want you to discuss how you used supervision when considering the case or where, looking back, you may have sought out additional supervision. In addition, they may ask you to point out areas where, in retrospect, you may have taken a different approach. Often, students worry about highlighting areas that demonstrate lack of expertise in a particular area. However, many programs recognize the development of clinical skills as an ongoing process and that these early case presentations represent a developmental point in your career. Therefore, being able to discuss how the case has helped to improve your therapeutic skills and any areas in which you may have acted differently may highlight your continued growth as a clinician rather than your failure as a therapist. This method of examination is beneficial because it allows the student to focus on one area of training and to receive feedback on a specific skill that is still being developed. However, this may mean that other areas, for example the student's own line of research, are not evaluated prior to the dissertation. In addition, since a comprehensive exam focused on clinical work does not pull the double duty of other methods of examination (i.e., a grant proposal), the student may feel a bit more pressure because of all the graduate school demands.

Preparing for Comprehensive Exams

Miller (1990) recommends that a graduate student begin preparing for comps from the first day of her or his graduate career. Though this advice might seem overwhelming with all the other responsibilities that come with beginning graduate school, it is a sage admonition. The first step is to identify the specific requirements of your department. Learn them early in your graduate career. Does your department require a written or an oral examination? Is this based on a compilation of information received during graduate training or some specific skill required? Knowing the requirements early allows you to prepare in two distinct ways. First, you know you can attend to information in courses and readings that you know traditionally appear on the comprehensive exam, and you can create a file in which the information is readily available during the preparation for the comprehensive exam. The second benefit is that it allows you to watch and learn as other students prepare. As other students in your program complete (and pass) comprehensive exams, do not be afraid to ask them about their experiences. Ask about the types of questions they were presented with (keeping your school's ethical principles in mind) and their manner of preparation. Advanced students can be a valuable source of information, and most people are willing to help. Just remember to pay it forward: If you have the privilege of learning important information about comprehensive exams from other students, be sure to share this information when other students ask you as well!

Dingfelder (2004) recommends the following strategies: read strategically, keep abreast of your field, take detailed notes, get organized, seek advice from older students, ask questions, read the directions, and be thorough but concise. Reading strategically and taking detailed notes both serve the same purpose; these strategies allow you to think critically about the material as you are reading it. In addition, by practicing these tips, you can organize the information as you like. Perhaps you remember information best by keywords, by author's name, and so forth. In reading strategically and actively, you are processing the information more thoroughly the first time around, thus saving time and energy during last-minute preparations. Even though this may seem like a lot of work in the beginning, in the long run, once you develop a strategy that works for you, this method of studying will pay off exponentially.

Dingfelder (2004) also suggested students get organized before the exam. Specifically, many universities may ask you to cite relevant works. Therefore, organizing the material as it comes through is just as important as reading the material closely. If the material is organized, then in the weeks before the exam, you can focus more on the content and less on locating pertinent articles. The flip side is to be detailed without being rote. Many people can recite memorized information, names of authors, important works, and the like. It is more important to show depth, breadth, and application of knowledge than to show the ability to regurgitate information other people have already presented. It is important to be able to demonstrate your ability to think critically about the material and provide well-reasoned answers. Even multiple-choice tests will likely require some interpretation of the material you learned.

Keeping abreast of your field is important because your exam may be tailored to your particular area of interest and may be focused on current issues and controversies rather than more seminal articles. In addition to reading journal articles, subscribe to listserves where people are discussing critical items relevant to your field. In addition to cueing you into important journal articles that you may have overlooked, the discussions on these e-mail chains will expose you to several points of view from some of the prominent people in the field.

It is also important to speak to advanced students (Dingfelder, 2004). These students can give you a summary of their experiences, perhaps help you prepare, and generally ease anxiety about expectations. In addition, do not be afraid to ask questions! Ask the department how they recommend you prepare. Ask if they have copies of previous examinations. Also, on the day of the exam, ask any questions that might arise. If you are unclear about what is being asked, how much time you will have, and so forth, ask the faculty present. The worst that will happen is that they will elect not to answer the question—they certainly will not fail you for asking for clarification. Finally, make sure to read and follow the directions. If there is a word or a time limit, those are not suggestions, so be sure to adhere to them. If the exam is a written exam, there may be specific formatting instructions. If the exam is timed, ask for a copy of the instructions in advance so that you do not waste time reading them on the day of the examination.

Sometimes the most difficult aspect of the process is not the intellectual preparation for the process but the emotional aspects. Managing your own stress and anxiety prior to and during the process can be crucial. Make sure you rely on your peer group who is going through the exact same process and experiencing the same anxiety and doubts. Use the same appropriate coping mechanisms you normally use, whether that means getting organized, going out for a run, or sitting in front of the television. Sometimes the anticipation is the worst part of these types of situations, but at other times, we tend to panic during the moment. If you notice that you are starting to let your emotions get the best of you as you stare at questions you don't think you have ever seen before in your life, take a deep breath, think some positive thoughts, and relax. You have prepared long and hard no matter the format of your particular examination, and you can do it.

Finally, Miller (1990) offers perhaps the most valuable piece of advice: sleep well. We extend this one step further, and recommend practicing good self-care in the weeks leading up to your comprehensive examination. Though it is important to spend time studying, it is also important to spend time making sure you are managing your stress properly so that on the day of the examination, you can perform to the best of your abilities.

Evaluation and Feedback

Once you have completed the exam, it becomes a waiting game in terms of learning if you passed or not. Some programs let you know right away, whereas others take time in reviewing the material submitted and let you know either at a specified date or when the review is completed. Typically, if the program intends to let you know on the same day, the committee will convene in private to ensure that there is consensus. In one graduate program, they ask you to step into the hall while they review the material you presented and discuss points of feedback they would like to share and invite you back into the room in order to have a discussion of your performance. However, in the same way the type of comprehensive exam varies greatly, the manner in which evaluation and feedback is presented varies greatly as well.

In a survey of counseling programs, Peterson, Bowman, Myer, and Maidl (1992) found that only 54% of the programs surveyed had written procedures describing how evaluation of the examination would occur. In general, the areas evaluated by the programs fell into three categories: content, style, and technical aspects (Peterson et al., 1992). Content included thoroughness, relevance, and accuracy of the information included in the response and represented the primary area of evaluation. Style included organization, grammar, and readability. Finally, technical aspects included things such as appropriate references, citations, and language. Depending on the type of exam, other areas may be evaluated as well. For example, if you present a clip of a therapy session, the committee may evaluate your therapeutic style. In some instances, it may be helpful to ask for a grading rubric prior to the exam so you can decide how to allocate your time and energy. It is likely that this rubric may not be available, but hopefully the program can give you some direction as to how you will be evaluated.

Peterson and colleagues (1992) also discovered in their survey that about 50% of the programs provided both written and verbal feedback to the students. Sometimes the feedback came from the committee, but other times, the feedback was synthesized and presented to the student by only his or her primary advisor. In one author's experience, written feedback was provided primarily to document the student's progress and tended to be in the form of a letter that was included in the student's departmental file. The real feedback came from oral sessions with the committee and then subsequent follow-up sessions with the advisor.

It is important to remember that receiving feedback is an excellent thing. When receiving feedback, typically both strengths and weaknesses are highlighted. Although everyone obviously loves to hear about their strengths, it is important that you pay careful attention when your weaknesses are highlighted. Graduate school is a time for you to hone your skills, and since comprehensive exams typically come sometime in the middle of training, there are skills that should still need to be improved. By carefully listening and responding to the concerns of your committee, you can help to improve your skills for future evaluation.

Postcomps Hangover

What If You Don't Pass?

You have spent the hours, days, or weeks required of you taking comprehensive exams and, upon completion, one of two things will happen: You will pass your exams or you will not. It is simply a fact of life that not everyone will pass her or his comprehensive exams. This phenomenon is both a good and a bad thing. It is a good thing because comprehensive exams are designed to ensure that only competent and well-qualified people enter the field. If there are some people that do not pass, then the exams are doing their jobs by acting as filters to protect the integrity of the field.

That being said, let's face it, being the person who does not pass would be terrible. The first thing to do is take a deep breath. Failing comprehensive exams does not necessarily mean that you have entered the wrong field or that you have wasted your time in pursuit of a degree you may never achieve. We all have bad days. Perhaps on the day of the exam, your nerves got the best of you. Maybe you were sick. Maybe you underprepared. There are a million reasons you may not have passed. At the beginning of the chapter, we stated that everyone who gets accepted into graduate school is capable of passing, and that remains true; however, many people do not pass because they may have picked the wrong career path and preparing was too tedious to be done properly. If you are certain you want to pursue a career in this field, it is important to be forward looking. What are the consequences of not passing comprehensive exams? Most programs will allow students another opportunity to take exams, though the time between the first and second testing may vary. Peterson and colleagues found that 44% of counseling programs surveyed required students to retake the portion of the test that they failed in order to progress in the program, whereas 13% of programs required students to retake the entire exam. In addition, they found that, typically, programs responded to failed exams on an individual basis. For example, some allow students to orally respond to failed written answers if this method is agreeable to the student. Similarly, if the exam was a paper or a proposal-type format, your committee may consider extensive revisions to the existing project to be sufficient instead of requiring you to rewrite the entire paper or may ask you to present an oral defense of the paper or proposal in lieu of rewriting it. Determine all of your options before you begin to consider them.

The first thing to consider is taking some time off (Gould, 2007). Perhaps the stress of graduate school is overwhelming at this particular juncture in your life. Perhaps taking some time off may help you clarify your goals and integrate other areas of interest into your career. Gould recommends acknowledging your feelings, figuring out what went wrong, practicing, and talking to other students. One of the biggest mistakes graduate students make is failing to practice good self-care rituals. It is important to recognize and honor the feelings of grief and self-doubt that may arise from failing an important exam. It is also important that you take the necessary steps to deal with these emotional states properly, including adequate rest, nutrition, exercise, and seeking professional help.

Once you have processed the initial news and are ready to continue with your graduate career, it is important to talk to the professors who were on your committee to discover where you went wrong (Gould, 2007). In seeing the questions and discussing your responses with professors, you can determine if your performance was due to a lack of knowledge or a misunderstanding of the question. Once you determine the origin of your poor performance, you will know where to begin in attempting to rectify it. In addition, consulting with professors gives them the opportunity to see that you are still invested and motivated to learn and do well, and it allows them a chance to provide you with additional material to help you prepare. Perhaps the professors can give you practice exams or study tips or set aside time to assist you in preparation. It is important to take whatever advice and feedback that they give you and integrate it into your study habits. Finally, Gould (2007) recommends that you talk to other students. Your peers may be able to provide you with information about their preparation and the stumbling blocks they discovered and even share their study notes and material with you. You do not have to broadcast your performance, but humbling yourself by turning to others for help may end up being a valuable experience toward your future success.

What Do I Do Now?

Passing your comprehensive examination is a big deal. It usually results in a master's degree, permission to advance in your program, or some other huge milestone. Therefore, it is important to celebrate once you have passed. Give yourself a chance to relax and do something you enjoy as well as acknowledge the fact that you have successfully accomplished a huge task.

Unfortunately, comps are usually not the end of the road. Typically, comps are just one hurdle on the long road to a Ph.D. So, although rest, relaxation and celebration are in order for the short term, after you have recovered, it is time to get back to work. The first thing to do is make sure you have submitted the proper documentation to your program showing that you have passed. This step may involve a trip to a university office (perhaps the office in charge of graduate affairs) to make sure they are aware you are progressing as well. After that, it is time to schedule a meeting with your advisor. Typically, comprehensive exams come prior to the start of dissertation. Though you and your advisor may have been discussing and planning for your dissertation preceding your exam, it is likely time to start hammering out specifics. A meeting with your advisor in the week or two after you have completed your comprehensive exams may help with the postcomps slump, which will likely hit. This slump is a period during which you may feel unmotivated or disorganized when you revisit your looming to-do list that you have put off while studying for comprehensive exams. A meeting with your advisor can help reignite some enthusiasm.

Conclusion

Completing comprehensive exams has become a rite of passage for graduate students. Different sites have implemented different formats in order to best meet the needs of students and the goals of the program. Regardless of the type of exam your school presents, preparation will take place over many months, and some students benefit from preparing from their first day of graduate school. It is reasonable to consult with your advisor, committee members, and past students about the best way to prepare for the exams. Further, it is important to manage stress and practice good self-care during the preparation period, as it tends to be a stressful time. Once you have completed the exam, it is important to take some time to celebrate this accomplishment if you passed. If you did not pass on your first attempt, you should take time to recompose yourself, handle the disappointment, and move forward, if that is what you choose to do. Though the task of completing comprehensive exams can be overwhelming at first, with proper preparation and planning, students can successfully navigate the ins and outs of these exams and pass.

❖ References

Anderson, W. P., Krauskopf, C. J., Rogers, M. E., & Neal, G. W. (1984). Reason for comprehensive examinations: A re-evaluation. *Teaching of Psychology, 11*, 78–82.

Bourg, E. F. (1986). Evaluation of student competence. In J. E. Callan, D. R. Peterson, & G. Stricker (Eds.), *Quality in professional psychology training; a national conference and self-study* (pp. 83–96). Washington DC: American Psychological Association.

Cobia, D. C., Carney, J. S., Buckhalt, J. A., Middleton, R. A., Shannon, D. M., Trippany, R., & Kunkel, E. (2005). The doctoral portfolio. Centerpiece of a comprehensive system of evaluation. *Counselor Education & Supervision, 44*, 242–254.

Department of Psychology, University of Washington. (2009). *Graduate school manual.* Retrieved July 12, 2011, from http://web.psych.washington.edu/graduate/files/MANUAL-09.pdf.

Dingfelder, S. F. (2004). Preparing for your comprehensive exams. *gradPSYCH, 2,* Retrieved July 12, 2011, from http://www.apa.org/gradpsych/2004/04/comps.aspx.

Gould, J. (2007). Didn't pass your comps? Even the best students sometimes fall short. Here's how to move on. *gradPSYCH,* Retrieved July 12, 2011, from http://www.apa.org/gradpsych/features/2007/didnt-pass.aspx.

Manus, M. B., Bowden, M. G., & Dowd, E. T. (1992). The purpose, philosophy, content, and structure of doctoral comprehensive/qualifying exams: A survey of counseling psychology training programs. *The Counseling Psychologist, 20*, 677–688.

Miller, P. W. (1990). Preparing for the comprehensive examination and writing the dissertation proposal: Advice for doctoral students. *Journal of Industrial Teacher Education, 27*, 83–86.

Peterson, S. E., Bowman, R. L., Myer, R. A., & Maidl, C. M. (1992). A survey of comprehensive examination practices among doctoral programs in counseling. *Counselor Education and Supervision, 32*, 116–129.

University of Wisconsin-Madison Department of Psychology. (n.d.). *Graduate Program, Preliminary Exam.* Retrieved July 12, 2011, from http://glial.psych.wisc.edu/index.php/gradmenucurrent/psychgradprelim.

Wolf, K. P. (1991). *Teaching portfolios: A synthesis of research and annotated bibliography.* San Francisco: Far West Laboratories.

❖ Suggestions for Further Exploration

Bourg, E. F. (1986). Evaluation of student competence. In J. E. Callan, D. R. Peterson, & G. Stricker (Eds.), *Quality in professional psychology training; A national conference and self-study* (pp. 83–96). Washington, DC: American Psychological Association. This is an empirical study examining various programs' methods of evaluating students across five different content areas. This chapter would be useful reading in order to examine how programs are assessing their students and what areas are frequently being examined. Further, if students are interested in empirical research in the area of student evaluation, this chapter would be a good starting place in order to examine both the methodology and criteria used in studies of this kind.

Cobia, D. C., Carney, J. S., Buckhalt, J. A., Middleton, R. A., Shannon, D. M., Trippany, R., & Kunkel, E. (2005). The doctoral portfolio. Centerpiece of a comprehensive system of evaluation. *Counselor Education & Supervision, 44,* 242–254. A fantastic resource if your program requires a doctoral portfolio. This chapter helps provide suggestions and ideas about how to manage this unique and, at times, overwhelming task. It is worth reading this chapter as early in your graduate career as possible as it provides many good suggestions for keeping track of certain items beginning in your first semester in graduate school.

18

Skill Development for Oral Presentations and Examinations

*Catherine E. Overson**
University of New Hampshire

Gary S. Goldstein
University of New Hampshire at Manchester

Prior to the growth in the 1970s of Writing-across-the-Curriculum (WAC) programs in higher education, writing was taught primarily in English departments (Russell, 1994). Commenting on this earlier practice, Russell (1994) suggested that the overall consensus of educators was that "writing skills could be taught separately from content, as a mere adjunct or service (in freshman composition, for example) or to a single course (in a research paper, for example)" (p. 6). As WAC programs began growing at a rapid pace in the 1970s in response to concerns about students' poor literacy skills, colleges and universities recognized the integral role writing has across the disciplines and in promoting learning and critical thinking.

More recently, faculty have recognized another area in higher education instruction that poses challenges for many students: oral communication. As is the case for limited writing skills, weak oral communication skills also hinder students' success in college and in their careers. Indeed, business and educational leaders often cite

---

*Author's Note: We thank Victor A. Benassi for reading and commenting on several drafts of this chapter.

poor oral communication (and writing) skills as a key to these failures (Cronin & Glenn, 1991; Dannels, 2001a; Wardrope, 2002). Boyer (1987) identified the broader consequence of enhanced oral skills. He wrote, "Language and thought are inextricably connected and as undergraduates develop their linguistic skills, they hone the quality of their thinking and become intellectually and socially empowered" (p. 73).

Just as educators at colleges and universities relied on the basic English composition course to ensure competency in writing, they also presumed a basic speech communication course would ensure competency in oral communication skills (Donofrio & Davis, 1997). Just as WAC programs supplemented the basic English composition course, oral communication programs across the curriculum (OCXC) have supplemented the basic speech communication course (Cronin, Grice, & Palmerton, 2000; Dannels, 2001a, 2001b; Friedland, 2004).

Inquiry into the field of oral communication skills historically has received limited empirical attention (De Grez, Vallcke, & Roozen, 2009). In our review of this literature, we found mostly anecdotal advice for improving oral performance, leading to a reliance on commonsense suggestions. Although these informal suggestions are useful to a certain extent, we expect that as the field matures, we will see an emerging body of empirical research. What follows, therefore, are a number of attainable suggestions for successful oral presentations derived from an assortment of empirical and practical findings. At the same time, we can draw on empirical outcomes from other disciplines that can be applied to the improvement of oral communication skills. For instance, existing clinical research can assist us in designing programs that aim to reduce public speakers' anxiety. Also, research findings in cognition and learning have helped us to design multimedia presentations that enhance oral skills and opportunities for learning in the classroom. Psychology graduate students should be particularly interested in OCXC programs. Their performance in graduate programs, course instruction, at conferences, and on job interviews depends heavily on oral communication skills.

In this chapter, we examine ways in which you, the graduate student, can enhance oral skills in various professional settings. First, we comment on what for many is a major impediment to successful presentations—fear of public speaking. From there, we identify particular considerations regarding presentation detail, topic preparation, use of multimedia, audience/evaluators, enhancing practice, and last-minute details.

Fear of Public Speaking

Think about an upcoming oral exam/presentation: You are about to give your first presentation in a graduate course, or perhaps your master's thesis or doctoral dissertation defense looms just around the corner. Recollections of your last public speaking assignment are overwhelming: "heart palpitations, shaky hands, dry mouth, abdominal pain, sweating, and head-ache" (Sarid, Anson, & Bentov, 2005, p. 294). It may be of little help to reassure you that these are all commonly reported feelings associated with public speaking (Sarid et al., 2005). Fear of public speaking, a type of social anxiety, can be debilitating and can markedly impair not only the actual presentation (Beatty & Behnke, 1991; Menzel & Carrell, 1994), but the preparation as well (Daly, Vangelisti, & Weber, 1995). Public speaking anxiety can have the power to trap individuals into a vicious cycle: anxiety about performance leads to poor performance and poor performance adds to anticipatory anxiety about future performance.

Even among the nonclinical population, "public speaking is usually near the top of any list of activities that most individuals dislike, fear, or avoid" (Breakey, 2005, p. 107), and oral exams are perceived as especially difficult, producing many of the debilitating symptoms noted earlier (Sarid et al., 2005). If you are concerned that your anxiety level may interfere with your performance during a presentation or oral exam, you might consider inviting a colleague, friend, or family member to attend the presentation, if permitted, to help allay your anxiety, as the presence of supportive others has been reported to be perceived by student presenters as helpful (Sarid et al., 2005).

If you feel that your anxiety reaches clinical levels, we suggest speaking with a clinical professional to address your fears. There are, however, several strategies that you might use if your anxiety is manageable without clinical intervention. For example, you might attend a traditional public speaking course designed to enhance skills (Ayres et al., 1993; Page, 1985; Robinson, 1997). These classes address presentation details such as preparation, practice, delivery, and presentation reflection in an effort to reduce anxiety (Pribyl, Keaten, & Sakamoto, 2001). Above all, ensure that you have mastered your topic; developing a working familiarity with your material will prepare you for exam questions and increase feelings of comfort during your exam (Robinson, 1997).

Aside from the necessary work of adequate mastery, many individuals worry that something negative might occur during the presentation itself, leading to unfavorable self-assessments (DiBartolo & Molina, 2010). Cognitive models of social anxiety suggest that individuals who fear public speaking hold dysfunctional beliefs and biases about their performance in social situations (Musa & Lépine, 2000). DiBartolo and Molina (2010) propose that these beliefs tend to give rise to an exaggerated self-focus on personal inadequacies, expectations of failure, and the audience's negative judgments. They suggest a number of cognitive restructuring techniques that might help you reduce performance anxiety. In particular, they encourage you to think critically both about specific fears you might have and about how anxious they make you feel. For example, the authors propose that you consider the real likelihood that your most feared prediction will actually occur. Further, how bad would it be if that negative outcome *did* occur? Consider past experiences with public speaking. How often did the feared prediction indeed occur? If the feared prediction did occur, "compare how horrible it would be . . . in comparison to other unpleasant things in life . . . How horrible would it be if/when you failed a course?" (DiBartolo & Molina, 2010, p. 164). Finally, the authors recommend that you generate a coping thought for use during your presentation, even if your feared prediction were to occur. Think about circumstances in which you might use that coping thought. Take time to revisit your anxieties about your upcoming presentation. How anxious do they make you feel now?

Preparation for an oral defense of a master's thesis or doctoral dissertation can be stressful. As described above, negative thoughts can pervade, contributing to anxiety. Try to eliminate negativity where you can. Kuhlenschmidt (1992), who has taught workshops on preparing and presenting a master's-level thesis, focused on the anxiety that many students experience when giving their oral defense. "Coping with anxiety," Kuhlenschmidt asserted, "involves acknowledging feelings, restructuring ways of thinking about the oral defense, learning ways to manage feelings" (p. 87). She suggested that students might begin the restructuring with basic terminology. She recommended that students use positive terms like an *oral meeting* rather than *oral examination* or *oral defense* and to "remind themselves of their expertise on their topic" (p. 87) as well as their past successes. Kuhlenschmidt also encouraged her students to use visualization techniques in which they imagined themselves doing very well at the oral meeting.

Although the commonsense view is that skill training and practice may reduce public speaking anxiety, research reviewed suggests that they may not be sufficient. By incorporating cognitive-behavioral techniques such as cognitive restructuring, along with training and practice, students may acquire a more effective means to manage public speaking fears.

Effective management of public speaking anxiety may be a primary concern for many; however, it is not sufficient for successful performance. Following are practical tips you may want to consider as you prepare for your oral exam/presentation.

Considerations Prior to Exam/Presentation

Preparation for your oral exam/presentation should be at least commensurate to that of a written exam. Considering, however, the nature of the oral platform, developing a more through working knowledge, along with a familiarity with the broader scope of the material than typically required for a written exam will be in your best interest. Whereas written exams allow for the comparative luxury of contemplating, drafting, and editing responses to a range of questions, oral presentations often call for more in-depth focus on a narrower theme, demanding an immediacy of retrieval and an inspired capacity for thinking on your feet.

Topic Preparation

As you work, be sure to master both supporting and principal materials, which will brace you for planned and impromptu questions/interactions from the examiner/audience. Attending to the full range of materials will provide you an opportunity to demonstrate a depth of knowledge beyond the required task. Additionally, you should be prepared for questions on material that you may not intend to present but that you might need to include if the interaction from the examiners/audience moves in that direction. Effective management of material drift and flow not only conveys your degree of preparedness but testifies also to your command of the material.

Plan to begin with an overview of your topic, outlining particular objectives that you intend to cover. From there, presentation requirements may govern the delivery and pacing of informational content. In the absence of specific requirements, you might consider organizing content according to the format of a standard scientific paper, beginning with background information leading to your research question (Miller, 2007). Refer, also, to Chapter 15, Developing Your Presentation Skills.

Adjunct Choice

Multimedia.

Effective presentation of material for your oral exam may call for or be augmented by the addition of multimedia. According to Mayer (2002), "Multimedia instructional messages [are] presentations involving words (such as spoken or printed text) and pictures (such as animation, video, illustrations, and photographs) in which the goal is to promote learning" (p. 56). In particular, when pictures and words are concurrently linked, more effective learning is achieved than when compared to traditional lecture alone (Mayer, 2002). Thus, multimedia affords you an opportunity not only to enrich a traditional oral presentation but also to facilitate a deeper understanding within your audience members.

An additional advantage of the multimedia format is that the development and production of your presentation presents an opportunity to clarify your thoughts and organize material content. At the outset, your content will need to comply with both your presentation objectives and the particular constraints regarding the choice of your multimedia delivery system. Such delivery systems can range from high- to low-tech, including software products, like PowerPoint or Keynote, to posters and even handouts.

Multimedia software.

Today's multimedia software eases the way for the insertion of charts, photos, video, and text, which you can use to facilitate a sound presentation and to which you can refer in response to questions. In addition, you may be tempted to take advantage of a multitude of bells and whistles that are believed to attract and hold viewers' attention. Rather than giving in to these temptations that can potentially distract from your message, take care to ensure that your selections are consistent with the presentation objectives. Refer, also, to Chapter 15, Developing Your Presentation Skills, for a review of appropriate and effective usage of multimedia software, especially PowerPoint presentations.

Posters.

The contextual backdrop for a poster presentation typically indicates a less formal setting for communicating information than, for example, that of a traditional lecture. Graduate students, for example, are often required to present learned material at a graduate seminar. These short presentations typically follow with informal sessions for questions and answers. Poster development and presentation can facilitate learning and prepare for unforeseen questions by promoting two principal functions. First, because of the limited space to present your material, poster development may help you to think about your material in novel ways. You, the developer, must constrain, hone, and configure your material in a manner that best represents your central theme within the specified constraints. Unlike a written report, the poster presentation culminates in a focused, concise format in which you will discard lengthy prose and elaborate tables in favor of streamlined, bulleted points and illustrative, colorful charts or hierarchical graphs highlighting your main points (Hardicre, Devitt, & Coad, 2007; Miller, 2007). Second, presenting your poster promotes interactive engagement of both presenter and viewer with the possibility of leading to deeper insights and a view toward wider ranging implications (Hardicre et al., 2007; Miller, 2007). You, the poster designer, determine the content, rhythm, and flow of your focused topic. Examiners, however, may find focus on a particular component of your presentation and ask questions that require you to step aside—to venture beyond your findings (Miller, 2007). Prepare notes that will facilitate your elaboration on the various components and that will ready you for these impromptu questions and explorations. Take advantage of these interactions, as they can generate compelling, related research ideas. Have a notepad ready to jot down thought-provoking particulars.

Yandell, in this volume (Chapter 15), presents additional details for improving a poster presentation, which we believe complements our comments on the topic. We refer the reader to those useful suggestions.

Handouts.

You may consider distributing handouts for examiners, detailing key aspects of your material otherwise not included in your presentation. Such material may comprise, for example, an abstract, images, tables and charts, and reference list (Miller, 2007). An outline of your presentation will provide the examiner with an orientation to your topic. If you are using presentation software, you may choose to use this option for printing your presentation as a handout.

The Audience

An important consideration is your audience. At the very least, when taking an oral exam, you will want to know how many assessors there will be, along with their specific roles. Will there be a lead assessor? Will each assessor be given an opportunity to ask questions? Will one assessor act as note taker for your later reference? Inquire as to whether you are permitted to extend personal invitations to your presentation. Although oral examinations can be stressful, some presenters have found, as noted earlier, the presence of supportive others to be a calming influence (Sarid et al., 2005). Your audience may be open to members of the institution at large or even to the public. Ensure that you have brought enough handouts for each assessor as well as other attendees. Your assessors will be able to inform you of a typical count for these events.

Presentation Preparation

Self-preparation

As noted above, ensure that you have mastered both planned and supporting materials for your oral exam. Inquire as to whether notes are permitted. Although you should refrain from reading directly from them, they can be useful in prompting you for upcoming topics.

Practice your presentation in front of others who are unfamiliar with the particulars of the material (Miller, 2007). You may consider providing these informal evaluators with an assessment instrument to complete. Lorentzen and Neal (1984) prepared an instrument that evaluators can use to document their impression of a presenter's content, presentation, delivery, voice, appearance, personal traits, and interaction. Finally, rehearse the pacing of your presentation until it is consistent with timing constraints.

Inquire as to whether there is a dress code, and dress appropriately. If there is no code, at the very least you will want to present a neat and clean appearance.

If possible, visit the location prior to your scheduled presentation. Doing so will help to orient you to your surroundings and forestall last-minute unanticipated complications. Familiarize yourself with the overall setting and feel of the space. Where will you present? Where will the examiners be seated in reference to you? What about invited others? Will you be able to see them, or will the room be darkened to facilitate viewing of the presentation software. Is there equipment that you will need to operate? Note the location of electrical sources, light switches, microphone, and so forth. How will you mount your poster? Is there an easel or mounting board? Do you need to bring along your own mounting implements?

The Presentation/Examination

Plan to arrive prior to your scheduled examination time in order to acclimate to the ambient environment and to prepare. Use the time to assemble your handouts for distribution, prepare and test accompanying multimedia software and props, mount your poster, and so on. Turn off your cell phone.

Pace yourself during the presentation and question sessions. Speak slowly, clearly, and with enough volume so that all attendees can hear. Make periodic eye contact with each of the audience members. If questions have not been posed during your presentation, invite questions at the end. Answer them fully—minimizing digressions—and to the best of your ability. If you do not understand a question, ask that it be repeated or stated in another way. If you do not know the answer to a question, acknowledge that you do not know the answer, and make note of the question with the assurance that you will make later inquiries into the matter.

Conclusion

Graduate students are often called upon to present material in a variety of settings, from informal classroom presentations to poster presentation of research findings to classroom lecturing of undergraduates to oral defense of a master's thesis or doctoral dissertation. Indeed, oral presentations are often a standard expectation throughout one's career. Thoughts about public speaking can provoke anxiety to the extent that they can interfere with and precipitate a negative impact upon performance; taking measures to assuage anxiety may help students to experience presentation preparation and delivery in a more positive light.

Careful planning and preparation also contribute to successful outcomes. Beginning with a methodical examination of available material, decisions about the use of presentation adjuncts should come early in presentation planning, as particular adjuncts may orchestrate the flow and delivery of topic material. Developing a familiarity with your presentation environment may also contribute to understanding presentation essentials and to forestalling last-minute confusions. Finally, preparing material beyond what is required will brace you for inevitable questions—whether the setting is a class presentation, examination, or part of a job requirement.

❖ References

Ayres, J., Ayres, F. E., *Baker, A. L., Colby, N., De Blasi, C.,* Dimke, D., . . . , & Wilcox, K. A. (1993). Two empirical tests of a videotape designed to reduce public speaking anxiety. *Journal of Applied Communication Research, 21,* 132–147. doi:10.1080/00909889309365362.

Beatty, M. J., & Behnke, R. R. (1991). Effects of public speaking trait anxiety and intensity of speaking task on heart rate during performance. *Human Communication Research, 18*(2), 147–176. doi:10.1111/j.1468–2958.1991.tb00542.x.

Boyer, E. L. (1987). *College: The undergraduate experience in America.* New York: Harper and Row.

Breakey, L. K. (2005). Fear of public speaking—the role of the SLP. *Seminars in Speech and Language, 26*(2), 107–117. doi:10.1055/s-2005–871206.

Cronin, M., & Glenn, P. (1991). Oral communication across the curriculum in higher education: The state of the art. *Communication Education, 40*(4), 356. Retrieved from http://search.ebscohost.com.libproxy.unh.edu/login.aspx?direct=true&db=ufh&AN=9111110312&site=ehost-live.

Cronin, M. W., Grice, G. L., & Palmerton, P. R. (2000). Oral communication across the curriculum: The state of the art after twenty-five years of experience. *Journal of the Association for Communication Administration, 29*(1), 66–87. Retrieved from http://search.ebscohost.com.libproxy.unh.edu/login.aspx?direct=true&db=ufh&AN=18014785&site=ehost-live.

Daly, J. A., Vangelisti, A. L., & Weber, D. J. (1995). Speech anxiety affects how people prepare speeches: A protocol analysis of the preparation process of speakers. *Communication Monographs, 62*(4), 383–397. doi:10.1080/03637759509376368.

Dannels, D. P. (2001a). Time to speak up: A theoretical framework of situated pedagogy and practice for communication. *Communication Education, 50*(2), 144. Retrieved from http://search.ebscohost.com.libproxy.unh.edu/login.aspx?direct=true&db=ufh&AN=4444008&site=ehost-live.

Dannels, D. P. (2001b). Taking the pulse of communication across the curriculum: A view from the trenches. *Journal of the Association for Communication Administration, 30*(2), 50–70. Retrieved from http://search.ebscohost.com.libproxy.unh.edu/login.aspx?direct=true&db=ufh&AN=18031289&site=ehost-live.

De Grez, L., Valcke, M., & Roozen, I. (2009). The impact of an innovative instructional intervention on the acquisition of oral presentation skills in higher education. *Computers & Education, 53*(1), 112–120. doi:10.1016/j.compedu.2009.01.005.

DiBartolo, P. M., & Molina, K. (2010). A brief, self-directed written cognitive exercise to reduce public speaking anxiety in college courses. *Communication Teacher, 24*(3), 160–164. doi:10.1080/17404622.2010.490230.

Donofrio, H. H. & Davis, K. (1997). *Oral communication across disciplines: Adding value to academic purist and marketability.* Paper presented at the Annual Meeting of the Southern States Communication Association, Savannah, G. Retrieved from http://www.eric.ed.gov/PDFS/ED411553.pdf.

Friedland, E. (2004). Oral communication across the curriculum: What's a small college to do? Report of a collaborative pilot by theatre and education faculty. *JGE: The Journal of General Education, 53*(3), 288–310. Retrieved from http://search.ebscohost.com/login.aspx?direct=true&db=aph&AN=16547082&site=ehost-live.

Hardicre, J., Devitt, P., & Coad, J. (2007). Ten steps to successful poster presentation. *British Journal of Nursing (BJN), 16*(7), 398–401. Retrieved from http://search.ebscohost.com.libproxy.unh.edu/login.aspx?direct=true&db=aph&AN=24911602&site=ehost-live.

Kuhlenschmidt, S. L. (1992). Teaching students to manage the oral defense. *Teaching of Psychology, 19*(2), 86–90. doi:10.1207/s15328023top1902_5.

Lorentzen, K. M., & Neal, R. B. (1984). Preparing health educators to be effective speakers. *Education, 105*(1), 62–65. Retrieved from http://search.ebscohost.com.libproxy.unh .edu/login.aspx?direct=true&db=psyh&AN=1985–29147–001&site=ehost-live.

Mayer, R. E. (2002). Cognitive theory and the design of multimedia instruction: An example of the two-way street between cognition and instruction. *New Directions for Teaching and Learning,* (89), 55–71. Retrieved from http://search.ebscohost.com.libproxy.unh .edu/login.aspx?direct=true&db=eric&AN=EJ645389&site=ehost-live.

Menzel, K. E., & Carrell, L. J. (1994). The relationship between preparation and performance in public speaking. *Communication Education, 43*(1), 17. Retrieved from http://search .ebscohost.com.libproxy.unh.edu/login.aspx?direct=true&db=ufh&AN=9405315250& site=ehost-live.

Miller, J. E. (2007). Preparing and presenting effective research posters. *Health Services Research, 42*(1), 311–328. doi:10.1111/j.1475–6773.2006.00588.x.

Musa, C. Z., & Lépine, J. P. (2000). Cognitive aspects of social phobia: A review of theories and experimental research. *European Psychiatry, 15*(1), 59–66. doi:10.1016/S0924–9338(00)00210–8.

Page, W. T. (1985). Helping the nervous presenter: Research and prescriptions. *Journal of Business Communication, 22*(2), 9–19. Retrieved from http://search.ebscohost.com.lib proxy.unh.edu/login.aspx?direct=true&db=ufh&AN=5777778&site=ehost-live.

Pribyl, C. B., Keaten, J., & Sakamoto, M. (2001). The effectiveness of a skills-based program in reducing public speaking anxiety. *Japanese Psychological Research, 43*(3), 148–155. doi:10.1111/1468–5884.t01–1–00171.

Robinson, Thomas E., II. (1997). Communication apprehension and the basic public speaking course: A national survey of in-class treatment techniques. *Communication Education, 46*(3), 188–197. doi:10.1080/03634529709379090.

Russell, D. R. (1994). American origins of writing-across-the-curriculum movement. In C. Bazerman and D. R. Russell (eds.), *Landmark essays on writing across the curriculum.* Davis, CA: Hermagoras Press. (pp. 3–22).

Sarid, O., Anson, O., & Bentov, Y. (2005). Students' reactions to three typical examinations in health sciences. *Advances in Health Sciences Education, 10*(4), 291–302. doi:10.1007/ s10459–005–6706–2.

Wardrope, W. J. (2002). Department chairs' perceptions of the importance of business communication skills. *Business Communication Quarterly, 65*(4), 60–72. Retrieved from http://search.ebscohost.com.libproxy.unh.edu/login.aspx?direct=true&db=ufh&AN= 8811940&site=ehost-live.

Suggestions for Further Exploration

Friedland, E. (2004). Oral communication across the curriculum: What's a small college to do? Report of a collaborative pilot by theatre and education faculty. *JGE: The Journal of General Education, 53*(3), 288–310. Retrieved from http://search.ebscohost.com/ login.aspx?direct=true&db=aph&AN=16547082&site=ehost-live. Friedland provides a case study of a small college's (Wheelock college in Boston) 2.5-year pilot of a coaching model designed to teach oral communication skills. Wheelock does not have a stand-alone communication department.

Ludwig, T. E., Daniel, D. B., Froman, R., Mathie, V. A. (2004, December). *Using multimedia in classroom presentations: Best principles.* Prepared for the Society for the Teaching of Psychology Pedagogical Innovations Task Force. Retrieved from http://teachpsych.org/ resources/pedagogy/index.php.

19

They Have My Money!

Applying for Research Funding

Leah Skovran Georges
University of Nebraska–Lincoln

Valerie M. Gonsalves
Fulton State Hospital

Matthew T. Huss
Creighton University

One of the most infuriatingly satisfying experiences you may have in your graduate student career is writing a grant. Granting agencies come in all shapes and sizes, but the one thing they have in common is that they *want* to give you money! During graduate school, one of us attended a presentation given by a program officer from the National Science Foundation (NSF). His overwhelming message was that granting agencies are in the business to give money away and that they have your money. You simply need to figure out how to get it! I left that presentation with my friend and fellow graduate student chanting, "We want our money" quietly, so as not to arouse suspicion, but it also gave us hope. These agencies and foundations, in both the private and public sectors, have monies allocated for the sole purpose of providing funding for creative, meaningful research by people just like you. They are not trying to hide it from you or keep it to themselves. They want to give it away! Of course, it is not that easy, but in this chapter, we hope to give you a little bit of information that might start to move your thinking into line with that presenter and make the task of applying for research funding less daunting. We hope to provide general information about where to find funding opportunities, our tips and tricks about how to play this game (and it *is* a game), and how to write and follow through on a research project that sets you apart from the pack.

Why Should I Apply for Funding?

Why should you, as an eager graduate student, apply for grants and outside funding? Why shouldn't you! We can collectively think of more reasons to apply for grant money than reasons not to, but besides the obvious motivation (money), ensuring funding for your research project, big or small, can be beneficial for a number of reasons.

Obtaining a grant may actually give you more time. Don't simply think of the grant in terms of the monies it can provide you. Think of it in terms of the time it saves you to seek out additional opportunities that may be better suited to your professional development. Many graduate departments offer only a 9-month stipend or tuition remission for graduate students. Grant monies can provide for the summer months that a student may go unfunded. Similarly, graduate departments often require a hefty amount of work to earn your stipend, which means the time you devote to department responsibilities may take away from time to complete your own projects. Securing your own funding may provide you the time you need to pursue your own research interests instead of completing other tasks unrelated to your own professional development simply to earn your bread and butter. You may find that with increased time for your research, the project will show higher levels of commitment and competence (Borkowski, 1996). Sustained, outside funding may give you the opportunity to carry out a long-term program of research that you may otherwise not have the opportunity to do. In short, if you provide your *own* funding, your departmental responsibilities may be less, thus increasing time available to work on your own projects and research.

Funding may also help pay for actual research materials. Even the most inexpensive project still costs something. Whether you are conducting drug studies with rats or jury studies with undergraduate samples, the money has to come from somewhere, and funding can help ensure that you get to conduct the research *you* would like to do. Grant monies may pay for copies of project materials, physical lab space and tools, online survey programs, statistics packages, and even help pay research subjects for their participation. Funding may also allow you to hire others to help you collect data or even help analyze the results. For example, a dissertation grant helped one of us pay an undergraduate student to enter all of our data and fund another graduate student for an entire year to continue collecting the data while away on clinical internship. As a graduate student, your time (and sleep) is precious, and if funding gives you the ability to delegate (i.e., pay) assistants to do your dirty work, you may have the opportunity to work on other, more significant facets of the project (Sternberg, 2004).

Applying for and receiving research funding is important for employment and employment advancement. By securing grant monies, you demonstrate the ability to write, develop innovative research ideas, work independently, and in some instances collaborate with well-established members of your field. Grant research is often the sign of a "serious scholar" and can be a "sine qua non" for advancement within a department and within the university (Sternberg, 2004). Similarly, poor economic conditions and the application of many business models to academia and social service jobs have only increased the importance of obtaining external funding for advancement. Although obtaining grants may have just been part of being a productive scholar before, it has become a necessity both within and outside of academia. Colleges and universities are renewing efforts to seek external funding not simply to expand or maintain their standing in the academic community but to survive. Private agencies are requiring staff to write grants to simply sustain their programs and services to the community. Recently, one of us has been conducting research with a state corrections department on their sex offender program. As part of the ongoing relationship, we agreed to submit grants for them not to simply continue and expand our research program but to provide for the basic necessities of staff. Specifically, we are writing a grant so they can obtain a truck to drive around and monitor recently released sex offenders. In the current economic conditions, whether you plan on working in academia, for a nonprofit, industry, or other public policy agency, a track record for obtaining external funding is increasingly valued.

Finally, the act of developing and writing a grant proposal is invaluable in and of itself. Grant writing is different from many other types of writing you will do as a graduate student, and the opportunity to develop a research plan and budget for your *own* research while still under departmental mentorship is an opportunity every student should take advantage of. For example, we have had the frustrating experience of working with a large university infrastructure to develop and coordinate a budget that pleases a variety of departments and people within the university. Having a skilled mentor to guide us through this process was invaluable. The skill set involved in grant writing is very similar to traditional academic writing, but the distinctions are enough that utilizing departmental resources while they are still available to you as a student will be to your advantage.

Where Can I Find Funding Opportunities?

The process of writing a grant may seem like a daunting one, but if you divide the process into baby steps, it can seem much more manageable. The first step is: where the heck do I find out about funding sources? Who is going to give me my money? One of the most important steps in the process is seeking out worthwhile funding sources, and the good news is that there are tons of ways to go about it.

First, begin with your best source for all information in graduate school, only said partially tongue in cheek: your advisors and mentors. Hopefully, the people training you have a track record of obtaining external funding and some idea of the grant funding landscape for your specific area. Is it better for you to start looking at the National Science Foundation? Should you look toward the National Institute of Mental Health? It may well be that if you look at a given call for proposals or program description, it seems like a good fit for your idea. However, your advisor may know some of the history and tradition of a grant source that may not be spelled out specifically and make a source less attractive to you and your research ideas. Your advisor or other professionals in the field should be able to save you some time and energy by guiding you in the right direction. However, make sure that you also do your own homework. We live in very dynamic times in the funding of research, and things are definitely changing compared to 5, 10, or 20 years ago. Utilize the knowledge of those available to you in your field to begin your search process.

In addition, large and increasingly smaller research universities typically have units set up on campus to assist in obtaining grants. Although a grants administration department may be set up specifically to help you obtain necessary signatures on a soon-to-be-submitted proposal or handle funding once a grant is obtained, they also are a great resource to discover potential sources for funding. They frequently will either identify general sources given your interest or identify specific grants seeking proposals. They may even keep you regularly updated on any information they receive in your discipline or specific area of interest. However, these agencies may not have discipline-specific knowledge that your advisor has and sometimes may cast a wide net that results in a lot of sources that are not appropriate for your particular research area.

Something else you can do in conjunction with contacting the grants administration at your university is conduct your own searches. First, there are specific databases set up for external funding. With a few key terms or phrases, you can identify hundreds of possibilities. Again, you are likely to yield a lot of sources that end up being unsuitable for your area of research. However, it can pay off for those one or two very relevant hits. Of course, besides searches set up specifically for grants, you can always use your favorite search engine such as Google, Yahoo!, or Bing. Our experience has been that even these crude searches can provide valuable information from time to time.

Besides specific ways to start your search, there are some additional conceptual issues to think about. Make sure you think both big and small. We have submitted and received grants from the largest federal agencies as well as small private foundations. Traditional sources like the National Institutes of Health, National Science Foundation, Department of Defense, and Department of Education are frequently the ones most people think about. However, more moderate-sized grants can also be obtained from smaller government-affiliated programs and private foundations such as the Society for the Psychological Study of Social Issues (SPSSI) or the Guggenheim Foundation. One source that we have not mentioned yet is your own university or even department. Many departments and universities have their own mechanisms for distributing small grants to graduate students that may simply fund the cost of materials or your stipend for an entire year.

Graduate students should also think outside of the box a little in terms of seeking out funding sources. The traditional model is to come up with an empirical question and submit a proposal outlining a particular study or program of study to a granting agency. However, there are also other types of grants such as training grants, career awards, and dissertation grants (Gerin, 2006). Training grants are grants that typically focus on funding an entire program or specific area of study. For example, one of our programs in graduate school historically was funded by a training grant from NIMH, and the focus of the grant shifted over the years to encourage research in a broad given area, not in a specific idea of study. Career awards are given to individuals based on general requirements such as being a graduate student or early-career professional and, again, tend to be broader in scope. Many agencies provide monies for specific populations that are underrepresented in that particular field, such as racial/ethnic minorities or women. There are even specific grants for dissertations.

These grants are only available to individuals who are planning on working on their dissertations, so you would only be competing with individuals in your career stage.

Another, less known source of funding is through traditionally nonacademic resources. Keep your eyes open for funding opportunities cleverly disguised as scholarships, stipends, or awards. One of us received a considerable scholarship from a national organization she was very involved with as an undergraduate. This organization had scholarship opportunities available for alumni members of the organization at both the regional and national levels, and oftentimes these types of awards are less competitive than traditional, research-based grants. Furthermore, the application process is often less time intensive and less research focused than similar sources. Take advantage of these national and community grants that you may be qualified for that are not necessarily related to your specific research interests. These funding sources generally do not specify how to spend the award money, so you may easily apply the funds to conduct your individual projects. The small amount of time involved in applying for these awards is often worth a hefty payoff!

There also are some practices that are accepted and even encouraged in grant writing that are contrary to the publication process that graduate students may be more familiar with at this stage. Although it is not acceptable to submit a manuscript to multiple journals simultaneously, it is perfectly acceptable to submit simultaneous grant proposals. Of course, although these submissions typically need to be geared to a particular funding source, it is not unusual for the bulk of a given proposal to be appropriately submitted to more than one source simultaneously. One of us submitted proposals for dissertation grants to multiple sources and was successful with one of them. You may also need to submit a proposal multiple times before being successful. It is not unusual for professionals to submit a proposal once, twice, or three times to a grant source before they are successfully funded. Of course, this can be a real issue in the finite world of a graduate education. Most of us hope to get out of graduate school in a reasonable amount of time and don't intend to spend years submitting grant applications. However, some agencies have multiple funding cycles in a given year and even have grants reviewed prior to the next funding cycle or deadline for submissions. In these cases, multiple submissions are a little more realistic.

Most larger granting agencies have a program staff available to answer specific questions about the submission and review process for you. Take advantage of this opportunity, as the program staff can guide you through some of the more complicated areas of the application process or even help you determine whether you are qualified for specific grants within their agency. If you are not sure whether your research ideas may be viewed with enthusiasm at a particular agency—ask! In fact, you should *always* contact the granting agency prior to your submission or even contact people you know who have reviewed grants for that particular agency before because it can be an invaluable resource.

Remember some of our initial comments? These granting programs and agencies are in the business to give money away, your money! They will normally bend over backward to help you navigate the process because they want to fund the best projects possible. One personal example of this is when one of us submitted a proposal to a large government agency for a dissertation grant. This agency had typically funded a broad array of dissertation grants across content and program areas.

However, it was beginning to change and was requiring dissertation grants to have certain overarching and specific content. After contacting the staff and one of the former reviewers for this agency, it became clear that the new mechanism for funding dissertations grants would not be as favorable as the prior process to the current idea. As a result of discussing the issue with the agency staff, the proposal was submitted under one program and then shifted to another content area for review by experts in the specific content area that would be much more favorable toward the idea. There is no doubt that this proposal never would have gotten funded without talking to the agency and figuring out the mechanism that would be most successful. On a side note, the program staff is available for general advice about the submission process and for clarification when necessary, not to design the specifics of your proposal. Be sure to do your homework before contacting a program officer, as many answers are available on the granting agency's webpage or within grant specifications materials.

You have many funding options available to you, large and small, and the key is to find the best fit for your area of research.

General Advice about Grant Writing: Our Not-So-Secret Tips and Tricks

One of the unique factors that sets grant writing apart from other academic writing is that it is not necessarily only about the quality of the writing that gets you recognition—or money, in this case. Many facets of grant writing are beyond the writer's control, including the political climate of the organization at the time you submit a project and funds available, among other things. However, there are several ways to play the game that will make your proposal more appealing, even to the most finicky reviewer. You might call these some of our favorite tips and tricks for getting your money.

One of the common myths about grant writing is that if you have the "best looking" horse in the race, the grant reviewers will jump at the opportunity to sing your praises. This isn't necessarily the case. Competition is stiff—some sources report that roughly 80% of reasonably *good* grants are initially rejected by granting agencies, and of the 20% of grants that were approved by agencies, very few of those will have been approved on their first submission (Borkowski, 1996). According to the National Science Foundation's 2009 funding statistics, some research areas received upward of 9,000 proposals, and acceptance rates ranged from approximately 15% to 33% (Data.gov, 2009). This certainly does not mean that most submitted grants were subpar but, rather, it illustrates that receiving grants is only part skill—and the rest depends on the reviewers, universal excitement about your proposed topic, amount of available funding, and sometimes even where your proposal fell in the stack of proposals the reviewer read that day. One of the authors has received such diverse comments from reviewers (i.e., "full support for funding," "does not hold enough intellectual merit as written," "unoriginal and largely implausible,") that it made her wonder whether the three reviewers had actually read the same proposal! Although there are some aspects of the process you can't control, focusing on the parts that you *are* able to control will increase your chances of success.

Once you have a clear sense of where and when you intend to submit a grant proposal, it's time to develop a clear sense of the expectation of the specific granting agency. Most major funding agencies (i.e., NIH, NSF, etc.) have specific and fairly unbending guidelines for the actual submission process. Although it may seem frivolous (i.e., font size, page limit, font *type*, etc.), stick to them rigidly, as the writer who cannot follow simple formatting instructions may not reach the reviewers' hands! Similarly, be sure you are *qualified* for the specific grant to which you intend to apply. We have heard horror stories about graduate students who submit well-written grants, only to find that the grant was not available to graduate students, but rather tenured faculty only, or even someone outside of their field of study! Another issue to think about is deadlines. For some agencies, their deadlines are target dates that serve only as a suggestion for a submission date. However, in most cases, these deadlines represent a very strict barrier. Even a minute, much less an hour or a day late, can mean that your proposal is not reviewed and that you may have to wait another 6 months, another year—or it may have been a one-time funding opportunity.

Grant writing certainly is *not* is an overnight project. First and foremost, do not underestimate the time it takes to put together a solid grant proposal. One of the most basic places to begin the process is with research—and not just the kind of research you might do for a class paper or project. Grant writing is a skill—a skill that takes practice—and one of the best places to start your research process is by reviewing grant proposals that have been successfully funded. Take time to review accepted projects from the granting agency and specifically in your area of interest (i.e., psychology, biology, etc.). What did those authors do particularly well? It can be a great place to begin your own research and writing process, but it also gives you an idea of the magnitude of the task that lies ahead.

Something else to think about that may seem pretty natural for a graduate student but counterintuitive on a different level is writing a grant without, in essence, getting any credit for it. Several of us have done this on purpose. The first experience with grant writing for one of the authors was without credit or authorship in any form. At an informal program brown bagger, the director of the program announced that he had an idea for a grant proposal based on the informal presentation he had just made and encouraged anyone interested in writing a grant with him to set up a meeting. A very young and naïve graduate student later approached him and expressed interest. Across several months, this graduate student assisted with writing the grant, and by *assisted*, we mean that the student wrote an entire grant in an area he had never studied before and that the faculty member submitted it and it was successfully funded! The graduate student did not get any credit in that the Principle Investigator on the grant had to have a Ph.D., and the student was therefore not eligible. However, the experience was invaluable, and even though the graduate student wrote the initial drafts of the grant, it became clear to the student that it was the feedback of the faculty member and his knowledge in knowing how to craft a grant submission that were key in getting it funded.

In a similar vein, although you may not have the gumption or simply the time to volunteer to assist on a grant, sometimes and often beyond your control, the task will be required of you. One of us has written countless biographical sketches for faculty she has never met and will likely never have the pleasure to meet; however, the experience was wholly worth the effort. Though it may not have initially been a volunteer endeavor, she has had the opportunity to appreciate, first hand, how a number of successful grants are written, edited, reviewed, and eventually obtained. Even if there was little (ok, zero) initial reward for the experience, several years down the line, writing her own grant has been far less stressful than for some of her peers because it is a familiar concept. Remember, the process of successfully obtaining funding is a marathon and not a sprint. Often, the satisfaction of a grant well written, albeit for somebody else, may come later during your graduate career and beyond.

One last but important tip that has served several of us well in obtaining funding is thinking about writing a grant from a multidisciplinary approach. Multidisciplinary research ideas can be very appealing. A project that can inform *multiple* areas of study can be very attractive for a review team. For example, a project that investigates a theory that appeals to the fields of psychology *and* law or sociology *and* women's studies may suggest farther-reaching implications than a psychology- or law-based proposal only. The research you plan to propose may already be multidisciplinary in a way you have not considered. Take a step back from your idea and receive some input about how you might present it in a way that relates to several areas of study.

Directly related to the idea of multidisciplinary studies is the topic of collaboration. One very important question you may ask yourself, especially as a graduate student, is whether one or two carefully chosen collaborators will help your odds in winning the funding game. Strategically selected collaborators could be the thing that sets your proposal apart from the rest—especially if you have chosen a multidisciplinary approach to presenting your ideas. For example, if you as a psychology graduate student present a new theory about jurors' understanding of expert witnesses in capital murder cases, it may be in your best interest to include a collaborator who has some expertise in the law surrounding capital murder. Including such collaborators may quell any question the reviewers have about your ability to complete the research—assuring them you have the expertise on board to successfully complete your proposed idea. Multidisciplinary research teams can certainly be appealing; however, be sure including collaborators in your study will in fact *help* your cause. If they are not necessary and would not add anything to the success of your grant proposal or to the implementation of the grant, perhaps it would be best to fly solo. There is such a thing as "too many cooks in the kitchen" in grant writing.

Now to Write the Thing!

Now that you have a plan—you know where to submit your proposal, understand the expectations, and have memorized our helpful tips—the fun part begins: writing the proposal! The rules of solid scientific writing are no different here than they are in other academic writing. As we said previously, writing a grant proposal is not an overnight process—it takes careful planning, research, writing, and feedback. Start early and plan to finish early—it will make the process far less stressful if you feel good about your timeline. Similarly, set both proximal and distal goals for your writing. What, specifically, do you plan to finish today? What should be done by the end of the week? Keeping a detailed schedule will make the task seem far less daunting than reading "write grant" on your to-do list each morning.

The Function of a Grant Proposal

A well-written, comprehensive grant proposal, regardless of how large or small the funding source, should function in at least three ways. It should serve as a way to communicate, as a plan for action, and as a contract between the researcher and the granting agency (Locke, Spirduso, & Silverman, 2007). One of the primary purposes of a grant proposal is to communicate your proposed idea to the granting agency generally and to the reviewers specifically. The quality of the writing, clarity of your methodology, and thoroughness of your ideas will depend on how well you communicate them to your readers. The best idea, lost in a sea of pages without direction or theory, is just that—a lost idea. Your 10- to 25-page proposal is the *only* information the reviewers have to understand completely your plan of research—be sure you present it as clearly as possible and in a way that excites your reviewers. It is important that you communicate exactly what you want your reader to understand.

A solid proposal will be thorough and factual with specific attention to detail, but there is more to communication in an excellent, fundable proposal than sentence structure and correct referencing. Solid communication also entails crafting and even selling a compelling story about your research. Remember, although the person reading your proposal may not be the most knowledgeable person in your *specific* area of research, that reader should finish your proposal with an understanding of the project you propose, its importance, but also a sense of excitement about your proposed project! A successful grant writer can take the most seemingly dull topic and make the most uninformed reader believe that not only is the research necessary, but it is also thrilling and the implications are real. Although the scientific merit of a proposal is at the core of this process, you are selling an idea and trying to prove it is necessary and should potentially get thousands or hundreds of thousands of dollars in order to make it a reality. Sometimes the way you say something is as important as what you say. What sets your project apart from the sometimes very large pack of other equally compelling studies? What are the long-lasting real-world implications of this research? Do they extend beyond your small research niche? If so, discuss them. Depending on the funding source, you have more or less freedom in the design of your proposal; however, even with the strictest formatting standards, well-thought-out writing with a plot twist or two will hook your reader and make her curious about the end of the story (i.e., fund your project)!

One of the best ways to communicate clearly is to have a sound research idea. Sounds simple enough, right? Well actually, it is. Your idea needn't be the most groundbreaking or earth shattering the National Science Foundation has ever reviewed. Rather, your idea should be novel and interesting to those in your field and should hold some theoretical implications for future research. Sternberg (2004) agrees; he advises that you simply need an idea you can sell to a granting agency. This is not to say that very simple ideas will cut it with the larger granting agencies. Rather, a new idea that integrates well-informed existing research with a novel application will be more appealing. Remember, your goal is not to fit the entire history of social psychology or biomedical ethics into a 10-page grant proposal. Rather, your goal should be to succinctly and clearly convey your expertise and excitement in the specific area of study.

Just as communication is one of the major functions of a grant proposal, your proposal should also serve as a plan for action (Locke et al., 2007). A hallmark of a solid proposal is the level of thoroughness and detail of the proposed execution of the study. Remember, to get the big bucks, you have to explain not only *why* you deserve the money to conduct your research but also *how* you will accomplish this research. Most granting agencies require some type of proposed design and methods summary—often detailed and specific. Be clear in your explanation of the independent variables, the participants, and your data analysis. Realize that reviewers are reading your proposal for the first time and have not thought about your particular idea for the last 6 months, received feedback from other experts in the area, written draft after draft, or gone back and forth consulting the literature. Part of being clear is keeping it simple; this can be difficult. A grant proposal is not the time to use convoluted language and discuss tangential ideas or implications. You have naturally thought about the next several steps in the process or the addition of a couple of other variables, but if these ideas become complex distractions to a reviewer, they are counterproductive. Do not be afraid of redundancy and extra care in organizing your proposal. A reviewer may be reading a stack of proposals, and you don't know whether he or she is reading your proposal while engaged and interested or after reading a series of poor proposals. Make sure you make your points clear and organize them in the fashion the reviewers are expecting so they don't have to go searching and can score your proposal easily.

A final function of a great grant proposal is its ability to function as a contract (Locke et al., 2007). A completed, signed, and submitted proposal implies that should you be awarded the funds and you intend to complete the study in the way you stated and within the budget you projected. This agreement is particularly important as you compose your proposal. Although you may have a fascinating proposal, be sure you can produce within the allowed timeline of the proposal you submitted. For example, if you are awarded a substantial amount of money to complete a 2-year, four-phase, 1,500 college student participant-as-subject study with multilevel modeling, this is what you would be expected to produce. If this seems unrealistic, pare back your proposed research in a way that is just as interesting, novel, and relevant without setting yourself up for burnout, or worse yet, having to return funds because you did not uphold your portion of the contract. Speaking with mentors and those who have received grants in the past can help a student set realistic goals about what is feasible within a particular timeline and budget.

Feedback and Revisions

So you have completed a solid draft of your proposal and, like climbing a mountain, now that you've reached this important milestone, it's compelling to stop and admire your work. Take a moment and congratulate yourself on a draft well written and then get back to work (insert groan here). Even the most seasoned writers stop and review their work and receive feedback during the writing process. It is important to get a fresh perspective at times. Remember, we said that your research idea needn't be the most novel or groundbreaking—but, rather, it should add something to your field of research and, most importantly, be interesting to you. If you show a passion for the research project, others will feel your excitement as well! One of the best ways to determine whether your idea seems realistic and fundable is to speak with those who have received grants in your specific area of interest in the past. Seek out feedback at each stage of the grant-writing process.

You do not want to find yourself with a 25-page finished proposal only to discover that your colleagues find serious flaws with your basic research idea.

Make feedback a frequent part of your writing process. Ask your fellow students and mentors to review your work and to give honest and constructive feedback about each aspect of the proposal. Gerin (2006) suggests providing a list of specific questions for your readers to answer as they review your grant, including: "Did the writing communicate a sense of my excitement about this project? Were you persuaded that this study should be done and that the results would help to answer the question or questions that it purports to ask? Did you find the story easy to follow? Were the methods appropriate to the study questions? What limitations do you feel I should have addressed?" (p. 64). He suggests setting a goal to finish the final draft of your proposal 6 weeks ahead of the deadline to allow for comments from colleagues and potential revisions. Gerin also notes that most will not follow through on this approach, as the deadline tends to sneak up more quickly than expected for most people, so keep this in mind when you set your own deadlines. Just be aware that you are asking a great deal of someone—to review up to 25 pages of writing. Be sure to offer to return the favor.

One of us has actually chosen to forgo a grant proposal deadline for the following submission date, 6 months later, based on the feedback she received on a project. After receiving quality feedback from several advisors, she realized that her chances of receiving the grant would be much greater if she submitted a more polished and focused project for the next deadline. Had she not received feedback on the project, she may have done herself a disservice by submitting a project that was in need of considerable revisions, especially because some funding agencies limit the number of times you can submit a proposal.

The End Game

Once you submit your grant, one of three things can happen: You receive funding, the agency recommends revisions and recommends resubmitting for the next deadline, or your project is not considered fundable. If you received approval, enjoy your funding and get to work to bring your project to life! Remember, one of the major functions of a grant is to act as a contract, and you may be required to send updates to the agency as your work progresses. Be sure to live up to your end of the bargain.

Much like submitting an article to a journal for publication, granting agencies may give you the opportunity to revise and resubmit. You should know prior to submission if this is the case for the agency to which you submit. If the agency allows for resubmission, it will often provide feedback about what the reviewers enjoyed about your proposal as well as what they think could be improved upon. If that is the case, you may have the golden opportunity to revise and resubmit your proposal for the following review date. If you do choose to resubmit the proposal (and you should), you will likely be asked to indicate how you addressed earlier comments by the reviewers (Sternberg, 2004). Follow the comments of the reviewers carefully, as they may be part of the board to review your revised proposal. Remember, the comments likely came from other well-respected professionals and will only serve to enhance your initial idea.

In the case that your proposal was not invited back for review, we still congratulate you! The experience of grant writing is invaluable, and the question "What now?" is actually rather wide open! Remember that most reasonably good proposals are rejected, especially on the first submission. In fact, Sternberg (2004) suspects that the correlation between the quality of ideas in a proposal and its getting funded hovers right around zero. Pride has no place in grant writing. No one enjoys being rejected, and it is easy to give up after the first or second, or even 12th try—especially after a few particularly scathing remarks from reviewers. Even the best writers and researchers in your field have had proposals go unfunded from both private and public funding agencies, and if they have not—they likely have not written any. We had one colleague that submitted 23 straight grants unsuccessfully. However, since those failures, he has become exceedingly successful, almost too successful to keep on top of all his projects. Persistence is the key to a successful granting career. If you know you have a great idea, continue working to convince granting agencies that it is worthy of their money. They will eventually see the novelty and importance in your idea and throw some funding your way.

Whatever you do, do not waste the time and effort you put into your proposal. One of the authors of this chapter gave another author some solid advice years ago—that is to never waste a thing you write. Take every class paper, research experiment, and rejected grant proposal and turn it into product. If you choose not to resubmit the proposal, you still have several options. First, put the proposal in your file cabinet for a bit (or even a few years) and revisit it only occasionally. You may stumble across some new literature or insight into how to modify the research to make it more appealing for granting agencies. Second, is it possible to modify the project in a way that you can still conduct the research sans funding? For example, instead of paying community members to complete a survey, is it possible to use a more available (and free) sample, such as college students? If the integrity of your study is still intact after several modifications, run that study anyway. If you wrote a solid proposal, at the very least you have a solid introduction, methods section, and perhaps part of a discussion already written—take advantage of the work you have already done.

Conclusion

In conclusion, many opportunities exist for those who search for them and want to put in the effort to write for them. Keep writing and chances are you will receive the funding to run that study. Start small with departmental or universitywide grants and work your way toward federal funding. The good news is that the odds are in your favor—you will likely receive funding, and the chances to make a meaningful impact on your research career, as well your field in general, are endless. And remember, they have your money, they want to give it away—you simply need to figure out how to get it!

❖ References

Borkowski, J. G. (1996). Applying for research funding. In F. T. L. Leong & J. T. Austin (Eds.), *The psychology research handbook: A guide for graduate students and research assistants* (pp. 342–350). Thousand Oaks, CA: Sage.

Data.gov. (2009). *National Science Foundation grant funding rates*. Retrieved October 8, 2010, from http://www.data.gov/raw/1598#.

Gerin, W. (2006). *Writing the NIH grant proposal: A step-by-step guide*. Thousand Oaks, CA: Sage.

Locke, L. F., Spirduso, W. W., & Silverman, S. J. (2007). *Proposals that work: A guide for planning dissertations and grant proposals*. Thousand Oaks, CA: Sage.

Sternberg, R. J. (2004). Obtaining a research grant: The applicant's vies. In J. M. Darley, M. P. Zanna, & H. L. Roediger (Eds.), *The compleat academic: A career guide* (pp. 169–184). Washington, DC: American Psychological Association.

❖ Suggestions for Further Exploration

Locke, L. F., Spirduso, W. W., & Silverman, S. J. (2007). *Proposals that work: A guide for planning dissertations and grant proposals*. Thousand Oaks, CA: Sage. This comprehensive text is useful not only for grant writing but also for any large research-based project, such as a dissertation. It covers topics that run the gamut from basic information about how to identify a fundable topic to developing a writing timeline and how to deal with acceptance and rejection of an award. It also includes an appendix of a variety of sample proposals.

Sternberg, R. J. (2004). Obtaining a research grant: The applicant's view. In J. M. Darley, M. P. Zanna, & H. L. Roediger (Eds.), *The compleat academic: A career guide* (pp. 169–184). Washington, DC: American Psychological Association. This chapter, situated in one of the must-read books for graduate students and young academics, reviews the application and grant-writing process from the perspective of an applicant. This relatively short chapter packs a large amount of insightful information about how to write a focused and comprehensive grant proposal.

SECTION III

Winding Down and Gearing Up (All at the Same Time)

As your graduate career begins to wind down and you start to gear up for the next phase of your professional journey, you are still faced with important challenges in the latter part of your graduate training. The authors in this section of the book offer excellent advice for success during this part of graduate school and beyond. Chapter 20 provides a sound framework for thinking about dissertation issues, an obvious and important milestone in completing your degree. Other chapters relate to developing a clear career plan for life after graduation or thinking through issues related to ADB status. The next two chapters, 23 and 24, are gold mines of practical information for successful application to academic and clinical and other applied positions. Finally, the book ends with advice on what to do if you don't land the job you want. We believe that if you carefully follow the advice in this book, from settling in to winding down, you will maximize your chances of turning your career dreams into reality. But if not, don't lose hope. As Chapter 25 suggests: Keep plugging away and you will ultimately find the position you have worked so hard to obtain. We wish you all the success in the world!

20

Working With Your Major Professor and Dissertation Committee

❖

Seraphine Shen-Miller
Belmont University

David S. Shen-Miller
Tennessee State University

I n this chapter, we share thoughts designed to be useful in working with your major professor and dissertation committee through one of the most exciting, challenging, and satisfying stages of your graduate career. A guiding theme of our approach to this topic is the importance of identifying your optimal environmental and relational conditions, so throughout we will be encouraging you to consider what works best for you. Above all, this is the time to be active. Often the dissertation is the last or next-to-last step in graduate training. It is a chance to pursue the research ideas you have been cultivating and an opportunity to put your graduate training into practice. You, your major professor, and your committee form a team that can help you produce a high-quality dissertation and a contribution to the literature. This may be the only time in your life that you will have access to a group of experts who are all giving their attention to your work—so try to enjoy it!

The dissertation committee is a team of faculty that provides you with guidance and critiques throughout the dissertation process and helps you form and develop your research. For example, at the proposal stage, your committee reviews and evaluates the feasibility of your dissertation topic, theoretical and empirical backgrounds of your research, and the methods you plan to use for data collection and analysis.

During the writing phase, your committee reviews and provides feedback for your drafts. And, when you are nearing the end of the project, your committee evaluates the scholarly merit of your work through the written document and your (typically oral) defense of the project.

A committee usually consists of four or five faculty members, including one chair (your major professor) and at least three other members. Typically, the committee will include two faculty from your own program or department as well as a member from somewhere else in the university. In the committee, your chair is particularly important as the person who will work most closely with you during the process. As you will see, the chair will be the major person who provides feedback for your drafts and determines when you are ready for your proposal and defense. The chair may also help you identify and recruit committee members.

A number of chapters in this book focus on the specific research, writing, and oral presentation skills necessary for completing a thesis or dissertation. In this chapter, we focus on supplementary yet essential skills such as self-assessment, professional comportment, and negotiation. We discuss how to develop strong relationships with your major professor and dissertation committee and how to get the most out of working with these experienced professionals who can add a great deal of expertise and dimension to your work. We start by focusing on the relationship with your major professor and continue with attention to the rest of the committee.

Selecting and Working With Your Major Professor

One of the most important parts of the dissertation starts with selecting a major professor from among your faculty. Your major professor typically works with you on multiple drafts of your dissertation before the proposal meeting and at every step in the process, from conceptualizing the study to selecting committee members, inviting committee members, and proposing and defending the dissertation. In other words, this person plays a central role—so choose carefully. We recommend beginning with a look inward.

Stage One: Begin With Self-Assessment

We suggest starting the process of selecting a major professor by thinking about the kind of relationship and environment that work best for you. Often this involves a frank and honest self-assessment. Take a look at your priorities—what is most important to you in terms of a major professor? What kind of role would you like this person to play in helping you with your research? For example, do you work best when going off on your own with a list of tasks and open-ended deadlines, or are you at your best when you have regular meeting times and established deadlines? Do you work best in a team environment where other graduate students will be contributing to your research (e.g., through data collection and analysis), or do you flourish when on your own? Krumboltz (1991) observed that the dissertation is a lonely process when students are expected to do all of the research on their own and suggested that team approaches can help students feel connected with others during the process.

Next, consider your communication preferences, including feedback and support. What kinds of feedback typically suit you best? Do you prefer point-by-point, specific feedback, or do you thrive on feedback that focuses on the "big picture"? Of course, you will likely need both kinds during the dissertation process, but think through which you will need more of—and identify the faculty member who is best at delivering it. Also, consider your interpersonal needs. Doing a dissertation is a long process that involves many different steps as well as a wide range of emotions. Consider what you might need from a major professor in terms of support. For some, connecting with a major professor who has not only been through the process but who has also helped many other students can be invaluable. And although some faculty can be highly responsive in meeting those needs, others may be less adept or willing to do so.

Make sure to include in your analysis an honest evaluation of your strengths and weaknesses in writing and research. In which areas (e.g., conceptualization, statistics, design, writing, analysis, or methods) are you the strongest? In which areas will you require the most support and help? What would you most like to learn during the process? Often there are additional areas in which a major professor can help you, such as locating funding (e.g., grants), writing proposals to support your research, and connecting with local, national, and international experts who can help with data collection, design, and conceptualization.

Finally, we conceptualize the major professor–student relationship as one that is in flux, including a number of different roles based on the needs of the given situation. Similar to Bernard's (Bernard, 1997; Bernard & Goodyear, 2004) model for supervision, during your dissertation, your major professor may serve as a teacher and at other times may be more counselor or consultant, depending on your needs and the needs of the project. Identifying a major professor who can move well among those roles is an important consideration.

Find a match of research interests. Of course, perhaps the biggest part of the equation has to do with finding a match with your research interests. We strongly recommend finding a faculty member whose research interests closely align with your own, as faculty who are doing research in your desired area (or close to it) can add a depth of knowledge of the field that will increase your potential for making an important contribution with your research. On the other hand, if no one is doing research in your area, you may consider connecting with a major professor whose expertise is closely connected in another way (e.g., research design, statistical analysis, intervention expertise, on a related topic).

Assess faculty strengths—and weaknesses. As you consider different faculty, keep in mind their individual strengths and weakness. In addition to the self-assessment needs noted above, consider faculty availability and responsiveness. How available is the professor? Is it relatively easy to set up an initial appointment for consultation? Chances are, if you have to work really hard to set up that first meeting, you will have a similarly difficult path to tread for setting future meetings. Ask a prospective major professor his or her typical timeline of turning drafts around. You may also ask this same question of students who have worked with this potential major professor. Although this may not seem the case today, the dissertation includes a number of significant deadlines and the process usually extends into summer vacation, holidays, and spring break. Finding out the extent to which a prospective major professor is available during those periods will help prevent time crunches and related meltdowns later.

Stage Two: Preparation and Consultation

Once you have completed your self- and faculty assessments, it is time to shift gears and get more information (think multimethod, multimeasure approach). We recommend consulting with student peers and meeting with a few faculty members to increase the amount of data on which you base your decision. If you have a good relationship with an advisor or faculty member, you may be tempted to skip these steps and simply select your major professor. Nevertheless, we recommend scheduling a meeting to talk over research ideas and working styles with a few faculty members. At the very least, you might identify a potential committee member or two.

Consult with peers. We strongly suggest talking with peers as well as asking any other mentors (e.g., clinical supervisors, contacts outside the program) about their experiences. Focus on the specific faculty you are considering and also on what does and does not work in general in terms of relationships with a major advisor. Ask other students, especially those working on their dissertations, about their experiences to get a sense of how helpful their major professor has been at each stage. What do they know now that they wish they had known at the beginning? What would they change? Do they have any recommendations about approaching the specific professor you are considering? Other questions could include: What was the working relationship like? Were your needs as a student prioritized? How accessible was this faculty member? What is her/his style of feedback? How was conflict managed (if it occurred)? Would you work with this person again?

Think systemically. It may be important to consider program and department dynamics. For example, does the professor you are considering have harmonious or contentious working relationships with other faculty? How are those types of relationships played out with students (if at all)? Does the potential chair have good facilitation skills (thinking ahead to the committee meeting; Van Slyke et al., 2003)? Although in our experience, faculty conflicts are not typically overt in dissertation committee meetings the last thing that you want is for some undercurrent of distress or conflict to be affecting interactions in the room. Asking questions such as the ones we have noted may give you some insight into the potential for such dynamics.

Get in touch—with advance notice. Next, get in touch with a few prospective major advisors. We recommend scheduling a formal meeting versus popping by during someone's office hours. Scheduling a formal meeting will let them know that you're serious and give them a chance to prepare for the meeting. E-mail typically works best, but if you decide to pop by, make sure you bring your schedule so if that person is not available at the moment, you can schedule a time to meet in the future.

Come prepared. Be as organized and prepared as possible for *every* meeting, especially in those initial meetings where you are screening potential major professors. They are going to commit significant time and energy to your project, so you want to convey that you are taking the process seriously. Remember, you are not only coming to get answers to your questions and figure out if you want to work with this person. You are also setting the tone for the relationship, and they are forming impressions of your readiness to work on the dissertation. Be prepared to talk about your interests and the role that you would like them to play, and have some questions ready about the topics that we have raised above. You might ask the faculty member how he/she views the role as a major professor. Does she see herself as a working partner, collaborator, or distant guide? In his opinion, how independently should the student operate? What does she see as her role in chairing the committee during meetings—is she an advocate for you or just another committee member? Knowing your major professor's beliefs about her or his role at all stages of the process will clarify your own role and help avoid potential conflicts and missed assumptions later on.

If you have a specific direction for your research, make sure to talk about that, and if you are passionate about a topic, hold strong to it. As with all else, use your negotiation skills—and be prepared to be a little flexible.

Decide. After your meetings, take a few days to think things over. Sometimes it can be useful to make a "pros and cons" list or to rank faculty members in terms of which of your priorities they meet—and the extent to which each one does so. Use your training as a scientist—consider all available data and think critically to make the best decision you can. Then, get in touch with that person via e-mail or meeting. Remember that although you can only choose one major advisor, other faculty were on your list for a reason and might be excellent additions to your committee. Finally, once you have secured your major professor and committee, contact those faculty you did not select. Acknowledge their expertise and express appreciation for their willingness to serve on your committee, yet let them know that you have decided to go in a different direction. Leave things on good terms and finish your interaction with them in a professional manner; it is always a good idea to have the door open for future collaboration.

Making the Most Out of the Relationship

Once you have chosen your major professor and made the match, revisit what you want to get out of the relationship. What would you like the relationship with your major professor to be? Consider your dissertation needs, but also think about life after graduate school—are you thinking about a career as a researcher or academic or working as a clinician? If you are thinking about a research or academic career, let your major professor know, since he or she can help you develop a dissertation that can set up the next few years of your research program. Your major professor can also work with you on your writing and research to strengthen your potential for an academic job postgraduation (see also Chapter 21 in this volume) as well as possible future grant applications. You may also want to seek other kinds of advice, such as asking about the kinds of approaches that have been most successful in completing dissertations in a timely manner. Other topics include preparing for meetings, asking for help, seeking feedback, and using your major professor as a resource throughout the dissertation process.

Prepare for meetings. As you know from other chapters in this volume, there are a number of different stages to the dissertation process. You'll likely have meetings and consultations with your major professor throughout. And, as we recommended for those initial screening meetings, be organized for all meetings with your major professor. Come prepared to talk about what you have been doing, where you are in the process, and what questions you have about next steps. Doing so will help you make the most of those meetings in terms of utilizing your major professor's expertise, and you'll be able to leave that meeting ready to keep moving forward. Being organized will also help keep your major professor up to date on your progress and will keep her or him "in the loop" about your work.

Ask for help/communicate. During your dissertation (and graduate school generally), you will at some point run into situations or moments in which you need help and/or are unsure how to proceed. For example, you may have had some changes in your family and more time and attention are needed to your life outside of school. You may be stuck in confusion about a particular statistical design that you think you should use and cannot get it straight. Later in the dissertation, you may uncover an error in data coding or analysis that needs correcting. In the course of one semester, you may be looking for jobs, applying for internship, getting married, and working part or even full time—and feeling completely overwhelmed in the process. In such instances, communicate with your major professor about your concerns. He or she will be more able to provide help, support, and feedback to you if he or she knows what is happening. Just like a clinical supervisor, major professors can often help students manage the anxiety, fear, depression, procrastination, anger, and excitement that accompany graduate school in general and dissertation writing in particular. Chapter 4 (Relationship Issues: Peers, Faculty, and Families) has more information on the importance of communication and tending to your relationships.

In terms of the dissertation, communicate directly with your major professor about how you will be working together. Find out if he or she prefers to see one chapter at a time, a draft of the whole project, outlines, or some other format. Clarify how often updates on your progress are expected. Generally it is a good idea to keep your major professor as informed as possible.

Of course, you are expected to spend time working through some problems, but do not spend days or weeks puzzling through a problem that may be fixable; your major professor has significant experience and expertise, so ask for it (Van Slyke et al., 2003). It is essential to keep your major professor "in the know" throughout the project, especially when you are considering methodological changes (e.g., design, number of participants, sites for data collection; Heppner & Heppner, 2004; Van Slyke et al., 2003). Heppner and Heppner (2004) discussed an example of a student who changed the number of participants needed for a dissertation without informing the major professor. When the student sent the proposal to the committee, it looked as though the student had not done enough homework and that the major professor had not read the final draft, which had negative implications for the committee meeting and the relationship between student and chair. Keeping in touch with your major professor and making such changes in consultation means that everyone on your committee will be on the same page and working in relative harmony.

Of course, a big part of the communication with your major professor will be in writing—in the form of drafts of your dissertation. We agree with Heppner and Heppner (2004), who suggested allowing ample time for your major professor to read and respond to multiple drafts. At the beginning of the project, develop with your professor a timetable for the proposal to be completed; be realistic, plan for three or four drafts to go back and forth between the two of you, and allow time for you to make revisions and for your major professor to read and comment. Revising and refining drafts are where the actual study develops. As you may or may not be aware, advisors have many responsibilities and often many students, so it may take awhile for them to comment on your draft, despite your desire and energy to keep things moving.

Seek feedback. Seeking feedback from your major professor is a central part of the process. Find out what is working, explore what is not, and identify any holes in your reasoning. Seeking feedback and incorporating it into your writing is a foundational skill that will invariably enhance your work throughout your career. At the same time, hearing feedback on one's writing is never easy. Our recommendation is to seek feedback, take notes (if it is in person), ask questions to make sure you understand what is being critiqued and what is needed to fix it, and remain calm throughout.

In some cases, you may need to set the feedback aside for a few days, but always come back to it. Once you do, you may realize that things are not as bad as they seemed and that you may have overlooked some positive points. Make sure to seek both positive and negative feedback—if you are hearing only positives, ask what could be strengthened; conversely, if you're getting buried under a mountain of things that need to be changed, make sure to ask about what is working. In addition, don't be afraid to give feedback to your chair. If you are not getting what you need during the process (e.g., time), asking for what you need is a necessary professional skill to develop. Of course, not all major advisors are welcoming of such feedback, so you will want to be thoughtful about how you deliver that feedback. Consulting with peers or another mentor and role playing prior to giving feedback may be helpful.

One final note about feedback: Make sure at the beginning of the relationship (and throughout) to discuss with your advisor the kind of feedback that will be most useful to you. Sometimes a major professor can overload you with one kind of feedback, negative or positive. Being very specific and having an upfront conversation about the kinds of feedback that will be most helpful to you can help shape the conversations, which will ultimately affect the working relationship as well as your progress on the project.

A Multifaceted Resource

Your major advisor may also be able to help in other ways. For example, if you are planning an intervention study, does your major professor have clinical expertise? Is the person currently licensed? Has she or he developed any materials, programs, or manualized treatments for a given population? Such expertise may change the course of your research as well as your professor's interest in your topic. You'll also want to find out whether your major professor has any connections to the community you are interested in studying.

Also, think about the range of experiences that comprise graduate training (e.g., clinical, research, teaching). You might consider consulting your major professor on issues in these areas as well. Topics that may seem far afield from the dissertation, such as balancing coursework, teaching responsibilities, outside work, internship applications, family, and life may be fair game for consultation. Some of the chapters in this book (e.g., Chapter 4) deal with these topics as well. Think ahead to your postgraduate career—are you interested in involvement with policy or organizational aspects of psychology? Some faculty are highly active on the local, regional, and national levels, and if you have interest in working on psychology at any of those levels, your major advisor may help you find ways to get involved.

If a Change Is Necessary

Of course, not all relationships work perfectly. In some cases, you may need to give feedback to get your needs met, and in some cases, you may find that you are not able to get what you need. As DiPierro (2007) pointed out, not all faculty approach their work as major advisors or committee members in the same way. You may have a number of concerns, such as having an advisor but being interested in someone else's research. In other instances, students may experience significant conflict with their major professor. Although some conflict is expected in any relationship, in some rare cases, the conflict may be serious enough to impair a student's (or professor's) ability to move the work forward. Indeed, researchers have found that conflict exists between students and faculty (e.g., Tantleff-Dunn, Dunn, & Gokee, 2002) and students and supervisors (e.g., Nelson, Barnes, Evans, & Triggiano, 2008), and there is no reason to assume that all dissertation relationships would be free of conflict.

When it does occur, we advise students first to consider the nature and seriousness of the conflict. Although it may seem overwhelming in the moment, take a few days to think things over. Is this something that is resolvable? Our first recommendation is always to try to work through whatever conflict exists. Remember that conflict in any relationship will often deepen the bond and can be a productive learning opportunity. Also, the focus should remain on generating the best study possible. Even if the fit between you and your major professor leaves something to be desired, things can still work out well. You may learn a number of new skills and may find some new dimensions to your work.

In some cases, however, a change may be necessary due to changes in research interests or (in rare cases) irreconcilable differences. Most faculty, particularly if the concern relates to change in research interests, are interested in seeing students connect with others who would best fit their needs. Of course, knowing the faculty member and how he or she would respond to such a request is important. In the case of irreconcilable differences (which we have seen only once), there is often the possibility of changing your major professor. Although doing so may be possible, it is unusual and may come with lost time as well as the potential for damaged relationships with other faculty and students. You may want to consult with a trusted mentor outside the program to gain additional perspective, and you should consult your graduate handbook or other documents about how such changes are made.

Working With Your Dissertation Committee

One of the most common mistakes we have seen students make is to approach the committee and chair with trepidation and dread. Doing so sets an unnecessary tone and perhaps adversarial relationship between you and the committee. Instead, we recommend seeing the group as a think tank that gets together to benefit your study and helps you with the final step in completing your training. Although most committees do provide challenging comments and ask tough questions to make sure you know your stuff, the members are almost always geared toward helping you. Keep in mind that when assembling your committee, you are actually recruiting people who possess a range of expertise (Hernandez, 1996); your study and future contribution to the literature depends on your committee. In particular, the outside member (typically from another department or college on campus) often provides alternate points of view, theoretical perspectives, strategies and sites for data collection, and expertise not found in your own department. In the following sections, we will provide suggestions on when to start looking, whom to invite, how to invite them, and how to work with your committee.

When to Start Looking

In most programs, once you officially pass your qualifying and/or comprehensive exams and become a doctoral candidate, you can begin forming your dissertation committee. If possible, start looking around even before then—when you are still in the early stages of your program. Create opportunities for yourself in which you observe and interact with faculty, which will provide useful data for you when you are putting a committee together. Getting involved in one or two research teams, getting to know a faculty member by being a teaching assistant, sitting in on courses taught by faculty with whom you are interested in working, and reading faculty's research are all good ways to identify potential members.

Deciding Whom to Invite

When deciding whom to invite onto your committee, we recommend a number of factors to consider. These include (but are not limited to): faculty members' eligibility, time and commitment, expertise, match with your self-assessed needs, and relationships.

Eligibility. When you begin to put a committee together, check the handbook of your doctoral program (or the website of your graduate school) and find out who is eligible to sit on your committee (e.g., tenure-track vs. adjunct, program faculty vs. department) as well as the requirements (typically, including a member from outside your department is required). If you are interested in working with someone who is not eligible to be on a dissertation committee in your department, find out the procedure (if there is one) to appeal for an exception and how long it would take.

Time and commitment. You want the members of your committee to be accessible and accountable and willing to provide constructive feedback, return drafts within a reasonably quick time (i.e., ideally 2–3 weeks), and attend important meetings. Keep in mind that faculty members typically have very busy lives, especially those working toward tenure. Faculty who are working toward tenure tend to be extremely busy working on their own research, writing articles for publications, and engaging in various responsibilities. Consequently, although they may be willing to be committee members, they may not be as accessible as you would like. You may also want to find out the number of committees on which each member is currently serving; those on more committees may have less time for you.

Committee members' career plans in the next few years may also affect your dissertation process. If a member is on sabbatical when you are completing your dissertation, there will be more details in your planning. The same issues apply if a committee member plans to leave the program in the next year or two (due to retirement, new position somewhere else, contract discontinued), which could be smack in the middle of your dissertation process. If that happens, you may run into situations that will delay your progress.

Expertise. As with your major professor, you will want to consider faculty's areas of expertise, strengths, and weaknesses when choosing committee members. You do not need committee members to have expertise in all aspects of your research, but your goal should be to have a committee with a *combination* of strengths and expertise that will help advance your research. For example, one or two members may be good at providing insights at the conceptual level, whereas others may have expertise with statistics, qualitative methods, research design, or types of studies (e.g., intervention, scale development).

Match with self-assessed needs. Remember your self-assessment and consider the qualities of a committee member that will facilitate you the most in the dissertation process. The same questions that you asked when choosing a major professor apply when selecting faculty to be on your dissertation committee. You want your committee to provide a balance of support and challenge. Although it is tempting to recruit committee members who will shower your work with praise and offer light editing only, having a relatively uncritical committee could spell disaster down the line, when it comes time to publish your work or present at a conference or in a job talk when you face more critical audiences.

Relationships. One of the less obvious aspects of assembling a committee involves relational harmony among committee members. A variety of factors may complicate relationships among committee members, including personality, relationship histories, differences in theoretical and methodological values, and standpoints. Find out whether potential committee members may be in conflict and, if so, whether they seem to be willing to work together. Although in most cases the focus is (as it should be) on helping the student, occasionally conflict among committee members is acted out in proposal meetings or even the dissertation defense.

Consult with your chair and other students. Finding out the answers to your questions about some of these criteria may involve some risk. For example, imagine asking a faculty member, "Are you in conflict with Dr. X?" Unless the stars are aligned perfectly, you're not likely to get a straightforward answer, and for good reason. Rather than asking these questions, consult your dissertation chair. Ask for a list of names of faculty members that you could consider inviting to be on your dissertation committee. Several advantages of doing so are that (a) You want to invite someone with whom your chair feels comfortable, (b) your chair knows more about the history of the department, its members, and its politics, and (c) your chair knows faculty research interests and areas of expertise and can provide advice on whose scholarly background would best facilitate your dissertation. You may also want to consult with other students about their experiences of working with specific faculty members.

Heppner and Heppner (2004) pointed out that one common mistake students make when choosing committee members is to listen to the rumor mill unquestioningly. Rather, they suggested listening with a grain of salt. Although word may get around that a certain faculty member is "difficult," try to find out the source of that rumor—it might be due to something that happened years ago, or it might be completely unfounded. Without asking, you might wind up avoiding the person who could add lots of excellent insights to the work.

Inviting Faculty to Be on the Committee

Once you have identified potential committee members, we recommend going through a similar process as selecting a major advisor—make a list of possible members based on your priorities. Consult with your major advisor about appropriate protocol to contact and invite members. Although sometimes you may be less formal (e.g., using a phone call or e-mail), other times there is an expectation that you make an appointment and prepare a brief prospectus of the project. Especially for the outside member and any faculty with whom you have had limited contact, preparing a brief overview of the project will make a good impression and allow them to make an informed decision. It may be especially important to have a conversation with potential committee members if you have unusual circumstances, such as access to existing data sets or existing relationships (e.g., work history) at a potential data collection or intervention site (Heppner & Heppner, 2004).

When you do issue an invitation, be sure to prepare faculty with tentative timelines for the proposal and defense dates. Also, let potential committee members know your reason for wanting them on the committee; for example, discuss the particular expertise that they bring and what they will add to the project.

Working With Your Committee Through Different Stages

Once you have chosen a major professor and assembled your committee, now the fun begins! In the following section, we provide points to consider as you work with your committee throughout different stages of the dissertation. We begin with scheduling a proposal meeting, follow with thoughts about managing impressions during the meeting, and clarify expectations about what is to happen after the meeting (i.e., when doing the dissertation).

Preparing for and managing the proposal meeting. In terms of the proposal meeting itself, we recommend consulting with your major advisor about how far in advance you need to get a copy of your proposal to the committee. Although you and your major professor will likely be passing drafts back and forth in preparing the document, your committee members may not see the document until your major professor has deemed it "proposal worthy." Once that happens, you'll need to get a copy to your committee members. At a minimum, get a copy of your proposal to your committee a week ahead of time, so they have time to read it and make comments. Also, we suggest providing a printed copy although sometimes faculty will accept or prefer an electronic copy.

When it comes to the proposal, there are a number of steps to ensure a productive meeting. First, consult your major professor to develop a sense of what to expect. What are the goals of the proposal meeting? What is expected of each person in the room? What are meetings like at your university? Are they more oriented toward problem solving or more adversarial in nature? Consult with other students and, if possible, attend a proposal meeting prior to your own. Seeing someone else sweating it out will provide you with a lot of information—and empathy—about how you'd like to prepare for this event. After your own proposal meeting, you should come out of the room with a clear sense of direction about any improvements or changes that are needed for you to begin your study and start those next steps toward completing your degree. Essentially, in this meeting, you will develop the contract with your committee about what you will do over the course of your project. We also recommend discussing with your major professor who will do what in that meeting—will you take notes or will he? Will you defend your ideas, choice of instruments, and so forth, or will she jump in? At what point would that happen?

Find out from your major professor about the typical length of time for presentations. Practice your presentation and get feedback (see Chapter 15 on presentation skills or Chapter 18 on oral exam skills), and be prepared to explain everything, including practical and theoretical issues, type of analysis, recruitment strategies, potential for attrition, number and demographics of participants, likelihood of recruiting a diverse and representative sample, potential limitations, and how you'll be handling internal and external validity threats. Also be ready to talk about your interest in the study; most committee members will be interested to learn about that as well. You may find it helpful to prepare a table in which you match each research question with a proposed analysis, including the instrument, subscales, type of relation you are measuring, and hypothesis (Heppner & Heppner, 2004). Be ready to talk about those analyses—although no one will expect you to know everything about every type of statistical and research design, you should know in depth the analyses you plan to run for the study, particularly their strengths, limitations, and assumptions.

Anticipate the kinds of questions you are likely to get from your committee members—and prepare to answer them. Most faculty will find it impressive if you have anticipated their questions and have an extra slide on hand to demonstrate your answer. Thinking through your project to anticipate these questions—especially the most difficult and critical ones—will also develop your critical eye and give you a chance to improve the project before the proposal even happens. Consult with peers and your major professor, and assess whether those problems are fatal flaws or can be addressed. Consider every possible flaw in your reasoning and design, from your choice of participants to your protection of human subjects, recruitment costs, instruments, and statistical approaches.

Managing impressions. Remember that it is likely that you are the expert in the room on the specific aspects of your study and topic (this may be especially true at the dissertation defense). Although your committee members represent a lot of expertise, projecting a confident image and appearing relaxed and upbeat about your study will convey to them that you are knowledgeable and capable of conducting the study and will keep the conversation moving. Of course, there is a fine line between being confident and appearing as though you do not feel you have anything to learn, so make sure that you are still conveying a sense of curiosity and respect to the committee. Be confident, but not overconfident.

If you find these types of meetings stressful (which is normal), find out what you need to do to remain calm and relaxed—and do it! Pay attention to your breathing, or do some relaxation or visualization exercises during practice sessions and prior to the actual meeting. When you are getting feedback, remember to take it in and have a conversation. Don't shut down, but also don't be too quick to accept committee members' concerns—doing either can convey that you have not thought things through seriously enough. Your committee may raise many suggestions, but keep in mind your original intent and consider whether their suggestions will add to your study or move you away from your original idea.

Clarifying expectations. Make sure you understand what is expected of you at the end of the proposal meeting. Your major professor should play a significant role in this process in terms of taking notes and clarifying what the committee expects. In most cases, some changes are required for the project to move forward; these can be in terms of participants, data collection methods, instrumentation, or statistical analyses. As we mentioned, the proposal meeting essentially functions as a contract meeting when you and your committee decide what you will do over the course of the study. So make sure you have a clear understanding. And make sure to be in touch with your major professor at any time when you are considering a change to the project, particularly during data collection and analysis.

After the Proposal

So, what happens next? After the proposal meeting, you might not see your committee again until the final defense. Alternately, you may be in contact with some or all of the members, depending on the specific expertise that they bring. We suggest keeping your committee informed and planning ahead.

Keep your committee in the loop. Given that this is the one time in your professional life that you have four people who are willing to act as free consultants on a project of yours, you may decide that you want more frequent contact with them. Although in most cases you'll want to talk with your major professor first, knowledgeable committee members may be able to help troubleshoot difficulties as well. Here again, pay some attention to cultural norms within your program and department. Consult your major professor about usual levels of interaction between doctoral candidates and committee members. At the end of the proposal meeting, ask whether committee members prefer individual chapters during the process or prefer to see only the final draft. If you are considering any major changes, definitely be in touch with your major professor first, and then with committee members. Even if things are going smoothly, you may want to drop them a line every couple of months with a quick update, especially if you have exciting news about completing data collection, receiving grant funding, or something else.

Plan ahead. As the end approaches, make sure to give your committee plenty of time to schedule a defense. We recommend scheduling at least a month ahead if possible. Get the draft to them at least 3 to 4 weeks ahead of the defense date, and send a friendly reminder about that date once it has been set. Do not assume that each member remembers the date, time, or location. We recommend setting a date in your own calendar to e-mail your committee members a reminder.

At the final defense, typically you will make a shorter, focused presentation based on what happened since the proposal; we suggest a quick presentation focused on results and discussion in which you relate findings back to your hypotheses and discuss implications (e.g., clinical practice, future research, training). As with the proposal meeting, try to anticipate questions and prepare slides. If you had any unanticipated experiences during the dissertation or any surprising findings, you may want to address those; if need be, you may also want to discuss nonstatistically significant findings as a potentially important contribution to the literature.

Concluding Remarks

In the final write-up of your document, make sure to show your appreciation to your committee. Typically this is done in the "acknowledgements" section of the dissertation. You will also likely want to include a quick thanks to your committee in an author note on any publications that emerge from the study. And in terms of publications, Van Slyke and colleagues (2003) suggested that students work with their major professors to determine publication expectations early in the process.

At the end, you may be so relieved to be finished (except for those revisions) that you may want to run from the room and your committee and never see them again. Alternately, you may have had a very difficult and trying experience, and so your desire never to see your committee again may come from a very different place. Either way, you would be missing an important opportunity if you did not consider debriefing the process with your committee and major professor (DiPierro, 2007). Of course, you will want to wait a week or two before having such a meeting—taking time to celebrate what you have just accomplished is important.

Debriefing can allow you the chance to clarify any points of contention, convey your appreciation to committee members, and learn from their feedback about your performance at all stages of the process. Particularly if you are thinking about conducting more research in the future or becoming a faculty member, having a postdefense discussion will be useful. Potential topics for this kind of meeting include the level and quality of communication between yourself and the committee, turnaround time for drafts, the number and usefulness of committee meetings, the level and quality of mentoring across all aspects of the project, committee members' availability, accessibility, and level of interest and commitment, and your level of preparedness and professionalism (DiPierro, 2007). Remember to remain calm, and take in the information as nondefensively as possible. And make sure to provide feedback in a similar manner. Focus on understanding their points of view.

Our final recommendation has to do with celebration. Make sure to celebrate along the way and not hold out for one giant party just after you plunge across the finish line. One of our major professors suggested that we buy a case of champagne at the beginning of the dissertation process, and that we share a bottle with friends or family after every major part of the dissertation was complete. So, after finishing the conceptual design, finalizing the committee, successfully proposing the project, collecting data, and so on, mark the moment with some time to relax, gain perspective, and set your sights on the next goal in the process. This is a long process, a marathon, and one in which you step out of the student role and into the professional one. Working with your major professor and committee as you transition into being a colleague and celebrating with them at the end are all important milestones in your professional career. Good luck!

❖ References

Bernard, J. M. (1997). The discrimination model. In C. E. Watkins, Jr. (Ed.), *Handbook of psychotherapy supervision* (pp. 310–327). New York: Wiley.

Bernard, J. M., & Goodyear, R. K. (2004). *Fundamentals of clinical supervision* (3rd ed.). Boston: Allyn & Bacon.

DiPierro, M. (Summer, 2007). Debriefing: An essential final step in doctoral education. *Journal for Quality and Participation, 14*–16.

Heppner, P. P., & Heppner, M. J. (2004). *Writing and publishing your thesis, dissertation, and research: A guide for students in the helping professions.* Belmont, CA: Brooks/Cole.

Hernandez, L. L. (1996). In search of a dissertation committee: Using a qualitative research approach to study a lived experience. *The Qualitative Report, 2*(4). Retrieved from http://www.nova.edu/ssss/QR/QR2-4/hernandez.html.

Krumboltz, J. D. (1991). The 1990 Leona Tyler Award address: Brilliant insights and platitudes that bear repeating. *The Counseling Psychologist, 19,* 298–315.

Nelson, M. L., Barnes, K. L., Evans, A. L., & Triggiano, P. J. (2008). Working with conflict in clinical supervision: Wise supervisors' perspectives. *Journal of Counseling Psychology, 55*(2), 172–184.

Tantleff-Dunn, S., Dunn, M. E., & Gokee, J. L. (2002). Understanding faculty–student conflict: Student perceptions of precipitating events and faculty responses. *Teaching of Psychology, 29*(3), 197–202.

Van Slyke, C., Bostrom, R., Courtney, J., McLean, E., Snyder, C., & Watson, R. T. (2003). Experts' advice to information systems doctoral students. *Communications of the Association for Information Systems, 12,* 469–478.

❖ Suggestions for Further Exploration

Glatthorn, A. A., & Joyner, R. L. (Eds.). (2005). *Writing the winning thesis or dissertation: A step-by-step guide.* Thousand Oaks, CA: Corwin. Glatthorn and Joyner cover the dissertation journey from beginning to end, starting almost immediately with attention to ethical choices in the dissertation. The authors provide a highly systematic means of progressing through the process, including questions about whether and how to involve peers and how to use technology to your advantage.

Heppner, P. P., & Heppner, M. J. (2004). *Writing and publishing your thesis, dissertation, and research: A guide for students in the helping professions.* Belmont, CA: Brooks/Cole. Heppner and Heppner provide a clear, well-written, and balanced approach to dissertation and thesis writing, using wonderfully compelling and concrete examples from their own experiences and from actual dissertations and theses. They also address issues related to using technology for literature searches and provide guidelines for Internet data collection.

Roberts, R. M. (2010). *The dissertation journey: A practical and comprehensive guide to planning, writing, and defending your dissertation.* Thousand Oaks, CA: Sage. Using the metaphor of mountain climbing, Roberts presents a systematic overview of the dissertation process, including attention to relationships with faculty as well as the elements of a successful approach to writing and defending your dissertation.

Single, P. B. (2009). *Demystifying dissertation writing: A streamlined process from choice of topic to final text.* Sterling, VA: Stylus. Single delivers an in-depth treatise on the writing process, with practical examples and a step-by-step approach to overcoming many common obstacles (e.g., anxiety, procrastination) to moving a dissertation forward. She also provides good information about choosing and working with your major professor and committee.

21

Developing a Plan for Your
Career After Graduate School

❖

Randolph A. Smith
Lamar University

T he title for this section of chapters, "Winding Down and Gearing Up (All at the Same Time)," captures this time of your graduate career well, although "winding down" is probably somewhat misleading. Few graduate students would consider dealing with all the work, stress, and worry involved with a dissertation as a true winding down process. Nonetheless, at some point during your graduate career, you are likely to be dealing simultaneously with two of the most important tasks of your life—working on your dissertation *and* attempting to launch your career. Thus, this time may be one of the most stressful times of your life. In this chapter, I provide some advice about your career path that I hope will help you deal with and, ideally, minimize that stress to some extent. My primary focus will be on preparing for an academic job, with some pointers toward applied fields as well.

What Works

Begin Thinking and Planning Early

One pointer that can help in a variety of situations is not to leave things until the last minute. Presumably this is a truism that you learned as you have gone through college and thus far in graduate school. Cramming the night before an exam is certainly not the most effective way to study and learn the material. Assuming that you will actually need to know and use things you have learned later in life, you have probably learned to begin studying well in advance of exams—in fact, you may have learned to study daily as you proceed in a course.

259

Developing a plan for your career is also something that you should work on earlier rather than later. Just as Chapter 3 advised you to begin your graduate career with your dissertation in mind, it is a good idea to begin your graduate career with your future career in mind. It is likely that you have already given some thought to your eventual career as an undergraduate. You certainly took career considerations into account when you applied to various graduate programs and when you made your final decision about which program you would actually enter. You had to choose a specialty as an undergraduate so that you would know where to apply.

Now that you are in your graduate program, you should gather information about the career options that will be open to you when you complete the program. It is entirely possible that career possibilities exist that you knew nothing about as an undergraduate. It is important for you to check out all your options so that you can make an informed decision about your future. Your graduate advisor can be an invaluable source of information in this process of making career decisions. At the same time, however, it is not uncommon for graduate advisors to have the goal of "remaking you in their image." In other words, graduate advisors may see no other career options than emulating them by choosing a career in academia—often a research-heavy career because that is typically what faculty in doctoral programs do.

Once you have a good idea of what you would like to do in your future career, it may have implications for your graduate program. For example, you may have options in your coursework. If you do have such options, you can choose your elective courses to better fit your intended career. Likewise, your program may have an array of different opportunities available to the graduate students; again, you can select the activities that are in keeping with your future plans. For example, if you anticipate a career in teaching, you should take advantage of any teaching opportunities available in the department. Buskist and colleagues have written several articles that can help you as you develop your career plan concerning teaching. Benson and Buskist (2005) surveyed representatives of 74 psychology departments that had advertised a position in November of 2000 or 2001 and had specified an excellent teacher (or some similar phrase). They found that quality of previous teaching experience, of publications and presentations, of an onsite presentation to undergraduates, and of a job talk were the highest-rated factors, although there were differences based on the level of the school that was hiring. For example, Clifton and Buskist (2005) found that baccalaureate and master's-level departments tended to stress teaching materials more in job ads, whereas doctoral programs tended to stress research materials more.

Although you may anticipate becoming a faculty member in a department that is similar to your graduate program, the odds are probably greater that you will begin your teaching career in a smaller department. If you do begin teaching in a smaller department, you typically have less of a chance of being a narrow specialist (as you are in graduate school) and teaching a narrow range of courses. Therefore, a good strategy during your graduate training is to teach multiple courses if you have that option; the more, the better according to Benson and Buskist (2005). If you cannot teach multiple courses, I advise you to make an effort to teach General Psychology. At the same time, I would warn you that General Psychology is one of the most difficult courses to teach in the psychology curriculum. *No one* is well prepared to teach this course, even with your fresh graduate education—only a few of the chapters will be very familiar to you. However, odds are high that your first teaching job will entail teaching this course. Even if your teaching job does not require teaching General Psychology, you might get brownie points in your new department by volunteering to teach the course. Irons and Buskist (2008) examined more than 200 position ads in 2006; they found that four courses accounted for 45% of all the specific courses listed: research methods, introductory psychology, developmental psychology, and statistics. Clearly, gaining experience in teaching these courses would be a major advantage for you.

If you plan a career in an applied field such as clinical, counseling, or industrial/ organizational (I/O) psychology, you should also look for opportunities to prepare for your future career. If you are preparing for practice as a clinical or counseling psychologist, this advice is somewhat easier to follow. During your graduate training, you will likely have practicum experiences that focus on practice simulations. For example, your department might have a counseling center in which you spend some time in supervised practice with actual clients. It is almost a given that you will spend a year-long internship that provides you with extensive experience in an applied setting after you complete your coursework. This advice may be more difficult for you to follow if you are in an I/O program. However, you can still look for practicum and internship experiences to provide you with hands-on experience that will be helpful in your career. If your graduate program does not include such experiences as a typical component, ask your faculty advisor and the head of your program about whether such opportunities exist and follow up on any leads that you get. Just as teaching experience is important to prospective faculty, applied experience is important to psychologists with applied specialties.

Be Flexible and Open to Change

Although I have advised you to begin considering career options early in your graduate program, I also advise you to keep your options open and be prepared to consider other options that come up. Most people with advanced degrees can probably relate how their career options or choices shifted several times during school and, perhaps, even after school.

Let me give you a case in point by examining my career path. As an undergraduate, I considered both I/O psychology and rehabilitation counseling; instead, I ended up in an experimental psychology Ph.D. program. When I applied to experimental programs, I applied for social programs; however, I ended up focusing on human learning and memory because a faculty member in that area had a research assistantship available. As a graduate student, I expected that I would end up as a faculty member at a large school, teaching and focusing on my research agenda; rather, I got my first teaching job at a small, private liberal arts college teaching 15 hours of courses. At the small college, I expected to teach there a few years and then move on to a large university; however, I spent 26 years there. After 20+ years at the small college, I thought I would end my career there, but I found an interesting and challenging chair's job at a much larger university several hundred miles away. After that move, I thought I was probably set for the end of my career; however, family health issues and a less-than-supportive dean led me to take a chair job at a moderate-sized university (Lamar University) 20 miles from where I grew up. If someone had told me in graduate school that I would end up teaching at Lamar, I would have laughed out loud. I expect that I am now set until retirement, but I have learned to expect the unexpected!

As you can see from my career path, I have been a lousy prognosticator about my future. If I had not been flexible and open to change, I would have been frustrated at many different turns, and my career would have been, I believe, much less fulfilling. I have learned important things and had important experiences at every stop along the way. The temptation is strong in graduate school to plot your career trajectory and vow not to vary from that trajectory. Based on my experience and the experience of many colleagues, I do not recommend that rigid, inflexible approach. Although I would not recommend flitting from job to job with no real pathway or goal in mind, I do advise you to be open to new and different possibilities.

Read Relevant Literature

One important skill you have learned during your graduate training is to consult the published literature before embarking on a research project. You should generalize that skill to your career preparation also. Although it is impossible in one book chapter to provide a comprehensive listing of all the literature that is relevant to your career plan, I will give you a representative sample of some potentially interesting sources. You can build on this list and find articles that are more specifically of interest to you.

Darley, Zanna, and Roediger (2004) have edited a book that could be useful to you, *The Compleat Academic: A Career Guide.* Of particular relevance to developing a career plan are the first four chapters in a section titled "Starting a Career." Lord (2004) provided pointers for graduate students about how to help move toward a successful academic career. Lord pointed out that both undergraduate and graduate grades (as well as GRE scores) have little predictive ability as far as which graduate students will eventually finish a Ph.D. However, he found strong correlations with Ph.D. completion and both number of publications and graduate research competence. Many students manage to wander through an undergraduate psychology degree, even with good grades, but still do not realize that psychology is a research-oriented discipline. The age-old lament of struggling undergraduate psychology majors who say "I just want to help people—I don't like all this research stuff!" falls on deaf ears, especially those of graduate faculty. If you do not like or understand research, then a graduate degree in psychology is going to be a difficult, if not impossible, process.

McDermott and Braver (2004) examined the question of whether to pursue a faculty position or a postdoctoral fellowship (a "postdoc") after graduate school. This choice is an example of one of those career options that I mentioned earlier—you should gather full information that will help you make this important decision along your career path. McDermott and Braver do admit in their chapter that they are strong proponents of postdocs because of the advantages that they provide—it is important to take this bias into account if *you* read their chapter to help you make a decision. The advantages (McDermott and Braver list seven) essentially fall into two categories: improving and broadening your research skills and experiences and increasing your marketability. If you envision an academic job at a college or university that is not a major research producer, then a postdoc is probably less of an issue for you.

Darley and Zanna (2004) presented a host of information about the academic hiring process that can be highly useful to you as you search, apply, and interview for an academic position. They cover the actual process of attempting to find suitable positions and applying for the ones that seem to be good fits—in this section, they address the question of many job applicants: "How widely should I apply?" They provide particularly useful and helpful information about preparing for a job talk, finding out about the environment in which you might live and work, and how to prepare to present yourself in the best possible light.

Kyllonen (2004) discussed broadening your job search to jobs outside of academia. Because this topic is not one that I address to any substantial degree in this chapter, Kyllonen's chapter could be of real interest to you. Although he covers some topics that are similar to Darley and Zanna's (2004), he focused primarily on outlining differences between academic and nonacademic jobs.

Another edited book that will be useful to you as you develop your career plan is *Your Career in Psychology: Putting Your Graduate Degree to Work* (Davis, Giordano, & Licht, 2009). As with the Darley et al. (2004) book, some chapters will be relevant to you at different times during your career, so this book would be a good investment. Hammer and Hammer (2009) listed "being too rigid in your plan" (p. 8) as one pitfall to avoid while you are in your graduate program. Their advice is aimed at the beginning of your graduate career—perhaps, for example, your advisor's interests have changed since you applied to the program. Still, as I noted earlier, flexibility is a key in developing at career plan; Hammer and Hammer's advice makes it clear that flexibility is a key anytime during your career planning process.

Papini (2009) stressed the importance of institutional fit in choosing your desired professional path and referred readers to Irons and Buskist (2009). Irons and Buskist provided a description and discussion of the different types of academic institutions available for faculty careers. They contrasted research institutions, master's institutions, small liberal arts colleges, and community colleges. Information such as this is helpful for planning your career because most graduate students do not have firsthand experience with all types of institutions that feature faculty positions. If you are more interested in teaching, liberal arts and community colleges may be more appealing to you. On the other hand, if your interests run more strongly to research, then you may prefer to look for a faculty position at a master's or research institution. Bear in mind, however, that the teaching and research responsibilities tend to vary along a continuum at these types of institutions. Although community colleges will have the heaviest teaching loads, they may also expect some type of scholarly work. Likewise, research institutions will have the highest research expectation but will also have teaching responsibilities as part of the position. If you find yourself at an institution for which you are mismatched (e.g., higher teaching or scholarship requirement than you prefer), you will likely be miserable in the position and not fare well there.

The remainder of the Davis and colleagues (2009) book has other chapters that might also be helpful in developing your career plan. For example, if you are a clinical or counseling psychologist, there are seven chapters aimed at topics such as licensure, beginning a practice, and combining research and teaching into working as a clinician. Finally, the book ends with chapters devoted to other applied areas: school psychology, forensics, I/O, neuropsychology, and continuing education.

Finally, there are many journal articles that you could consult as you develop your career plan. Such articles are so numerous that there is no way to do them justice or cover them comprehensively in a short chapter such as this. Instead, I will simply note that searching the literature for career-related articles is just as good a strategy as searching the literature for articles related to your research focus. For example, remember the several articles by Buskist and his colleagues that I cited earlier. *Teaching of Psychology* is an excellent source for articles that relate to graduate students and their career preparations.

What Doesn't Work

As you can imagine, what *doesn't* work is the opposite of what *does* work in developing a career plan. Waiting until the last minute to develop a career plan is a bad idea because you will probably miss out on some steps you should have taken along the way. For example, I am invariably surprised when students come to see me in their final semester and tell me that they are interested in going to graduate school. As you read the last sentence, you probably chuckled to yourself. However, the notion of not developing a career plan as early as possible should seem just as ludicrous to you. Knowing "where you want to go" increases the odds significantly that you will get there. And, of course, the sooner you decide where you want to go, the longer you have to plot your route.

Being inflexible about your career plan can send you down a road that you have little interest in traveling. Again, in my personal experience, I have seen undergraduates who have plotted their career from before college; although their interests have changed over time, they believe that they need to stick with that early choice. The most difficult choice students tend to face is when they realize that their career interests have shifted, but they are close to graduation based on their earlier interest. If they shift their educational plans to match their new interests, they will have to delay their graduation for a semester or more. Although it is difficult to realize at the time, delaying graduation is a wise move in this case. Graduating a little later is preferable to not having the proper training for a career that you actually want to pursue.

Choosing not to read literature that is relevant to your career plan is tantamount to not asking mentors and friends for any advice. Given the importance of the decisions that you are making in developing a career plan, the more sources of information you consult, the better. Clearly, not everyone you know is familiar with the career options facing graduate students. The advantage of conducting a literature search on various career options is that you will be getting input from people who *do* know the ins and outs of a specialized career plan such as the one you are developing.

I leave you with one last piece of advice that goes back to being flexible and open to change. If you develop a career plan, or even embark on a career option, it is not necessarily permanent. If you realize that you have made a less-than-optimal choice, you can always develop a new career plan. Popular wisdom holds that many people will make several career changes during their lifetimes. Clearly, you should not take such a decision lightly, but realizing that change is possible may help ease some of the pressure that you feel. Good luck as you plan your future!

❖ References

Benson, T. A., & Buskist, W. (2005). Understanding "excellence in teaching" as assessed by psychology faculty search committees. *Teaching of Psychology, 32,* 47–49.

Clifton, J., & Buskist, W. (2005). Preparing graduate students for academic positions in psychology: Suggestions from job advertisements. *Teaching of Psychology, 32,* 265–267.

Darley, J. M., & Zanna, M. P. (2004). The hiring process in academia. In J. M. Darley, M. P. Zanna, & H. L. Roediger, III (Eds.), *The compleat academic: A career guide* (2nd ed., pp. 31–56). Washington, DC: American Psychological Association.

Darley, J. M., Zanna, M. P., & Roediger, H. L., III. (2004). *The compleat academic: A career guide* (2nd ed.). Washington, DC: American Psychological Association.

Davis, S. F., Giordano, P. J., & Licht, C. A. (Eds.). (2009). *Your career in psychology: Putting your graduate degree to work.* Malden, MA: Wiley-Blackwell.

Hammer, E. D., & Hammer, E. Y. (2009). Maximizing your graduate training: Issues to think about from the start. In S. F. Davis, P. J. Giordano, & C. A. Licht (Eds.), *Your career in psychology: Putting your graduate degree to work* (pp. 3–12). Malden, MA: Wiley-Blackwell.

Irons, J. G., & Buskist, W. (2008). Preparing the new professoriate: What courses should they be ready to teach? *Teaching of Psychology, 35,* 201–204.

Irons, J. G., & Buskist, W. (2009). Preparing for a career at a teaching institution. In S. F. Davis, P. J. Giordano, & C. A. Licht (Eds.), *Your career in psychology: Putting your graduate degree to work* (pp. 117–131). Malden, MA: Wiley-Blackwell.

Kyllonen, P. C. (2004). Broadening the job search: Jobs outside of academia. In J. M. Darley, M. P. Zanna, & H. L. Roediger, III (Eds.), *The compleat academic: A career guide* (2nd ed., pp. 57–76). Washington, DC: American Psychological Association.

Lord, C. G. (2004). A guide to PhD graduate school: How they keep score in the big leagues. In J. M. Darley, M. P. Zanna, & H. L. Roediger, III (Eds.), *The compleat academic: A career guide* (2nd ed., pp. 3–15). Washington, DC: American Psychological Association.

McDermott, K. B., & Braver, T. S. (2004). After graduate school: A faculty position or a postdoctoral fellowship? In J. M. Darley, M. P. Zanna, & H. L. Roediger, III (Eds.), *The compleat academic: A career guide* (2nd ed., pp. 17–30). Washington, DC: American Psychological Association.

Papini, D. R. (2009). Your advisor and department chair: Key figures in your early career. In S. F. Davis, P. J. Giordano, & C. A. Licht (Eds.), *Your career in psychology: Putting your graduate degree to work* (pp. 45–58). Malden, MA: Wiley-Blackwell.

❖ Suggestions for Further Exploration

Darley, J. M., Zanna, M. P., & Roediger, H. L., III. (2004). *The compleat academic: A career guide* (2nd ed.). Washington, DC: American Psychological Association. Given that I cited four chapters from this book, you should not be surprised to see it listed as a suggested reading. In addition to the chapters covering the job search and early career issues, you will also find chapters aimed at helping you maintain your career over the long term. This book's true strength lies in the authors' insights into academia's implicit rules.

Davis, S. F., Giordano, P. J., & Licht, C. A. (Eds.). (2009). *Your career in psychology: Putting your graduate degree to work.* Malden, MA: Wiley-Blackwell. Like the first suggested reading, I have cited several chapters from this book. Its strength is its comprehensive coverage of a wide variety of career options for people with graduate degrees in psychology—not only academic jobs, but also clinical or counseling positions, as well as other applied areas of psychology such as forensics, industrial/organizational, and neuropsychology.

22

To ABD or Not to ABD?
That Is the Question

❖

Jeffrey S. Bartel
Washington and Jefferson College

Kimberly M. Christopherson
Morningside College

Graduate students are used to answering questions from their advisors, their professors, their students, and even their families ("How's that dissertation coming?"). Among the more important questions you may have to answer, though, is one you may be asking yourself: Is it advisable to leave your graduate program for a job before you have defended your dissertation? The answer is, like most of the answers you have to give in graduate school, complicated. In this chapter, we discuss some of the common roadblocks to dissertation completion, important considerations for those deciding whether to complete their dissertation before beginning a full-time job, and general suggestions for completing the dissertation.

How Long Does Graduate School Take, Anyway?

As with undergraduate students, not all students who matriculate into a graduate program will complete their degrees. The sobering statistic is that roughly half of students entering doctoral programs will leave without graduating (Bowen & Rudenstine, 1992, cited in Leatherman, 2000). Although this may seem like a dreary statistic, for students who persevere long enough to complete their coursework and pass their qualifying or preliminary examinations—obtaining the unofficial status of ABD or "all but dissertation"—the completion rate is a much more promising 80 percent.

While there are many reasons students may not complete the degrees they started, one explanation for attrition from graduate programs is that students feel that it was taking too long to complete their degrees. The duration of graduate school varies considerably by discipline, with doctoral students in the natural sciences completing their degrees more quickly than those in the humanities or social sciences (Leatherman, 2000; Wilson, 1965).[1] Whereas the median number of years elapsed from starting a bachelor's degree to completion of a doctoral degree is 10.4 years (National Center for Education Statistics, 1991, cited in Hanson, 1992), doctoral students in the physical sciences can expect to spend a total of about 7.1 years in college, while students in education programs average 16.2 years. Assuming that a typical undergraduate degree can be completed in approximately 4 years, a graduate student can, therefore, expect to spend from about 3 to more than 12 years working toward a doctoral degree.

If you talk to a Ph.D. who earned his or her degree 30 or more years ago, you might get the impression that the lengthy time it takes many students to complete a degree is a recent phenomenon. However, lamenting over doctoral students' feet-dragging dates back at least five decades, as Berelson (1960) argued for enforcement of the 4-year norm for completion of the doctorate (and, to the joy of graduate students everywhere, that shorter dissertations should replace the even then burgeoning tomes). Indeed, unlike an undergraduate degree, which can be completed in a fairly predictable timeframe (X total courses needed for graduation divided by Y courses per year), Wilson (1965) noted that the 3 to 4 calendar year expectation for completing a doctorate must be weighed against the fact that the completion of a dissertation is not itself "couched in terms of specific time limits" (p. 2).

So . . . Why Is It Taking so Long?

One of the great difficulties of being a graduate student is that many of your friends and family do not understand the process of graduate school. Questions like "Why is it taking so long?" are often from those who have no experience writing a dissertation. To your friends, family, and even your significant other, it can be difficult to understand why the progress is slow, especially now that your coursework is completed. Answering the question of what takes some graduate students so long to complete their dissertations is complicated, but several researchers have examined the reasons for late or delayed completion (e.g., Bowen & Rudenstine, 1992; Jacks, Chubin, Porter, & Connolly, 1983; Kluever, 1997; Muszynski & Akamatsu, 1991; Truitt & Wong-On-Wing, 1991). In this section, we will discuss some of the most common roadblocks to dissertation completion.

Dissertation Roadblocks

Many graduate students will begin their dissertation process with the attitude that their topic must be revolutionary in their field and that their results must enlighten the scientific community with some profound insight. Developing a topic of this magnitude is unlikely even for many seasoned researchers, much less someone just starting in the field. The pressure that some graduate students put on themselves to develop this "next best idea" can be potentially paralyzing (Bowen & Rudenstine, 1992). The reality is that while you should develop a topic that helps to further the knowledge in the field, it is not necessary for this to be an earth-shattering discovery. The trick here is to narrow the topic to investigate just a few of the possible variables that might contribute to the phenomenon and not to attempt to measure and explain all variables that might be involved. Overly broad or comprehensive topics lead to difficulties further along in the research process, including the integration of the existing literature, the development of a clean research design, and data analysis.

For graduate students in the natural and social sciences who conduct experiments for their dissertations, another frequent cause for delay in completing the dissertation is the tendency to develop an overly complicated research design. Developing a large-scale study with a multitude of variables can lead to students delaying their completion of their dissertations (Sanchez-Hucles & Cash, 1992). Studies that attempt to address all possible factors related to the phenomenon of interest may lead both to a more complicated design (Muszynski & Akamatsu, 1991) and to more difficult data analysis (Jacks et al., 1983).

Psychological Roadblocks

Along with difficulties encountered relating to the process of creating the dissertation, graduate students' own psychological characteristics might also contribute to their delay in completing the dissertation. For example, students may struggle with psychological disorders such as depression or anxiety. Counselors recommend that graduate students who begin to experience psychological distress seek psychological assistance, and most universities provide free or low-cost counseling to students. Two common psychological factors that contribute to the delay in completion of the dissertation are the issues of procrastination and perfectionism (Flett, Blankstein, Hewitt, & Spomenka, 1992). Although these factors may seem to be unrelated concepts at first, research demonstrates that individuals with perfectionistic tendencies are particularly likely to procrastinate when a fear of failure is present (Flett, et al., 1992). Perfectionists may avoid beginning real progress on their dissertations because they will not settle for anything less than perfection in the development of a topic and design.

Situational Roadblocks

Though the difficulties of developing a research idea and managing a difficult data analysis impede graduate students' progression toward graduation, it is more common that other situational factors contribute to a delay (Jacks et al., 1983). We discuss most of these in greater detail in the next section of this chapter, but a few of the more common situational factors that contribute to delays in completion include one's teaching responsibilities (Wright, 1991), a nonsupportive advisor, geographical distance from the school, and financial difficulties leading to the necessity to take on additional employment during school or leave the graduate program to take full-time work (Jacks et al., 1983).

Summary

The dissertation is undoubtedly one of the most intimidating projects that doctoral students will face. There are several barriers that you might face when attempting to complete your degree, including the development of a topic and research design and other individual psychological and situational factors. With all of these various roadblocks to the completion of the dissertation, it is no surprise that ABD students are so numerous. It is also common for graduate students to find themselves in the situation in which they must decide whether to complete their dissertations before taking a job, or to even complete their dissertations at all. In the next two sections, we will discuss in more detail some of the situational factors to consider when deciding whether to leave your graduate program ABD and give you some suggestions for completing your dissertation in a timely manner.

Should You Leave ABD?

For most graduate students, the primary goal of graduate school is not to earn a doctoral degree. Although important, that goal is secondary to the ultimate end: securing a job for which that degree is required. When you are close to finishing your dissertation, it obviously makes sense to begin looking for a job so that when the degree is awarded, you can begin the job immediately. The question you may be asking yourself, though, is whether you should consider taking a job if it means you will have to leave graduate school ABD. To answer this question, there are a variety of factors you will need to consider.

Academic Program and Logistical Considerations

One of the most important considerations in determining whether to accept a job while ABD is how easily and quickly you will be able to complete your dissertation from a distance. Your evaluation of this probability is dependent on three key issues related to your major professor and your graduate program.

1. How close are you to finishing your dissertation? How close does your major professor think you are to finishing? Many graduate students are surprised to learn that these answers may not be the same! Talk to your major professor to get his or her estimate of how much longer you will take to complete your dissertation. Although you may believe that you only have a little more to do, ultimately, it is your major professor— and probably your committee—who will have to sign off on your dissertation. It would be in your best interest to get these folks' opinions before you find out the hard way that you are really not as far along as you had thought.

2. Does your major professor support your move? Even if you are relatively close to completing your dissertation, your major professor will have to work with you from a distance (and perhaps a considerable one). Does she or he support your decision and exhibit a willingness to work with you? When you leave campus, it makes your major professor's job of advising you on your dissertation more difficult, so you will want to make sure that you have his or her support.[2]

3. What are the requirements of your graduate school? For most graduate schools, finishing your dissertation while you are off campus is not a problem. However, you should check with your graduate school's policies to be certain. Generally, you will have to remain enrolled in at least one credit hour of dissertation research, but there may be a limited number of semesters that you can do that. Other schools may limit the number of semesters from completion of your preliminary or comprehensive exams until graduation, so you need to familiarize yourself with these rules before you consider leaving ABD.

New Job Considerations

Of course, your current academic program is not the only factor you will need to consider in making your decision. You also need to think about a variety of aspects of your new job. Although most of these apply primarily to jobs in academia, others are more broadly applicable.

1. What are the policies of the institution to which you are considering applying? For some jobs, particularly those outside of academia or academic jobs for which a master's degree is sufficient (e.g., at many community colleges), your status as ABD may not be a concern to your employer. Alternately, some positions will state that you must complete your degree to be considered for tenure (do not take that to mean that they would prefer you wait until your tenure review year to finish, however!). However, an increasing number of job ads are explicitly stating that ABDs are expected to complete their degrees by the time their appointment begins. You should be sure to find out the employer's policies before you make a decision about whether to leave ABD.

2. What type of job is it? All jobs are not created equal, and that should be part of your thought process when considering taking one while ABD. For example, a tenure-track academic position would be much more enticing than a full-time temporary or part-time adjunct. If you have no reason to believe that you have job security beyond one or two semesters, you should seriously reconsider whether you want to leave graduate school. Completing your degree is considerably more difficult away from campus and, as we will discuss later, when you are taking on a four- or five-course teaching load. One of the worst things you could do would be to leave campus ABD for a teaching job that lasts only a year or so, find that you are too busy to complete your dissertation, and then end up both without a job and *still* ABD a year later.

3. Will you earn less as an ABD than if you finish first? Some schools pay less to ABDs (the rule of thumb is about $5,000 to $10,000 less), often because ABDs start as instructors rather than assistant professors. A full year at the instructor pay scale will hurt you both in the short term (though your salary will undoubtedly be larger than your teaching or research stipend) and in the long term, as future pay raises may be based on how many "steps" or years of service you have accrued at each level.

4. What classes are you going to be expected to teach? It makes more sense to accept a job ABD if you will be teaching classes that are in your research area or, even better, that you have already taught before. However, be on the lookout for new preparations, especially those that are outside your area of focus. Smaller schools with smaller numbers of faculty in your new department often have expectations of more diverse teaching assignments.

5. How many classes will you be teaching? Many graduate students who teach are responsible for one or maybe two courses. Although a large, research-focused university may only expect a 2–2 courseload, more typical are teaching loads of three, four, or even five classes per semester. You may be able to negotiate with your dean or department chair to get a release from a course or two while you complete your dissertation, but if not, you need to contemplate when you are going to have time to complete your lecture preparation and write your dissertation at the same time.

6. Will you have a teaching assistant, or will the grading duties be yours alone? Those four classes you are teaching are not going to grade themselves. Departments with graduate programs may have TA support available to you, but even new professors who *did* complete their degrees are often overwhelmed by grading.

7. Will your new job support your completion of the degree? You may get lucky and find that you are allowed to use resources such as copying, office supplies, or mailing at your new job if they will serve to help you finish your degree. If not, expenses that might have been covered by your graduate program may come out of pocket.

8. If you are in an academic position, when does the "tenure clock" begin? For many institutions, your tenure evaluation will occur a fixed period of time after your employment begins. If you are working toward your dissertation during this time, you may be able to include this in the research component of your tenure application. However, some institutions go on the assumption that your dissertation was a minimum requirement for the position and, therefore, only work completed in addition to your dissertation will be considered.

9. In which field are you? Some fields hire ABDs regularly, while others seldom do. If yours is an area in which hiring ABDs is rare, time that you allotted to the job hunt may be better served finishing up your dissertation. Related to this is the issue of your specialization. If your focus is extremely specialized, job openings may not open up very frequently. You might find that taking the job when it becomes available is beneficial.

Personal Considerations

In addition to factors related to your current school and the new position, naturally you have to consider personal factors that may make starting your career right away a more or less attractive option.

1. What is your family situation? Assuming that the position you are considering is not nearby, you will likely have to move. Obviously, making a cross-state or cross-country move is considerably easier if you are single than if you have a family to consider. If you are a nontraditional graduate student, you may have children in school; you may need to time the start of your job with their academic calendar (fortunately, most academic positions start in August or September, so this makes it less likely you would have to switch your children's school system in the middle of the school year).

2. Are you moving somewhere familiar? A move, especially to a distant or unfamiliar part of the country, will slow down your progress, as it may take you a while to get acclimated to the area. Conversely, if you are moving nearby or somewhere familiar, the acclimation process should be easier.

3. How flexible are you? Some people are limited geographically. Maybe you want to stay near your family, or perhaps you prefer a particular city or region for other reasons. Regardless, if you are less flexible, then you should consider taking that "perfect" position when it opens up even if you are still ABD because you might not be able to count on a similar one next year. Taking that job while ABD is even more tempting if you are part of the growing number of academic couples. If your significant other is offered his or her dream job, leaving your graduate program while ABD might become a much more appealing option.

Other Considerations

Economists talk about the concept of opportunity costs. These are the resource expenses incurred when you make one choice instead of another, and one resource that will be in short supply when you start a new job is time. Every minute working at your new job, trying to impress your new employers (and possibly begin working toward tenure) is one minute you are not working on your dissertation. Conversely, every minute you work on your dissertation is a minute taken away from committee assignments, advisees, new research, writing letters of recommendation, serving as the department's faculty representative on campus (e.g., at an open house) and, of course, prepping classes and grading. The fact is, even if you cut back considerably on sleep, hobbies, and recreation, your time is still a finite resource. For reasons we discussed earlier, finishing your dissertation is difficult even in the best of circumstances. While still in graduate school, most graduate students have multiple roles that tug at them. When you add to that the obligations associated with a new job, it could become even more difficult. Taking a job ABD is much easier if you have a history of effective time management.

In sum, there are some situations for which leaving your graduate program ABD to take a job may make sense. Conversely, there are other times when leaving ABD would likely cause more problems than it would solve. These are summarized in Table 22.1. If you have talked to your peers and the faculty at your institution,

Table 22.1 Best- and Worst-Case Scenarios for Taking a Job While ABD	
Best-case Scenario	*Worst-case Scenario*
• You are very close to completing your dissertation and your advisor both believes you can finish quickly and supports your leaving ABD. • Your potential employer does not recognize your ABD status as a liability. • The job is exactly what you were looking for long term, in a place you would like to live, and appears to be a good match to your qualifications. • Your new position will support your completion of your dissertation both financially and by giving you temporarily reduced responsibilities.	• The job you are considering is part time or has little chance of extending beyond one to two semesters. • You will have to teach numerous courses outside of your primary research area. • The position is tenure track, but working toward your dissertation will not count toward tenure. • Most people hired in your field have already completed their doctoral degrees. • You have a spouse or significant other who will have to move with you but who does not yet have a solid job opportunity.

you have probably noticed that most people in academia have strong opinions about whether students should leave ABD. The fact is, though, that these strong opinions are based on a variety of both historical and hypothetical situations that may not apply to your particular case. Ultimately, students considering this move should strive to find the best fit for their own circumstances.

Reasons to Finish Your Degree Before You Leave Graduate School

Having read through the list of things to consider, if you feel that your situation is one that is well suited to completing a dissertation while starting a new job, there still may be other reasons to consider completing your degree before you leave graduate school.

The first reason to complete your degree before you leave campus is that some academic positions will not even consider you if you are ABD. For example, at the University of Minnesota, unless the job ad specifically states that those who are ABD are invited to apply, it is assumed that applicants will have completed their degrees prior to applying. Should you apply to a school with a similar policy while ABD, it is possible your application would not even be considered. Other schools, such as Missouri State University, have a policy that ABDs can be hired only when both the department head and dean can make an argument that hiring an ABD is necessary. As you will see in Chapter 23, you never want to make things difficult for the people who are reviewing your application.

A second reason not to leave ABD is that the applications for academic jobs are extremely competitive. ABDs are competing not just against each other but also against those with postdoctoral research experience, visiting professors with considerable teaching experience, and tenure-track professors looking for new positions. Each of these individuals likely has a beefier curriculum vitae than the average newly minted Ph.D. However, that newly minted Ph.D. does not have any strikes against him or her (most hiring committees will forgive you for not having a Nobel-worthy CV right out of graduate school), whereas the ABD candidate has one glaring deficiency.

A final reason to complete your degree before you leave grad school is one to which we alluded previously: money. An ABD in business, for example, can expect to earn between 7% and 14% less than a new Ph.D., with most institution types paying new business ABDs approximately $10,000 less per year than new Ph.D.s (LeClair, 2004). The rewards for completing your degree before leaving graduate school, then, are not only abstract emotional ones but also those of the tangible financial variety.

How to Finish Your Dissertation

A full discussion on the best practices for completing your dissertation is beyond the scope of this chapter. However, we would like to provide three general tips for those working to finish their dissertations.

The first tip is something to consider long before you even begin debating whether to leave ABD, and that is to decide on a research topic that is of a practical scope and design so that you are able to complete your dissertation (see Chapter 3). As mentioned earlier, this may be one major reason why doctoral students find themselves delayed in graduation (Bowen & Rudenstine, 1992; Jacks, et al., 1983; Sanchez-Hucles & Cash, 1992). Keep in mind that your dissertation does not need to change the world or develop a theory of everything. The best research helps answer just a piece of the greater puzzle. Choose a topic that you are passionate about and then choose one or two specific variables to investigate.

Second, try to control the situational factors that you can. Limit your teaching load, avoid extra work responsibilities, and try to create a constructive working relationship with your advisor, whether on campus or from a distance. Most importantly, you need to make time to work toward the completion of your dissertation. Schedule large blocks of time to allow you to do the reading, analysis, and writing necessary to complete your dissertation. Additionally, be sure that you and your dissertation committee work together to help you keep on track (see Chapter 20).

Finally, look for assistance when needed. Group therapy specifically for those working on their dissertations, available at some institutions, can be effective in helping you overcome real or perceived obstacles. Also, seek out the assistance of your graduate student colleagues, your advisor, and other mentors in your graduate program. Additionally, there are several books available giving advice on how to complete your dissertation (see Additional Resources). It is common for dissertation writers to feel isolated through the process of writing their dissertation (Bowen & Rudenstine, 1992), but keep in mind that you are not the only person to go through this process. Seek out those who have successfully completed their dissertations, perhaps recent graduates of your department, and request their advice. You will probably find that these people have experienced the same anxiety and fear that you have. Also seek out people who are currently working on their dissertations and discuss the problems and successes that each of you has had. This level of communication can potentially be useful to help you accomplish some of your major goals, work toward improving your relationship with your advisor, and help you feel more satisfied with the progress that you have been making (Pauley, 2004).

Final Advice for Those Leaving ABD

Leatherman (2000, p. 7) quoted an anonymous recent Ph.D. as saying, "Two things are hanging over your head when you're A.B.D.—the dissertation and the job market," and both are "brutal institutions." For some graduate students, however, one of these "brutal institutions," the job market, seems more pressing, and as a result, many ABDs apply for jobs. If you are among those contemplating joining their ranks, we hope that the information we have presented has been helpful in making a decision. Let us leave you with some parting thoughts. First, if your CV and letters of reference stand out enough that you can get an interview while you are ABD, you will almost certainly be an even more competitive candidate when you change those three letters after your name from ABD to Ph.D. Second, do not accept a job unless you are *really* close to being done. Again, you should check with your major professor and committee to get their thoughts on how close you really are. Accounting faculty who were hired ABD and completed their degrees within the first year were more likely to be at the same school 5 years later than faculty who took longer to complete their degrees (Truitt & Wong-On-Wing, 1991), so if you want to stay at the place that hires you, completing your degree quickly is the best way to assure that happens. Overly optimistic projections may help you secure a job, but there may be negative consequences later if you are not able to deliver. Rather than tell yourself and your new colleagues your best-case scenario timeline, build in a cushion to account for Murphy's Law. This cushion will help you look even more motivated if you complete the dissertation earlier and prevent you from looking deceptive when the inevitable delays occur.

Notes

1. Consistent with the hypothesis that duration of graduate program is related to attrition, Lovitts (2000) notes that graduate school attrition is highest in the humanities and lowest in the natural sciences.

2. Related to this question is the issue of your advisor's level of comfort with technology. Working with someone who is okay marking up your Word document and e-mailing it back is much faster, not to mention less expensive, than snail mailing hard copies back and forth.

References

Berelson, B. (1960). *Graduate education in the United States.* New York: McGraw-Hill.

Bowen, W. G., & Rudenstine, N. L. (1992). *In pursuit of the Ph.D.* Princeton, NJ: Princeton University Press.

Flett, G. L., Blankstein, K. R., Hewitt, P. L., & Spomenka, K. (1992). Components of perfectionism and procrastination in college students. *Social Behavior and Personality, 10*(2), 85–94.

Hanson, T. (1992, October–November). *The ABD phenomenon: The "at risk" population in higher education and the discipline of communication.* Paper presented at the Annual Meeting of the Speech Communication Association, Chicago, IL. Retrieved from ERIC database.

Jacks, P., Chubin, D. E., Porter, A. L., & Connolly, T. (1983). The ABDs ABCs of ABDs: A study of incomplete doctorates. *Improving College and University Teaching, 31*(2), 74–81.

Kluever, R. C. (1997). *Dissertation completers and non-completers: An analysis of psychosocial variables.* Paper presented at the Annual Meeting of the American Educational Research Association, Chicago, IL. Retrieved from ERIC database.

Leatherman, C. (2000). A new push for ABDs to cross the finish line. *Chronicle of Higher Education, 46*(29), A18–A20. Retrieved from ERIC database.

LeClair, D. (2004, March/April). The professor's paycheck: U.S. business school salaries continue to rise, but the increases are relatively modest. *BizEd,* 58–60.

Lovitts, B. E. (2000). Context and attrition. *Research News on Graduate Education, 2*(3). Retrieved from http://ehrweb.aaas.org/mge/Archives/6/context.html.

Muszynski, S. Y., & Akamatsu, T. J. (1991). Delay in completion of doctoral dissertations in clinical psychology. *Professional Psychology: Research and Practice, 22*(2), 119–123. doi: 10.1037/0735–7028.22.2.119.

Sanchez-Hucles, J., & Cash, T. F. (1992). The dissertation in professional psychology programs: A survey of clinical directors on requirements and practices. *Professional Psychology: Research and Practice, 23*(1), 59–62.

Truitt, J., & Wong-On-Wing, B. (1991). An examination of degree completion and turnover rates among accounting doctoral candidates employed at the ABD stage. *Issues in Accounting Education, 6*(2), 214–220.

Wilson, K. M. (1965). *On time and the doctorate: Report of an inquiry into the duration of doctoral study.* Atlanta: Southern Regional Education Board.

Wright, L. M. (1991 April). Full-time teaching and the ABD phenomenon. *Association for Communication Administration,* 49–55.

Additional Resources for Completing Your Dissertation in a Timely Manner

Cone, J. D., & Foster, S. L. (2006). *Dissertations and theses from start to finish: Psychology and related fields* (2nd ed.). Washington, DC: American Psychological Association. This dissertation guide focuses on dissertations in psychology and other social sciences. The authors draw on skills that graduate students have learned through their training and apply these skills to writing a dissertation. A detailed description of each step of the dissertation writing process is included.

Glatthorn, A. A., & Joyner, R. L. (2005). *Writing the winning thesis or dissertation: A step-by-step guide* (2nd ed.). Thousand Oaks CA: Corwin Press. This book provides a step-by-step guide to writing a thesis or dissertation, beginning with securing resources and ethics to defending your thesis or dissertation and publication. The authors rely upon their experiences in chairing dissertation committees to assist graduate students through this process by addressing the common struggles that they saw their students experience.

Hawley, P. (2003). *Being bright is not enough: The unwritten rules of doctoral study* (2nd ed.). Springfield, IL: Charles C. Thomas. A "how to finish your dissertation" book that focuses on the different types of "smarts" that are needed to be successful in graduate school, including being perceptive, knowing how to "play the game," having an entrepreneurial spirit, and engaging in self-management. Other topics include how graduate study is different from college or university study, how to "divorce" your chair, and addressing different family issues that graduate students might experience.

Miller, A. B. (2009). *Finish your dissertation once and for all! How to overcome the psychological barriers, get results, and move on with your life.* Washington, DC: American Psychological Association. This guide focuses on common barriers to completing one's dissertation, including procrastination, anxiety, self-doubt, and perfectionism, and how to combat these obstacles. This book helps graduate students learn how to break down the task of the dissertation into smaller and more manageable pieces, how to manage the dissertation committee, and how to take care of their personal lives as well.

Roberts, C. M. (2010). *The dissertation journey: A practical guide to planning, writing, and defending your dissertation* (2nd ed.). Thousand Oaks, CA: Corwin Press. This book uses the analogy of high-altitude mountain climbing to describe the dissertation process. It begins with a discussion about the choice to begin graduate school and moves to writing a dissertation, including topics such as necessary characteristics for success, common difficulties, and what a dissertation is. It then continues to break down the process of writing a dissertation from topic inception to dissertation defense.

23

Applying for Academic Positions

❖

Krisztina Varga Jakobsen
James Madison University

As you come to the close of your graduate career, many things will keep you busy. Of course, you are working on your dissertation and are also likely in the process of looking ahead to the next step. Although for some it makes sense to complete postdoctoral training, for others, the next step is to get a job. As overwhelming as this task may seem, it doesn't have to be as painful as you might expect. In this chapter, I will outline what to think about and prepare prior to the search process. I will also describe the search, interview, and offer processes.

Things to Consider Before Applying for an Academic Position

Before you start the search for an academic position, you need to consider a number of factors. First, think about the setting in which you want to work. Do you want a position in which your primary responsibility is research or teaching, or a combination of both? Once you've decided, it will make it easier to identify positions for which you wish to apply. For example, if you are interested in continuing your line of research, don't apply to positions in which your sole responsibility is teaching, with no curriculum or resources for your research.

In addition to thinking about the type of position you'd like, determine whether you are geographically restricted, or whether you're flexible in where you live. If you are generally open to positions around the country—or even the world—you will have many more options to consider than someone who is geographically limited; however, don't apply to positions in locations where you would never move or positions that aren't a good fit. This is a waste of your time as well as a waste of the search committee's time. If you are geographically limited—due to a personal preference, a significant other, or your research population—look for job listings on the websites of schools in the particular area where you wish to live. In addition, you should send each of the schools a letter stating your interests, even if they do not have a vacancy, because a position may unexpectedly become available (Darley & Zanna, 2004).

While thinking about these things, keep in mind your training and what you're qualified to do. Think very realistically about where you can get an offer. For example, do you have sufficient teaching experience to apply for a position at a liberal arts school? Does your publication record indicate to research-oriented schools that you will be a productive faculty member? You don't want to put yourself in a situation in which you're applying for every position that is announced. Instead, think about how you and your qualifications fit with the requirements in the job ad. For example, if the ad requires research in a specific area, is that an area that truly interests you? Also, read the school's mission; if you don't agree with the values of the institution, you probably should not apply to that institution.

Think about what *you* want to do. Don't worry about pleasing other people. As difficult as it may be for you to decide on a path for which you receive little support, in the end, you are the one who will have to live with the decision. Make a decision that works well for you and don't let others force you into a decision with which you would be unhappy.

Typically, faculty positions are announced starting in August and continue to be announced through the spring, and even through the summer in some cases. There are several sources through which you can find advertisements for academic positions, including APS Employment Network, APA PsycCareers, *The Chronicle of Higher Education*, and HigherEdJobs. The APS and APA websites provide psychology-specific options, while the *Chronicle* and HigherEdJobs provide job ads for all fields of higher education and joint positions. These four sites are great places to start your job search, but look at the websites of your specific field through domain-specific societies and relevant divisions of APA, which often also have job postings. Another source through which you can learn about job postings is listservs such as Psychteacher (http://teachpsych.org/news/psychteacher.php) or even the graduate listservs within your department.

Components of the Application

Applying for an academic position is at least a year long process, if not longer. However, you don't have to—and shouldn't—wait until August to start compiling the materials you will need to apply for an academic position. You may not realize how time consuming it is to prepare all of the materials that are required for applying for an academic position; therefore, start to prepare your application materials well in advance of when you expect to go on the job market. The most commonly requested materials for academic positions are a cover letter, a curriculum vita (CV), a teaching statement, a research statement, and letters of recommendation

(Clifton & Buskist, 2005). Additional materials requested might include preprints or reprints, evidence of teaching effectiveness (e.g., course evaluations, sample syllabi), undergraduate and graduate transcripts, and evidence of scholarly activities (e.g., participating in workshops and conferences). Getting started early on preparing these aspects of your application will help you be on the ball when positions in which you are interested are posted.

Cover Letter

The cover letter is one of the most important components of your application; it is your opportunity to *show* (not just say) how you are a good fit for the position for which you are applying. In addition, it is generally the first piece of your application—and often the only piece—that is examined by the search committee. Make it count! Devote time to writing, obtaining feedback, and revising your cover letter. In this section, I outline things to keep in mind when writing your cover letter.

You should have one cover letter for each position to which you apply (Wilbur, 1998). This means that you need to tailor a basic cover letter for each position. For example, have a brief paragraph about the school's mission statement and describe how you plan to contribute to it. Another simple way to tailor your letters is to put your research experiences and interests before your teaching for research positions, and your teaching experiences and interests before your research for teaching positions. Although some of the criteria cited in job ads are similar (e.g., teaching experience, research background, academic qualifications), not all of the criteria will be identical. Think about the criteria for each position and be sure to address all of them in your cover letters. For example, if the job is at an institution at which there is a diverse student population, it would be to your benefit to highlight strengths or experiences you have working with diverse populations (e.g., students, participants) or incorporating diversity into your teaching, research, or service.

It is crucial that you demonstrate in the cover letter the fit between you and the position, as this is one of the most important factors search committees consider when hiring a new faculty member (Landrum & Clump, 2004; Sheehan, McDevitt, & Ross, 1998). The extent to which your qualifications fit the needs of the department can make or break your application; so if you think you're a good fit, make it explicit. Consider whether your background and training will make sense for the department for which you are applying. For example, if you are applying to a small school, explain why you are interested in a small school, particularly if you are coming from a large university. My graduate training was at a large research-oriented university, and I found myself having to explain why I wanted to work at smaller schools with mainly a teaching focus. I demonstrated to the committee that even though my training was at a large research-oriented university, I had experience in teaching at a smaller liberal arts university and that I was drawn to smaller schools for very specific reasons (e.g., smaller class sizes). I also highlighted my research experience with undergraduate students and focus on the mentoring aspect of the research process.

As part of your responsibility as a faculty member, you will be expected to teach particular courses. Demonstrate in your cover letter that you are a good candidate to teach those courses. If you have taught the courses outlined in the job ad, state clearly that you have. If you haven't taught the courses before, identify other experiences that qualify you to teach the course. Have you taught other similar courses? Have you taught a laboratory section on the topic? Have you conducted research in that area? Be creative when thinking about your relevant qualifications; you may be more qualified than you think!

It is also important to investigate the research interests of faculty in the department. You will want to tailor the presentation of your research so that it is complementary to others in the department. Do your homework: Check the department website, look at the research interests of faculty members, get a sense of what research productivity (e.g., publications) is expected, and get ideas about what resources are available. Most departments are not looking for a new faculty member who does the same research as someone else in the department. If you find yourself in a situation in which there is someone else already doing similar research to what you do, you may have to be creative. Think about putting a different spin on your research to show that your research is not the same as that already being conducted in the department. One other point that you want to demonstrate in your cover letter with regard to research is that you can conduct research independently as well as collaboratively.

You also want to make sure your research is a good fit for the department in terms of resources. If you require lots of laboratory space, expensive equipment, or a special population for your research, make sure that the institution can provide these resources. Do other faculty members have lab space? Is it a big city where special populations would be easy to recruit? Are there other facilities nearby that have resources you could use? For example, I have a colleague who conducts neuroimaging research; however, he also has a line of behavioral studies, which could be done with very little funding. When he is applying to schools with fewer resources, he describes his line of behavioral studies rather than others that involve expensive equipment. If you apply for a position that isn't an exact fit, justify why you are applying and how you are a good fit for the department.

You may have written the perfect cover letter, which clearly demonstrates how you fit with the department and their needs, but there are a number of things you can do (or forget to do) that can cost you the interview (Brems, Lampman, & Johnson, 1995). First, be sure that the cover letter is addressed to the correct individual(s) and that you include the name of the correct school within the cover letter. Second, be sure you don't have grammatical mistakes and typos. Proofread! Proofread! Proofread! Once you have a draft of your cover letter and CV, have several people edit them and give you feedback. One of the greatest mistakes you can make when submitting your application is submitting materials with grammar and spelling mistakes. These types of mistakes could result in your application not being taken seriously.

As a final note, you may want to create a website on which you can put additional information about yourself, including your teaching portfolio, reprints, syllabi, student work samples, and teaching evaluations. Provide the link in the cover letter and on your CV. If you are not Web savvy, use a Google account to create a profile (www.google.com). Also, consider using professional social networking sites—such as Academia.edu (www.academia.edu) and LinkedIn (www.linkedin.com)—to showcase your strengths and to network professionally. Search committees look at this type of information for the top candidates they are considering for the position; after all, this is additional information that they have about candidates. Again, have others review your website to check it for grammatical and spelling errors. In addition to considering what you *do* want the search committee to see about you, also consider what you *don't* want them to see. Consider making nonprofessional social networking sites (e.g., Facebook, Twitter) private so that search committees cannot view your profile. Think about other ways in which you might show up online: Do you have YouTube videos? Reviews of books on Amazon .com? Do you blog? Whatever you do, if it's not professional, take it down or make it private!

Curriculum Vitae

When applying for academic positions, you are competing with many other qualified individuals. How will the search committee narrow down the applicant pool to only those individuals with whom they want to conduct a phone interview? In some cases, search committees start with looking at applicants' CVs.

Writing a professional CV takes time. One of the simplest ways to start preparing your academic job application is to keep your CV up to date throughout your graduate training by keeping track of all of your accomplishments in teaching, research, and service (Jackson & Geckeis, 2003). I suggest that you keep a document in which you jot down your accomplishments as you achieve them and update your CV only once a month. You'll be surprised at how much you actually accomplish, and you'll be more surprised at how many of your accomplishments you forget if you don't keep track of them.

Be sure that your CV is organized in a professional manner; in other words, avoid strange fonts, purple paper, and spraying your CV with perfume or cologne. Your CV should have sections that describe your teaching, research, service, and any other relevant information that shows your experience and qualifications. As with your cover letter, tailor your CV to the school to demonstrate that you are a good fit. For example, if you're applying for a primarily teaching position, put your teaching accomplishments first, followed by research, and vice versa. When describing your honors and awards, include a phrase that describes for what reason you received them. For example, I received the Charles L. Darby Award, but no one outside of my graduate department would know the significance of the award based on its name; therefore, I wrote a brief description of the award so that the search committee would know that this award is presented to the graduate student who was recognized as the outstanding graduate teaching assistant in the department. Similarly, when describing your teaching experience, list the name of the course and your role (e.g., Developmental Psychology, Instructor of Record) rather than just the course number (e.g., PSYC 4220); you can also include the number of students you taught in each course, which may help justify your fit at a small or large school. At the end of your CV, include your list of references and their contact information.

As with all other parts of your application, proofread! If you have another publication or receive a grant after submitting your application materials, send a brief cover letter and an updated CV to inform the search committee of additional accomplishments.

Teaching and Research Statements

Teaching and research statements are also commonly requested for academic positions (Clifton & Buskist, 2005). These statements allow you to describe your teaching and research experiences and to *show* your understanding and enthusiasm for these aspects of the position. It takes time to write thoughtful teaching and research statements, so start early. For example, you can begin to write a teaching statement (or teaching philosophy) early in your graduate career. You may want to write a teaching statement after teaching your first course. You will very likely overhaul it—or even start over—as you gain more experience. Nonetheless, preparing a teaching statement early in your teaching career gets you thinking about it.

Teaching statements typically include your teaching philosophy, which is a very personal statement that typically includes points such as why you teach, what you find most rewarding, and what you consider to be effective teaching (Davis & Huss, 2002). Such a statement conveys how your teaching is "conceptualized, implemented, and assessed" (Rasmussen, 2006, p. 301). Teaching statements should also contain specific information about what courses you've taught, class sizes, what types of students were in your classes (e.g., nontraditional), and the types of institutions at which you have taught (e.g., community colleges, private liberal arts colleges). Don't simply state what's important to you—give concrete examples of things you do that illustrate your teaching values. State your teaching goals, strategies, and experiences. Ideally, provide a link to your personal website where you can post additional supporting information, as already suggested. Read teaching statements written by successful job applicants to get ideas about the type of writing style and content of teaching statements. If you have one, consult your school's center for teaching and learning.

Excellence in teaching is important not only for schools whose main focus is teaching but also for research schools (Irons & Buskist, 2008). When evaluating your dedication to teaching, schools will want to see your previous teaching experience, student evaluations, and teaching philosophy statements (Benson & Buskist, 2005). You can demonstrate your excellence in teaching by preparing a teaching portfolio (see Seldin, 1991), which includes all aspects of your teaching, helps you reflect on your teaching (Korn, 2002), and helps you present your teaching accomplishments. Seek out opportunities to teach and to improve your teaching throughout your graduate career, whether it is in your department, college/university, or community. Also, take advantage of professional development opportunities focused on teaching (e.g., teaching workshops and conferences).

In addition to your teaching statement, you may be required to write a statement of research. In your research statement, tell a story that clearly demonstrates that you have a systematic research agenda and show how one study leads to the next, as these are good predictors of your ability to get tenure, especially at a research-oriented university. Explain your research in easy to understand terms (e.g., don't use jargon). Include information about any grants that you have written and/or received. If you have publications—even poster presentations or manuscripts under review—you can cite them within your research statement. Try to avoid citing too many other papers in which you are not an author; you don't want your research statement to sound like a literature review. At the same time, if there are key publications in your area that would be good to cite, go ahead and do so.

If you are applying for a teaching-focused position but have the opportunity to conduct research, focus on the importance of involving students in your research. As a graduate student, you probably worked with undergraduates who were involved in various aspects of research. Describe how you got undergraduate students involved and the ways in which you mentored them to become competent researchers.

Remember to tailor your research and teaching statements to the particular schools to which you apply. Although your views of teaching and your lines of research won't change depending on where you apply, there may be specific requests in the job ad that you should address in your teaching and research statements. You should also tailor the length of your research statements to the position: if you're applying to a research-focused institution, a longer (no more than five pages) research statement is fine, but if you're applying to a teaching-focused institution, a briefer research statement (no more than two to three pages) is more appropriate.

Letters of Recommendation

Typically, academic positions require three to five letters of recommendation. Throughout your graduate career, you likely have worked with several professors who have gotten to know you, your research, and your work ethic. Before asking any of these individuals to write you a letter, speak with them about the type of position for which you are searching: primarily teaching, primarily research, or a little of both. You want to make sure that your letter writers can—and are willing to—talk about your abilities in the domain(s) that are most important for the schools to which you're applying. Once your letter writers know the types of positions for which you are applying and have confirmed that they can support you in your endeavors, approach the topic of recommendation letters. Ask these individuals early (as soon as you know you're going on the job market) if they can write you a *strong* letter of recommendation. This is actually one of the best pieces of advice I got when I was in graduate school, because you don't want someone to write you a weak letter that doesn't demonstrate your qualifications. Asking the person to write you a *strong* recommendation—rather than just a recommendation—gives them an "out" if they do not feel comfortable in writing you a recommendation. After all, you want your reference writers to highlight your assets, as the letters of recommendation may be a critical aspect of the initial screening of applicants (Sheehan et al., 1998).

Sometimes letter writers may want to gain more experience with or knowledge about you in a certain domain (e.g., teaching, research) before they feel confident in writing a letter. Find out if there's something you can do to make their knowledge of you more complete. For example, offer to give a guest lecture in one of your mentor's classes during which you talk about your research. This way, your mentor can learn more about your research and see your teaching in action. Also, no matter the number of letters required by the position, it is a good idea to have one extra letter writer just in case. Things happen that cause letters to be delayed—often outside of your control—and you don't want to not be considered for a position because your application was incomplete due to a missing letter of recommendation.

After you know who will write your letters, it is time to get organized yet again. Make things as easy as possible for your letter writers by providing them with all the information they need to write you a strong letter. For each position, prepare a packet of information that includes the job ad, your cover letter, CV, and teaching and research statements for the particular school. These materials will help your letter writers tailor their letters for individual schools.

Point out to your letter writers if there is something particular that you want them to mention in their letters. This piece of advice can be particularly important if you have a top choice, and you want your letter writers to know that this is the place you want to work. It is also helpful if you are applying to schools with somewhat different levels of responsibility with regard to teaching and research. For example, you don't want your letter writers to go on and on about how great a researcher you are when the position for which you are applying is solely a teaching position.

You need to be clear with your letter writers about aspects of your applications. Most importantly, be sure that they know the deadline for each application. To ensure that your letters of recommendation are received on time, make a checklist for your letter writers that includes the name of each school, the position for which you are applying, the type of institution (e.g., research-focused, teaching-focused), the name of the search committee chair (or the person to whom the letter should be addressed), the departmental address (for writing a professional recommendation), the mode of turning in the application (e.g., online, mailed, returned to you), where it should be sent (e.g., e-mail or mailing address), and the deadline. Your letter writers may also find it helpful if you include the website to the institution, department, or program to which you are applying, where they can go for additional information. Even if all of this information is in the job ad, it is helpful to your letter writers if you organize it in a spreadsheet by due date, especially if you are applying to many positions.

When you give your letter writers their packets, ask them if they want a reminder before the deadline. You will find they often appreciate the offer and ask you to remind them before the deadline. Keep in mind that writing a strong letter of recommendation takes time, so be sure you give your letter writers at least 3 to 4 weeks to complete your letters.

Interviews

Phone Interviews

If you get a phone interview, you're likely one of 7 to 10 individuals being interviewed. Typically, the search committee chair will call you to ask if you are still interested in the position. If you are, she or he will ask to schedule a phone interview with you. Once you are asked to do a phone interview, do your homework and familiarize yourself with the school, department, and faculty (e.g., look at the school's website). However, you may not have much time between when you schedule the phone interview and when the phone interview takes place, so it's not a bad idea to start preparing for phone interviews before you start receiving them. You should be prepared to answer the interviewers' questions (Table 23.1) and also prepare a list of questions to ask your interviewers (Table 23.2).

When scheduling a phone interview, ask with whom you will be speaking during the interview. You may interview with just the search committee chair, or you may

Table 23.1   Questions You Should Be Prepared to Answer

Why did you apply here?

What are you looking for in a position?

How would this position differ from your current position?

What do you think is the ideal balance of teaching, research, and service for you?

What are your strengths and weaknesses?

What is your teaching philosophy?

What student requirements do you have in your courses?

How would you describe your teaching style?

What does a typical class period look like?

What type of teaching experience do you have?

What courses are you willing to teach?

How do you incorporate diversity into your teaching?

What do you think are some challenges of teaching this generation of students?

What kind of assignments do you give in your classes and why?

Now that you have reviewed our curriculum, what kinds of courses could you foresee providing to round out the breadth of our classes?

What are your research interests?

How would you incorporate undergraduates into your research?

Why is your research important?

How do you feel about student advising? What role do you see yourself taking?

What types of service would you be interested in becoming involved in, in the department, college, community, and profession?

What are your outside interests?

Table 23.2   Questions You Should Ask

Is this a 9-month or 12-month position?

Is there opportunity for summer salary?

What type of technological support is there in the department? In the university?

Is there a place on campus that helps with preparing grants?

Is there a participant pool of undergraduates available to use for research?

How many courses would I be expected to teach each year?

What does a successful faculty member look like?

What are the students like?

What is there to do in the area?

interview with a group of people. What should you expect from a phone interview? Phone interviews vary a lot. In some cases, the interviewers have scripted questions that they are going to ask you. This type of interview can be especially awkward because the interviewers may not reply to your answers and just move on to the next question; however, this doesn't mean that you're not doing well; it's just that they have a particular way that they are interviewing all candidates. On the other hand, you may have phone interviews that are much less formal. For example, I had several phone interviews that felt like relaxing conversations about my research and teaching. A word of caution is in order for less formal phone interviews: You are still being evaluated, so continue to be professional in all of your interactions with committee members.

On the day of your phone interview, ensure that you are in a location in which you feel comfortable. For example, I decided to do as many of my phone interviews as possible from home because it was less likely that someone would disturb me. It's okay to have papers/websites in front of you during your interview, but don't let them distract you.

Following the phone interview, send a thank-you e-mail to the person(s) who interviewed you to convey interest in the opportunity to speak with the interviewers and to let them know that if they have questions, they can contact you.

After your phone interview, a number of things can happen. You may receive an e-mail or a letter that states you are not one of the candidates to be invited for a campus interview. Although this news may be disappointing, it is better than not hearing anything from the school, which is extremely frustrating. Keep in mind that there may be no rhyme or reason for why you weren't offered a campus visit or why you weren't informed that the position has already been filled.

The best-case scenario is being invited for a campus interview. The committee typically invites three to five candidates for a campus interview, so if you receive an invitation, you've made it a long way, but your job is still not done. The campus interview can come very quickly after the phone interview, sometimes within a few days. This means that you must be ready for your campus interview. The campus interview is a chance for the faculty, students, and administrators at the school to get to know you, so you need to impress them, but it's also an opportunity for you to be able to get a feel for the culture of the department, school, and larger community.

Campus Interviews

As soon as you are offered a campus interview, think about what you are going to wear. Be sure to dress professionally and present yourself in a favorable light, as you only get to make one first impression! Although you want to look professional, also be sure that you are comfortable in what you are wearing. Neither men nor women can go wrong wearing a suit; however, not everyone is comfortable in a suit. Women can choose to wear a skirt or pants and a jacket as an alternative to a suit, and men can choose to wear slacks and a sport coat. Be sure to wear comfortable shoes, as you may be doing a lot of walking around campus! As a general guideline, don't dress any lower than business casual.

What can you expect from an on-campus interview? In brief, campus interviews are typically 1 or 2 days long. During this time, you will meet with the search committee, department head, other faculty, students, and administrators. You should be provided with an itinerary that gives you an idea how your day(s) at the interview will be spent. If you are not sent an itinerary, it is okay to ask for one. You will likely feel nervous and anxious as you wait for your campus interview day(s); these feelings are perfectly valid! From my experience, waiting for campus interviews to start was the most stressful part. Once the interview started, my anxiety decreased and I became excited about the opportunity to learn about the schools where I was potentially going to work. The key to decreasing your anxiety is to be prepared!

While at the interview, keep in mind that you're "on" the whole time. This means that you're "on" even during social events and when you're meeting with students. While it's okay to be yourself and show your sense of humor and your ability to get along with faculty, students, and administrators, remember to be professional.

Job Talks

A major component of the campus interview is a job talk. Job talks come in two forms: a teaching demonstration or a research talk. Either way, the job talk is your opportunity to demonstrate your ability to communicate information. When you are setting up your campus interview, ask for specifics about the job talk, including the type of job talk (e.g., teaching or research), who your audience will be (e.g., faculty, students, or both), how many people are expected to attend, and what type of equipment will be available (e.g., a computer).

Before your interview, practice your job talk! Practice it for yourself in front of a mirror, videotape yourself and watch yourself to see what you need to work on, practice it in front of your committee, in front of undergraduate and graduate students, or in the class(es) you teach (if the topic is relevant). Practicing your job talk is critical in catching typos on your PowerPoint, making sure the presentation flows logically (specifically for those not familiar with the topic), and in ensuring that you are within the time limit of the presentation.

If you are presenting a teaching demonstration, you will likely be told a topic—either narrow or fairly general—that you should address. If you are presenting a research talk, tell a story about your research. You know why your research is important, but others may not, so be explicit about where and how your research fits within a larger context. Show your audience how one study relates to the next and have a clear indication of where you plan to take your research in the future. Be sure to balance numbers and ideas, and demonstrate your ability to conduct research independently and collaboratively.

Remember that you are being evaluated even during the question-and-answer session, particularly with regard to how you handle questions. If you have practiced your job talk in front of many different people, you can anticipate some of the questions the audience may have; however, be prepared to demonstrate your ability to think on the spot to answer new questions. Remember, you are the expert in your research area, so have confidence in your ability to field questions. When answering questions about your research, make sure you're not coming across as defensive; be friendly and open to discussing new ideas and interpretations, even if they are different from your own interpretations.

Make your job talk memorable! I have seen many job talks throughout the years. Most candidates present job talks that are engaging and convey their enthusiasm about their research. In one case, the candidate may have blown his chance for a position due to his job talk. He may have had a very interesting job talk and may have been enthusiastic about his research, but the only thing I remember from his job talk was the jingling of the change that he was playing with in his pocket during the entire presentation. It is understandable that you will be nervous during your job talk, but be sure that you are not distracting the audience due to your nerves.

Have a backup plan for your presentation; e-mail your presentation to yourself, put it on a CD and flash drive, or bring your own computer. In the case that the equipment fails, you may want to have back-up overhead slides. Prepare for the worst, because you don't want to be left unable to present your talk. You may have some time before your talk, so check that all of the equipment is working. For further thoughts about presentation skills, see Chapter 15 of this book.

Meeting Faculty, Administrators, and Students

During your campus interview, you will meet with a lot of different people, all of whom will have questions for you. In many cases, you will be answering the same three to five questions for each person with whom you meet; but remember that they haven't heard your answer to the questions, so be just as sincere about answering the question the sixth time as you were the first time. I will discuss some commonly asked questions below and have listed others in Table 23.1.

The department head may ask you about what kind of space, equipment, and resources you will need to conduct your research. You likely don't need a full list during a campus interview, but you should have a general idea of the big items you will need. Some of the standard things that you will ask for are a laptop and/or desktop computer for your office and lab, including special software that you need to conduct your research. Don't assume that the school has the programs you may use on a regular basis. In addition to hardware and software, you will likely need lab space. Be sure to describe the type of space you need and ask to see some potential lab spaces. Prior to your visit, check out the library's website to see if they have the journals you will need to conduct your research. If they don't, ask that the library subscribe to the journals so that you can continue to do your research. Keep in mind that smaller schools and schools with limited funding may not have the resources to offer you a lab space or the journals you may need. If you conduct research with a special population (e.g., children, elderly, prisoners), determine if you will be able to recruit them in the way that you have previously. If not, prepare alternate ways in which you could recruit them in the area.

There are certain questions that interviewers should not ask you and you do not have to answer! For example, the interviewers can't ask you about your marital status, if you have kids (or plan to have them), sexual orientation, or age. If you are faced with questions about your personal life, particularly ones that are illegal to be asked of you, you can politely ask how the question is related to the position or ask if that is something that the department would be concerned about. Alternately, you can address the concern brought up in the questions rather than the question itself.

The campus interview is your opportunity to determine whether the school is a good fit for *you!* Prepare questions for the search committee, other faculty, the department head, and school administrators with whom you will be meeting. These questions should show your interest in the position and the school. One thing you should ask the department head is about the expectations for the position with regard to teaching, research, and service and about the tenure and promotion process. Ask if there were any cases in which individuals did not receive tenure in the last 5 to 10 years and why. Also, ask questions about the future of the department. For example, ask how the department head sees the department changing in the next 10 years and if the department intends to hire more faculty over the next 5 years. How the department head answers these questions can be especially telling about the department. Ask the people with whom you meet about *their* research interests, which shows your interest in what they do and gives you a better idea about what kind of research people are doing in the department and whether there is any potential for collaboration. Also prepare questions for the students with whom you will likely meet. Ask them about what they look for in an instructor, their research interests, their future academic plans, and how they like the school.

Another question you may consider asking is whether there is an internal candidate for the position. Internal candidates can have an advantage over external candidates if they have demonstrated that they are good fit for and meet the needs of the department. On the other hand, if internal candidates do not meet the standards of the department, they are likely not favored by the department, so external candidates have the advantage.

The exit interview—which is the last interview—is your chance to ask the department head remaining questions and to offer to address anything in your application that may have been concerning to the committee. It is appropriate at this time to ask about when you might expect to hear the outcome of the search. If you have time frame constraints, you can mention these. For example, if you have other interviews or already have an offer, you can let the department head know; however, don't name the other places. See Table 23.2 for additional questions you should consider asking.

Following your interview, send a thank-you e-mail to those with whom you met expressing your interest in the department and the university and appreciation for the opportunity to meet with the faculty, students, and administration. In addition, send receipts for any travel expenses promptly so you can be reimbursed. Also, finalize your start-up criteria so you have them ready in the event that you get an offer. Your start-up criteria include a list of all of the equipment you will need, including prices and where the items can be purchased. This is particularly important if you have to present your offer within a short period of time (e.g., you might have to send it back within 24 hours of receiving the offer).

Offer, Negotiations, and Decision

After your interview, the search committee will meet to discuss the candidates who visited campus. This process may take some time, from days to months. While you are waiting for an offer, look up the salary range for the position and type of school at which you applied and finalize your start-up requests. Typically the department head or the dean will contact you with the offer either over the phone or through e-mail. When you receive an offer, convey interest, but never accept it right away. Once the offer has been made, you need to negotiate! Think of the negotiation process in terms of the school's needs, not just your own. After all, the school wants to hire you to do a service for them. Therefore, don't be afraid to phrase negotiations by saying "X and Y are what I need in order to do my research and teaching."

Because you have already done your research on what a typical salary range is for the position to which you applied and have compiled your start-up requests, you should be ready to negotiate. You can find salary tables for negotiation purposes on the *Chronicle* (http://chronicle.com/stats/aaup/) and APA (http://www.apa.org/workforce/index.aspx; http://www.apa.org/workforce/publications/10-fac-sal/index.aspx) websites. After examining these websites, you can be specific in stating that "for X position, at Y university, in the Z region, the average salary is A." Keep in mind that any raises you may receive in the future are based on your starting salary, which means the higher your starting salary, the higher your raises! Don't be afraid to negotiate your salary. The worst thing that happens is that they are not able to meet your request. Particularly if you are a female, don't be afraid to ask. Women on average have lower starting salaries than men because they are less likely to negotiate (Barron, 2003).

At your campus interview, you have already likely given the department head an idea about the types of equipment and space you will need to conduct your research. After an offer is made, you may have to turn in your request for start-up within a very short period of time. Again, because you have prepared your start-up requests while you were waiting for an offer, you should not have any problems having your start-up request ready to go. Take into consideration the position for which you applied and the resources the school may have. For example, if you have been offered a position at a smaller school, they may not have the resources to buy you expensive research equipment such as an fMRI or eye tracker. If you received an offer from a school with more resources and you are requesting expensive equipment or software, talk about others in the department who might also be able to use it. Once you have come to an agreement on your start-up, ask about when you have to spend it. Often, you have to spend your start-up money during your first year.

Some other things for which you might consider negotiating are moving expenses, a course release during your first year, summer salary, and travel money. You might consider negotiating for time if you need to make a decision, particularly because you typically have only a week or two to make a decision. Let's say that you have interviewed at at least two schools and you have a top choice and a second choice between the two schools. What should you do if you have been offered a position at the second-choice school but have not received an offer from your first-choice school? This is a case in which you would want to negotiate for time. Regardless of the initial timeframe, contact your first-choice school and let them know that you are still interested but have received an offer from another school. Hopefully they will be able to let you know whether you are still being considered for the position and can give you a timeline. Based on what your top choice says, you can negotiate more time to give your response to your second-choice school. Make sure you get everything in writing! If the offer is made over the phone, ask for a follow up e-mail stating the terms of the offer; you should not consider a verbal offer an official offer.

Once you have taken a position, let the other schools where you interviewed know that you are withdrawing your application. In the event that you don't receive an offer, don't fret. You should have thought about a Plan B, which could involve staying in school for another year to finish up your dissertation and improve your CV through further teaching and research experiences. Sometimes positions are announced later in the year if someone has decided to retire or has left a position unexpectedly, so new positions may become available. Chapter 25 discusses in more detail how to proceed if you don't land a job.

Summary

As you have seen throughout this chapter, applying for academic positions is a long and usually stressful process. Here are three Ps that will help make the process less stressful: prepare, practice, proofread! If you keep these in mind, you will not only be less stressed, but you should also be more likely to prepare a successful job application and to have successful phone and/or campus interviews, which in the best case will lead to several offers. Also keep in mind that you will experience many emotions as you go through this process, some positive and others negative. Finally, keep in mind that there is often no rhyme or reason for why a strong candidate did not receive a phone or campus interview. The key is to remain optimistic during the process and not to get discouraged.

❖ References

Barron, L. A. (2003). Ask and you shall receive? Gender differences in negotiators' beliefs about requests for a higher salary. *Human Resources, 56,* 653–662. doi: 10.1177/00187267030566001.

Benson, T. A., & Buskist, W. (2005). Understanding "excellence in teaching" as assessed by psychology faculty search committees. *Teaching of Psychology, 32,* 47–49. doi: 10.1207/s15328023top3201_11.

Brems, C., Lampman, C., & Johnson, M. E. (1995). Preparation of applications for academic positions in psychology. *American Psychologist, 50,* 533–537.

Clifton, J., & Buskist, W. (2005). Preparing graduate students for academic positions in psychology: Suggestions from job advertisements. *Teaching of Psychology, 32,* 264–266. doi: 10.1207/s15328023top3204_8.

Darley, J. M., & Zanna, M. P. (2004). The hiring process in academia. In J. M. Darley, M. P. Zanna, & H. L. Roediger (Eds.), *The compleat academic: A career guide* (p. 31–56).

Davis, S. F., & Huss, M. T. (2002). Training graduate teaching assistants. In S. F. Davis & W. Buskist (Eds.), *The teaching of psychology: Essays in honor of Wilbert J. McKeachie and Charles L. Brewer* (p. 141–150), Mahwah, NJ: Lawrence Erlbaum Associates.

Irons, J., G., & Buskist, W. (2008). Preparing the new professoriate: What courses should they be ready to teach? *Teaching of Psychology, 35,* 201–204. doi: 10.1080/00986280802186185.

Jackson, A., & Geckeis, K. (2003). *How to prepare your curriculum vitae.* New York: McGraw-Hill.

Korn, J. H. (2002). Beyond tenure: The teaching portfolio for reflection and change. In S. F. Davis & W. Buskist (Eds.), *The teaching of psychology: Essays in honor of Wilbert J. McKeachie and Charles L. Brewer* (p. 203–213), Mahwah, NJ: Lawrence Erlbaum Associates.

Landrum, R. E., & Clump, M. A. (2004). Departmental search committees and the evaluation of faculty applications. *Teaching of Psychology, 31,* 12–17.

Rasmussen, E. B. (2005). Creating teaching portfolios. In W. Buskist & S. F. Davis (Eds.), *The handbook of the teaching of psychology* (p. 301–306). Malden, MA: Blackwell.

Seldin, P. (1991). *The teaching portfolio: A practical guide to improved performance and promotion/tenure decisions.* Bolton, MA: Anker.

Sheehan, E. P., McDevitt, T. M., & Ross, H. C. (1998). Looking for a job as a psychology professor? Factors affecting applicant success. *Teaching of Psychology, 25,* 8–11.

Wilbur, H. M. (1988). On getting a job. In A. L. Deneef, C. D. Goodwin, & E.S. McCrate (Eds.), *The academic's handbook* (p.63–76). Durham, NC: Duke University Press.

Suggestions for Further Exploration

Darley, J. M., Zanna, M. P., & Roediger, H. L. (2004). *The compleat academic: A career guide.* Washington, DC: American Psychological Association. This book is a guide for starting and maintaining an academic career.

Johnson, W. B., & Huwe, J. M. (2002). *Getting mentored in graduate school.* Washington, DC: American Psychological Association. This book is a guide for graduate students that can help make their graduate experiences with their mentor(s) positive, which can help put you on a great career path.

Rheingold, H. L. (1994). *The psychologist's guide to an academic career.* Washington, DC: American Psychological Association. This book provides guidance for a successful academic career in psychology.

Sternberg, R. J. (1997). *Career paths in psychology: Where your degree can take you.* Washington, DC: American Psychological Association. This book describes career paths in a number of fields related to psychology.

Vick, J. M., & Furlong, J. S. (2008). *The academic job search handbook.* Philadelphia: University of Pennsylvania Press. This book is an in-depth guide to applying for academic positions in any field.

Websites

APA PsyCCareers (http://www.apa.org/careers/psyccareers/). This website offers listings for psychology-related academic and postdoctoral positions.

APS Employment Network (http://www.psychologicalscience.org/index.php/employment). This website offers listings for psychology related academic and postdoctoral positions.

The Chronicle of Higher Education (http://chronicle.com/section/Jobs/61/). This website offers listings for academic and postdoctoral positions across all fields.

HigherEdJobs (http://higheredjobs.com/). This website offers listings for academic and postdoctoral positions across all fields.

24

Applying for Clinical and Other Applied Positions

❖

Janet R. Matthews
Loyola University New Orleans

Lee H. Matthews
Private Practice, New Orleans, LA

T his chapter addresses best practices in applying for clinical and other applied positions. We use *clinical* to refer to health service provider positions, including but not limited to clinical, counseling, school, clinical neuropsychology, clinical geropsychology, and clinical health psychology. We will also address issues related to applying for positions in industrial-organizational and consulting psychology. These positions are also applied, but the application process may be somewhat different from that found in the clinical positions. Another term used for the specialties included in this chapter is *license-eligible* specialties. Although there is a separate chapter (Chapter 23) on applying for academic positions, this chapter will address some of the unique issues of academic positions in graduate training programs for which licensure is needed for trainee supervision and academic positions in medical centers that carry academic rank in addition to clinical duties. We have included relevant websites in several places within this chapter. These websites are not the only ones of use in the application process, but they are used to illustrate the range of helpful sources available to applicants.

Traditionally, much of the material covered in this chapter has been transmitted orally. It is not usually the subject of research projects or journal articles but, rather, part of either the mentoring experience or what has been experienced by the individual psychologist as both an applicant and employer over a career. Thus, the reference section for this chapter is somewhat briefer than for many of the other chapters in this volume.

Applications

Starting Your Search

There are a variety of sources for identifying potential positions. Optimal searches require time so that you have a complete picture of the offerings. A good strategy is to schedule yourself at least an hour of computer time several days each week for the job-search process. This is a *minimum* time commitment for the initial part of the process. A good starting point is the American Psychological Association (APA) website (www.apa.org) and then PsychCareers. Although these positions are also listed in APA's monthly *Monitor on Psychology,* you will find them sooner on the website. Positions are also listed in APA's *GradPsych.* The American Psychological Society (APS) website (www.psychologicalscience.org) lists positions under Employment Network. During their conventions, professional associations may also have bulletin boards on which positions are listed. In addition to these national associations, most states have applied jobs listed under the appropriate state website. If you are interested in moving to a particular state or region of the country, go to the state government website and search under employment opportunities. For example, for clinical positions, this may be under the Department of Health and Human Services or similar title.

Specialty organizations also list available positions on their websites. For example, clinical neuropsychology positions are often advertised at the conventions of the National Academy of Neuropsychology and the International Neuropsychological Society. The National Association of School Psychology lists jobs under the title of Career Center on its website (www.nasponline.org). School psychology jobs are also listed on the APA Division 16 website (www.indiana.edu/~div16/indix.html). These positions are subdivided into academic, K–12, and other. Divisions of APA as well as state, provincial, and territorial psychological associations (SPTPAs) also post information about positions on their listservs with not only position information but also the offer of further information by contacting the person posting the notice. Thus, becoming a student member of some of these groups may add to your information pool. Usually, student membership is relatively inexpensive and allows you access to these listservs as well as starts you on the road to professional activity. In addition to their listservs, some APA divisions also list jobs on their websites. These are free services. Candidates looking for industrial/organizational jobs might go to the Division 14 website (www.siop.org) and use JobNet, which is part of the Jobs link. Consulting psychology positions are listed under Jobs on the Division 13 website (www.div13.0rg). Some applied positions, especially those in medical schools, are also found in the *Chronicle of Higher Education* (www.chronicle.com/section/jobs). Finally, if there are specific urban areas of interest to you, try the classifieds in the local newspaper under the *employment* section; you can access many of these online.

An important and often overlooked source of employment information is your faculty mentor. Although there are many psychologists in this country, in some ways, we are a small community. Let your faculty mentor know of your interests in terms of both type of job and preferred locations. If you have a good mentor relationship, you might consider scheduling an appointment to discuss the range of potential positions that match your skill set and personality. Do not be afraid both to do some self-assessment about your personal characteristics and to ask your mentor about how they may be relevant to different types of positions.

A broader term that is also part of your job search is *networking*. A brief example illustrates how this might work. Dr. Jennifer Nardozzi noted that she got her first position as director for admissions for a multisite eating disorders facility through a somewhat circuitous route (American Psychological Association, 2005). She knew someone whose mother knew other people who were connected to the facility. After talking to about five different people, she learned about the position she wanted as well as the name of the appropriate contact person. This process led to her first job. Using this process may not lead to a job for you, but these initial contacts may know other people who do know about positions.

Another issue to consider is timing. When should you start this job search? University applied positions typically begin with the fall term. Other applied positions are advertised year round. Thus, start your search for faculty positions in doctoral training programs in the fall before you actually plan to start. Although some of these positions may be advertised in the summer, many will wait until administrative approval, which often comes after the beginning of a fiscal year. The same can be said of most postdoctoral fellowships. They often have a starting date of September 1 and therefore may start taking applicants 10 or 11 months prior to that date. Postdoctoral fellowships located in medical school settings may actually begin July 1, as that is the traditional starting date for medical residents. For many applied positions, the employer is seeking applicants who can begin within a reasonably short period of time after the offer is made. It is important to monitor such positions early, but you may not want to apply until a bit closer to your graduation date. You will also want to have a solid idea about whether your dissertation will be completed and, thus, you will actually have your degree prior to beginning your employment. Degree status is an issue for both salary and qualification for some applied positions.

An important issue to address early in the search process is the relative importance of the type of job and its geographic location. Some people decide where they really want to live and then look for jobs in only those areas. For others, the position is more important than the location. In a tight economy, or when you are part of a dual-career couple, location may not be as easy to include as a criterion as when jobs are plentiful and only one person is looking. However, if you already know that you will have major adjustment issues if you try to live in certain types of communities (e.g., rural rather than at least near a city), do not apply for jobs in those settings. If you consider jobs in places where you find the locale interferes with your ability to perform, you are not as likely to perform in a satisfactory manner. In this case, it may become difficult to obtain your second position, as you will not have a good reference from the initial employer. Regardless of the variables, however, take some time to consider the importance of community in addition to the match between your abilities and the demands of the position.

Dual-career couples face some additional points to consider when starting the job search. Such couples need to have a general discussion about the topic prior to doing the initial phases of the job search. Although some dual-career couples locate jobs in the same community at the same time, this is not always the case. Are you willing to have a commuter relationship for the sake of your career? Are there some distance limitations to an acceptable commuter relationship? For couples who are unwilling to have a commuter relationship, decisions about hiring priorities need to be made prior to active job hunting. This discussion needs to include the comparative difficulty of each in finding an acceptable position if a move is made for one position. For example, if your significant other is in the nursing profession, you should probably concentrate on your position as primary because there is currently a shortage of nurses in most communities. On the other hand, if you are looking for a position in organizational consulting and your significant other is a school psychologist, hiring deadlines for the school system may be much different from those of consulting firms.

Type of Job

Although this chapter addresses only applied positions, there are still some decisions you need to make. If you are in a *license-eligible* specialty, you need to decide if you really want to look for a permanent position or whether a postdoc would be a better match for your long-term goals. Despite the fact that some jurisdictions now allow licensure immediately upon completion of your doctorate (as of December 2009, there were 10 states in this category), others do not. Your first job may not be your lifetime position. Even if you can obtain a license immediately, it is a good option to document supervision for 1 year postdegree to allow you maximum career mobility. When making this decision, remember that the common licensing board definition of postdoctoral supervision includes the fact that the hours do not count until AFTER the doctoral degree has been granted. We have each served on our state licensing boards and have seen the licensure applicant denied candidate status because the degree was not granted until some time after the start of the postdoc. For example, consider the applicant who completed a predoctoral internship in a medical center at the end of June. The university's graduation date, however, was in May, and therefore she had not met graduation requirements at that time. The next scheduled graduation at her university was in August. Because she had completed all requirements for her degree, she began a postdoctoral fellowship on July 1. Her doctoral degree was granted on August 15. When she applied for her license to practice, she was denied candidacy because the licensing board did not accept the experience from July 1 to August 15. She was considered to have had only 10.5 months of supervised postdoctoral experience rather than the mandated 12 months. Regardless of when you complete your degree requirements, it is important to have a year of supervised experience after the date on your diploma to qualify for licensure in many states.

If you do not elect to do a formal postdoc or cannot find one, it is still important to include in your job search requirements the availability of supervision at your site. Although you may find tempting positions where you will be the only psychologist on site, we strongly urge you to bypass them for the first year in order to get that supervision. Depending on state law for supervision, you may be able to negotiate about the provision of supervision with the facility. Here's an example of what may meet the legal requirements. You are interested in working in a sexual trauma inpatient program. You have had considerable experience in this specialty during your graduate training and a facility where you live and know people has an opening. They offer you the position as their staff psychologist upon receipt of your doctorate. There are no other psychologists in the facility. You have two problems with this offer in your state. First, you cannot call yourself a *psychologist* until you are licensed. Thus, if you accept the position as offered by the human resources department, you are violating state law. Second, you will have no one to supervise you because state law requires that supervisors have *administrative control* over your clinical work. This means that you cannot just have someone in the community agree to supervise you. You really want this position; what do you do? You locate someone in the community who has expertise with sexual trauma and is willing to supervise you for a year. You then explain the situation to the human resources director at your proposed place of employment. You ask them to give this community psychologist a 1-year contract for the number of hours per week of supervision that is required by your state's law and a title, such as Director of Clinical Psychology. This psychologist is then able to view all patient records as an employee of the facility, to observe you in treatment settings, and to discuss your clinical care with you. As soon as you have completed your postdoctoral hours and received your license, the position of Director of Clinical Psychology is deleted from the roster.

Depending on your specialty, you may be looking at a range of types of position. If that is the case, consider developing multiple versions of your *curriculum vitae* (CV) that emphasize different facets of your background. There is no standard format for your CV. Of course, the basic demographics (name, educational history, etc.) will be included on all forms. For positions that include some academic responsibilities, such as academic medical centers, you may wish to note your research interests and production more prominently than for purely applied positions. For the latter, you may need to have more detailed information about your applied experiences that are relevant to that site. Since you may wish to use different references depending on the position, you should not list references in your CV. At the end of your CV, note: References available upon request. Be certain to contact those people you plan to use as references and let them know of the types of positions you are considering. You may want to vary who serves as a reference for which types of position. It is a *red flag* to employers if they see a name on your CV and that person does not submit a letter of support. With a competitive job market, this factor may be sufficient to remove your name from the top candidate list. In your cover letter for each position, include the names and affiliations of the people who will be sending references under separate cover. Then do follow-up with the potential employer to determine that all letters have arrived. If they tell you they have only two of your three letters, ask them for the names so you can contact the missing endorser and let that person know the letter did not arrive.

When considering the type of job for which you may be a successful candidate, think in terms of skill sets rather than specific experiences you have had. It is possible that your experiences may be a good fit for settings you had not considered. For example, Dr. Nabil El-Ghouroury noted that although he had considered himself a clinical child psychologist, his first job after his postdoc was as a pediatric psychologist. He obtained this position because of the match between his skills and the medical center's needs (Matthews & Anton, 2008, p. 432). It may be a good idea to actually read some of the books on careers in psychology to help you broaden your concept of potential jobs (e.g. Davis, Giordano, & Licht, 2009; Sternberg, 2007).

Applying for Jobs

Before actually filling out the formal application or sending a letter, visit the facility's website if one is available. Although many websites provide only a position description, others may have considerably more information. For example, the

University of Michigan Medical School website has an entire section for *Prospective Faculty*. Scanning the various links in this section gives you an overview of expectations and resources that may prove useful in writing your application letter.

Some positions will use online applications. It can be easy to make typographical errors when you are doing this on your computer. Be certain to carefully review what you have written before sending it. Sloppy applications can be seen as an indication of sloppy work. Prepare responses to common questions in advance. Such responses are useful for sites that allow uploads. For example, you may wish to develop descriptions of your assessment and intervention experience, your past research and proposed future work, and your personal career objectives. Even if you either can't upload this information or it needs a degree of modification for a particular position, having these bits of information handy can facilitate your application and probably make it both stronger and more representative of your abilities. It is also possible that even if you can't upload, you can copy and paste rather than risk errors.

Some job descriptions are quite clear in their explanation of expected duties, while others seem to be looking for a range of skills with no way for the candidate to determine which of those skills are actually the key elements of the search. Thus, it is not always easy to determine whether you are a good match for each position. There are two major errors applicants tend to make at this point. Some applicants tend to assume that because they are early-career psychologists (ECPs), they have minimal skills. These applicants do not make a sufficiently strong case for their candidacy. Others take the opposite extreme and overestimate their abilities. It is important to give a realistic picture of your current level of skill development and experiences.

The cover letter for each position to which you apply needs to be individually crafted. Letters that are obviously generic do not make a good impression on potential employers. Do not begin your application letter with "Dear Employer" unless no name is provided in the advertisement. Even when no name is provided, start your letter with something specific to that site, such as "Dear NAME OF FACILITY." Use the cover letter not only to describe your skills but also to show why you are a good match for the position and why you want to be employed in that setting.

Selection of references is important. Although you will want to have one of your letters come from a member of your doctoral training faculty, the other two letters should come from psychologists who are familiar with your applied skills. Remember, this is why you did not list references on your CV. If you are applying for a variety of different positions, be certain to let your references know of these differences so that they do not use the same letter for each position. Do not just ask if the person is willing to write a letter for you. Be specific about the types of skills you would like to have addressed in the letter. If you note some hesitancy by the person, find another reference. Let's see how this might work. If you are applying for positions in medical centers in which you will be working with professionals from many different disciplines, you want your reference to note your prior experience with those disciplines as well as your ability to work effectively on an interdisciplinary team. It is certainly appropriate to remind your references of the specific relevant experiences you have had so they may include them in your letter. Many of your references will keep a letter on file so they can just print it repeatedly with a new inside address. If they are using this approach, you might discuss with them the possibility of moving paragraphs around depending on the specific employment site.

The Interview Process

Phone Interviews

In order to maximize the use of limited funds for job searches, many employers will do an initial candidate screening and then select a pool of candidates for phone interviews. These interviews are used to determine the final candidates who will actually be interviewed in person. Phone interviews require as much preparation as on-site interviews. Some of this preparation can be done immediately after you apply, while other information needs to wait until the phone interview is scheduled. Relevant information on employer websites is not always found where you initially search. For example, the Department of Medical Education page at the University of Michigan Medical School has such relevant links as *dual career hiring* and *how to prepare for tenure*. A review of these links may provide information that will allow you to show both your interest and knowledge of the facility. For other information, you may have limited time to gather data. It is important, if possible, to find out the names of the specific people who will participate in the interview. Make a list of these names and have that list with you during the call. Get information about each of the interviewers. You can use the website of the facility as well as professional websites. You may want to do a quick literature search and/or Google each of them and then make notes on the sheet for the call. Typically, each interviewer will be introduced at the beginning of the call. Try to respond to each individually and make some note for yourself about the voice so you can recognize who is asking questions if the person does not self-identify. Knowing something about the person's background and interests can help you understand the rationale for the question as well as suggest a direction for your response. These interviews use technology of varying quality. If you do not hear a question sufficiently well, indicate that the communication was not clear rather than giving a response that is not adequate for the question.

Make yourself as comfortable as possible during this interview to maximize the way you come across to the interviewers. Have water handy so that you can clear your throat if needed. Spread out the material you have prepared about the interviewers, the position, the facility, and the community so that you can locate whatever you may need to respond quickly. Have a copy of all the materials you submitted in case one of the interviewers asks you about some item from your packet. Candidates who do not seem to be familiar with their own material are not likely to move beyond the phone interview stage.

Also, have your own questions ready. Many interviews end with the opportunity for the candidate to ask questions. Since there is no such thing as a perfect interview, merely indicating that they have provided all of the information you need is giving the potential employer the wrong message. It seems that you are either not really that interested or possibly not sufficiently bright to be a good candidate. Cross out those questions that are answered during the phone interview as you go. Thus, it is important to have many questions prepared. A basic question, regardless of the type of position, involves the timeline under which they are operating. Although specific dates may not be realistic, try to clarify when decisions are expected regarding invitations to visit the site.

In some cases, employers will notify those who are not going to be invited shortly after the phone interview. Other employers, however, wait to contact those who had telephone interviews until after they have made a job offer and the candidate has accepted. For example, consider a university counseling center that has invited three candidates to campus for an interview. They offer the counselor position to their first choice. That person takes a week to think about it and then declines. They now offer the position to their second choice. This candidate also takes a week to decide and then accepts an alternative position. By this time, the third candidate who had visited the center has also taken another position. Because of their strong need for a psychologist, the administration approves bringing another candidate to campus. The search committee reviews those who had phone interviews and selects their next choice. This person is then invited to visit. Thus, there may be considerable time between the date of your phone interview and final notification that you will not be offered a position. If the starting date for the position was not listed in the ad, this is also a relevant question. There are questions that are specific to the site. For example, suppose you are applying for a staff position in a university counseling center. Unless it was clear on the website, ask about how medication evaluations are handled. Do they have a consulting psychiatrist, or is a referral made to the university health center? This process is handled in a variety of ways depending on the campus. Your questions show that you have looked at their materials and also that you are familiar with the variability of the process. Another area to pursue in this case is the length of intervention time permitted and whether individuals who seem to merit more long-term counseling are handled. Most university counseling centers provide campus programming on relevant topics. This is fertile ground for the candidate to not only ask questions but also to show an interest in participation and program development related to prior experiences. In the case of a position at a community mental health center, you might ask about how inpatient referrals, when needed, are handled. If you have done a sufficiently good Web search, you might ask if they use specific facilities you noted in your search of facilities that are in the geographic area.

You may wish to send a *thank you* e-mail to the person who arranged the interview. This e-mail does not require much of your time but is typically viewed as an indication of your interest in the position.

On-Site Interviews

Do not wait until you are contacted about visiting sites to determine the availability of flights from your community to those locations. It will save you some extra calls if you already know, for example, that the earliest flight arrival time you can get is in the middle of the day or what time in the evening the last flights arrive. Having this information when you are contacted about the interview will allow you to discuss arrival and departure time to meet the demands of the site. For example, one of us was invited for an interview at a facility that was more accustomed to having local candidates than those from out of town. They suggested a day-long interview and had no plans for hotel accommodations. Although that schedule was technically possible, it would have required taking a return flight that left slightly after midnight with the necessity to sit at the airport from the end of the interview day until flight time.

Learn as much as you can about both the facility and the community before you arrive. You never know what seemingly unrelated factor may be the difference between you and another candidate being offered the position. For example, we know of a candidate who was not offered a position because the search committee decided the candidate would just not be comfortable in their community. The candidate had shown some surprise about the climate during the interview, and this concern was viewed as indicating the person would not be happy there and thus more likely to leave than the other candidate, who commented positively about the locale. By the time you have reached the level of the on-site interview, it is often the intangibles that lead to the final selection.

Ask for an overview of the interview schedule and process. Be certain to ask if you will be expected to give an in-service talk or case presentation during your interview. If so, determine what equipment will be available and plan accordingly. If a case presentation is involved, select your case carefully. Find a case that highlights your range of skills but is not too complicated. You do not want to be in the position of needing to defend what you did or be second-guessed by a trainee who is eager to impress the supervisor. Your case presentation should showcase your talents and be indicative of why your skills are a good match to the people served by the facility. Thus, select a type of case that might be seen there.

Candidates for industrial/organizational positions may find they are given a case in advance, and their job talk will be an analysis of that case. Your work product can then be compared to that of other candidates who are invited for an interview. In these settings, you may even be asked to take personality and cognitive tests as part of the candidate evaluation process (Attenweiler, 2009). Such assessment is much less likely to be part of the interview process for clinical positions.

Bring a range of clothing, but only what you can fit into carry-on luggage. You do not want to arrive at your destination only to discover that your clothing and/or presentation material is in another city. Observe attire on the first day of your interview and make any necessary changes for the next day. Strive for professional attire, but do not look like you have a million-dollar wardrobe.

Dinners provide an opportunity for you to learn the informal structure of the setting as well as to determine the strength of your fit with potential colleagues. Don't be afraid to order a drink if others do so. When everyone at the table is having a drink and the candidate does not, there is often an underlying concern about the reason for this decision (e.g., is this person concerned about control when drinking). Don't be the first one to order a drink but, rather, take your cue from the interviewers. Often these dinners occur in restaurants that are considered special and/or representative of the local cuisine. This does not mean that you should order the most expensive item on the menu. If you have special dietary needs, let your hosts know well in advance, as these reservations are usually made before you arrive in the community. For example, if you are a vegetarian or have specific food allergies, there is no reason not to mention this when finalizing your interview schedule with the host. Your courtesy will be appreciated.

Meals are also a good time to learn about *quality of life* issues in the community. Depending on your circumstances, you may want to ask about housing costs and where your colleagues live. We failed to ask this question during one of our moves. The result was that we rented what we thought was a lovely home in what appeared to be a typical neighborhood and were the victims of two home invasions within a 6-month period. One of our colleagues noted that the particular area was one where we should not live—after the fact. Another *quality of life* issue involves daycare and schools. These topics are often covered over dinner during interviews.

Although you are being hired for your professional skills, you are also in an interpersonal profession. Thus, part of the interview also involves your interpersonal skills. A situation from the experience of one of us as a potential employer involved a candidate who "flunked lunch." This candidate had excellent credentials and solid letters of recommendation. On the other hand, the two of us who picked him up at the airport decided by the time we reached his hotel that we would get one of our junior colleagues to have dinner with him as we found him so obnoxious. After he had lunch the next day with a group of us, the number of faculty members who did not want to interact socially or professionally with him increased enormously.

As with the phone interview, be prepared with questions you want to ask. When meeting with the department head or administrator, ask about the time line for their decision process, available funds for any specialized equipment you may need (e.g., computer test scoring programs), moving expenses, whether computers and printers are individual or shared, and allocated salary range for the position. Today, most ads only use phrases such as *competitive salary*. Also ask about the benefits package. This question may lead to a referral to human resources but get the Web address and/ or phone number so you can do your homework prior to any potential job offer. If you will need to have supervision for licensure, ask about ways that can be acquired. If you have already done a postdoctoral year and are either licensed or license eligible, find out the time line allowed for you to obtain a license there if you are hired.

In medical centers, psychologists have several unique salary issues that need to be clarified. In some of these settings, psychologists are expected to essentially *earn* part or all of their salary through clinical services provided in a range of settings. There may also be an internal *private practice* that allows you to use your office to see individuals privately, and then you receive a percentage of the income while the medical center or the department gets the rest for their expenses. It is important to ask about these processes so any ambiguity can be clarified while you are talking to them rather than trying to address them over the phone during a job offer or finding out after you arrive that their expectations are too much for you.

As soon as you return to your hotel for the night or when you get home, depending on your interview schedule, make a list that summarizes your experiences. This list should include what impressed you and what raised concerns. If your on-site interview is multiday, raise as many of the concerns as you can on the second day of your visit. If not, save them for the possibility of a job offer and then raise them. Also note what you would need to accept an offer should one be made. This part of the list includes a minimum salary, equipment, support, supervision, and so on. If you have had multiple on-site interviews, start ranking them in terms of your interest in both the position and the community. You may find that you liked some communities more than others or that certain positions and/or potential colleagues have an especially strong appeal at this time. Thus, if one near the bottom of your list is your first offer, you will have information to help you decide whether you want to try to wait for more preferred positions.

The Job Offer

Job offers are typically made over the phone. Except in very rare situations, it is best to think about the offer before making a decision. It would be a most unusual offer to which you must immediately respond. The amount of time you are given, however, varies widely. The employer does not want to lose the second-choice candidate because the first choice has taken so long to respond that the other person is no longer available. There are no standard time lines for a response period. Asking for a week is not unreasonable. During that time, you can contact potential employers at other positions for which you have applied to determine whether their decision timeline will fit into your current offer. Asking for an extension on the response time for an offer can be risky. The message you are giving is that you are really not that eager for employment there. If you really would prefer another position or are waiting for an offer for your partner, you may choose to ask for an extension. However, realize that the offer may be withdrawn if you do so. Such a delay may also impact your negotiations for salary extras that were not included in the initial offer (e.g., start-up funds). If you delay and then finally do accept that offer, your new colleagues will also wonder how much you really wanted to join them and view you as just not getting another offer. This is not a positive way to start your first job.

Once you accept a position, make sure you get everything in writing that is discussed over the phone. For example, if relocation funds are provided, that information may not be in your actual contract. This information, however, should be in a letter or e-mail regarding the offer, so in addition to your contract, ask for written confirmation about relocation funds, whether they are to be billed to the employer or reimbursed, and whether there are any restrictions on the way they are spent. Depending on the amount of material to be moved, you may consider renting a truck and moving your own belongings only to learn that the employer covers only professional movers. The written offer should also include any start-up monies to be provided. If the position has a probationary period prior to full employment status, be sure you understand the evaluation process. Clarify such factors as the date of benefits coverage, such as health insurance and contributions to retirement. Some retirement plans require a period of employment prior to starting in those plans. Others require a period of employment before you are *fully vested* in the program. These factors have fiscal implications for consideration of your second job as well as your financial planning.

Summary

Looking for an initial applied position seems quite straightforward initially. When you consider the process, however, you quickly learn that it is not as simple as it seemed. Following some simple steps can maximize the success of the experience.

Step 1 is self-analysis. Before you even apply for positions, take some time to really decide the range of positions to which you plan to apply as well as the importance of such factors as location, salary, and benefits.

Step 2 involves your resources. Do not limit yourself to the traditional advertisement sites. Use various networks you may have developed, including friends and relatives in addition to faculty and peers. Spend time talking to potential reference letter writers to help them understand the range of positions of interest and whether they would be able to write you a strong letter for some or all such sites.

Step 3 is homework. Homework is necessary at each step of the application process. Take time to evaluate who your employers are, what they want in a new employee, and how you fit their requirements.

Step 4 is evaluation. What are your personal strengths and weaknesses related to each position for which you either intend to apply or for which you have actually applied? What questions do you have about the position? Don't hesitate to make lists for each position. Comparison of these lists can help you if you receive multiple offers.

Step 5 occurs after you start your first job. Give yourself time to adjust to the position. Listen and learn before being too vocal. Although you should not hesitate to provide input when asked or to ask questions when information is needed, the new psychologist who seems to be trying to change the culture of a setting is less likely to be accepted than one who wants to know how best to fit into the culture. Even if you determine that this is not really the job for you, try to fit in sufficiently well that you will be able to get a solid letter of recommendation for your next position.

❖ References

American Psychological Association (APA). (2005). How to land your second job. *Monitor on Psychology, 36*(9), 58.

Attenweiler, W. J. (2009) Industrial and organizational psychology. In S. F. Davis, P. J. Giordano, & C. A. Licht (Eds.), *Your career in psychology: Putting your graduate degree to work.* (pp. 259–269). Malden, MA: Wiley-Blackwell.

Davis, S. F., Giordano, P. J., & Licht, C. A. (Eds.). (2009). *Your career in psychology: Putting your graduate degree to work.* Malden, MA: Wiley-Blackwell.

Matthews, J. R., & Anton, B. S. (2008). *Introduction to clinical psychology.* New York: Oxford.

Sternberg, R. J. (Ed.). (2007). *Career paths in psychology: Where your degree can take you.* (2nd ed.). Washington, DC: American Psychological Association.

❖ Suggestions for Further Exploration

Davis, S. F., Giordano, P. J., & Licht, C. A. (Eds.). (2009). *Your career in psychology: Putting your graduate degree to work.* Malden, MA: Wiley-Blackwell. Parts II and IV of this edited book are specifically relevant to those seeking positions in applied areas of psychology. Specific chapters address working in medical centers and community clinical settings, medical centers, and industrial/organizational settings. The chapter on industrial/organizational psychology has a detailed description of the hiring process.

Sternberg, R. J. (Ed). (2007). *Career paths in psychology: Where your degree can take you.* (2nd ed.). Washington, DC: American Psychological Association. This edited volume addresses many applied careers, including working in medical schools and hospitals, independent clinical practice, child clinical psychology positions, and public and government service. Of particular interest are the "day in the life" segments, which give the reader a view of the rewards and challenges of the careers for which they may be interviewing.

25

When Things Don't Go According to Plan

❖

What If You Don't Find a Job?

Jared Keeley
Mississippi State University

By now, you have poured countless hours of blood, sweat, and tears into completing your degree. You've made it through, and you have faced the scary question of what you will do next. You made your decision and applied for several different positions. You have followed the good advice presented in this book, and yet, after the trials and tribulations of the application process, you still don't have a job. Everyone has a different emotional reaction at this point, ranging from bewilderment to outrage to despair. Nonetheless, it is probably best to follow the advice printed in bold friendly letters on the back of the *Hitchhiker's Guide to the Galaxy* as written by Douglas Adams (1979): "DON'T PANIC!"

This chapter is designed to help you through that next step of determining what to do when your best-laid plans for finding a job go awry. It is the last in the book because, hopefully, you will not get to this point. However, if you do, it is best to have read the suggestions in this chapter beforehand and have a plan in mind.

My first piece of advice is to breathe; it is easy to forget how vitally important that is when faced with so seemingly terrible a calamity. My second piece of advice is not to take it too personally. Given that you have more or less successfully navigated graduate school, I am willing to bet you are a high-achieving individual with lots of positive qualities. It can be easy to make an internal attribution regarding your inability to find a job, and although it is useful to consider what you could have done better in the process, do not forget that external factors also likely played a role. For example, in difficult economic times, finding a job can become much like searching for a needle in a haystack—the odds at least can feel very similar. We will consider below what you might be able to do about some of those factors. The good news is that, according to the U.S. Bureau of Labor Statistics (2008), positions in secondary education and professional psychology are expected to increase at a rate of 11 to 15%, which is outpacing many other sorts of jobs.

Although my first two pieces of advice are mandatory, everything else I say should be taken as a suggestion. It is my hope that this chapter will help you to think about some of your options and to consider carefully issues germane to the next stage of your career. However, I hope that you are also seeking advice from other sources, like your dissertation advisor, your family, professional contacts, and friends who might have also gone through the job hunt.

Suggestion 1: In Times of Trouble, Turn to Old Friends

You have a variety of very important resources at your disposal for helping you to find a job. Hopefully, you have taken the advice presented earlier in this book (e.g., Chapters 1, 2, and 4) to develop a network of colleagues in your field. To start, these individuals would include your dissertation advisor, dissertation committee, and other faculty members in your graduate program or university. Beyond that, you may have made some connections at conferences, meetings, or other professional organizations. You may have had the opportunity to work in a limited capacity in the field, either in a practicum for applied students or some other sort of part-time job or position, and your coworkers or supervisors can be valuable contacts (see Chapters 13 and 16). Odds are other graduate students from your program have had success (or not) in finding jobs as well, and both would have important perspectives about your current situation.

All of these individuals, let us call them your professional network, are resources for hearing about or even creating positions. Let these individuals know that you have been having trouble finding employment and that you would be interested in hearing about opportunities that cross their desks. Some of them might even be in a position to create a temporary opportunity for you. For example, they may be able to find a few classes for you to teach in the department or perhaps include you as a research assistant on a grant or other project. For those in an applied field, professional contacts may have additional work they could delegate to you under their supervision or find a part-time or temporary position in their practice/organization. Social networks are powerful; harness some of that power to work for you.

Suggestion 2: Consider Postponing Graduation

Depending upon where you are in the process, you may have the option of postponing your graduation. This option has a few advantages. Depending upon the nature of your program, you may be able to secure an assistantship while taking extra classes, improving your vitae, or otherwise improving your application for the next year (see *Suggestion 4* for more discussion on this topic). Staying in your program has the advantage of keeping you in contact with many of those individuals in your professional network. Staying close to them helps to remind them to continue looking for possible positions for you.

Of course, you have to eat. Depending upon your financial situation, delaying graduation may be an unattractive option, because you would potentially continue to pay for tuition while also not having a more lucrative source of income. Many people have taken student loans, and you may be reluctant to increase your amount of debt. However, by postponing graduation, depending upon the nature of your loans, you have also postponed needing to pay them back, which would be truly difficult without gainful employment. If you decide not to postpone graduation, you may want to try to find some other type of employment outside of your field. Although it would pay the bills, anecdotally some individuals have said that obtaining employment outside of your field can look bad when you apply the next time. Potential employers may ponder why you did not work "closer to home," and they may count it against you in their decision process. We certainly would hope that employers would not think like that, but we have to consider the possibility that they might. Therefore, if you do decide to get a job, I strongly recommend that you find a job related to the field of psychology (see *Suggestion 4* for more). It might be useful at this point for you to revisit Chapter 22, "To ABD or Not to ABD."

Suggestion 3: Continue the Search

Heretofore, I have assumed that you have been looking for a permanent position, either in academia or in an applied setting. If that is the case, your search is not over. Bear with me for a moment, as our discussion will diverge slightly depending upon searching for an academic or applied job.

In the case of academia, most permanent positions are advertised and hired relatively early in the academic year. Many places might have deadlines as early as September or October. Some searches might continue into the spring, but usually the majority have concluded by February or March. However, temporary positions like lecturers, adjuncts, or visiting professors might not be advertised until later in the year, often after the time frame of permanent searches. The reason for the difference is that the budget at many institutions (especially if they receive state or federal funding) would not be complete until later in the year, and so departments would not know if they have the money available to cover temporary positions until spring or even summer. Additionally, sometimes individuals retire or move, and departments must then fill those classes quickly. Be on the lookout for those sorts of jobs, as again they are often advertised with a relatively quick turnaround time before the new semester. The best place to find advertisements for temporary academic positions is on e-mail listservs. It is rare that these job ads find their way into traditional sources like the *APA Monitor* or *APS Observer* because of the quick turnaround time. If you have not already, join professional listservs in your specific field as well as the Society for the Teaching of Psychology's (APA's Division 2) PsychTeach listserv (go to http://www.teachpsych.org/news/psychteacher.php for instructions on how to join).

Another option is to look for jobs in areas you might have otherwise not considered. By default, I imagine you have looked for academic positions in departments of psychology. Depending upon your specialization, you may be able to find a home in less traditional places, like a business school, generalized social sciences department, medical school, or education program. Broaden your search, and you may find appropriate opportunities. Places to search include the *Chronicle of Higher Education* and specialized academic job websites like www.higheredjobs.com and www.academiccareers.com.

For applied settings, these jobs operate on a far less rigid schedule than academia. Applied jobs tend to come available and be advertised throughout the year. Whereas your academically oriented colleagues have to wait until the next year to apply for permanent positions again, you have the advantage of being able to continuously apply as new jobs become available. For you, then, it becomes even more important to stay vigilant regarding those sources that advertise applied jobs and to solicit help from your professional network to alert you to new positions. Professional listservs are a great way to go. Some electronic job databases even have an e-mail alert system. For example, www.USAjobs.gov is a database of all federal jobs in the country. Relevant to psychology, this includes all Veterans Affairs (VA) and Department of Defense (DoD) positions. You can sign up to receive e-mail alerts any time a job relevant to your field is advertised. General job-search engines like www.career builder.com and www.monster.com also list relevant positions that may not be advertised in other formats.

As with academic jobs, if you have training in an applied area, you may wish to consider expanding the definition of a job you would be willing to take. You may have been looking for positions in a particular clinical area, like anxiety disorders. It might be worth your while to work in a different area for a limited time and then reapply as more attractive jobs become available. Similarly, you may choose less traditional roles like working in the business world in an employee assistance program (EAP) if your training is in the counseling or clinical area. Now is the time to broaden your horizons, not limit them.

For both academics and applied individuals, another option is to pursue a post-doctoral position (see Chapters 21–24 for more information). Again, these sorts of jobs do not have the same deadlines as other positions. Some are early in the year, but some are not. Some come available only once, others offer admission on a rolling basis. Postdocs come in two major flavors: formal and informal. Formal post-docs are those positions that are advertised as postdocs. There will be a specified mentor (or mentors) to supervise your work. The position usually has a set start and end date. Some postdocs last for a single year, but others might specify an expectation for 2 or 3 years of work. Some might even have the option of extending for an additional year. If you happen to be on a postdoc now while looking for jobs, it is important to explore the option of extending your postdoc as a backup plan, in case you find yourself in the position of an unsuccessful job search.

To find a formal postdoc, there are several places to look. First, some are advertised in print in the *Monitor* or *Observer*. For applied postdocs, there is a special listserv managed by the Association of Psychology Postdoctoral and Internship Centers (APPIC) explicitly designed to announce and find postdocs. To join, go to http://www .appic.org/email/index.html. For research-oriented postdocs, look to e-mail listservs in your specific discipline. This is another good time to utilize your professional network, as they will hear about opportunities for postdocs from channels you might not, such as colleagues or reviewing grant proposals.

Informal postdocs are a different creature. There is usually no application process or advertisement of an available position. Instead, it is an agreement between yourself and the individual who will be mentoring you. When you are in the position of having exhausted more traditional options, an informal postdoc offers an acceptable outlet to find work that will allow you to stay within your area and gain additional experience. To find an informal postdoc, you may solicit directly from individuals with whom you would be interested in working. For example, there might be a big-name researcher in your area, and you could contact that person to ask if he or she would be interested in supervising you in a postdoctoral position. It might be a good idea to have someone in your professional network (like your dissertation advisor) act as a go-between, introducing you to the potential mentor and facilitating the negotiation. On the other hand, your professional network might be able to drum up some opportunities for you directly. They might have funding available or know of someone who does.

The tricky part about an informal postdoc is the funding. If someone happens to have money available and no one to fill it, then you are in luck. But let's be honest . . . how often is that kind of money just lying around? It might be that you have to take an unfunded or partially funded position. If so, then you are faced with the same dilemma with which we wrestled earlier. To take an unfunded position, you may have to work in addition to your postdoctoral duties or you may have to secure additional student loans. One other alternative exists: the National Science Foundation (http://www.nsf.gov/funding/education.jsp?fund_type=3) and National Institutes of Health (http://grants.nih.gov/training/) offer training grants that essentially fund postdoctoral positions. This option takes some planning ahead, but if you are reading this book, you are likely planning ahead and can deal proactively with the eventuality of not finding a job. When you apply for one of these training grants, you need to have a precursory agreement with your mentor, who will need to agree to take you on for the specified time. However, you will find that possible mentors will be much more willing to talk with you if you come with money attached.

Suggestion 4: Prepare for Next Time

Regardless of what you do in the meantime, be it a postdoc, part-time teaching, or working at McDonald's, you need to focus on how you will improve your chances of success the next time you apply for jobs. First, revisit the advice offered in Chapters 23 and 24, respectively. The next step is to critically consider what you did this time to identify areas you might improve. The number one factor that leads to unsuccessful job searches is limiting yourself geographically. By only applying to jobs in a particular area, you are handicapping yourself by seriously limiting your job pool. Understandably, you probably have very good reasons for wanting to stay within a particular geographic location, like family, climate, or access to amenities. If you choose to limit yourself geographically, you will have to simultaneously broaden your definition of jobs you would be willing to take. Alternatively, you might consider expanding the area of your search. I do not envy you the task of weighing your priorities against the possibility of successfully finding a job. It will take careful consideration and reflection on your part, but remember the old adage: Do not expect a different outcome if you do everything the same.

Next, reflect upon the aspects of the application process that you can improve. If possible, you might solicit feedback from places to which you applied. They can provide invaluable information about how your application was perceived, what weaknesses it evidenced, and what they would have liked to see different. However, do not expect a response. These individuals are busy and they might not feel comfortable offering such candid feedback. In certain situations, they may not be ethically or legally able to give you the feedback. In the absence of getting feedback directly from the places to which you applied, turn to your professional network to get a sense of what you can improve. Hopefully, you already had someone review your materials before applying. This time, have someone new look at your application with a fresh set of eyes. The odds are that the individual(s) who reviewed your materials the first time will not find anything new.

In some cases, you may find a particular area of your application that needs improvement. For instance, perhaps you struggled during your interviews. You may have been inadequately prepared for the types of questions you received, or maybe you simply have a hard time in those sorts of social-evaluative situations. Either way, practice is the key for next time. Set up mock interviews and walk through your responses to questions. Exposure is the best therapy for anxiety, and this situation is no different.

However, it is more likely that you will find your application was overlooked due to factors of quantity rather than quality. Depending upon the type of job you are seeking, you need to get more experience in the relevant areas. For research-oriented positions, this means you need to try to publish more papers and complete more professional presentations. Continue working in your own line of research, but also look for opportunities to become involved with other researchers, especially those who seem to be very productive. For teaching-oriented positions, you need to get a few more classes prepared and taught. The most frequently requested courses in job ads for psychology are Introduction to Psychology (or General Psychology), Research Methods, Statistics, and Developmental Psychology (Irons & Buskist, 2008). If you do not already have a couple of these in your repertoire, try your best to get experience with these courses. For applied positions, find a job as closely analogous to the career you desire as you can. Work in that area and get more experience. It may also be helpful to broaden your skill set by gaining experience in additional areas beyond a narrowly focused ideal career. For example, if you want to work with anxiety disorders, perhaps also work in a substance abuse clinic for a time, as these disorders are commonly comorbid.

Finally, carefully consider the fit of your application to the sorts of positions to which you applied. For example, if you applied for a position where research is heavily emphasized, your research experience should be the part of your application that stands out most. Your publications should be one of the first things on your curriculum vitae, and you should describe in detail what sorts of projects you have completed and what sorts of research skills you have. Alternatively, if you are interested in applying for a primarily teaching position, your teaching skills should be highlighted. In your cover letter and statement of teaching philosophy, you want to convey your interest and passion for students and education. The type of institution matters as well. For example, small, liberal arts colleges tend to be interested in how you will engage and interact with your students. Some may specifically ask how you will be able to engage students in the research enterprise. Other institutions may be more interested in your classroom skills and consider involving students in research as superfluous at worst or an unnecessary perk at best. Be mindful of your audience and tailor your materials accordingly.

Try to maximize the fit between your application and the institution to which you are applying. However, you also want to present yourself in an accurate light. It does not help anyone, including yourself, to misrepresent your abilities or interests. If you get a position because you presented yourself in a favorable but inaccurate light, it is highly likely that you will not perform well in that position, you will be unhappy, and your employer will be unhappy. You will then be back to having to look for another job with a potentially negative evaluation coming from your last boss.

Instead, be favorable but honest. In your cover letter, discuss the ways in which you would fill the needs of the institution and talk about how the structure of the position fits with your interests. For example, if a job ad indicates that they value engaging undergraduate students in the research process, discuss how you would include students in your own work and ideally recount a time when you have successfully done so. You do not have to go into great detail about ways that the job isn't exactly what you want or ways that you might not be the perfect match for what they are looking for, but you should be prepared to discuss in an interview any weaknesses you might have or areas of least fit and how you are planning on dealing with them. Remember that employers are looking for someone who will be successful in their eyes, but they also are not expecting perfection. They know that even the best candidates will have limitations or ways in which they are not perfect fits. However, demonstrating a level of insight that you are aware of those limitations regarding yourself and the nature of the job to which you apply will likely score you points in the interviewer's final considerations.

Conclusion

As I said at the beginning of this chapter, the most important thing you can do is remember to breathe. The job search process can be arduous, and you must marshal your forces for a second campaign. It becomes vitally important that you take care of yourself as well (see Chapter 10). Make sure that you are making time for fun activities and rest; it can be all too easy for the job search to consume all of your spare moments. That is also why it is important not to become too demoralized; keep your energy up to do your best the second time around. It will be a busy time for you as you continue to look for jobs, prepare new materials, work to improve your vitae, and possibly have some other form of employment as well. The only way you will be able to do all of that is to remember to take care of yourself. Get good sleep, eat well, exercise, maintain a healthy social network, and do all of those other things we know are important for general well-being. Although I can't promise that you will have success in the job market, I imagine that if you follow the advice in this chapter and the others I refer to, you will at least increase your chances of successfully finding a job.

❖ References

Adams, D. (1979). *The hitchhiker's guide to the galaxy*. United Kingdom: Pan Books.

Irons, J., & Buskist, W. (2008). Preparing the new professoriate: What courses should they be ready to teach? *Teaching of Psychology, 35*, 201–204.

U.S. Bureau of Labor Statistics. (2008). Occupational Employment, Training, and Earnings Database. Retrieved from http://www.bls.gov/emp/home.htm#data.

❖ Suggestions for Further Exploration

Darley, J., Zanna, M., & Roediger, H. (2004). *The compleat academic*. Washington, DC: American Psychological Association. This excellent book offers a thorough exploration of the academic career and includes chapters relevant to the job search and career selection. It is a good source for understanding the nature of academic jobs, planning ahead, and concrete advice on approaches that lead to success.

Society for the Teaching of Psychology E-books. (2010). Retrieved from http://www.teach psych.org/resources/e-books/index.php. The Society for the Teaching of Psychology publishes a variety of free e-books on its website. These books offer concrete advice on improving your teaching (e.g., *A Guide for Beginning Teachers of Psychology, Preparing the New Psychology Professoriate: Helping Graduate Students Become Competent Teachers*) and examples of successful professionals and how they reached that point in their careers (*Teaching in Autobiography*, Volumes 1–3).

Conclusion

We hope this book has helped you navigate all the phases of your graduate training, from settling in to maturing and developing to launching out into life after graduate school. Our hope is that the chapters in this volume have helped you understand what it takes to be a successful graduate student in psychology. As Chapter 2 suggested, your ultimate goal is to finish your degree in a timely fashion, and we hope this book has helped in this regard.

Graduate training in psychology offers lots of challenges and rewards. Think about some of the topics addressed in this book: learning the unwritten rules of success; navigating professional and personal relationship issues; becoming an effective writer, teacher, presenter, and researcher; developing clinical and counseling skills; passing your comprehensive exams; completing and defending your dissertation; and applying for professional jobs. It's no wonder that your graduate training years are so full of challenge, exhilaration, and feelings of personal accomplishment. You have grown a great deal during your graduate school experiences.

If you are near the end of your graduate training, then be sure to celebrate your accomplishments, as some of our chapter authors suggest. If you are midway through your training, then continue to use this book as a resource. We thank you for taking the time to look through and read the chapters in the book. We have enjoyed preparing it and working with the excellent authors who have contributed chapters. Next to our names below, we have listed our e-mail addresses. We would love to hear about how this book has helped you become a successful graduate student and, even more importantly, a successful psychologist after you obtain your graduate degree.

With all good wishes for your graduate training and beyond,

Peter J. Giordano (pete.giordano@belmont.edu)

Stephen F. Davis (davis122@suddenlink.net)

Carolyn A. Licht (calicht@msn.com)

Name Index

Brethower, D., 29, 31
Brewer, C. L., 138, 145, 171
Brewer, M., 165
Brewster, M. E., 54, 66
Brown, C. S., 13
Brown, M. C., 63, 66
Bruner, K.F., 118, 130
Bryson, W., 118, 130
Bubb, R., 133
Buckley, T., 133, 145
Burke, C., 68, 81
Burkhalt, J. A., 214, 215
Burns, S. R., 33, 83
Busch, J. W., 63, 66
Buskist, W., 68, 81, 133, 137,
    138, 139, 140, 142, 145, 146,
    260, 261, 263, 264, 265, 281,
    284, 293, 312
Byerly, S., 164, 172

Cacioppo, J. T., 164, 171
Caffarella, R. S., 27, 31
Callahan, J. L., 194, 201
Caplow, J. H., 62, 66
Carlson, R. G., 147
Carney, J. S. 214, 215
Carr, A. C., 151, 157
Carrell, L. J. 218, 225
Cash, T. F., 269, 275, 277
Cathey, C., 125, 130
Cautin, R., 171
Chamberlain, J., 43, 44, 51, 52, 100
Chin, E., 185
Cho, K., 125, 130
Christensen, A., 112
Christopherson, K. M., 267
Chubin, D. E., 268, 276
Cialdini, R., 165
Clark, J., 54, 67
Clark, W.H., 124, 130
Cleveland, M., 179, 183
Clifton, J., 260, 264, 281, 284, 293
Clump, M. A., 281, 293
Coad, J. 221, 224
Cobia, D. C. 208, 214, 215
Cohen, A.L., 137, 145
Cohen, N., 70, 81
Collins, F.L., 194, 201
Committee on the College Student,
    Group for the Advancement of
    Psychiatry, 70–81
Cone, J. D., 277
Conolly, T., 268, 276
Cooper, B.J., 123, 131
Corts, D. P., 23
Courtney, J., 257
Covill, A.E., 125, 130
Coyne, J., 86, 90

Crandall, C., 165, 171
Crittenden, K.S., 133, 145
Cronin, M. 218, 224
Crosby, F. J., 10, 12
Cross, K.P., 137, 145
Cuetara, J., 25, 31
Cullen, M.J., 120, 131
Cusus, A., 63, 66

Daly, J. A., 218, 224
Daniel D. B., 179, 183, 225
Daniels, D. P., 218, 224
Daniels, M. H., 71, 73, 75–76, 81
Darley, J. M., 52, 173, 262, 263,
    265, 280, 293, 314
Davis, B. J., 135, 136, 140, 145, 146
Davis, D. D., 151, 157
Davis, G. L., 63, 66
Davis, K. 218, 224
Davis, M., 105, 106, 112
Davis, S. F., 5, 54, 55, 60, 67, 140,
    145, 168, 172, 263, 265, 284,
    289, 293, 306
DeAngelis, T., 44, 46, 47, 49, 51, 52
DeGrez, L, 218, 224
Delamont, S., 12
Dermer, M. L., 125, 130
desJardins, M., 44, 45, 51
deValero, Y. F., 27, 31
Devitt, P., 221, 224
DiBartolo, P. M. 219, 224
Dingfelder, S. R. 209, 210, 214
DiPierro, M., 249, 256
Dlugos, R. F., 102, 112
Donald, J. G., 159, 171
Donaldson, J. F., 62, 66
Donofrio, H. H., 218, 224
Dore, T. M., 25, 31
Dowd, E. T., 204, 214
Driscoll, D. M., 164, 172
Dunn, D. S., 56, 66, 125, 130, 160, 169, 171
Dunn, M. E., 250, 256
Dunsmuir, S., 119, 130

Eisenberg, M.B., 120, 131
El-Ghourourey, N., 299, 306
Elman, N. S., 104, 105, 106, 108, 112
Elton, L., 123, 130
Epting, K., 137, 145
Eshelman, E. R., 105, 106, 112
Evans, A. L., 250, 256
Ewing, H. M., 65, 66
Examples of Plagiarism, 126, 130

Fairchild, J. A., 34, 35, 38
Fallahi, C. R., 125, 131
Fallahi, H., 131
Feist-Price, S., 35, 36, 38

Subject Index